Shakespeare and Gender

Shakespeare and Gender
A History

Edited by

DEBORAH BARKER

and

IVO KAMPS

VERSO
London · New York

First published by Verso 1995
This collection © Verso 1995
Individual contributions © the contributors 1995
All rights reserved

Verso
UK: 6 Meard Street, London W1V 3HR
USA: 180 Varick Street, New York NY 10014–4606

Verso is the imprint of New Left Books

ISBN 0 86091 458 5
ISBN 0 86091 669 3 (pbk)

British Library Cataloguing in Publication Data
A catalogue record for this book is available from the British Library

Library of Congress Cataloging-in-Publication Data
Shakespeare and gender : a history / edited by Deborah Barker and Ivo
Kamps.
    p.   cm.
Includes bibliographical references and index.
ISBN 0–86091–458–5. — ISBN 0–86091–669–3 (pbk.)
1. Shakespeare, William, 1564–1616—Political and social views.
2. Shakespeare, William, 1564–1616—Knowledge—Psychology.   3. Sex
differences (Psychology) in literature.   4. Masculinity (Psychology)
in literature.   5. Femininity (Psychology) in literature.   6. Man
–woman relationships in literature.   7. Gender identity in
literature.   8. Sex role in literature.   I. Barker, Deborah.
II. Kamps, Ivo.
PR3069.S45S53   1995
822.3'3—dc20   95–3581
                                                                       CIP

Typeset by Solidus (Bristol) Limited
Printed and bound in Great Britain by Biddles Ltd, Guildford and King's Lynn

For Malcolm

Contents

Acknowledgements

The editors gratefully acknowledge permission of various journals, presses and individuals to reprint the following materials: Coppélia Kahn, 'The Rape in Shakespeare's *Lucrece*', *Shakespeare Studies* 9 (1976): 45–72; Gayle Greene, '"This That You Call Love": Sexual and Social Tragedy in *Othello*', *Journal of Women's Studies in Literature* 1 (1979): 16–32; Marianne Novy, 'Shakespeare and Emotional Distance in the Elizabethan Family', *Theatre Journal* 33 (1981): 316–27; Carol Cook, '"The Sign and Semblance of Her Honor": Reading Gender Difference in *Much Ado about Nothing*', *PMLA* 101 (1986): 186–202; Jacqueline Rose, 'Hamlet – the *Mona Lisa* of Literature', *Critical Quarterly* 28 (1986): 35–49; Valerie Traub, 'Jewels, Statues, and Corpses: Containment of Female Erotic Power in Shakespeare's Plays', *Shakespeare Studies* (1988): 215–40; Gabriele Bernhard Jackson, 'Topical Ideology: Witches, Amazons, and Shakespeare's Joan of Arc', *English Literary Renaissance* 18 (1988): 40–65; Ann Thompson, '"Miranda, Where's Your Sister?": Reading Shakespeare's *The Tempest*', in Susan Sellers, ed., *Feminist Criticism: Theory and Practice*, Toronto: University of Toronto Press, 1991, pp. 45–55; Joseph Pequigney, 'The Two Antonios and Same-Sex Love in *Twelfth Night* and *The Merchant of Venice*', *ELR* 22 (1992): 201–21; Catherine Belsey, 'Love in Venice', *Shakespeare Survey* 44 (1992): 41–54; Leah Marcus, 'The Shakespearean Editor as Shrew-Tamer', *ELR* 22 (1992): 177–200; William Van Watson, 'Shakespeare, Zeffirelli, and the Homosexual Gaze', *Literature Film Quarterly* 20:4 (1992): 308–25; Phyllis Rackin, 'Engendering the Tragic Audience: The Case of *Richard III*', *Studies in the Literary Imagination* 26 (1993): 47–65; William C. Carroll, 'The Virgin Not: Language and Sexuality in Shakespeare', *Shakespeare Survey* 46 (1994): 107–20.

The essays by Gabriele Bernhard Jackson and William Van Watson are revised, updated versions of the original articles.

We would like to thank Mark Derenzo for helping to proof this book.

Shakespeare and Gender: An Introduction*

Deborah Barker and Ivo Kamps

Shakespeare gender criticism is a doubly significant site of exploration into developments in the field of literary criticism. On the one hand, because Shakespeare is still regarded as one of our culture's most central icons and because his plays continue to draw the attention of an extraordinarily wide range of scholars, Shakespeare studies continually feature important trends and innovations in the field of literary criticism. As Lynda E. Boose observes:

> Shakespeare is a site of such competitive jostling because Shakespeare is a site of enormous cultural power. As such, he is not only a universally available but likewise a dangerously charged locale, where maneuvers for appropriation, displacement, erasure, and the institutionalization of both cultural and academic privileges are invested with a particular energy that makes the politics within this field the more recognizable and, simultaneously, perhaps the more crucial to recognize. (p. 708)

On the other hand, because of its increasing academic power and prestige, feminist criticism has made a significant impact in the field of Shakespeare studies, and it is there that we can turn to explore not only innovations in literary criticism in general but also innovations in gender criticism in particular.

Feminist critics of Shakespeare, however, have been in both a precarious and a privileged position *vis-à-vis* gender criticism in general and Shakespeare criticism specifically. Particularly in the early stages, feminist critics of Shakespeare have had to operate on the fringes of a fairly homogeneous and privileged domain of male scholarship. Certainly, in writing about Shakespeare they did not have to defend his reputation as an author, or make a case that his writing was truly literary. Unlike feminist critics working in other fields trying to introduce female

---

* We are grateful to Lisa Schnell for commenting on an earlier draft of this Introduction.

authors into the canon, Shakespearean feminists never had to answer the question 'But is it [the author's work] any good?' (Tompkins, pp. 186–202). On the other hand, feminist Shakespeareans have had to face a different kind of resistance: they have had to overcome the obstacles presented by the powerful indifference of a predominantly male critical establishment content to ignore feminist critics as long as they did not encroach on their turf. Or – when such marginalization proved ineffective, and feminist criticism was perceived as a threat to the academic/political status quo – feminist critics have had to (and still have to) weather the full force of the old guard's critical acumen aimed at censuring, ghettoizing and/or ridiculing their modes of literary analysis. As a result, perhaps more than in any other field, feminist Shakespeare critics have had to examine and re-examine their political and theoretical positions, and to respond to attacks from both left and right.[1] This responsiveness to criticism has led to rapid innovations in the field, innovations which have been thoroughly documented and analysed through a series of articulate, self-conscious and self-critical overviews of feminist influences in Shakespeare studies (see, for example, Belsey, 1991; Boose; McLuskie; Neely, 1988).

In the spirit of this self-scrutiny, Marianne Novy assessed the gender dynamics of Shakespeare criticism in 1981 and suggested that feminists had responded to Shakespeare 'with the loyalty that a dutiful daughter might have for her father' (1981a, p. 25), portraying Shakespeare as the perfect parent. One could extend Novy's point to suggest that feminists – initially, at least – have responded as dutiful daughters not only to the image of Shakespeare, but also to the institution of Shakespearean criticism, by correcting and criticizing their own work; unlike some of their more radical sisters (like Luce Irigaray), who have more blatantly broken with their mentors in both style and substance. Feminist critics, however, have certainly not responded to the Shakespeare establishment as Cordelia does to Lear's demand for filial devotion. Instead of saying nothing, they have criticized the question, challenged Lear's position as patriarch, reconsidered the position of women in Renaissance society, and so on. If feminists have not thrown Lear out of doors, they have certainly made him share the kingdom.[2]

This anthology is about that sharing of the kingdom – about the redistribution of power in Shakespeare studies, and about the exciting new questions and concerns that can now be raised in the criticism of the plays. Yet despite engendering these changes, feminist scholarship also exhibits a great deal of continuity in its socio-political aims. In putting together this anthology, one thing we discovered was that although the terminology of feminism has changed (and clearly there have been important innovations), many of the most salient arguments put forth by early feminist critics still carry significant weight today, except that they have in some respects been translated or updated to a more theoretical level. If the motto of seventies feminism was 'The personal is the political', today's maxim seems to be 'The personal is the theoretical'.

One of this book's chief purposes is to make available for classroom use a single volume charting the recent history of feminist critical practice since the late 1970s. The essays anthologized here (most of them reprinted for the first time) have been chosen for their variety of voices, but also because they exemplify important moments in the trajectory of feminist critical thought. Although we have conceived this anthology as a historical survey – like its companion, *Materialist Shakespeare: A History* – we have shied away from seeking to transform the chronology of the essays into a succinct, purposive narrative. By gathering from the last two decades a broad range of essays with a gender orientation, this collection offers its reader a (necessarily) circumscribed historical record of feminist critical practice. The pieces speak for themselves, but in this introduction we will use them as markers to chart some of the currents and countercurrents in feminist criticism from the 1970s to the present.

In keeping with the familiar seminar format that combines a Shakespearean text with one or more pieces of literary criticism, several of the essays offered here are sustained readings of single plays. But there are also several essays that take up important new gender concerns and trace these across a broad range of the playwright's *oeuvre*. To respond further to the needs of seminar students and teachers, the articles selected cover a broad spectrum of Shakespeare's dramatic writings while focusing for the most part on the most frequently taught plays.

I

Early feminist criticism was clearly a reaction, not only to Shakespeare and the literary canon, but to literary criticism to date. Many of the earliest feminist critics were trained by New Critics and traditional Freudians who looked at the world of the play and its characters in either aesthetic or psychological terms; or by 'old historians' who, in the manner of E.M.W. Tillyard, posited a strong mirror-like correlation between the play and the Elizabethan world, the former passively reflecting the latter. As Linda Boose explains in her 1987 essay on Renaissance literary research on the family, marriage, and sex:

> Until roughly ten years ago, 'the family' was still contained by the definition of its proper place that critics like E.M.W. Tillyard had, years earlier, extrapolated unquestioned from the hierarchical discourses of the

> Elizabethan state and promulgated as truths that were unproblematic
> because still firmly in evidence, hence 'natural'. . . .
>
> Until recently, the men who defined the scholarly establishment we
> were all trained within never imagined that terms of discourse were
> needed to separate cultural ideas *about* sexual identity ('gender') from
> the register of biological differentiation ('sex'). (pp. 710–11)

Rereading Shakespeare from a feminist perspective, therefore, also meant
rereading the canonical critical reading of Shakespeare, and the most
obvious and acceptable place to begin was with the many interpretations
of Shakespeare's women characters. This task was necessary not only for
feminist Shakespeare critics but also for feminist critics in general, given
the importance that Shakespeare's female characters have played in
assessing the nature of women. In the countless nineteenth-century debates
on the nature of women, for example, Shakespeare's women were often
discussed alongside historical figures, with the fictional characters given
equal weight and often even prominence over actual women. John Ruskin,
for instance, turned to the works of the 'wisest and greatest men' (of whom
Shakespeare is his prime example) in order to establish 'some clear and
harmonious idea . . . of what womanly mind and virtue are in power and
office' (pp. 63, 62). An ideological corollary to Ruskin, Mary Cowden
Clarke's 'Preface' to her nineteenth-century edition of Shakespeare's
plays, underscores Shakespeare's unparalleled capacity to depict ideal
womanly behaviour. Clarke declares:

> Shakespeare's works are a library in themselves. . . . A poor girl, studying
> no other volume, might become a lady in heart and soul. Knowledge,
> refinement, experience, in men and manners, are to be gathered from his
> pages in plenary abundance. (p. v)[3]

At a glance, the Ruskin–Clarke phenomenon is in part a tribute to the
complexity of Shakespeare's female characters, as well as a demonstration
of a conception of literature as a mirror held up to nature; but it is also
indicative of a dearth of in-depth historical knowledge of the lives of real
women. In order to produce a public record of what women 'thought' and
'felt' (or what they 'ought' to think and feel), one had to turn to literature
– literature almost exclusively written by men. That this was accepted in
the past as almost a given underscores the seeming impossibility of
obtaining historical information about real women and the unseemliness of
a living woman conveying her feelings in a public format, a condition
rather analogous to the use of boy actors to play women's parts on the
Renaissance stage.

It has been suggested (often none too subtly) that the so-called 'images
of women' criticism that emerged in the 1970s is not at the same level of
sophistication as 'real' literary criticism. The early emphasis on images of

women was deemed to produce naively realistic, essentialist and ahistorical interpretations of the plays, and thought capable of generating only thematic presentations of female characters. Part of the charge of naivety arises from the emphasis placed on 'reading as a woman', and the allegation that feminists treat the female characters as if they were real women with whom they can identify. This position assumes that 'femaleness' is transhistorical, and hence captures some essential quality to which all women can relate at all times. One criticism of this type of approach is that it often focuses on the female characters without placing them in the context of the play and/or the historical situation out of which the play arose. A somewhat more historical version of stressing the woman's point of view assumes that female characters can be read as examples of how women were treated in the period in which the work was written. In this case, literature is treated as a history of the times, and a one-to-one correspondence between reality and the text is assumed. A survey of these kinds of interpretations shows that there are various possible outcomes for 'images of women' criticism depending on how the characters are viewed and whether they (the female characters), the male characters, the patriarchy, or the author are held accountable for their presentation.

While it is productive to analyse the underlying theoretical assumptions of feminist criticism, and while many of the objections are cogent, the unfortunate problem with the labelling and dismissal of early feminist criticism as 'images of women' (and thus unsophisticated) is its tendency to read feminist critics thematically, and thus to give hostile critics licence not to deal with the specifics of the arguments raised by feminists. It should be stressed that many early feminist readings are hardly accurately described by such labels as 'not rigorous', 'naive', 'simplistically mimetic', and 'theoretically unsophisticated'. Gayle Greene's essay on *Othello*, published in *Journal of Women's Studies in Literature* in 1979 (p. 47 below), is an example of superb 'early' feminist criticism of Shakespeare. It is 'early' feminist criticism because it deals in images of women and men, and because it does not bother with a careful consideration of historical conditions and conceptions of women's and men's lives. Yet this essay, and other early feminist essays like it, continue to have considerable critical currency because the images of women are implicitly grounded in a largely unarticulated yet remarkably accurate sense about women's actual historical conditions. Greene's essay reflects the crucial distinction between biologically determined sex and culturally constructed gender roles as delineated by Gayle Rubin in her immensely influential 1975 essay 'The Traffic in Women: Notes on the "Political Economy" of Sex'. Rubin's distinction facilitates the analysis of Shakespeare's plays as cultural representations of gender norms rather than simple reflections of the inherent differences between men and women. For Greene, *Othello* is a play in which love turns to death because of certain unexamined definitions of the 'ideal of manly and womanly behaviour' (p. 60). It is precisely Desdemona's striving, encouraged by the patriarchal society, to embody the feminine ideal – selflessness, solicitousness and obedience – that leaves her without an effective defence against a destructively jealous Othello, whose martial and 'masculine' traits lead him away from introspection and towards insecurity and ultimately violence.

Like Greene's essay, Coppélia Kahn's seminal study of the rape in Shakespeare's *Lucrece* (p. 22 below) continues to be relevant today. What is implied in Greene's essay – a move towards history – takes on a visible shape in Kahn's. First published in 1976, it draws on both secondary (Lawrence Stone) and primary (John Florio) historical sources to construct, albeit briefly, a historical understanding of the overdetermined and contradictory position women occupied in late-sixteenth-century England – a position which, Kahn asserts, Shakespeare found mirrored in his Latin sources, and which he inscribed in his poem. Carefully woven into this understanding of history is an anthropological analysis of the role of women as commodities of exchange in patriarchal societies.[4] Kahn's analysis of the construction of Lucrece's gender clearly stands as a prophetic instance of the kind of theoretically sophisticated, self-consciously historical, feminist-inspired scholarship practised today.

Feminist criticism's increasingly rapid response to a demand for theoretical and historically grounded readings of Shakespeare is beautifully exemplified in Marianne Novy's essay 'Shakespeare and the Emotional Distance in the Elizabethan Family' (p. 63 below). Novy does not merely demonstrate a growing feminist interest in the historical conditions of actual women; she also manifests a keen concern with literature's relationship to history – a subject that was typically the provenance of male-dominated literary theory and historical criticism. Novy takes issue with Lawrence Stone's thesis about the Elizabethan family as one marked by 'distance, manipulation, and deference', and argues – echoing a central concern of Gayle Greene's in her essay on *Othello* – that Stone has identified less a normative characterization of family relations than 'a cultural ideal of Elizabethan society', an ideal notion of 'emotional control'. Novy discusses half a dozen of Shakespeare's plays – not to argue that the emotional complexities and excesses depicted in them constitute a refutation of Stone's evidence, but to suggest that they 'permit the vicarious experience of emotions latent and too threatening to acknowledge in everyday life'. The plays, she argues, appeal to that which the culture encourages the individual to suppress. Novy's understanding of the relationship between drama and culture, it is worth noting, skilfully pre-empts the charge of 'naive realism'. For Novy, Shakespeare's female characters clearly do not represent real women;

rather, they are the playwright's fictional meditations on familial attachments submerged in an ideology of control.

II

Reassessing critical interpretations of Shakespeare's female characters has often meant valorizing both Shakespeare and his fictional women. Marianne Novy explains the impulse to read Shakespeare as a 'champion of women' as follows: 'For all the limitations on his feminism, he is one of the few widely honored culture heroes who can be claimed as a supporter of women at all' (1981a, p. 24); that is, feminist scholars *needed* to come to terms with Shakespeare. Rereading Shakespeare as sympathetic to women's concerns often involved genre as well as gender issues. Early feminist critics almost invariably turned to the strong-willed, intelligent and emotionally vital female characters of the middle and late comedies to make their case for a feminist Shakespeare. But Rosalind, Viola, Beatrice and Helena are not, of course, Shakespeare's only female characters, as Linda Bamber has pointed out in *Comic Women, Tragic Men*, which charges that Shakespeare's treatment of his tragic heroines is misogynistic. Another reaction to the valorization of the comic heroines was to rethink their critical reputations. In her seminal essay on *Much Ado about Nothing* (p. 75 below), Carol Cook openly questions the commonly held feminist assumption that 'Beatrice['s] feminine charity triumphs over' Messina's masculine values (p. 75), and goes on to demonstrate that for all her apparent independence, defiance and witty repartee, Beatrice is more representative of Messina's oppressive patriarchal order than of any ostensibly feminine values. Two prominent materialist feminists, Kathleen McLuskie and Ann Thompson, share Cook's reservations about a 'feminist' Shakespeare. In her much-cited contribution to *Political Shakespeare* (1985), McLuskie argues that celebratory readings of Shakespeare cannot ignore the staging of the play and the male viewpoint imposed on the dramatic presentation of events (cf. Woodbridge, p. 295). And Ann Thompson closes her essay on *The Tempest* (p. 168 below) with the following disturbing question: 'what kind of pleasure can a woman and a feminist take in this text beyond the rather grim one of mapping its various patterns of exploitation?' (p. 177).

Indeed, the essays by Cook, Thompson, and William Carroll (p. 283 below) may offer feminists some real satisfaction in their criticism of some basic principles of patriarchal discourse, but they do not offer them an easy path to changing that discourse. Cook and Carroll openly question the possibility for a genuine female presence in the male-dominated world of the dramas they inspect. William Carroll pursues the thesis that female

sexuality is presented only through male discourse, and examines the
'linguistic transgressions' (puns, malapropisms, riddles) which reveal
significant slippage between 'the ordinary relation between signifier and
signified', a type of transgression through which female sexuality enters
into discourse in the form of absence or negation. Riddles, for instance,
Carroll argues, can represent a kind of '"epistemological foreplay",
leading to the riddler's clarifying and satisfying solution to the problem –
providing the absent signified' (p. 285). What is more, by discussing
various uses (literary and medical) of the word 'hymen', Carroll demonstrates that even when female sexuality (specifically, discussion of female
genitalia) does enter into the plays' 'high discourse', it does so obliquely,
veiling the 'realm of the referential' in mystery (p. 287).

Carol Cook's essay resembles William Carroll's in so far as it adopts a
comparable stance on the absence or presence-only-through-negation of
female values/sexuality, but Cook also makes it her business to explore the
consequences of this premiss for a political feminism. She explicitly
questions feminism's ability to uncover or create an authentic feminine
presence in patriarchal societies that defines what constitutes the feminine
in the first place. Embracing a position akin to that of French feminist
theory, Cook argues: 'The construction of femininity within an economy
of representation governed by the phallus ... obviates the possibility of
"feminine values" or of a feminine alternative to the "predominately
masculine ethos"', and that 'alternatives cannot be generated from within
the binary structures by which patriarchy figures gender' (p. 82). Since
there is no available method that allows us to return to first causes or
origins in the history of gender construction – indeed, all analysis
necessarily commences *in medias res* – Cook's claim packs a real,
potentially paralysing punch. How can one produce female values from
within a binary system in which *both* terms are defined by a masculine
ethos?

Jacqueline Rose's well-known essay on *Hamlet* (p.104 below) puts an
intriguing spin on arguments about the negative presence of female values
in the plays. Rose extends the troubling issue of female absence or negative
presence in masculine discourse to the activities of several prominent
twentieth-century literary critics, most notably T.S. Eliot and Ernest Jones.
Central to her argument is the claim that Eliot accounts for what is, for him,
most baffling about Hamlet the character and *Hamlet* the play – that which
causes the play's aesthetic failure – by conjuring up a category of the
'feminine', which, like the *Mona Lisa*, is presumably 'enigmatic and
undecipherable' (p. 104). In particular, Rose points to Eliot's argument
that Gertrude is insufficient as a character to serve as an 'objective
correlative' for Hamlet's powerful emotions. But what is more important,
Gertrude is also the *cause* of Hamlet's inexpressible and excessive

emotions: 'Gertrude is ... disgusting, but not quite disgusting *enough*.'[5]

If *Hamlet* is an aesthetic failure for Eliot, it is not so for the Freudian critic Ernest Jones, who finds a perfectly sound psychoanalytic solution to the problem by reading Hamlet as a 'little Oedipus who cannot bring himself to kill Claudius because he stands in the place of [Hamlet's] own desire, having murdered Hamlet's father and married his mother' (Rose, p. 111). Once again Gertrude is the cause of aesthetic excess, both as the source of Hamlet's conflicted desire and hate for his mother and as the cause of his inability to act, his repression of desire. As Rose demonstrates, femininity becomes the key to aesthetic coherence in the psychoanalytic reading of *Hamlet* because the psychoanalytic concentration on the mother makes her the 'cause of all good and evil, and her failings responsible for a malaise in all human subjects – that is, in men *and* in women – which stems from their position in the symbolic order of culture itself' (p. 116). Rose notes Lacan's attempt to redress this problem by focusing 'resolutely on the side of the symbolic ... on the side of the father' (p. 116). But while Lacan does not make the mother the key to understanding, he does this by leaving her out of the picture. The psychoanalytic readings of *Hamlet* follow an all-or-nothing interpretation of the mother.

Valerie Traub's essay 'Jewels, Statues, and Corpses: Containment of Female Erotic Power in Shakespeare's Plays' (p. 120 below) also employs a psychoanalytic model that makes use of earlier studies of male anxiety about female power. But Traub proposes to look more specifically at the 'strategy of containment' by which 'male anxiety towards female erotic power is channelled' (p. 121). Traub also positions her essay within the debate about feminists' relationship to Shakespeare. She aligns herself with Kathleen McLuskie and Carol Cook in their rejection of a 'feminist Shakespeare', yet she also rejects McLuskie's charge that feminist psychoanalytic criticism is 'mimetic essentialism',[6] while she criticizes Cook for posing 'patriarchy as a monolithic, transhistorical entity that can be transformed only with the destruction of phallogocentrism' (p. 136). Traub asserts that 'a politicized and historically attuned psychoanalysis is a valuable tool for exploring those anxieties and attitudes towards women which have endured through time. . . . However delimited and inscribed by patriarchal codes our resistances, rebellions, and women's movements and communities may be, their very existence argues that alternatives can be generated from within "the binary structures by which patriarchy figures gender"' (p. 136). She holds out the hope that by 'analysing the expression of sexual anxieties with Shakespearean drama' we can 'begin to exorcize them' (p. 137). It is the apparent ahistoricism of Cook's argument that bothers Traub, and she offers the historical example 'of various communities of women, particularly lesbian separatists' who have 'successfully if temporarily disengaged themselves from patriarchal values and structures ...' (p. 141, n. 41) to underscore the possibility that non-patriarchal definitions of femininity *can* be generated from 'within' the system.[7]

This is not the occasion to try to settle this question, but because we begin our analysis of social structures *in medias res*, it seems that all categories of original or authentic maleness or femaleness we look for are already reciprocally determined. It is important, therefore, to get away from essential conceptions of gender altogether, no matter how male-dominated a society may be. The real crux lies in the distribution of power – the power to own, to define, to name, to interpret, to determine one's life, and so on. Quite obviously, in Western civilization this power has resided disproportionately with the male gender; but from that it does not follow that its values, which the society labels 'masculine' or 'rational', and so on, are essentially male. As Traub puts it: 'what it means to be female [or male] can be theorized only in the context of social inscriptions' (p. 141).

Without a doubt, a conception of gender as socially constructed obfuscates the clarity of early feminism's political agenda. For instance, the most positive things Traub can conclude from her reading of *Hamlet*, *Othello*, and *The Winter's Tale* is that the romance is less rigorous in its disallowance of 'femaleness' than are the tragedies. At best, the plays perpetuate 'defensive structures of dominance instituted by men', while they explore the masculine anxieties that prompt them and present 'the tragedy of masculinist values' (p. 137). As we noted above, Ann Thompson expresses genuine distress over 'grim' rewards for feminists in such small favours. Yet Thompson recognizes that this may be the price feminists have to pay if they want to move beyond 'privileging the woman's part or ... special pleading on behalf of female characters' (McLuskie, p. 106). It may mean that *The Tempest*, *The Taming of the Shrew*, and similar texts, which were presumably staged to entertain their audiences and afford pleasure, can perhaps do so only as long as audiences share their retrograde suppositions about gender roles. Despite her palpable ambivalence about producing largely 'negative' readings (p. 177), Thompson's essay on *The Tempest* answers Kathleen McLuskie's call to extract from a play an 'ideology of femininity' even if it features only one woman whose role is 'small and comparatively passive' (p. 170). Thompson points out that in *The Tempest* the ideology of femininity is determined largely by the absence of female characters, and by how the play and its male characters respond to this absence. She shows that despite her small role, Miranda's sexuality, her chastity and her fertility, are absolutely crucial to Prospero's machinations to reclaim his dukedom and to achieve, through his daughter's marriage, 'a counter-usurpation of Naples by Milan' (p. 175). But Miranda's importance does not, of course, lead to her empowerment, merely to the necessity of her submission to Prospero's authority. Thompson's cheerless conclusion closely resembles Cook's findings *vis-à-vis*

Beatrice (p. 82 and *passim*) and Traub's *vis-à-vis* Hermione (pp. 134–7).

Our discussion so far has centred on 'feminist' studies, but it is time to recognize that, as the title of our volume suggests, 'gender' has emerged as a powerful term that allows for the analysis of masculinity and femininity as mutually defining constructs. The term 'gender studies', which has recently come to replace 'feminist studies', recognizes that issues of gender are not limited to a focus on women. Gayle Rubin's questioning of any fixed link between gender and sexual orientation has been crucial for the development of gender studies because it exposes the heterosexual bias implicit in various feminist discussions of eroticism.[8] As Valerie Traub asserts in her important essay 'Desire and the Difference it Makes':

> To assume that gender *predicates* eroticism is to ignore the contradictions that have historically existed between these two inextricably related yet independent systems. While they are always connected, there is no simple fit between them. Gender is not equal to sexuality. (1991, p. 84)

This kind of conceptual leap in gender studies has paved the way for exciting new readings of texts deemed generally heterosexual in their outlook. As he did in his groundbreaking book on Shakespeare's sonnets, *Such is My Love*, Joseph Pequigney (p. 178 below) confronts the question of homosocial desire and homosexuality in Shakespeare's comedies *The Merchant of Venice* and *Twelfth Night*. Pequigney is quick to acknowledge that homoeroticism in Shakespeare has been discussed before, but he stresses that even those critics (mostly feminists) who did perceive homoerotic impulses in the two Antonio characters in *Merchant* and *Twelfth Night* generally argued that the 'impulses are suppressed; that the love returned by the other is non-erotic; and that the characters are finally ostracized and marginalized' (p. 178). On the basis of close textual analysis, Pequigney counters these assumptions and, among other things, offers a perfectly plausible reading of the 'nature to her bias drew' passage from *Twelfth Night* which refutes Stephen Greenblatt's assertion that the only licit sexuality in the play is heterosexuality. For Pequigney, 'homoerotic swerving or lesbian deviation from the heterosexual straight and narrow cannot be considered unnatural, since it is effected by nature itself'. Pequigney, however, does not reject the concept of 'Renaissance friendship' (often used by critics to diffuse questions of homosexuality) which, he argues, does accurately describe the Bassanio–Antonio relationship in *Merchant*.

In 'Shakespeare, Zeffirelli, and the Homosexual Gaze' (p. 235 below) William Van Watson revises Laura Mulvey's classic feminist analysis of the male gaze disclosing its heterosexual assumptions and limitations. Van Watson demonstrates the ways in which the tacit male heterosexual perspective circumscribes the application of Mulvey's theory of the male gaze by ignoring the possibility of a male-to-male or female-to-female gaze. Van Watson combines Shakespeare criticism with innovations in film theory, analysing Franco Zeffirelli's film adaptations of *Othello*, *Hamlet*, *Romeo and Juliet*, and *The Taming of the Shrew*. He uses Shakespeare's and Zeffirelli's biographies to account for their ambivalent presentation of homoeroticism, in which their political conservatism 'closets' the homo-erotic dimension. As he states: 'Admittedly, such male bonds in Shake-speare's plays usually remain safely within the realm of heterosexual male behaviour patterns, any homoerotic undercurrents remaining precisely that – undercurrents' (p. 236). Like Pequigney, Van Watson rejects critics who attempt to dismiss the homosexual element in Shakespeare by displacing it to the conception of 'Renaissance Friendships' between males: 'The point is simple. Homosexuality existed in Renaissance society, and Shakespeare knew it' (p. 237).

Rejecting the limitations of an exclusively heterosexual male gaze, however, 'does not necessarily remove the agenda for control from scopophilia itself' (p. 243). In analysing Zeffirelli's films, Van Watson perceives the same issues of domination within male-to-male and female-to-male relationships. Within the homosexual gaze, 'The axis of control merely shifts from the male–female polarity to the more Oedipal older male–younger male polarization' (p. 243). As with the male heterosexual gaze, the homosexual gaze has the potential to express not only desire, but also hatred: 'As by-products of the same phallocratically repressive society, homophobia and misogyny derive from a similar source' (p. 244). Zeffirelli's production of *Taming of the Shrew* is a case in point: 'Zeffirelli invites the derision of the feminine in the caustic effeminacy of a variety of male characters' (p. 245). In his most recent Shakespeare production of *Hamlet*, according to Van Watson, 'the more acceptable but ultimately equally deadly "patriarchal father–son bond" fully displaces the homoerotic tensions and intimate male friendships of his *Romeo and Juliet*' (p. 255).

III

It is impossible to deny that psychoanalytic theory has had an enormous impact on gender studies; as Traub points out: 'Feminists, materialist feminists, cultural materialist and new historicists implicitly draw on a psychoanalytic construct whenever they pose the question of "desire"' (1991, p. 85). What we saw in McLuskie's above-mentioned censure of psychoanalytic critics and Traub's defence of it, however, is the dispute over the role of history in feminist criticism. Graham Holderness, in his contribution to *Shakespeare Left and Right*, maps out the debate between

British materialist critics and American psychoanalytic critics using Kahn's and Bamber's readings of *Richard II*.[9] What differentiates Holderness's reaction to Kahn and Bamber from McLuskie's is that his criticisms do not lead him to dismiss their work outright. Instead, despite harbouring certain reservations, he claims that Kahn's and Bamber's arguments 'have been neither exhausted nor superseded by subsequent theoretical work', and he proposes 'not to oppose but to expand and develop' them 'by linking their arguments more formally with a historical approach' (p. 168; see also Cohen, p. 24).

The strong connection between women's issues and historical analysis is most evident in the work of feminist materialists like Catherine Belsey, who have reappropriated terms like 'experience' and 'meaning' into a feminist theoretical framework which draws both on Althusser's concept of 'ideology as the lived relationship to real' and on his rejection of a strictly economic analysis of culture. As Belsey points out in her afterword to *The Matter of Difference*:

> To privilege the material as economic over meaning and culture is simply to reaffirm, by reversing it, the conventional idealist opposition between consciousness and the 'real' world. . . . Culture exists, in a word, as meanings. But the cultural meanings of man and woman, experience at the level of consciousness, have also been lived precisely as material practices; not only as rape and violence, but as the slower, more tedious and more insidious oppression of women's bodies by regimes of beauty, by corsetry and crippling footwear, by marital availability, domestic labour and continual childbirth. (in Wayne, p. 259)

Many recent feminist essays make use of 'early' feminist insights because, combined with historical analysis, they remain as relevant as ever. The essays by Catherine Belsey, Phyllis Rackin, Gabriele Bernhard Jackson and Carol Thomas Neely included in this anthology are some outstanding examples. In her essay on *The Merchant of Venice* (p. 196 below), Catherine Belsey presents a reading of the sexual politics of the play. Like William Carroll, Belsey studies riddles, but to a different purpose. If for Carroll riddles point to the absence of the feminine, for Belsey 'the riddle of the rings [in Act V] is . . . a utopian vision of the new possibilities of marriage'. Similarly, she views the riddle of the caskets as hopeful because Bassanio recognizes in it 'the appropriate emblem of desire'; by answering the riddle correctly, he shows that he is 'motivated by desire [as opposed to "his own desert" or "Portia's value"] and knows that lovers give and hazard all they have' (p. 199). But the answer to the riddle in *Merchant* does not provide a solution to the complexities of identity and desire: 'The full answer to the riddle of the rings is that Portia has more than one identity'; and the 'equivocations and doubles entendres of Act V celebrate a sexual indeterminacy, which is not in-difference but multiplicity' (p. 205). It is evident through the casket episode and the marriage that eventually follows it that Portia is not the meek princess we usually encounter in fairy tales, but a woman with strong sexual desires of her own who challenges 'an archetypal yet vanishing order' by cross-dressing, travelling 'from Belmont to Venice and, uniquely in Shakespearean comedy, interven[ing] not only in the public world of history, but specifically in the supremely masculine and political world of law, with the effect of challenging the economic arrangements of the commercial capital of the world' (p. 202).

The tone of optimism evident in Belsey's essay contrasts sharply (but does not *per se* contradict) Cook's and Thompson's frustration over the severe constraints patriarchal structures place on the feminist search for female values in the plays. Drawing on her own work on the changing family in Renaissance England (1985), Belsey puts forth the thesis that *Merchant* participates in a historical moment during which 'the meaning of marriage is unstable, contested, and open to radical reconstruction' (p. 205). Turning its back on the older notion of dynastic marriage, in which the woman was merely a vehicle to produce a male heir to whom title, wealth and honours could be passed on, *Merchant* concerns itself with 'the meaning of gender difference within a new kind of marriage, where a wife is a partner and a companion' (p. 202).

Phyllis Rackin's contribution, an essay on *Richard III* (p. 263 below), is similarly concerned with the shifting structure and function of the Renaissance family, and the redefinition of masculinity within it. Rackin links these changes directly to the immanent demise of the history play genre and the emergence of tragedy. This shift, she argues, is enacted in *Richard III*, a play that displays a movement 'from historical chronicle to tragical history' (p. 274). Significantly, contemporary responses to the genres suggest that Renaissance audiences considered history plays depicting the valiant acts of our forefathers to be aimed primarily at males, while tragedy, though aimed at both sexes, was determined 'to inspire womanly emotions in its spectators' (p. 264). Indeed, the effects of tragedy were thought to be feminizing (p. 266). Rackin links this phenomenon to the historically gradual move from 'the masculine ideal of the hereditary feudal aristocrat to that of the self-made capitalist man', a shift which concomitantly inaugurated a new

> conception of women. Women became a form of property: acquiring a woman, like acquiring any other property, became a means of validating masculine authority and manhood.... [Hence] [o]nce a man's status came to be defined [not by his family genealogy but] by his own *performance* ... the ideal woman became the marriageable heiress, the prize to be attained by a man's own efforts, the material basis for the establishment of his own wealthy household. (p. 276; emphasis added)

Richard III, Rackin demonstrates, not only delivers such a performance but genders it in ways commonly associated with the tragic genre, not with the history play.

Gabriele Bernhard Jackson, in her reading of *1 Henry VI* (p. 142 below), is not interested in condemning Shakespeare's misogyny or defending him against that charge; her point is that the play's presentation of Joan of Arc, like its dominant ideology, is not clear-cut. Employing a careful analysis of historical, literary and mythological allusions, she argues against traditional interpretations of Joan as simply a negative foil to set off the English hero Talbot: 'Although she triumphs over the English, and so must be negative, she carries with her a long positive tradition reaching back to Plato's assertions that women could and should be trained for martial exercise, and to the figure of the armed goddess Minerva' (p. 152). Joan's contradictory presentation allows her 'to perform in one play inconsistent ideological functions that go much beyond discrediting the French cause or setting off by contrast the glories of English chivalry in its dying moments' (p. 144). While the play does draw on 'the current controversy about the nature of women', Shakespeare maintains his negative capability in his creation of Joan through his use of culturally relevant and 'interrelated types of the Amazon, the warrior woman, the cross-dressing woman, and the witch' (p. 145). Although Jackson agrees that the structure of the play 'points in the direction of synthesis' and presents an increasingly negative representation of Joan, she illustrates how the use of '*exempla* point towards differentiation, the temporally disjunctive reading' (p. 150).

Carol Thomas Neely's contribution to this volume imparts a good sense of feminist criticism's historical trajectory. It is a reconsideration of her much-celebrated and widely critiqued essay on *Othello*, first published in 1977 and reprinted in *The Woman's Part* (1980). Today, eighteen years after it first appeared, Neely readily admits to what she calls the 'blind spots' in her earlier essay; she comments on the 'glaring omissions of race and of historical context'. Her present revisitation of *Othello* reflects her response not only to critiques of her own essay but also to more recent interpretations of the play by other critics, which are historical and have introduced race, but have also reified it. While Neely agrees that race must be part of any substantive discussion of the play, she rejects the notion that race can be elevated over gender; that is, she views a search for any single 'cause' of the tragedy as too simple. Instead, she disperses causality into a wider cultural field in which race and gender are precarious and mutually constitutive. As a result, her essay typifies the type of current criticism which places strong emphasis on literature's inextricable link to historically determined cultural systems that do not by any means lend themselves to convenient binary division.

The present turn to history should not, however, be seen as a cure-all, or even as a palliative, for the perceived woes of essentialism. Historical analysis as it is practised today is not without its own built-in pitfalls. New Historicism or cultural poetics revel in historical detail and favour a synchronic approach to 'cultural systems' (Montrose), but are still prone to the privileging of historical anecdotes and their interpretation in a largely preconceived 'understood' context which is not explicitly derived from a wide range of historical data. Anecdotal materials are often held up as moments of cultural revelation because they constitute condensed instances or re-enactments of broader cultural tensions, anxieties or processes; but it is generally not sufficiently acknowledged that the historicist critic must already have a fairly definite image of Renaissance culture before she or he is able to identify the anecdotal materials as re-enactments of that culture. This two-way reading of Renaissance culture needs to be theorized more thoroughly if it is to circumvent an implicit (though of course less ponderous) reliance on the much-maligned 'history as background' of old historicism.

Like New Historicism, cultural materialist criticism cannot really be said to essentialize history in the same way as psychoanalytic criticism often does, but cultural materialism, like New Historicism, has a tendency to *generalize* history. To generalize is not, of course, the same as to essentialize (the former does not evoke the transhistorical quality of the latter), but historical discourses that do generalize (and they all do) necessarily efface data (knowingly or unknowingly) in order to make affirmative statements about the past. In the context of current historicist-materialist criticism this is unavoidable, because literary criticism, unlike the physical sciences, does make the concept of probability an integral feature of its theory or analytic practice. In other words, if psychoanalysis and deconstruction can drop the 'feminine' or 'femaleness' from their discourses, a generalizing historical criticism can easily do the same. Neely goes so far as to assert: 'In spite of all that the new theoretical discourses seem to have in common with feminist criticism ... their effect – not necessarily a deliberate or inevitable one – has been to oppress women, repress sexuality, and subordinate gender issues' (1988, p. 7).[10]

As our discussion so far illustrates, it is undeniable that feminist criticism has made impressive inroads into Shakespearean criticism. Yet one of the areas where feminism has lagged somewhat behind is in one of the last strongholds of male scholarship: textual editing. Although feminists are beginning to have an impact on this most conservative bastion of Shakespeare studies, the current situation can hardly be called satisfactory. We know of no currently available college edition of the complete plays that is edited by a woman, let alone by a feminist – male or female. One troubling consequence of this is that undergraduates in

particular, most of whom come to Shakespeare either innocently or with
the preconceived conservative, patriarchal views still prevalent in our
culture, have to rely on the kindness of teachers for a fuller consideration
of gender complications in the text. What is more, most undergraduates
probably come away believing that editing and annotating the text is a
male prerogative. But positive changes are on the horizon. Feminist
scholars are involved in the forthcoming Norton edition of the plays,
Barbara Mowat is busy re-editing the *New Folger Library Shakespeare*,
and Ann Thompson, a dedicated feminist, is one of the general editors
of the forthcoming Arden 3 series (where its predecessor, the New Arden
Series, shows a systematic neglect of gender issues and of female editors).
In the last several years we have also seen the emergence of critical
scholarship converging on questions of gender. Gary Taylor's 'Textual
and Sexual Criticism: A Crux in *The Comedy of Errors*' and Margreta
de Grazia's *Shakespeare Verbatim* are brilliant instances of this recent
trend. In her contribution to the present volume, Leah Marcus takes up
the question of the Shakespearean editor as Shrew-Tamer, and
demonstrates that the way editors conceive of the textual relationship
between Shakespeare's *The Taming of the Shrew* and the anonymous *The
Taming of a Shrew* depends on 'shifting views of male violence and
female subordination'. Specifically, she argues that Shakespeare's play
may stand much closer to *A Shrew* (either because Shakespeare used this
less misogynistic version as a source or because he had a hand in writing
it) than modern editors are willing to admit. This reluctance Marcus
attributes to an 'affinity between shrew-taming as valorized in *The Taming
of the Shrew* and what editors have traditionally liked to do with texts'
– tame them.

The potent voices in the present volume, however, as well as those in
gender studies at large, leave no doubt that gender scholarship is now
untameable. Although it is certainly not free from the still powerful forces
of conservativism and patriarchy within both the academy and culture,
gender studies has left the critical margins and justly taken a position at the
very centre of academic discourse. Occupying the centre often brings with
it the inevitable danger of institutional co-optation, but even the most
cursory glance at the actual work done in gender studies confronts us with
its radical *difference* from the scholarship produced in any other moment
of our history. Indeed, the rapidly increasing volume, scope, and vehe-
mence of antagonistic approaches to gender scholarship are a sound
indication that the establishment perceives gender scholarship as *different*,
and as corrosive of masculine prerogatives.

Notes

1. As Richard Levin, Brian Vickers, Jonathan Goldberg, and other critics of feminist criticism have recently learned, they need to be equally self-conscious about their critical assumptions and methods. For attacks on Levin's work, see Cook; Graff; Greene; and Sprinker.

2. Novy goes on to reject the metaphor of Shakespeare as father figure, and suggests that it might be more useful to think of him as a brother to women: 'The brother–sister metaphor does not give men primacy, and it emphasizes what people of both sexes have in common' (1981a, p. 25). While admittedly all familial metaphors can be seen as limiting, a father can at least leave a legacy to a daughter, while – particularly in Renaissance culture – if a woman has a brother she has no hope of inheritance or independent access to that legacy.

3. Cf. Thompson, p. 170. Clarke makes an identical claim for 'poor' boys who wish to become 'gentlemen'.

4. Kahn's anthropological reading echoes the work of Gayle Rubin's and Luce Irigaray's critique of Lévi-Strauss, although only Mary Douglas's *Purity and Danger* is acknowledged as an explicit influence.

5. Eliot is clear, however, that he is not asking for a stronger woman character on the stage, since he recognizes that it is the nature of the problem dealt with in this play – a son's feelings towards a guilty mother – that they should be 'in excess of their objective cause' (p. 36). What lies behind Gertrude's failure, therefore, is 'precisely unrepresentable, a set of unconscious emotions which, *by definition*, can have no objective outlet and which are therefore incapable of submitting to the formal constraints of art'. Recalling that Eliot's famed concept of the 'objective correlative' was introduced in the essay on *Hamlet*, Rose points out that Eliot's local views regarding *Hamlet* are really symptomatic of a much more pervasive inclination to posit the 'feminine' as the cause of artistic failure in general.

6. British materialist feminists like Kathleen McLuskie have distanced themselves from liberal feminists who, she claims, have 'co-opted Shakespeare' to fit their own agenda. She criticizes the psychoanalytic work of Coppélia Kahn and Janet Adelman, as well as Juliet Dusinberre's ideological analysis of contemporary discourse, as equally 'unproblematically mimetic', and maintains that despite their references to feminist anthropology and philosophy, Marilyn French and Linda Bamber are ultimately essentialist (p. 89). McLuskie rejects 'claiming Shakespeare's views as feminist' and calls instead for a 'procedure [which] would involve theorizing the relationship between feminism and the plays more explicitly ... refusing to construct an author behind the plays and paying attention instead to the narrative, poetic and theatrical strategies which construct the plays' meanings and position the audience to understand their events from a particular point of view' (p. 92).

7. In fairness to Cook, two things should be noted here. First, it is somewhat ambiguous whether her description of the patriarchal world in *Much Ado* should be used to extrapolate a general definition of patriarchy. It is not clear that Cook wants this. Secondly, it is none the less clear that her dim hopes for 'feminine values' in a patriarchal world highlight a significant ontological difficulty in the feminist project. All the same, Cook may be guilty of a linguistic sleight of hand which imperils the veracity of her claim. Initially, she speaks of Messina's 'predominately masculine ethos', but when she makes her pronouncement concerning the impossibility of 'feminine values' the term 'predominately' apparently comes to mean 'exclusively', and this is a mistake, for 'predominately' precisely denotes a space for a non-masculine (feminine?) ethos within the society of the play. In this way, Cook privileges and essentializes patriarchy in *Much Ado* (even though she clearly understands that many of the anxieties males experience in Messina result not from some essential maleness but from a frantic desire to control female sexuality, a control which is necessary within the patriarchal scheme of inheritance). Cook is surely right to reject the suggestion of some feminist critics that 'Beatrice's feminine charity triumphs' over Messina's masculine values (p. 75), for she cogently demonstrates that Beatrice's views and Claudio's final acceptance of Hero reinscribe rather than subvert or displace Messina's patriarchal value system, but she does not consider the possibility that the absence of genuine feminine values does *not* necessarily mean that all values are masculine. She challenges the play

world's binary principles of maleness and femaleness, but only to demonstrate the apparent impossibility of the latter and to privilege the former.

Although she tries hard not to, Traub likewise utilizes essentialism when she argues that certain women's groups have been able to 'disengage themselves from patriarchal values and structures'. At the very least, such disengagement signifies a rejection of a male dispensation, and is therefore a gesture in some way occasioned by that dispensation.

8. For critiques of such heterosexual bias, see Goldberg, 1992, 1994; Smith; Traub, 1991.

9. As Holderness points out, Bamber constructs the relationship between 'femininity' and 'history' 'as a binary opposition of mutually incompatible contraries' (p. 168); 'history is a grand narrative of male achievement' which 'specifically denies any significant space to "feminine Otherness"' (p. 167). Bamber therefore looks to 'a female principle apart from history' (p. 140, quoted in Holderness, p. 167) in order to challenge the male historical narrative. Coppélia Kahn, on the other hand, is concerned not with the representation of women but with the 'dramatic explorations of masculine ideology' (Holderness, p. 168). For Kahn there is no 'irreconcilable split between masculine and feminine principles'; she is interested in the 'dramatized historical context as a patriarchal structure, the ideological site of a crisis of masculine identity' (ibid.). While Kahn states her methodology as both psychoanalytic and historical, Holderness maintains that psychoanalysis prevails over history, and that 'both family relationships and problems of identity tend to be seen as independent of history, gravitating towards the immanent structure of a psychological archetype' (ibid.).

10. Neely goes on to declare that despite many points of commonality between feminism and the new theoretical discourses, 'All of the topoi of the new approaches: the historicity and intertextuality of texts; the constriction of history to power, politics, and ideology; the denial of unity, autonomy, and identity in authors, subjects, texts; the displacement from women to woman to sexual difference to textuality; the view of man/woman as just one more of the outmoded, interchangeable parade of binary oppositions, have the effect of putting woman in her customary place, of re-producing patriarchy – the same old master plot' (1988, p. 7).

References

Althusser, Louis, 'Ideology and Ideological State Apparatuses (Notes towards an Investigation)', in *Lenin and Philosophy and Other Essays*, trans. Ben Brewster, New York and London: Monthly Review Press, 1971, pp. 127–86.

Bamber, Linda, *Comic Women, Tragic Men: A Study of Gender and Genre in Shakespeare*, Stanford, CA: Stanford University Press, 1982.

Belsey, Catherine, 'Disrupting Sexual Difference: Meaning and Gender in the Comedies', in *Alternative Shakespeares*, ed. John Drakakis, London: Methuen, 1985, pp. 166–90.

—— 'Love in Venice', *Shakespeare Survey* 44 (1992): 41–54.

—— 'A Future for Materialist Feminist Criticism?', in Wayne, pp. 257–70.

Boose, Lynda, 'The Family in Shakespeare Studies; or – Studies in the Family of Shakespeareans; or – The Politics of Politics', *Renaissance Quarterly* 40 (1987): 707–72.

Bray, Alan, *Homosexuality in Renaissance England*, London: Gay Men's Press, 1982.

Carroll, William C., 'The Virgin Not: Language and Sexuality in Shakespeare', *Shakespeare Survey* 46 (1994): 107–20.

Clarke, Mary Cowden, 'Preface', *Shakespeare's Works*, New York and London: Appleton & Trubner, 1861.

Cohen, Walter, 'Political Criticism of Shakespeare', in *Shakespeare Reproduced: The Text in History and Ideology*, ed. Jean E. Howard and Marion F. O'Connor, New York: Methuen, 1987, pp. 18–46.

Cook, Carol, '"The Sign and Semblance of Her Honor": Reading Gender Difference in *Much Ado about Nothing*', *PMLA* 101 (1986): 186–202.

―――― 'Straw Women and Whipping Girls: The (Sexual) Politics of Critical Self-Fashioning', in Kamps, pp. 61–78.

Douglas, Mary, *Purity and Danger: An Analysis of Concepts of Pollution and Taboo*, London: Routledge & Kegan Paul, 1966.

Eliot, T.S., *Selected Prose of T.S. Eliot*, ed. Frank Kermode, London: Faber, 1975.

Graff, Gerald, 'Ordinary People and Academic Critics: A Response to Richard Levin', in Kamps, pp. 99–113.

de Grazia, Margreta, *Shakespeare Verbatim: The Reproduction of Authenticity and the 1790 Apparatus*, Oxford: Oxford University Press, 1991.

Goldberg, Jonathan, *Sodometries: Renaissance Texts, Modern Sexualities*, Stanford, CA: Stanford University Press, 1992.

―――――, ed., *Queering the Renaissance*, Durham, NC: Duke University Press, 1994.

Greenblatt, Stephen, *Shakespearean Negotiations: The Circulation of Social Energy in Renaissance England*, Los Angeles and Berkeley: University of California Press, 1988.

Greene, Gayle, 'The Myth of Neutrality, Again?', in Kamps, pp. 23–30.

―――― '"This That You Call Love": Sexual and Social Tragedy in *Othello*', *Journal of Women's Studies in Literature* 1 (1979): 16–32.

Holderness, Graham, '"A Woman's War": A Feminist Reading of *Richard II*', in Kamps, pp. 167–83.

Jackson, Gabriele Bernhard, 'Topical Ideology: Witches, Amazons, and Shakespeare's Joan of Arc', *English Literary Renaissance* 18 (1988): 40–65.

Jones, Ernest, *Hamlet and Oedipus* (1949), New York and London: W.W. Norton, 1976.

Kahn, Coppélia, 'The Rape in Shakespeare's *Lucrece*', *Shakespeare Studies* 9 (1976): 45–72.

Kamps, Ivo, ed., *Shakespeare Left and Right*, New York and London: Routledge, 1991.

Lacan, Jacques, 'Desire and the Interpretation of Desire in *Hamlet*' (1959), in *Literature and Psychoanalysis, The Question of Reading: Otherwise*, ed. Shoshana Felman, *Yale French Studies* 55/56 (1977): 11–52.

Levin, Richard, 'Ideological Criticism and Pluralism', in Kamps, pp. 15–22.

McLuskie, Kathleen, 'The Patriarchal Bard: Feminist Criticism and Shakespeare: *King Lear* and *Measure for Measure*', in *Political Shakespeare: New Essays in Cultural Materialism*, ed. Jonathan Dollimore and Alan Sinfield, Ithaca, NY and London: Cornell University Press, 1985, pp. 88–108.

Marcus, Leah, 'The Shakespearean Editor as Shrew-Tamer', *ELR* 22 (1992): 177–200.

Montrose, Louis, 'Professing the Renaissance: The Poetics and Politics of Culture', in *The New Historicism*, ed. H. Aram Veeser, New York and London: Routledge, 1989, pp. 15–36.

Mulvey, Laura, 'Visual Pleasure and Narrative Cinema', *Visual and Other Pleasures*, Bloomington and Indianapolis, IN: Indiana University Press, 1989, pp. 14–26.

Neely, Carol Thomas, 'Constructing the Subject: Feminist Practice and the New Renaissance Discourses', *English Literary Renaissance* 18 (1988): 5–18.

―――― 'Circumscription and Unhousedness: *Othello* in the Borderlands', this volume, pp. 302–15.

Novy, Marianne, 'Demythologizing Shakespeare', *Women's Studies* 9 (1981a): 17–27.

―――― 'Shakespeare and Emotional Distance in the Elizabethan Family', *Theatre Journal* 33.3 (1981b): 316–27.

Pequigney, Joseph, *Such is My Love: A Study of Shakespeare's Sonnets*, Chicago and London: University of Chicago Press, 1985.

―――― 'The Two Antonios and Same-Sex Love in *Twelfth Night* and *The Merchant of Venice*', *ELR* 22 (1992): 201–21.

Rackin, Phyllis, 'Engendering the Tragic Audience: The Case of *Richard III*', *Studies in the Literary Imagination* 26 (1993): 47–65.

Rose, Jacqueline, 'Hamlet – the *Mona Lisa* of Literature', *Critical Quarterly* 28 (1986): 35–49.

Rubin, Gayle, 'The Traffic in Women: Notes on the "Political Economy" of Sex', *Toward an Anthropology of Women*, ed. Rayna R. Reiter, New York and London: Monthly Review Press, 1975, pp. 157–210.

—— 'Thinking Sex: Notes for a Radical Theory of the Politics of Sexuality', in *Pleasure and Danger*, ed. Carole Vance, London: Routledge & Kegan Paul, 1984, pp. 267–319.

Ruskin, John, 'Of Queens' Gardens', in *Sesame and Lilies*, Cambridge, MA: Riverside Press, 1900.

Smith, Bruce R., *Homosexual Desire in Shakespeare's England: A Cultural Poetics*, Chicago and London: University of Chicago Press, 1991.

Sprinker, Michael, 'Commentary: "You've Got a Lot of Nerve"', in Kamps, pp. 115–28.

Taylor, Gary, 'Textual and Sexual Criticism: A Crux in The Comedy of Errors, *Renaissance Drama*', n.s. 19 (1988): 195–225.

Thompson, Ann, '"Miranda, Where's Your Sister?": Rereading Shakespeare's *The Tempest*', in *Feminist Criticism: Theory and Practice*, ed. Susan Sellers, Toronto, Buffalo: University of Toronto Press, 1991, 45–55.

Tillyard, E.M.W., *Shakespeare's History Plays*, New York: Collier Books, 1962 (1944).

Tompkins, Jane, '"But Is It Any Good?": The Institutionalization of Literary Value', in *Sensational Designs: The Cultural Work of American Fiction 1790–1860*, New York and Oxford: Oxford University Press, 1985, pp. 186–201.

Traub, Valerie, 'Jewels, Statues, and Corpses: Containment of Female Erotic Power in Shakespeare's Plays', *Shakespeare Studies* (1988): 215–40.

—— 'Desire and the Differences it Makes', in Wayne, pp. 81–114.

Van Watson, William, 'Shakespeare, Zeffirelli, and the Homosexual Gaze', *Literature Film Quarterly* 20:4 (1992): 308–25.

Vickers, Brian, *Appropriating Shakespeare: Contemporary Critical Quarrels*, New Haven, CT and London: Yale University Press, 1993.

Wayne, Valerie, ed., *The Matter of Difference: Materialist Feminist Criticism of Shakespeare*, Ithaca, NY: Cornell University Press, 1991.

Woodbridge, Linda, 'Afterword: Poetics from the Barrel of a Gun?', in Kamps, pp. 285–98.

2

The Rape in Shakespeare's *Lucrece*
Coppélia Kahn

I

The central problem in Shakespeare's *Lucrece* is rape – a moral, social, and psychological problem which Shakespeare sets before us in all its ambiguities and contradictions, but which criticism has so far failed to confront, for several reasons.[1] In *Venus and Adonis*, traditional sex roles are reversed, with humorous effect; in *Lucrece*, they are taken with deadly seriousness and carried to a logical and bitter extreme, which makes it painful to confront the poem squarely. Furthermore, the rhetorical display-pieces invite critical attention for their own sake, offering readers a happy escape from the poem's insistent concern with the relationship between sex and power. That relationship is established by the terms of marriage in a patriarchal society. The rape is ultimately a means by which Shakespeare can explore the nature of marriage in such a society and the role of women in marriage. Therefore, the poem must be understood in a psychosocial context which takes account of sex roles and cultural attitudes towards sexuality.

In this context, the terms 'patriarchal' and 'sex role', rather than being modern impositions on a Renaissance sensibility, accurately reflect both the Elizabethan and the Roman reality. Because Shakespeare's own society was patriarchal in the means by which it maintained degree as the basis of the social order, it would be surprising if he had not sensed a strong kinship between Rome and England. As M.W. MacCallum states:

> Thus Shakespeare, in his picture of Rome and Romans, does not give the notes that mark off Roman from every other civilization, but rather those that it possessed in common with the rest, and especially with his own.[2]

It is a critical commonplace that Elizabethans regarded Rome as a political mirror of their own times, finding in it a series of lessons about the fall of princes, the dangers of mob rule, the horrors of rebellion – lessons which they considered to have more than theoretical value. The story of Lucrece as Shakespeare found it in his Latin sources is also a mirror – a mirror of the patriarchal marriage system obtaining in England, in which matches were arranged so as to ensure, through the provision of legitimate male heirs, the proper continuance of wealth and status. In marriage as the propertied classes of the sixteenth century knew it, women were to serve the interests of their fathers' and their husbands' family lines; only in that way could they acquire their own rights and privileges. According to such an authority as Lawrence Stone:

> This sixteenth-century aristocratic family was patrilinear, primogenitural, and patriarchal: patrilinear in that it was the male line whose ancestry was traced so diligently by the genealogists and heralds, and in almost all cases via the male line that titles were inherited; primogenitural in that most of the property went to the eldest son, the younger brothers being dispatched into the world with little more than a modest annuity or life interest in a small estate to keep them afloat; and patriarchal in that the husband and father lorded it over his wife and children with the quasi-absolute authority of a despot. None of these features was new, but the first two became more marked in the later Middle Ages and reached their extreme development in the sixteenth century.[3]

Shakespeare's interest in rape lies in the consequences of the crime for the victim, rather than in the act of committing the crime; hence the poem's original title is simply *Lucrece*; *The Rape of Lucrece* was an addition by the editor of the 1616 quarto. Shakespeare focuses our attention on the curious fact that Lucrece acquires a moral stigma from *being* raped. Though innocent of the crime, she finds herself disgraced, ruined, an object of shame to herself and the world. In the language of the poem, she is morally 'stained' and sexually 'tainted'. Why should Tarquin's crime pollute Lucrece? Why should she bear, in more than the physical sense, the 'load of shame' which he 'leaves behind'?

A summary of the plot will help us to place Lucrece's stigma in context. First, a prose argument relates how Collatine, Lucrece's husband, boasted of her 'incomparable chastity' to his fellow officers in Tarquin's tent. To verify his and others' claims for the virtue of their wives, the men post to Rome that very night and find all the women save Lucrece 'dancing and revelling'; she is spinning with her maids. At this first meeting, Tarquin conceives a lustful passion for Lucrece, but hides it. Later he returns to Collatine's house alone; at this point the poem begins. On a pretext he stays the night and, after an agonizing debate with himself (126–356), forces his way into Lucrece's chamber. He threatens to kill her and posthumously slander her as an adulteress if she resists him, but promises not to tell anyone if she submits peaceably to his will. She pleads with him at length

(561–666); he rapes her anyway and immediately departs. She then delivers several tirades in the high style of the complaint poem: apostrophes to Night (764 ff.), to Opportunity (876 ff.). Attended by her maid, she composes a letter to Collatine summoning him to Rome and bids her groom carry it to him. Then begins the most famous set-piece of the poem, a description of the defeat of Troy as painted on a wall hanging (1366–1568). When Tarquin and other lords arrive, she declares that she has been raped but insists that they swear to avenge her before she names Tarquin as her assailant. Thereupon, she stabs herself to death. Brutus urges the grief-stricken husband and father to their mission of revenge, and in the last stanza we learn that Tarquin has been banished for his crime.

The central metaphor in the poem is that of a stain, which is repeatedly and forcefully attached to Lucrece.[4] The words 'stain' or 'stained' are mentioned eighteen times in the poem's 1855 lines, and synonyms such as blot, spot, blur, blemish, attaint, scar, and pollution are frequently used. Other words denoting either moral error, social disgrace, or both occur with great frequency: shame, blame, infamy, offence, disgrace, sin, guilt, crime, trespass, defame, fault, and corruption. Tarquin introduces the metaphor as he is contemplating the rape, using it to characterize the effect of the act on her:

> Fair torch, burn out thy light, and lend it not
> To darken her whose light excelleth thine;
> And die, unhallow'd thought, before you blot
> With your uncleanness that which is divine;
> Offer pure incense to so pure a shrine.
>   Let fair humanity abhor the deed
>   That spots and stains love's modest snow-white weed.[5]

He again employs it to describe the disgrace which will follow her death if she resists him:

> Then for thy husband and thy children's sake,
> Tender my suit; bequeath not to their lot
> The shame that from them no device can take,
> The blemish that will never be forgot,
> Worse than a slavish wipe or birth-hour's blot.

$$(533–7)$$

After the rape, the idea that she is 'stained' becomes the leitmotiv of all her laments and the motivation for her suicide.

The poem's major concern is expressed through the metaphor of the stain, but it is expressed ironically. Whatever the stain is, Lucrece believes it to be indelibly hers and tragically lives out the implications of her belief. But Shakespeare has moulded the poem so as to examine and question her belief from many angles, as I shall show. First of all, the simple moral facts

of the rape impel us to doubt Lucrece's self-indictment. In the poem, as in
its sources, Lucrece is wholly innocent of any provocation or complicity
in the crime; therefore, the stain cannot indicate her guilt.[6] In fact, it is hard
to find any single term or moral category which encompasses Lucrece's
conception of how the rape has stained her, as this passage, one of several
similar passages, shows:

> He in his speed looks for the morning light,
> She prays she never may behold the day:
> 'For day,' quoth she, 'night's scapes doth open lay,
>   And my true eyes have never practis'd how
>   To cloak offences with a cunning brow.
>
> They think not but that every eye can see
> The same disgrace which they themselves behold;
> And therefore would they still in darkness be,
> To have their unseen sin remain untold.
> For they their guilt with weeping will unfold,
>   And grave like water that doth eat in steel,
>   Upon my cheeks, what helpless shame I feel.'
>
>   (745–56)

On the one hand she mourns her 'disgrace' and 'helpless shame', terms
which might indicate a fear of social disapproval or loss of prestige but do
not necessarily imply that she has done anything to deserve such moral
judgements. On the other hand she refers to 'sin' and 'guilt' which must,
in the rhetorical context, be hers, the result of her own moral failing. To
complicate the matter further, she reviles Tarquin as the one who
committed the crime, but declares herself equally guilty of a crime against
Collatine:

> Feast-finding minstrels tuning my defame,
>   Will tie the hearers to attend each line,
>   How Tarquin wronged me, I Collatine.
>
>   (817–19)

Our difficulties in comprehending the basis on which Lucrece judges
herself guilty of such a crime arise from her conception of herself as a
woman in a patriarchal society, a conception which renders irrelevant for
her the questions of moral responsibility and guilt in rape. Though Lucrece
uses moral terms such as sin and guilt, she actually condemns herself
according to primitive, non-moral standards of pollution and uncleanness,
in which only the material circumstances of an act determine its goodness
or evil. In doing so, she embodies the attitudes towards female sexuality
underlying Roman marriage. Shakespeare poises these attitudes against
another standard of judgement, radically different from Lucrece's but more

familiar to us. He weaves through the narrator's comments and through the heroine's speeches suggestions of a Christian ethic which disregards material circumstances and judges an act wholly according to the motives and disposition of the agent. His point of view, as a result, is a blend of ironic distance from Lucrece's materialistic conception of chastity and compassionate respect for her integrity in adhering to chastity as the only value which gives meaning to her as a Roman wife. What the poem conveys above all is the tragic cost Lucrece pays for her exquisite awareness of her Roman duty. She upholds the social order by accepting her stain and dying for the sake of marriage as an institution.

II

The poem deals with the rape of a *married* woman. Lucrece's chastity is emphatically that of the wife who has dedicated her body to her husband. This dedication has so rarefied and sanctified her sexuality that she seems virginal or even unsexual. She is imbued with a modesty so profound as to make us wonder, perhaps, what sexual satisfactions the marriage bed could hold for Collatine. The vocabulary of purity and holiness surrounds her like a halo throughout the poem. In the second stanza, she is

> that sky of his [Collatine's] delight;
> Where mortal stars as bright as heaven's beauties,
> With pure aspects did him peculiar duties.

                                                          (12–14)

She is called 'This earthly saint' (85), a 'heavenly image' (288), 'the picture of pure piety' (542). In a stanza already quoted, she is 'divine', 'so pure a shrine', and her chastity is 'love's modest snow-white weed' (190–96). The wifely chastity of later Shakespearean heroines, such as Desdemona, Imogen and (to a lesser extent) Hermione, is also depicted in hyperbolical terms which serve not merely to defend them against slurs on their sexual honour but to make them seem 'enskied and sainted' – above and beyond sexuality.

It is precisely such virginal qualities which make Lucrece the paragon of wives. The sexual act in marriage has not altered the perfect innocence which presumably characterized her before she married, and it has hallowed in Collatine the desire which is evil in Tarquin. The marriage bed which Lucrece shares with Collatine is, before the rape, 'clear' (382) and 'pure' (684) – free of any carnal sin; and her breasts are 'maiden worlds' (408), a phrase which strikingly expresses the anomaly of this conception of woman in marriage. Though she is supposedly her husband's sexual partner, she is also untouched, unchanged by her participation in the sexual act.[7] Marriage has invested sex with a prelapsarian sinlessness, and herein lies its psychological value for man. It is his defence against sexual desire, with its risks, perils, and humiliations, and Lucrece is the embodiment of that defence. In her, woman made wife, desire is legitimized; it is made a habit and a right instead of an adventure into the illicit. No longer taboo, desire is now shrouded in the pieties of domestic life.

As Shakespeare would have known from his two main sources, Ovid's *Fasti* and Livy's *The History of Rome*, the national cult of Vesta, goddess of the hearth, virtually institutionalized the virginal wife.[8] This cult duplicated on a national scale the values and rituals of the ancient Roman domestic religion, in which the household altar fire was identified with the ancestral gods of the family and with the earth from which the family drew its sustenance; thus the fire symbolized the continuity of the family itself. When Numa, who according to legend succeeded Romulus as king, founded the temple of Vesta, the tending of the sacred altar fire was entrusted, significantly, to virgins, who enjoyed high public honours. It was believed that catastrophe would befall the state if the vestal fire were ever allowed to go out, and any breach of chastity by the vestals was punished by their being buried alive.[9] The symbolic social value of their chastity is noted by Cicero:

> And since Vesta ... has taken the city hearth under her protection, virgins should have charge of her worship, so that the care and guardianship of the fire may be the more easily maintained, and other women may perceive by their example that their sex is capable by nature of complete chastity.[10]

At least one Elizabethan saw in the vestals the same kind of social importance. John Florio, in his *First Fruites* (1578), after praising Queen Elizabeth's virginity, declaims on vestal worship in imperial Rome:

> O golden worlde ... then was chastitie knowen in the Temple of Vesta. Then the Emperours dyd frequent the Chappel of Iupiter, then Lust durst not come to the Court of Caesar, then abstinence walked through the markette in euerye Cittye, then the world was chaste, then the world dyd triumph, but nowe euery thyng goeth contrary. Certis it is a lamentable thyng, to consider the state of this world.[11]

Florio might have found this vision of a chaste imperial Rome in Ovid's *Fasti*, in the verses celebrating Augustus' election as pontifex maximus, whose duty it was to preside over the vestals and their temple. In them he pictures the eternal fire of Vesta's hearth next to the 'fire' of Augustus' divinity, 'the pledges of empire side by side'.[12]

The two descriptions of Lucrece's person in the poem, both remarkably non-erotic, elaborate a paradoxical desire to desexualize the woman who, by virtue of her status as wife, is entitled to be sexually possessed. I will discuss them in some detail. The first is the narrator's account of the heroine greeting Tarquin on his arrival at her house in Rome, lines 50–84. This description is so heavily encrusted with heraldic terminology and so burdened with the conceit of a chivalric contest between the lady's beauty and her virtue that nothing of a plausible female face or body survives. Shakespeare is trying to convey the impression that she is surpassingly beautiful without admitting any suggestion that she might be physically desirable – a difficult task. In order to accomplish it, he has recourse to chivalric conventions and to allegory, the battle between red and white representing the parity of beauty and virtue in Lucrece. The result is confusion, in physical reference (is the red and white her habitual complexion, or a succession of blushes?) and in syntax (especially in lines 57–63). But if this contest tells us nothing about Lucrece physically, it does hint at the tension between two conceptions of her, as sexual object and as sexually taboo, which is shortly to explode. It is interesting that she is characterized in terms of two qualities, beauty and virtue, which are necessarily opposed in this context. In so far as she is beautiful, it is inevitable that men should desire her; but in so far as she is a virtuous wife, she belongs to Collatine and no other man may have her.

As T.W. Baldwin has shown, Shakespeare draws his emphasis on the erotic quality of Lucrece's chastity, as distinct from her beauty, not so much from his sources as from the commentary on Ovid by Paulus Marsus in the edition he used.[13] For instance, the Argument prefacing the poem states: 'Collatinus extolled the incomparable chastity of his wife Lucretia.' In Livy the terms of Collatine's praise are vague and general; in Ovid, 'Each praised his wife' for her 'loyalty to the marriage bed'. Marsus interprets this phrase to mean *pudicitia*, and relates this praise directly to Collatine. To give but one more of many possible examples, Marsus' commentary on Ovid's description of Tarquin's mounting desire:

> verba placent et vox, et quod corrumpere non est,
>   quoque minor spes est, hoc magis ille cupit
>
> [pleasing, too, her words and voice and virtue incorruptible;
>   and the less hope he had, the hotter his desire]

singles out the phrase *quod corrumpere non est* (*Fasti*, II.765–6), stating '*hoc est ipsa spectata pudicitia*'.[14] It is clear that Shakespeare was not the first to discern the peculiar element built into the dramatic situation, the power of chastity to arouse desire. But Shakespeare goes further than Ovid or Marsus in relating this phenomenon to Lucrece's status as the wife of Tarquin's friend.

Shakespeare begins the poem by announcing in the first stanza that Tarquin

> lurks to aspire
> And girdle with embracing flames the waist
> Of *Collatine's fair love, Lucrece the chaste*.
>
> (5–7; emphasis added)

In the next stanza he suggests that Collatine's praise of his wife's 'unmatched red and white' has inspired Tarquin's lust. But it is not only the fact that Lucrece is both beautiful and unavailable which arouses Tarquin; it is the fact that Collatine's proprietorship over Lucrece *makes* her unavailable.

Notice how heavily Shakespeare emphasizes the husband's private possession of his wife:

> For he the night before, in Tarquin's tent
> Unlock'd the treasure of his happy state:
> What priceless wealth the heavens had him lent,
> In the possession of his beauteous mate;
> Reck'ning his fortune at such high proud rate
>   That kings might be espoused to more fame,
>   But king nor peer to such a peerless dame.
>
> (15–21)

The strong similarity, in image and in situation, between this boasting contest and that in *Cymberline*, written some sixteen years later, attests to Shakespeare's enduring perception of the chaste wife as an aspect of her husband's status amongst male rivals. Posthumus, it is said, has asserted Imogen to be 'more fair, virtuous, wise, chaste, constant, qualified and less attemptable' than any woman in France. Iachimo challenges this claim, contending that one so fair cannot possibly remain chaste against the attempts of other men to possess her: 'You may wear her in title yours, but you know strange fowl light upon neighbouring ponds,' he insinuates.[15] In both works, the chaste wife is seen as a precious jewel which tempts the thief; in both works, the husband's boasts initiate the temptation, in effect challenging his peers to take that jewel.

The conventional metaphor of jewels, treasure or wealth to represent the value of the lady to her lover has an additional meaning in *Lucrece*. The frequent references throughout the poem to Lucrece as 'treasure', 'prize', and 'spoil', and the comparison of Tarquin to a thief (134–40, 710–11, to cite two of many examples) constitute a running metaphorical commentary on marriage as ownership of women. As the elegiac stanza lamenting the destruction of Collatine's marital happiness tells us:

> Honour and beauty in the *owner's* arms
> Are weakly fortress'd from a world of harms.
>
> (27–8; emphasis added)

Marriage is no fortress against the greedy lust of Tarquin, just as the rich man's coffers cannot prevent his gold from being robbed.[16] If Collatine even speaks of Lucrece to another man, he invites competition for possession of her; Lucrece is 'that rich jewel he should keep unknown / From thievish ears, because it is his own' (34–5).

For the husband, his wife's sexuality is both neutralized and protected by marriage; for other men, it is heightened in value because another man, a potential rival, possesses it. When Tarquin considers 'his loathsome enterprise' before departing for Lucrece's chamber, he devotes only one stanza to abstract moral arguments against the contemplated rape (the stanza already quoted on p. 24), as an act that would unjustifiably harm the good, as embodied in Lucrece. Otherwise, he thinks of the act as a social disgrace to himself as a nobleman and to his family (196–210), and as one which would place him in a morally disadvantageous position *vis-à-vis* Collatine:

> If Collatine dream of my intent,
> Will he not wake, and in a desp'rate rage
> Post hither, this vile purpose to prevent? –
> . . .
> O what excuse can my invention make
> When thou shalt charge me with so black a deed?
>
> (218–20; 225–6)

He then considers hypothetical circumstances which would have justified the deed and made it honourable:

> Had Collatinus kill'd my son or sire,
> Or lain in ambush to betray my life;
> Or were he not my dear friend.
>
> (232–4)

That is, he is primarily concerned not with the absolute moral quality of the rape, nor with the harm it will do to Lucrece specifically, but with the possible damage it may cause to his status as a nobleman of honourable reputation. This status, of course, is relative to Collatine's power to accuse him of a dishonourable act, and shame him thereby. Tarquin regards Collatine as ultimately the judge of his (Tarquin's) acts, and the only real obstacle to his desire:

> Within his thought her heavenly image sits,
> And in the self-same seat sits Collatine.
> That eye which looks on her confounds his wits;

That eye which him beholds, as more divine,
Unto a view so false will not incline. . . .

(288–92)

Basically, Tarquin considers the rape a violation not of Lucrece's chastity but of Collatine's honour. It is an affair between men, as the ending of the poem will reveal.

The competition between these two men for possession of Lucrece is exacerbated by the difference in their status, for Tarquin is the king's son and Collatine is merely of a noble family (39–42). But Livy relates that Tarquin's father seized the throne unlawfully, brutally murdering his father-in-law and simply naming himself king without observing the custom of calling on the senate for their approval. *Tel père, tel fils*; both men display a kingly disregard for the legitimate sanction of power, and take power into their own hands. Tarquin's private conduct in seizing his friend's wife is parallel to his father's public conduct in seizing the throne; both actions are inimical to a just and ordered society. Another parallel between the realms of sex and politics is notable; the structure of both is patriarchal, with authority over subordinates designated to certain individual men. But authority cannot withstand the strains exerted against it by rivalry between the men, and breaks down in violence and disorder. The rape of Lucrece not only parallels the abuse of kingship in Rome but also precipitates its end. Thus the revenge against Tarquin with which the poem concludes involves (as an educated Elizabethan familiar with Livy would know) not only his banishment but the exile of all the Tarquins, the end of monarchy, and the election of Collatine and his fellow-avenger Brutus as the first consuls of the new republic.

Women in Livy frequently appear as victims of the incessant struggle for political power.[17] For example, in the early days of the monarchy, Amulius deposed his older brother and proclaimed himself king of Alba. To prevent his brother's family from asserting their claim to the throne, he murdered his nephews and made his niece a vestal virgin, 'thus, under the pretence of honouring her, depriving her of all hopes of issue' (I.3). Again, in the well-known episode of the rape of the Sabine women, the women rush into the midst of battle, appealing to their fathers on the one side and their husbands on the other to stop the fighting (I.9). In the story of Appius and Verginia (well-known to Elizabethan audiences from Chaucer's version), which is the longest single episode in Book I, the assaulted virgin assumes a symbolic importance quite similar to that of Lucrece; her plight illustrates the patricians' wanton trespass against the legitimate rights of the plebs. When her father stabs her rather than allow Appius to violate her, he declares to his supporters: 'In this the only way in which I can, I vindicate my child, thy freedom' (III.48).

Shakespeare also calls attention to male rivalry over the proprietorship of women in a curious episode immediately following Lucrece's suicide, when the heroine's father, Lucretius, and her husband indulge in a contest of grief:

> Then one doth call her his, the other his,
> Yet neither may possess the claim they lay.
> The father says, 'She's mine,' 'O mine she is,'
> Replies her husband, 'do not take away
> My sorrow's interest; let no mourner say
> He weeps for her, for she was only mine,
> And only must be wail'd by Collatine.'

(1793–9)

The egotistic competitiveness of the two male guardians over their lifeless 'claim', who now belongs to the ages, is academic. But the metaphors of possessing a 'claim' and having 'interest' in sorrow remind us of the actual legal position of women in marriage, in Rome as in Shakespeare's England.[18] This 'emulation in their woe' between father and husband is checked only by the vigorous efforts of Brutus, who reminds the men that their real task is revenge. Here as in the major conflict of the poem, Shakespeare questions the wisdom and humanity of making property the basis of human relationships.

The second description of Lucrece raises similar issues concerning marriage and the competition for ownership and power between men. Unlike the first, it portrays Lucrece's body directly, viewed as Tarquin sees her sleeping in her chamber (386–420), but again, it fends off erotic suggestiveness. Since the heroine is being described through Tarquin's lustful eyes, we might expect the titillating detail which the poet handles so deftly in *Venus and Adonis*. Instead, he portrays her as 'a virtuous monument' or gravestone effigy, her head 'entombed' in her pillow, with a hand like an April daisy and eyes like marigolds, 'Showing life's triumph in the map of death, / And death's dim look in life's mortality' (402–3).[19] Even her breasts convey no impression of soft and inviting womanly flesh. They are depicted in legal and political terms, as venerable emblems of her status as Collatine's wife:

> Her breasts like ivory globes circled with blue,
> A pair of maiden worlds unconquered;
> Save of their lord, no bearing yoke they knew,
> And him by oath they truly honoured.
> These worlds in Tarquin new ambition bred;
>   Who like a foul usurper went about,
>   From this fair throne to heave the owner out.

(407–13)

But the whole stanza disturbingly portrays Lucrece's sexuality politically, as the colonization of her very flesh by the men who would 'lay claim' to her.[20] As at the beginning of the poem, here it is Collatine's proprietorship which provokes Tarquin's desire to rape Lucrece. The last three lines depict his desire in political language; the sight of her naked bosom breeds not new lust but 'new ambition'. The heroine becomes an image for two fields of political conquest, the expanding Roman Empire and the New World (similarly, Virginia is named for a virginal woman), and Tarquin, correspondingly, is a rival power who would snatch the newly won territory from its rightful possessor. In lines 3 and 4, the marriage of Lucrece and Collatine is metaphorically a feudal contract in which she swears fealty to him as her lord. Its awesome legality is sharply contrasted to the lawless 'usurpation' of Tarquin's rapine. But both forms of conquest over woman, legal and illegal, involve force. Notice the 'bearing yoke' of marriage, an allusion both to the husband's right to subjugate his wife and command, by force if necessary, that she serve him, and to childbearing, the wife's duty to her husband.

In the action of the poem, force is a primary element in both the sexual and political realms, and Tarquin is the primary embodiment of it. I have already discussed the background of political force from which Tarquin emerges. From the beginning he can conceive of taking Lucrece only by force; because of her undoubted chastity and because Collatine would never voluntarily surrender his rights, seduction and persuasion never figure as alternatives:

> His falchion on a flint he softly smiteth,
> That from the cold stone sparks of fire do fly;
> Whereat a waxen torch forthwith he lighteth,
> Which must be lodestar to his lustful eye:
> And to the flame thus speaks advisedly:
>   'As from this cold flint I enforc'd this fire,
>   So Lucrece must I force to my desire.'
>
>   (176–82)

He forces open all the locked doors between his chambers and hers (301–2), and when he places his hand on her breast, it is compared to the invasion of a conquering army (435–9), 'a rude ram, to batter such an ivory wall!' (464). He announces his purpose to Lucrece in the language of feudal conquest, saying 'Under that colour am I come to scale / Thy never-conquer'd fort' (480–81), a common figure in Renaissance love poetry which regains its martial undertones in this context. He concludes his announcement by shaking 'his Roman blade' over the defenceless Lucrece (505–6), a familiar gesture of military victory. In Shakespeare's sources, Tarquin's sword also serves as an emblem of the excessive force by which he frightens an unarmed woman into submission. Livy mentions the sword twice, Ovid four times, in the bedroom scene; both prominently juxtapose the sword with the image of the prone, defenceless Lucrece in her bed.[21] Needless to say, in this context the sword symbolizes phallic as well as military power.

In the end, of course, his victory is hollow, and the 'Roman lord' who marched to Lucrece's bed creeps away guiltily, 'A captive victor that hath lost in gain' (730). He is vanquished, as he knew from the beginning that he would be, by his own conscience. But in political terms, he is destroyed by Lucrece's avenging guardians. After she kills herself, Brutus ritually legitimizes counter-violence against Tarquin by asking the assembled nobles to swear, by the bloody knife she used, vengeance against Tarquin. On this level, woman is but a pawn in the struggle of the state to maintain its laws (represented by marriage) against the arrogant individual who would seize what he wants in scorn of the law.

Ironically, Tarquin is driven to risk all for Lucrece *because* the law makes her taboo to anyone but her husband. Officially, as a chaste wife, she is desexualized, but to one who desires her despite the law, because she is forbidden she acquires a high erotic potency totally extraneous to her sense of herself as Collatine's wife. Thus the poem suggests that the rape represents in part the failure of marriage as a means of establishing sexual ownership of women. That marriage does not succeed in eradicating illicit desire is conveyed forcefully in Tarquin's tortured debates with himself as he approaches Lucrece's bed. Scrupulously, he enumerates the perils of robbing another man's treasure, then recklessly denies them in frenzied rationalizations (127–441). Honour, piety, reason, and self-respect melt before his desire and bear witness to the destructiveness of this woman's erotic power over him, of which she is wholly unaware.

III

Tarquin, however, can wield a far greater power over Lucrece, and does so with great cunning. This power rests not in his 'Roman blade' but in the nature of his threat against her, which derives its coercive strength from the conditions of Roman marriage, conditions implied in the threat itself. If she refuses to submit to his lust, he will force her and then kill her. But even worse, he will slander her posthumously by killing a slave, placing him in Lucrece's arms, and claiming that he killed them both for their sexual trespass. This slander will do irreparable damage to Lucrece's reputation as a chaste wife, but that is not its cutting edge. What matters to Lucrece, as Tarquin knows well, is that it will destroy Collatine's honour and his family's:

So thy surviving husband shall remain,
The scornful mark of every open eye;
Thy kinsmen hang their heads at this disdain,
Thy issue blurr'd with nameless bastardy.

                                                        (519–22)

In conformity with the patriarchal idea of woman, Lucrece has perfectly identified herself with her husband and sees herself as the seal of his honour. Therefore she cannot forcibly resist Tarquin (though she pleads with him), not because it would result in her death, but because it would dishonour Collatine and all his kin. On the other hand, if she submits to Tarquin, he will say nothing and Collatine's honour will remain unblemished. Neither alternative allows her to remain chaste, if chastity is considered a physical state. The first means death but, more importantly, public dishonour. The second allows her to live, presumably with the secret knowledge of dishonour.

Lucrece's pleas are useless, and she does not struggle when at last the rape occurs. Tacitly, she has chosen the second alternative of not resisting Tarquin and could now simply keep her secret. But because chastity for Lucrece is not merely a matter of social appearance but a physical reality, she cannot pretend to be the exemplary wife once she is no longer technically chaste.[22] Her extended apostrophe to Night, usually criticized on aesthetic grounds as undramatic and cumbrously rhetorical has firm psychological justification as an illustration of her profound sense of the reality of chastity and of its loss. She begs Night to conceal her from 'the tell-tale day', contending that in the light all would see the evidence of rape (746–56; 806–9). Of course they would not; the topos is intended only to convey her belief in the stain; *she* knows it is there and assumes that everyone else could see it. As she dilates upon her grief, it becomes evident that she thinks of the rape as comprising two crimes, that which Tarquin committed against her and that which she committed against Collatine:

The nurse to still her child will tell my story,
And fright her crying babe with Tarquin's name.
The orator to deck his oratory
Will couple my reproach to Tarquin's shame.
Feast-finding minstrels tuning my defame,
    Will tie the hearers to attend each line,
    How Tarquin wronged me, I Collatine.

Let my good name, that senseless reputation,
For Collatine's dear love be kept unspotted.
If that be made a theme for disputation,
The branches of another root are rotted,

And undeserv'd reproach to him allotted
    That is as clear from this attaint of mine
    As I ere this was pure to Collatine.

(813–26; emphasis added)

Whatever Lucrece believes that she has done to her husband, terms such as 'offence' or 'crime' do not exactly fit it. Her word 'attaint' and the prevailing metaphor of the stain come much closer to describing it. Marriage makes sex, and woman as sexual object, clean; outside of marriage sex is unclean. Once the pure, unsexual wife is brought into contact with sexuality outside of marriage, though it be beyond her powers to avoid that contact, she is a polluted object. According to the anthropologist Mary Douglas, 'Pollution rules are unequivocal, [and] do not depend on intention or on rights and duties. The only material question is whether a forbidden contact has taken place or not.'[23] 'A forbidden contact' is exactly what has taken place, and it is understandable that Lucrece sees it as such and does not take into account what for us would be paramount: the moral questions of intention and responsibility. She is the perfect patriarchal woman, content to be but an accessory to the passage of property and family honour from father to son; she has no sense of herself as an independent moral being apart from this role in marriage. Thus she views her chastity as a material thing, not as a moral attitude transcending circumstances.

In the Rome of *Lucrèce*, the social order depends on the institution of marriage as the boundary line between legitimate and illegitimate procreation, another way of defining what is sexually clean or unclean. As Dr Johnson pointed out, female chastity is of the utmost importance because 'upon that all the property in the world depends'; a man trusts that a chaste wife will produce legitimate heirs.[24] Certainly this factor is important in the rape of a married woman. It figures in the first alternative Tarquin offers Lucrece; as a way of coercing her into submission, he threatens that her 'issue will be blurr'd with nameless bastardy' (522). It also provides a subsidiary motive for Lucrece's suicide, for she resolves that

> He shall not boast who did thy stock pollute,
> That thou art doting father of his fruit.

(1063–4)

In anthropological terms, place in the caste structure is biologically transmitted through the mother; under a patrilineal system of descent, wives are the door of entry to the group, and the wife's adultery introduces impure blood to the lineage.[25]

As is well-known, the honour of a patrician depended in great measure on the purity of his genealogy, his descent from an unbroken line of patricians with respectable reputations. Honour was collective as well as individual; all in the line shared honour and dishonour. The biological importance of female chastity is thus inseparable from its social importance. Furthermore, whether or not a woman introduced bastards into the line, she could dishonour it by adultery or sexual misconduct. Any alteration in her chastity polluted her permanently and was contagious, passing down through the line from generation to generation, as Tarquin's threat makes clear:[26]

> Then for thy husband and thy children's sake,
> Tender my suit; bequeath not to their lot
> The shame that from them no device can take,
> The blemish that will never be forgot,
> Worse than a slavish wipe or birth-hour's blot.

(533–7)

Finally, once a man assumed guardianship of a woman in marriage, the chastity of his wife became a primary component of his honour. He then became vulnerable to dishonour through any threat to his wife's purity, as the many jokes about cuckoldry in Elizabethan drama attest. Since honour was to be gained through competition between individuals and between patrilineal clans, men could dishonour each other by exposing any breach of chastity in their wives. The first alternative Tarquin offers to Lucrece (which involves publicly accusing her of sleeping with a slave) is a way of striking at Collatine through her. Tarquin is well aware that if it is known that he has raped Lucrece, his posterity will also be shamed. But if he can contrive to hide his crime by a lie and publish Lucrece's unchastity by the same lie, only Collatine will lose in the competition for honour.[27] Again, Lucrece's fate as a woman is but incidental to a struggle for power in which only men compete.

Only Lucrece, of all the characters in the poem, fully understands her importance to the Roman social system, possessing an insight which transcends that of an ordinary wife and makes her 'a singular patterne of chastity, both to hir tyme, and to all ages following'.[28] Lucrece's 'singularity' is most marked when, after revealing the rape to her kinsmen, she rejects the forgiveness they hasten to offer and plunges the knife into her breast, on the grounds that

>   no dame hereafter living
> Shall claim excuses by my excuse's giving.

(1714–15)

They are persuaded by her narration of the particular circumstances surrounding the rape that she is innocent, but she sees herself as a 'patterne', a paradigm for all ages of the meaning of female chastity in a patriarchy. In the terms of that paradigm, when a chaste wife is polluted by sexual contact outside of marriage, no matter what the circumstances, she is forced across the line between sexuality and innocence which marriage has drawn for her, and becomes a marginal and dangerous person. Furthermore, given Lucrece's total identification with this paradigm, no alternative identity is possible for her once she can no longer call herself a chaste wife. The tragedy of Lucrece is that only by dying is she able to escape from marginality and regain her social and personal identity as a chaste wife.

IV

The suicide of Lucrece was a nexus of controversy long before Shakespeare wrote his poem. In Book I of *The City of God*, Augustine questions Livy's presentation of her suicide as the proof of her virtue. His way of articulating the problem is relevant to Shakespeare's Lucrece in two ways. First, the poet has woven suggestions of the Augustinian viewpoint into his heroine's speech and into the narrative commentary. Second, these suggestions form a contrast to Lucrece's attitude, distinguishing it sharply and enabling us to understand its peculiarities. Augustine's discussion touches some of the same points of contrast, which fall under the broad headings of patriarchal versus moral, or pagan versus Christian attitudes towards chastity.

Augustine's conception of chastity is built on the dichotomy of mind and body:

> In the first place, then, let the principle be stated and affirmed that the virtue whereby a good life is lived controls the members of the body from its seat in the mind, and that the body becomes holy through the exercise of a holy will, and while such a will remains unshaken and steadfast, no matter what anyone else does with the body or in the body that a person has no power to avoid without sin on his own part, no blame attaches to the one who suffers it.[29]

Nothing could be further from the view of chastity represented by Lucrece herself, for whom the only important consideration is material: what Tarquin did with her body. For Augustine, the only important consideration is spiritual: whether Lucrece's will remained steadfast in mental opposition to the rape, or whether she consented to it. If she remained steadfast, then as far as Augustine is concerned, her chastity is intact, and she had no defensible reason for committing suicide. If she inwardly consented to the rape, presumably because she took carnal pleasure in it, then she sinned and added to her guilt by the sin of self-murder. Augustine is not convinced that Lucrece did not consent, but assuming for the sake of the argument that she did not, he concludes that her death was motivated 'not by her love of chastity, but her irresolute shame. For she was ashamed of another's foul crime committed on her person, even though not committed with her ...' (I.xix, p. 89) and declares that she was 'a Roman lady, too greedy of praise [who] feared that if she remained alive, she would be thought to have enjoyed suffering the violence that she had suffered while alive' (ibid.). The shame and love of praise that he sees in her are in his eyes mere worldliness, for he dwells in the city of God and she in the city of Rome. He regards her as a moral agent whose will is free and whose will determines all; she finds herself trapped by the obligations of her marital role, a role crucially important to the social order. Roman she certainly is, but Augustine is wrong in calling her 'too greedy of praise', for she dies not to save her honour but to save Collatine's.[30] Indeed, her honour *is* Collatine's. Thus she declares

> Let my good name, that senseless reputation,
> For Collatine's dear love be kept unspotted.

> (820–21)

> If, Collatine, thine honour lay in me,
> From me by strong assault it is bereft.

> (834–5)

She is not greedy but selfless in terms of the values by which she lives. Though, generally speaking, Shakespeare distrusts honour as a social ideal which is easily perverted, becoming an excuse for political expediency, blind egotism or vicious rivalry (some of the many forms it takes in the Roman plays), his realistic tolerance impels him to distinguish between the quality of personal commitment to the ideal and the ideal as shaped by a social milieu. In *Lucrece*, he may deplore the social order which requires dishonoured women to martyr themselves or be despised, but he sees in Lucrece's suicide a brilliantly successful attempt to re-create Collatine's honour by symbolically restoring to herself the sexual purity on which it depends.

Lucrece stage-manages her death so as to maximize its social effectiveness for this purpose. She summons her husband cryptically by letter, hinting at some disaster connected with herself but not mentioning the rape (1314–23). First, to tell Collatine she was raped is to risk or invite public knowledge of that fact before she can rally her public to Collatine's cause. Second, she fears that even Collatine would suspect *her* of 'gross abuse' were she to tell him plainly that she had been raped. Even to relate the extenuating circumstances, she feels, would be a 'stain'd excuse' – stained, perhaps, by his suspicion that she protests too much to cover up her own possible guilt (1314–16). She therefore plans to delay her revelation until she can counteract the social prejudice against her by a histrionic demonstration in which the stain of her rape will be obscured by the stain of her blood in suicide.

When she first resolves on suicide, it is evident that Lucrece understands the blood she will shed as the literal equivalent of the stain which she so laments; she is determined to 'let forth my foul defiled blood' (1029). The idea that her moral value and social purpose as a wife have been destroyed is for her as literal as a physical change in her blood, and is symbolized for the reader when her blood eerily divides into two streams upon her death, one red and one black, the latter congealing into a black substance and 'a watery rigol' (1737–50). The Elizabethans knew from Aristotle that wholesome blood was red, while diseased blood turned black.[31] William Harvey, writing in 1651, attributed the separation of coagulated blood into thick clot and water serum to corruption in the body. Thus, as one critic has suggested, it is possible that the extreme literalism of Lucrece's moral self-analysis seemed quite plausible to Shakespeare's audience, to whom magic and medicine were hardly distinct, and thus escaped that strained, overly schematic quality which may bother a modern reader.[32]

It is significant, though, that the heroine's blood is not *wholly* corrupted, as she believes it to be. The division of her blood into two streams is a detail not found in Livy, Ovid, or any other possible source for the poem. Through it Shakespeare symbolizes a tragic duality in Lucrece which she does not perceive. While she regards herself merely as a polluted object, he sees her as a moral agent whose mind remains pure, whose courage and integrity in taking her own life testify to that purity and make her death tragically ironic. In the final scene Lucrece does distinguish firmly between the staining of her blood – that is, her body consecrated to Collatine – and the purity of her mind:

> Though my gross blood be stain'd with this abuse,
> Immaculate and spotless is my mind;
> That was not forc'd, that never was inclin'd
> 　　To accessory yieldings, but still pure
> 　　Doth in her poison'd closet yet endure.

　　　　　　　　　　　　　　　　　　　　　　　(1655–9)

But for her it is a purely intellectual distinction, irrelevant to her vision of herself as a 'singular patterne of chastity', whose value does, therefore, reside in her body.

The shedding of Lucrece's 'defiled blood' is based on a clearly worked out social rationale. When she submitted to Tarquin instead of resisting, she thereby saved her husband from public disgrace, but only by incurring her private stain. This stain brought upon her an existential crisis in that it deprived her of her *raison d'être*: being a truly chaste wife. Integrity to the ideal of married chastity prevents her from continuing to be Collatine's loyal wife in name only; thus the sole course of action for her is to renounce her role and die. The problem then facing her is how to accomplish this renunciation, which necessarily involves confessing the rape, without bringing disgrace on him and on their families. This problem she solves by contriving her death in such a manner that she symbolically restores her body to its previous sexual purity by the purgation of shedding her blood, thus removing the stain which would dishonour Collatine.

She also wrests from the degradation of rape a considerable moral triumph for herself. Addressing the hand which will wield the dagger, she declares: 'For if I die, my honour lives in thee, / But if I live, thou liv'st in my defame' (1032–3), and later adds:

> O that is gone for which I sought to live,
> And therefore now I need not fear to die!
> To clear this spot by death, at least I give
> A badge of fame to slander's livery,
> A dying life to living infamy.

(1051–5)

The paradoxes of life and death, honour and 'defame', slander and fame indicate Lucrece's imaginative understanding of the potential in her situation. She sees that the death made necessary by the rape can be the means of re-creating that ideal self which the rape destroyed and of restoring Collatine's honour (implied in 'badge' and 'livery' in the above lines), which becomes the theme of the following three stanzas (1058–78).[33]

On a larger scale, the social rationale for the heroine's death is that she must sacrifice herself for the survival of marriage as the strongest bulwark against lust. This aspect of her death is revealed in the last scene, when Shakespeare makes her step out of character in reversing her previous attitude towards the stain. After describing the circumstances of the rape, she declares that she will reveal her assailant's name only if the assembled lords swear to avenge her. They do so, and then she pauses melodramatically to ask:

> How may this forced stain be wip'd from me?
>
> What is the quality of my offence,
> Being constrain'd with dreadful circumstance?
> May my pure mind with the foul act dispense,
> My low-declined honour to advance?
> May any terms acquit me from this chance?
>   The poisoned fountain clears itself again,
>   And why not I from this compelled stain?'

(1701–8)

Her questions are predicated on the Christian idea, voiced by Augustine, that the 'Pure mind' can rule the body and transcend 'dreadful circumstance'. For nearly a thousand lines previously, Lucrece has seemed unaware of such a distinction. Furthermore, in referring to the stain as 'forced' and 'compelled', she deviates from her previous, amply elaborated belief that it is the inevitable consequence of the rape for her and her appropriate moral burden. Here Shakespeare simply forsakes consistency of characterization, as he often does, to clarify an idea which the character represents. This dramatic last-minute appeal to a moral justice untainted by sexual prejudice is only the rhetorical prelude, however, to Lucrece's final enactment of her selflessly patriarchal conception of the role of woman in marriage.

Not trusting the easy forgiveness of her audience, which immediately follows the above lines, she declares 'No dame hereafter living / By my excuse shall claim excuse's giving' (1714–15). She hereby rejects any attempt to make married chastity for woman conformable with rational moral standards which take into account the intention of the accused and the circumstances in which the crime occurred. There is simply no excuse for a raped wife, because the social order depends upon pure descent as a mark of status, legitimate heirs as a means of ensuring property rights, and the control of male sexual rivalry through the ownership of sexual rights to women in marriage. In addition, as I have argued, marriage enables man to cope with his ambivalence towards his sexual desire by dividing women into two classes, clean and unclean sexual objects. It could be argued that all of these goals, while beneficial to men in particular, are also beneficial to society as a whole. But they all require women to sacrifice themselves, to live or die for the sake of marriage. Lucrece's last words charge Tarquin with guilt for her death as well as for the rape, but her last action, plunging the knife into her breast, indicates her final acceptance of the ultimate female responsibility: to keep herself sexually pure for the sake of her husband and of Rome.

Shakespeare's sensitive understanding of the social constraints which force Lucrece into a tragic role informs the whole poem. But it is made explicit in a passage which I have never seen quoted. In the three stanzas of narrative comment following the pathetic episode in which the heroine and her maid weep together, he clearly blames men for exercising several kinds of unfair advantages over women. I see no reason not to identify the author's point of view with that of his narrator in this passage. The first stanza leans heavily on the traditional conception of woman's physical, moral and intellectual inferiority to man:

> For men have marble, women waxen, minds,
> And therefore are they form'd as marble will;

The weak oppress'd, th'impression of strange kinds
Is form'd in them by force, by fraud, or skill.
Then call them not the authors of their ill,
  No more than wax shall be accounted evil,
  Wherein is stamp'd the semblance of a devil.

(1240–46)

Because woman is so relatively weak, man can mould her to whatever purposes he wishes. In the second stanza, the metaphor changes from the stamping of marble on to wax, male force imposed on female weakness, to open space, smooth surfaces or clear glass, all of which easily reveal impurities:

Their smoothness, like a goodly champaign plane,
Lays open all the little worms that creep;
In men as in a rough-grown grove remain
Cave-keeping evils that obscurely sleep;
Through crystal walls each little note will peep:
  Though men can cover them with bold stern looks,
  Poor women's faces are their own faults' books.

(1247–53)

Women are no more innocent than are men; rather, their simplicity or artlessness prevents them from concealing their faults by a bluff show of strength ('bold stern looks') as men do. The third stanza is a passionate plea that women not be blamed for the abuses perpetrated on them by men. Again Shakespeare stresses, in a very traditional vein, that women are weaker than men:

No man inveigh against the withered flower,
But chide rough winter that the flower hath kill'd;
Not that devour'd, but that which doth devour
Is worthy blame; O let it not be hild
Poor women's faults, that they are so fulfill'd
  With men's abuses! those proud lords to blame
  Make weak-made women tenants to their shame.

(1254–60)

He imputes a sort of natural inevitability to the relationship between men and women as the relationship between the strong and the weak, through the metaphors of 'rough winter' killing the flower, or one beast devouring another. The evil that concerns him is that men not only abuse women but also hold women guilty of those very abuses. The last three and a half lines relate this concern directly to Lucrece. The surname 'Superbus' or 'proud' applied to Tarquin's father (mentioned in the first line of the Argument), which might fittingly apply to Tarquin as well, is alluded to in the phrase 'proud lords'. The word 'shame', connected with Lucrece so many times in the poem, recalls her predicament. The metaphor of woman being the tenant of man's shame suggests that Lucrece as the chaste wife, subservient to and dependent on patriarchy, suffers for a crime she did not commit.

Notes

1. J.W. Lever summarizes the issues to which twentieth-century criticism of the poem has directed itself in 'The Poems', *Shakespeare Survey* 15 (1962): 18–30. He lists the relationship of *Lucrece* to *Venus and Adonis*, the function of rhetoric, the problem of whether the poem is 'dramatic' or 'narrative' in method, Shakespeare's relationship with Southampton at the time it was written, hints of Shakespeare's later work, and the poem as a tragedy. For the purposes of this essay, I will comment only on the few essays which deal with the sexual and moral issues of the rape *per se*.

Those critics who do take up these issues find Lucrece in some sense guilty of her own rape. Don Cameron Allen's scholarly examination of sixteenth-century humanistic attitudes towards chastity leads him to characterize Shakespeare's viewpoint as Christian, and to criticize the heroine's suicide on the same grounds as does Augustine (see pp. 38–9 above), as motivated by her 'maculate body' and 'love of pagan honour' ('Some Observations on *The Rape of Lucrece*', *Shakespeare Survey* 15 [1962]: 89–98). J.C. Maxwell's Introduction to the new Arden edition of *The Poems* (Cambridge: Cambridge University Press, 1966) concurs in this view. The most thorough and polemical elaboration of the contention that Shakespeare wants us to judge Lucrece by Christian standards is Roy W. Battenhouse's 'Shakespeare's Re-Vision of Lucrece' in his *Shakespearean Tragedy: Its Art and Christian Premises* (Bloomington: Indiana University Press, 1969), pp. 3–41. He reads the poem as a critique of Lucrece's typically Roman 'inordinate love of glory' (p. 14). Battenhouse finds a contemptuous rejection of Roman moral and social standards in every detail of the poem, and reveals considerable bias against Lucrece, remarking on her 'feminine proclivity to self-pity and evasive argument'. He finds the sweat on her hand in the bedroom scene evidence of her 'subconscious preparation' for Tarquin's visit, and interprets her long plea to Tarquin before the rape as 'her way of escaping from calling for help' (p. 16). So far as I am aware, only Kenneth Muir, '*The Rape of Lucrece*', *Anglica* 5 (1964): 25–40, explicitly disputes the point of view represented by Allen and Battenhouse, stating: 'It was not fear of death that made her give up the struggle, but fear for her reputation after death.... When one considers the high value set by the Elizabethans on reputation, and also that this story [Tarquin's threatened slander of Lucrece] would be more damaging to her husband than her actual rape, one can see that in the circumstances Lucrece's duty was not clear ...' (p. 38). Professor Muir does not develop this argument any further, however.

2. Mungo W. MacCallum, *Shakespeare's Roman Plays and Their Background* (London: Macmillan, 1910), pp. 84–5.

3. Lawrence Stone, *The Crisis of the Aristocracy: 1558–1660* (London: Oxford University Press, 1971), abridged edn, p. 271.

4. It should be noted that the metaphor is also used three times of Tarquin, in lines 221–4, 654–5, and 719–28. Apart from these few instances, the stain is associated with Lucrece.

5. Lines 190–96. This and all subsequent quotations from *Lucrece* are taken from the New Arden Shakespeare edition, *The Poems*, ed. F.T. Prince (London: Methuen, 1960).

6. For a view completely at variance with mine on this point (and on many others), see Battenhouse, cited in n. 1.

7. Steevens, mischievously attributing his comment to Amner, remarked on the phrase: '*Maiden worlds!* How happeneth this, friend Collatine, when Lucrece hath so long lain by thy side? Verily, it insinuateth thee of coldness.' Quoted in *A New Variorum Edition of Shakespeare: The Poems*, ed. Hyder Edward Rollins (Philadelphia, PA: Lippincott, 1938),

p. 155. Curiously, Shakespeare employs the same idea, that a chaste wife is in effect a virgin, and uses the same word, 'maiden', to express it, near the end of his career. In *Henry VIII*, after the divorce, Queen Katherine elegiacally says:

> When I am dead, good wench
> Let me be used with honour. Strew me over
> With maiden flowers, that all the world may know
> I was a chaste wife to my grave

(IV.ii.167–70)

8. See Geoffrey Bullough, ed., *Narrative and Dramatic Sources of Shakespeare*, I (New York: Columbia University Press, 1966), pp. 179–80. Relying on previous scholarship by Ewig and Baldwin, he states: 'Ovid remains the chief source' and 'The dramatist seems to have had before him a copy of Titus Livy's *History of Rome*.'

9. In Book I, chapter 20 of *The History of Rome*, Livy describes Numa's appointment of virgins as priestesses to Vesta, noting: 'He gave them a public stipend so that they might give their whole time to the temple, and made their persons sacred and inviolable by a vow of chastity and other religious sanctions.' See Titus Livius, *The History of Rome* (London: J.M. Dent, 1926) I, 24. Shakespeare found the story of Lucrece in chapters 57–60, which conclude Book I.

Ovid's *Fasti* describes the rituals of the first six months of the Roman festive year, drawing upon their origins and on legends surrounding them. Among the observances connected with Vesta are the lighting of a new fire in her shrine on the Kalends of March (III.141–4), and the celebration of her day on the twenty-eighth Kalend of April (IV.949–54). More extensively, he discusses the founding of her worship by Numa, her function as goddess of the hearth, and her virginity and virgin ministers (VI.249–348). The version of the Lucrece story which Shakespeare consulted is found in the *Fasti*, II.721–852. I have used The Loeb Classical Library edition, trans. Sir James George Frazer (London: William Heinemann, 1931).

10. Cicero, *De Legibus*, trans. Clinton Walker Keyes, The Loeb Classical Library (Cambridge, MA. Harvard University Press, 1959), II.27.

11. Quoted in Frances Yates, 'Queen Elizabeth as Astræa', *Journal of the Warburg and Courtauld Institutes*, 20 (1957), 27–82, esp. p. 73.

12. Ovid, *Fasti*, III.421–8.

13. T.W. Baldwin, *On the Literary Genetics of Shakespeare's Poems and Sonnets* (Urbana: University of Illinois Press, 1950), pp. 110, 114.

14. I quote from the Paulus Marsus edition of the *Fasti* published in Milan by Antonius Zarotus for Johannes de Legnaro, 1483.

15. *Cymbeline* I.iv.59–61, 88–9.

16. The futility of sexual gain or conquest is likened to the futility of gaining wealth in several passages (127–56; 687–93; 710–11; 855–68).

17. Subsequent quotations in this paragraph are taken from the Everyman edition, cited in n. 9 above.

18. Under Elizabethan marriage laws, when a woman was married she passed from the legal guardianship of her father to that of her husband, as she had under Roman law; thus the claim of Lucrece's father is technically invalid, and he may be understood as referring to an emotional 'claim' in her as a father. Nevertheless, the metaphors of legal possession and financial interest recall the marriage portions which Elizabethan fathers settled on their daughters. See Stone, pp. 273–5.

19. We might ask why Tarquin sees no specifically erotic qualities in Lucrece at this rather erotic moment. I would argue that for Tarquin, Lucrece's appeal resides as much in the fact that he must 'steal' her from another man to whom she does, in every sense, 'belong', as in her physical attributes. Tarquin, like his fellow Romans in Livy, finds women and territory equally exciting fields of conquest.

20. In attending to Ovid's account of the Lucrece story, *Fasti*, II.721–86, Shakespeare could hardly have avoided making this connection between sex and politics. As Tarquin contemplates the possibility of rape, he directly compares it to a previous Roman military conquest:

Exitus in dubio est: audebimus ultima dixit.
   Viderit: audentes forsque Venusque juvant.
Cepimus audendo Gabio quoque talia fatus.

'The issue is in doubt. We'll dare the utmost,' said he. 'Let her look to it! God and fortune help the daring. By daring we captured Gabii too.'

(II.781–3)

(Loeb edition, trans. Sir James George Frazer, cited in n. 9 above)

21. Livy, I.58; Ovid, II.784, 793, 795, 802.

22. Somewhat similarly, Richardson's Clarissa refuses to marry Lovelace after he has raped her, though she is advised by all her friends to do so, because she does not subscribe to their 'marriage-covers-all' morality. But in contrast to Lucrece, Clarissa asserts that her virtue remains untainted by the rape because her mind never consented to the act. She declares: 'Have I not reason, these things considered, to think myself happier without Mr. Lovelace than I could have been with him? *My will too unviolated* [*sic*]; and very little, nay not anything as to him, to reproach myself with?' (Samuel Richardson, *Clarissa* [London: Chapman & Hall, 1902], VII, 197).

23. Mary Douglas, *Purity and Danger: An Analysis of Concepts of Pollution and Taboo* (New York: Praeger, 1966), p. 130.

24. Quoted in 'The Double Standard', by Keith Thomas, *Journal of the History of Ideas*, 20 (1959): 193–216, a learned and most intelligent discussion of the legal and social manifestations of the double standard in England from the Middle Ages through the nineteenth century.

25. Douglas, p. 126.

26. The rape is also reckoned as a lasting blot on Tarquin's lineage, in II.197–8, 204–10, but unlike the dishonour imputed to a raped woman, this dishonour has a clear moral rationale; it results from a crime deliberately committed by Tarquin.

27. Julio Caro Baroja, 'Honour and Shame: A Historical Account of Several Conflicts', in *Honour and Shame: The Values of Mediterranean Society*, ed. J.G. Peristiany (Chicago: University of Chicago Press, 1966), pp. 79–137, provides a lucid analysis of this kind of competition for honour in patriarchal society.

28. Quoted from the entry under 'Lucretia' in Thomas Cooper's *Thesaurus Lingae Romanae & Britannicae*, first published in 1565. See DeWitt T. Starnes and Ernest W. Talbert, *Classical Myth and Legend in Renaissance Dictionaries* (Chapel Hill: University of North Carolina Press, 1955), pp. 125–34, for a discussion of Shakespeare's use of Cooper, whose phrase 'singular patterne' sums up the poet's conception of Lucrece as exemplary, and thus rare, verging on eccentric, in her chastity.

29. St Augustine, *The City of God Against the Pagans*, trans. George E. McCracken, The Loeb Classics (London: William Heinemann, 1951), I, 75. All subsequent quotations are taken from this edition.

30. Edward Hubler, in the introduction to his edition of *Shakespeare's Songs and Poems* (New York: McGraw-Hill, 1959), maintains that *Lucrece* is a tragedy of honour and reputation, stating: 'Lucrece's concern for her good name is Shakespeare's first full statement of this attitude, and it motivates her resolve to die' (p. xxxi). Like Muir (cited in n. 1), he does not carry the argument further.

31. Aristotle, *The History of Animals*, trans. A.L. Peck, The Loeb Classics (London: William Heinemann, 1965), I, 67.

32. See Bickford Sylvester, 'Natural Mutability and Human Responsibility: Form in Shakespeare's *Lucrece*', *College English*: 26 (1965), 505–11.

33. Later she also plans that her death will benefit her husband in providing an example of the bloody revenge he should take on Tarquin (1177–83; 1191–7). To ensure support for him in that action, she delays the revelation of her assailant's name until the assembled nobles pledge their faith to avenge the rape. Brutus' speech rousing Collatine to move against Tarquin (1818–41) returns the domestic tragedy to a historical context, in which the announcement of Tarquin's offence to the people and the banishment of his family marks the end of the monarchic era in Rome. Thus Lucrece, in effect, provides her husband with a heroic mission.

3

'This That You Call Love': Sexual and Social Tragedy in *Othello*

Gayle Greene

I

> Thy husband is thy lord, thy life, thy keeper,
> Thy head, thy sovereign ...
> And craves no other tribute at thy hands,
> But love, fair looks, and true obedience ...
> I am ashamed that women are so simple
> To offer war where they should kneel for peace,
> To seek for rule, supremacy, and sway,
> Where they are bound to serve, love, and obey.

The Taming of the Shrew

> Truly, an obedient lady.

Othello

The revilement and murder of Desdemona by her husband is an excruciating experience, so relentless is his 'tyrannous hate',[1] so outrageous the assumptions that motivate it, so defenceless is she against it. Emilia's version of human relationships –

> 'Tis not a year or two shows us a man:
> They are all but stomachs, and we all but food;
> They eat us hungerly, and when they are full
> They belch us.

(III.iv.103–6)

– though hardly complete, does have a certain terrible validity as description of what we see happening. Iago's redefinition of love, or 'this that you call love' (I.iii.331), as 'a lust of the blood and a permission of the will' (334), also has its weight. Though neither of these views is adequate to the complexity and variety of possibilities in love, the love that we see in this play seems inexorably linked to brutality; the violence unleashed in the last acts is in direct consequence of and proportion to

47

Othello's adulation of Desdemona, the release of a powerful destructive energy against which it has no defence.

From beginning to end, the play focuses on love. Its first words concern elopement; its last, 'the tragic loading of this bed' (V.ii.363), a bed which has been present throughout much of the play, in the language and imagery. The love of Othello and Desdemona defies world and time, barriers of social and parental opposition, and is consecrated by some of Shakespeare's greatest poetry, terms which are the absolute expression of those feelings:

> O my soul's joy!
> If after every tempest come such calms,
> May the winds blow till they have waken'd death!
> ... If it were now to die,
> 'Twere now to be most happy; for I fear
> My soul hath her content so absolute
> That not another comfort like to this
> Succeeds in unknown fate.

> (II.i.182–93)

G. Wilson Knight calls them 'essential man and essential woman' in this scene: 'Othello is a prince of heroes, Desdemona lit by a divine feminine radiance, both of them transfigured.'[2] Yet theirs is a *Liebestod*, a love which is, like Romeo and Juliet's, wedded to death: within a scene, Othello has, on the basis of allegation, 'prove[d] her haggard' (III.iii.260), his 'fond love' turned to 'tyrannous hate' (445–9), his eloquent adoration turned to 'I'll tear her all to pieces' (431), 'I will chop her into messes' (IV.i.200). But it is not a hostile social order that destroys them – this is overcome in the first act – nor a quirk of timing, nor even the slow, wasting time which is love's enemy in *Troilus and Cressida* and the sonnets. It is, rather, Othello himself who deliberately and premeditatedly murders his love, and though he has powerful instigation in Iago, Iago has power only because his insinuations ring deeply true to him: 'I told ... no more / Than what he found himself was apt and true' (V.ii.176–7). Shakespeare's tragic vision has matured in the ten years between *Romeo and Juliet* and *Othello*, and we must look for the flaw in the couple themselves, in the man, in the woman, and their love – a love that, as Othello's intimation indicates, hovers on the edge of perdition, whose 'absolute content' makes him think of death.

II

For her sweet, silent submission, Desdemona has been praised by generations of critics: 'a maiden never bold; / Of spirit ... still and quiet ...'

(I.iii.94–5). Selfless, solicitous of her husband at the expense of herself, obedient to the 'fancies' of her 'lord': 'Be as your fancies teach you / What e'er you be, I am obedient' (III.iii.88–9), she has struck many as an ideal of femininity. A.C. Bradley praises her 'helpless passivity': 'She can do nothing whatever. She cannot retaliate even in speech. . . . She is helpless because her nature is infinitely sweet and her love absolute'.[3] Robert B. Heilman sees in her 'the dynamics of the personality under the magic influence of love, the full ripening of outward-turning love which we may call the magical transformation of personality'.[4] What do we do, then, with our outrage, as we suffer through the last half of the play, our attention riveted with horror on Othello's violence, a violence motivated by assumptions that his wife is a 'thing' (III.iii.272) which, 'stain'd' or 'spotted' (V.i.36), must be murdered for 'Justice[s]' (V.ii.17) sake? There is no question, of course, that we are meant to condemn him, but it is the basis and extent of our outrage that we must question, testing our 'modern' responses against those which can be supported by the play. Shakespeare, we are told, was deeply traditional, a believer in the hierarchical order which was even in his time a thing of the past. Does he see in Desdemona, this woman who goes lyrically to her death, and is, next to Ophelia, the least capable of his women of defending herself, the ideal that so many of his critics have seen?

Just as we look to Othello's character for cause of his vulnerability to Iago, so must we look to Desdemona's character for her vulnerability to Othello. She too is a tragic figure with a flaw analogous to his. Neither is simply a victim; rather, they are manipulable because they are responsive to and co-operative with their victimizers, a view which, according them some responsibility for their fates, accords them more stature. It is in part Othello's very nobility that makes him vulnerable: being of 'a free and open nature', he 'thinks men honest that but seem to be so' (I.iii.339–40). The play is concerned, as Terence Hawkes suggests, with an ideal and standard of manly behaviour. Hawkes sees Othello as the epitome of this ideal, an ideal expressed in his splendid rhetoric, 'manly language' which breaks down, becoming abusive and incommunicative under Iago's influence, but which is regained at the end.[5] But I think that the 'manly ideal' embodied by Othello is, like the rhetoric that sustains it, suspect from the start. Mixed with his nobility is a habit of self-dramatization, a tendency to observe his life as an adventure fiction, a concern with a heroic self-image: 'I ran it through, even from my boyish days' (132).[6] The 'tale' he tells in defence of his marriage, 'the story of my life', 'the battles, sieges, fortunes, / That have pass'd' (I.iii.129–31), reveals a naivety and romance splendid but dangerous. We hear, also, in words like 'never', 'all', 'forever', a tendency to absolutes which points to an inability to tolerate ambiguity or uncertainty, a failure of irony. His account of their love – 'She

lov'd me for the dangers I had pass'd, / And I lov'd her that she did pity
them' (167–8) – indicates considerably more interest in what made
Desdemona love him than in what made him love her, and a reliance on
what Heilman calls certain 'props of assurance':[7] a dependence on the
esteem of others for his sense of himself apparent also in his concern with
honour, and his idea of honour as 'reputation'.[8] Othello's life of action and
adventure has ill equipped him for the human complexities he is about to
encounter, complexities related in part to language, which is, as Brabantio
says in this scene, 'equivocal' (217). There is at the centre of his selfhood
an insecurity related to his position as black man in a white society. Though
he is an outsider, this 'extravagant and wheeling stranger' (I.i.135)
embodies the essence and extreme of certain qualities which are conventionally 'masculine': a vision that looks without, a nature that expresses
itself in action and, when threatened, in violence, which has been
conditioned by his 'occupation' as soldier. Circumscribed by this ideal of
character and conduct, Othello is deficient in self-awareness and judgement of others.

Desdemona is his counterpart, in love and in tragedy. She is, like him,
too noble for the world, and vulnerable because she is virtuous, unable
to understand his accusations because incapable of imagining the evil of
which she is accused, powerless to challenge him because conditioned
to obey, she remains 'Truly, an obedient lady' (IV.i.248). Her
defencelessness is a function of an ideal of womanly behaviour that makes
her co-operate with him in love and in destruction: as he is 'essential
man', she is 'essential woman'. They are, as Maud Bodkin calls them,
'archetypal fantasy of man and woman',[9] a fantasy that turns to nightmare.
Women and relationships are prominent in this play to an unprecedented
degree in Shakespeare's tragedies: each of the male characters is shown
in relation to a woman, their relationships emphasized by verb forms:
'wiv'd' (II.i.60), 'woman'd' (III.iv.194), 'bewhor'd' (IV.ii.115). As the
play is concerned with a standard of manly behaviour, so is it concerned
with an ideal of womanly character and conduct, with the question of
what women are, what they might be and should be. Such an ideal is
suggested by the interplay of the three women characters, and is defined,
like the men's, partly in terms of what it is not, partly in terms of language,
and related – again like the men's – to the capacity for survival. The
tragic vulnerability of both male and female protagonists is rooted in
ideals and illusions they bring to one another which create their love and
destroy it, ideals related to conventional conceptions of man and woman
– conceptions which, Shakespeare suggests, are misconceptions. Othello's
confusion regarding 'honesty', a word that rings through the play with
insistent irony, with different meanings for man and for woman, involves
more than a personal error: Shakespeare implies a criticism of the ideals

themselves, that man's worth is contained in his 'honour' and woman's in her 'chastity'.

III

Othello is concerned, in action and theme, with men's misunderstanding of women. Throughout the play, we hear men telling us what women are, and what strikes us most about their terms and definitions is their inadequacy. Whether adulating them as goddesses or reviling them as whores, their generalizations tell us more about themselves than about the women they are describing. Iago's slander is simple and all-inclusive, encompassing men as well as women: women are whores, men are knaves. His 'alehouse paradoxes', in his exchange with Desdemona as they await Othello's arrival in Cyprus, reduce all to a lowest common denominator:

> You are pictures out a'doors,
> Bells in your parlors, wild-cats in your kitchens,
> Saints in your injuries, devils being offended . . .

                                                                    (I.ii.109–11)

Fair and foolish, foul and foolish, even 'a deserving woman indeed' (145) are 'fit to suckle fools and chronicle small beer' (160), to wear themselves out in child-rearing and housekeeping, and all alike in bed: 'Players in your huswifery, and huswives in your beds' (112).

Cassio's attitude is slightly more complicated, though equally destructive of the individual, human reality: some women are whores, some are goddesses. His idealization of Desdemona contrasts to Iago's debasement; to him, she is 'the riches of the ship' (II.i.83), to Iago, she is 'a land carract' (I.ii.50), and it is distanced and abstract: 'a maid that paragons description', 'divine' (II.i.61–2, 73), 'most exquisite', 'indeed perfection' (II.iii.18, 28). But Cassio reserves his revilement for the 'other kind', the woman with whom he is involved: 'He, when he hears of her, cannot restrain / From the excess of laughter' (IV.i.98–9). Though Bianca shows herself devoted and willing to risk herself for him, it suits him to see her as 'caitiff' (and 'customer', 'monkey', 'fitchew' [IV.i.108, 119, 127, 146]). Cassio, we hear, is 'A fellow almost damn'd in a fair wife' (I.i.21), an enigmatic reference which draws attention to Shakespeare's change in the source: whereas in Cinthio, Cassio was married, Shakespeare shows him in relation to a prostitute, and needing to see her as such.

Cassio divides women into two types, Desdemona and Bianca, but Othello directs his confusions at one woman, his wife. There is no question that Othello is in love with her: 'there, where I have garner'd up my heart . . . / The fountain from the which my current runs or else dries up'

(IV.ii.57–60). But there is a question as to whether he loves her – whether, in human terms, he loves her at all: she is an idea, an ideal, a symbol. Thus even his adulation is curiously egocentric, showing more concern with the feelings she inspires in him – 'my soul', 'my content' – than with Desdemona. Many of his terms for her are conventional and stereotyped: images like 'rose', 'balmy breath' (V.ii.13, 16), and the recurrence of the adjectives 'sweet' and 'fair' indicate a simplistic and primarily physical response. Shakespeare has elsewhere, in the early Romeo and certain of the sonnets, used such Petrarchan terms to indicate immaturity and self-love, a response to one's own projected image rather than to the loved one.[10] Othello's adulation screens out a considerable portion of human reality, and as Maud Bodkin observes: 'If a man is wedded to his fantasy of a woman ... he grows frantic and blind with passion at the thought of the actual woman ... as a creature of natural varying impulses.'[11] From conceiving of Desdemona as one 'type' it is a short distance to imagining her as the other 'type' – only a matter of a turn in perspective, which Iago accomplishes, and adulation reverses itself to as extreme a revilement.

Othello's language indicates, as well, certain ambivalences about sexuality. There is suggestion, in images like 'monumental alabaster' (V.ii.5) and 'perfect chrysolite' (145), of what Traversi calls a 'monumental frigidity'.[12] Othello is never at ease in speaking of sexuality: his terms indicate strain or self consciousness, a conception of love which is either idealized or reductive, making it more or less than it is – 'absolute content', or a physical, trifling matter. Certain statements strike a wrong tone: 'The purchase made, the fruits are to ensue / The profit's yet to come 'tween me and you' (II.iii.9–10) – and his terms of affection for Desdemona, such as 'honey' (II.i.204) and 'sweeting' (II.iii.253), are not unlike his derisive term 'chuck' (IV.ii.24). Comparing the straightforward ease of Desdemona's request to accompany him to Cyprus, with his extended protests, we can hear how much more comfortable with their love is she than he. Her declaration of devotion and desire to be with him is simple and direct:

> I saw Othello's visage in his mind,
> And to his honors and his valiant parts
> Did I my soul and fortunes consecrate.
> So that, dear lords, if I be left behind ...
> The rites for which I love him are bereft me.
>   ... Let me go with him.

(I.iii.252–9)

His is hedged with protests that he does not want her with him to 'please the palate of my appetite / Nor to comply with heat'; that neither 'light wing'd toys / Of feather'd Cupid' nor 'disports' will 'corrupt and taint my business', lest 'housewives make a skillet of my helm' (268–73). The statement amounts to a denial of the ennobling effects of love, and his terms 'heat', 'appetite' and 'housewives', terms Iago will use, are present in his mind before Iago suggests them.

Implicit in Othello's language is a suspicion of sexuality and the physical being of woman and man, which Iago turns easily to loathing. The swiftness with which Othello leaps to Iago's conclusions indicates that Iago is hardly necessary to convince him of these calumnies; 'they are all there' – as Leslie Fiedler puts it – 'in his head, picked up in the same army camps where Iago himself had learned them.'[13] Thus Iago offers his example of generalized abuse – 'In Venice they do let God see the pranks / They dare not show their husbands' (III.iii.201–3) – supplementing his slanders with vivid images of animal copulation: 'Were they as prime as goats, as hot as monkeys ...' (403). Within a few lines, Othello, too, is generalizing –

> O curse of marriage!
> That we can call these delicate creatures ours,
> And not their appetites!

$$(267–9)$$

– and the rank, sexual images have been 'engend'red' (I.iii.403) in his language: 'Goats and monkeys!' (IV.i.263). We can see that this sort of thing is not merely a matter of Iago's influence, since we hear it first from Brabantio, who reacts to Desdemona's elopement with a sense of betrayal and a warning – 'Fathers, from hence trust not your daughters' minds' (I.i.170) – and a wish indicating revulsion from the physical fact of paternity: 'I had rather to adopt a child than get it' (I.iii.191). It is these shared male assumptions that make Othello 'know' so certainly that Iago is 'honest' and Desdemona is not.

Othello's response to Iago's insinuations is a righteously vindicated recognition that 'the forked plague' is 'destiny unshunnable' (III.iii.275–6), a certainty possible only because woman has been suspect from the start. Iago seems so wise to him – 'O, thou art wise, 'tis certain' (IV.i.74) – because he confirms things Othello has known all along. Othello demands 'satisfaction' – 'Would I were satisfied' (III.iii.385) – a peculiar word to describe his request for proof, and one which is repeated five times within the next eighteen lines. However, in the confirmation of his deepest fears it is a 'satisfaction' which takes the place of the consummation which never seems to occur with Desdemona. The language which was frigid in its adoration takes fire from jealousy, and the cold and conventional turns to passionate anguish: 'O ay, as summer flies are in the shambles / That quicken even with blowing' (IV.ii.66–7). Only in the desire to destroy and the assurance of loss does Othello's language attain conviction.

This deep certainty of woman's faithlessness accounts for his obsession with possessing her. Knowing that possession can never be sure – that 'we can call these delicate creatures ours / And not their appetites' – his passion, in both its loving and its destructive aspects, is more involved with Desdemona as possession than as woman, as a 'thing' to which he has exclusive privileges: 'I had rather be a toad ... than keep a corner in the thing I love / For others' uses' (III.iii.270–73). He thus speaks of her in terms of 'exchange' (I.ii.25–8), 'purchase' (I.iii.9–10), something of which he has been 'robb'd' (III.iii.342), which he would 'not have sold'; and though he progresses to an awareness that he 'threw' (V.i.146) her away, a verb indicating more recognition of responsibility, still, he is thinking of her as something that is his to discard. Offended vanity mingles with his motives for murder; he reveals a concern that she has made him appear a 'figure ... of scorn' (IV.ii.54) which follows from his concern with reputation: 'false to me?' (III.iii.333), 'Cuckold me!' 'With mine officer!' (IV.i.200, 202).

It is Othello's failure to see Desdemona as a person or to recognize his own uncharted areas that accounts for his easy acceptance of Iago's terms. Men's misconceptions of women are, in Desdemona's words, 'horrible fancies' (IV.ii.26), projections of their own worst fears and failings. Man defines woman as 'the other', in Simone de Beauvoir's term: 'He projects upon her what he desires and what he fears, what he loves and what he hates.'[14] Only once does Othello attempt to 'say what she is' (IV.i.187), and though wrenched with 'the pity of it' (195), he is unable to hold this reality in focus. The final speeches in which he summons the old rhetoric in self-justification and evocation of his heroic past – 'speak of me as I am' (V.ii.343) – make no mention of the human being he has loved and killed, and are concerned, like so much of what he says, with his tragedy rather than hers. The women, on the other hand, do attempt to adjust their visions of the men and to temper their ideals. Emilia has thought about 'jealous souls' and their 'cause' (III.iv.159–60), and Desdemona tries to excuse Othello's anger – 'Nay, we must think men are not gods' (III.iv.148) – and to understand the human being with concerns besides herself:

> Something sure of state ...
> Hath puddled his clear spirit; and in such cases
> Men's natures wrangle with inferior things
> Though great ones are their object.

(III.iv.140–45)

But none of the men succeeds; Othello himself only once even tries to adjust his ideas and 'images' of women to the human reality.

IV

The characters of the three women illuminate aspects of one another, Emilia and Bianca providing potentials of character and behaviour available to Desdemona. In this system of contrasts and parallels, an association between Desdemona and Bianca is established by the juxtaposition of the eavesdropping and 'brothel' scenes, analogous in the cruelty with which men impose 'fancies' on women. Bianca enters the scene, which Iago has devised, in the midst of the laughter characteristic of Cassio's habitual response to her; in a feeble attempt at self-assertion she returns the handkerchief she believes to be from another woman, but ends by begging him to accompany her home, an incident which constitutes 'proof' for Othello of his own wife's adultery. Though the scene is comic in tone, it provides comment on the next scene, which is not. As Cassio has called Bianca 'caitiff' and 'customer' (IV.i.108, 119), Othello imposes the same 'fancy' on Desdemona, reducing the reality of a woman who loves him to 'strumpet' and 'whore' (IV.ii.81, 83, 85, 89), a role and relationship that justifies his abuse. Though least alike in terms of innocence and experience, Bianca and Desdemona are analogous in that to which they are subject, and in an ability to return devotion for revilement which is simultaneously virtue and folly.

We watch Desdemona progress, in the course of the play, through a variety of roles traditionally assigned to woman: she is defined and disowned as daughter, then adulated as lover and wife, reviled as whore, and finally deprived of all designations. Her first words define her carefully within the social order, as daughter and wife; in her description of herself as 'divided' in 'duty' between father and husband she provides an emblem of her situation. The words she uses to describe these relationships – 'bound', 'duty', 'due' (I.iii.182–8) – indicate circumscription, a deeply engrained obedience for which she is finally literally strangled. (Othello's first plan is to poison her, but he eagerly accepts Iago's suggestion that he strangle her: 'The justice of it pleases' [IV.i.210].) Only in relation to her love for Othello does her language assume the more active qualities of 'storm', 'violence' (294), and 'challenge' (188), but her elopement, though a challenge to the social order, is still a circumscribed form of rebellion which follows the prescribed path from father to husband, a husband whom she nearly always addresses as 'my lord', true to the filial relationship determined by their difference in years. And though her love for Othello is touching, bold, wonderful, hers is still that romantic illusion of the merging of identity – 'My heart's subdu'd / Even to the quality of my lord' (I.iii.250–51) – and the verb 'subdued' is accurate, since, as de Beauvoir notes, it is an ideal that must result in the obliteration of self: if, as Catherine says, 'I am Heathcliffe', that leaves only one of them.[15]

Defined by men and in relation to men, woman's identity is precarious, and we see how precarious within this scene when Brabantio dissolves his ties to Desdemona, casting her off as daughter: 'Dead ... to me' (I.iii.59); 'I give thee that ...' (193). Having betrayed him, she is no longer his daughter, nor even a person, but a 'that'. (So, for that matter, is Othello called a 'thing' [I.ii.71], and the dehumanizing terms suggest a similarity between racial and sexual stereotyping which we have come to recognize.) Brabantio's warning – 'Look to her, Moor, if thou hast eyes to see; / She has deceiv'd her father and may thee' (I.iii.292–3) – suggests similarities between Desdemona's relations with both husband and father, though not those which Brabantio imagines. Othello, too, will dissolve his ties to her, and redefine her – no longer as his wife, but as 'that cunning whore of Venice / That married with Othello' (IV.ii.89–90), a redefinition that strips her of identity, and finally of life: 'My wife? ... I have no wife' (V.ii.97).

Though Desdemona's 'divided duty' may represent orthodox Elizabethan doctrine, it is her acceptance of these terms and assumptions that leaves her powerless to understand her situation, let alone deal with it. We watch the course of her love for Othello – from simple adoration, to confusion ('What shall I do to win my lord again?' [IV.ii.149]), through attempts to justify him ('something sure of state ...'), to justify herself: 'You do me wrong' (IV.ii.82); 'I have not deserv'd this' (IV.i.241). We watch her struggle with her sense of outraged worth, subduing her rebellion, remaining solicitous of him at the expense of herself ('Am I the motive for these tears, my lord?' [IV.ii.43]), siding, finally, with him against herself: 'My love doth so approve him, / That even his stubbornness, his checks, his frowns ... have grace and favor in them' (IV.iii.19–21); 'Let nobody blame him, his scorn I approve' (52); and ending, finally, resolutely faithful in her acceptance of blame: 'Nobody; I myself ... / Commend me to my kind lord' (V.ii.124–5). Her defencelessness is partly a patter of naivety, and partly linguistic: she cannot pronounce the word 'whore' – 'I cannot say "whore". / It does abhor me now I speak the word' (V.ii.161–2). As Othello 'throws despite and heavy terms upon her' (IV.ii.116), she can barely understand them – 'What doth your speech import?' – let alone defend herself against them: 'I understand a fury in your words, / But not the words' (IV.ii.31–2). For this she has been praised by a critic as astute as Heilman:

> She does not fly off into the loud vehemence of offended self-love [or] rise above a hurt amazement and a mild earnestness of assertion.... Instead of looking around for someone to blame, she tries to make a case for Othello's incredible conduct, and she rebukes herself for blaming him.... But she does not ... subordinate devotion to self-pity and self-justification.[16]

But though this mildness may have appeal in the abstract, to approve it is contrary to our experience of these last scenes, to the tension and frustration created as Desdemona is brought together with her raving husband and is unable to rise above 'hurt amazement'. What began as the 'archetypal fantasy of man and woman' turns to another 'complementary mythic fantasy', what Fiedler calls 'the male nightmare of unmerited betrayal and the female dream of patient suffering rewarded'.[17] Precisely what is required of Desdemona is 'self-love' and 'self-justification', defiance of the role in which Othello has cast her; we long to hear her ask, inquire, answer, challenge, shout, to find a voice by which she can express her innocence and defend herself, but it is her acceptance of his terms – not 'whore', but the premisses and assumptions that make her 'inferior thing' – that renders her helpless and inarticulate. What has been lost in her 'divided duty' is duty to herself, and Othello's irony strikes a terrible truth: 'And she's obedient, as you say, obedient; / Very obedient' (IV.i.225–6). Though, to his question, 'What art thou', she can reply: 'Your wife, my lord; your true / And loyal wife' (IV.ii.33–4), she is not able to find a language strong or clear enough to counteract his 'fancy', and in fact manages consistently to say just the wrong thing, pursuing Cassio's suit at the moment when it does her most harm, struggling for life when the desire to live convicts her of guilt: 'Kill me tomorrow, let me live tonight!' (V.ii.80). We cringe as she finds just the words to infuriate him: 'He [Cassio] will not say so' (71); 'Alas, he is betray'd and I undone!' (76). 'Bewhor'd', she is bewildered, 'half asleep' (IV.ii.96), and overcome.

Is this her 'wretched fortune' (IV.ii.128), as she calls it, and as her name implies? In a sense, it is her fate as a woman, quintessential woman, the 'jewel' (I.iii.195) of her father, 'pearl' (V.ii.347) of her husband, treasure, but possession, and her acceptance of her position, that render her incapable of self-defence. That defiance is what is required in her situation, and is an Elizabethan as well as a modern possibility, is indicated by Shakespeare's structuring of the murder scene in such a way that expression is given the rebellion we have longed to hear, and an alternative mode of behaviour is provided. Bursting in on the scene, demanding 'a word' (V.ii.90), it is Emilia who finds the voice of protest that makes itself heard: 'You told a lie, an odious, damned lie! / Upon my soul, a lie! a wicked lie' (V.ii.180–81), a voice which is contrast and antidote to the muffled silence of her mistress. From the beginning, Emilia has had this ability to name things clearly, precisely, if at times a bit crassly. Speaking on her own behalf, she gives expression to the human reality which we have heard stereotyped:

> But I do think it is their husbands' faults
> If wives do fall . . .

Why, we have galls; and though we have some grace,
Yet have we some revenge. Let husbands know
Their wives have sense like them: they see, and smell,
And have their palates both for sweet and sour,
As husbands have ... And have we not affections,
Desires for sport, and frailty, as men have?
Then let them use us well; else let them know
The ills we do, their ills instruct us so.

$$(IV.iii.92-103)^{18}$$

A simple truth, yet beyond any of the men in the play: that woman is neither goddess nor whore, but a being with 'frailty', desire, and point of view, combined of both 'grace' and 'gall'. Not that Emilia's is a perspective to which we wholly ascribe, entrenched as it is in a material reality, but her vision complements Desdemona's, and represents some of the body and toughness that Desdemona lacks: 'The world's a huge thing ... and the wrong is but a wrong i' th' world; and having the world for your labor, 'tis a wrong in your own world, and you might quickly make it right' (IV.iii.69–83). Such relativism has its strengths: an acknowledgement, like irony, of other points of view; and it is irony of which Desdemona and Othello are tragically incapable; but that relativism plays no part in Emilia's actions is seen in her unhesitating sacrifice of her life. If we try to account for her character, we may speculate that this clarity is partly a matter of social class: never adulated, no one's 'jewel', she has remained clear-eyed and without illusions, although she is, like Desdemona, too tolerant of her husband's 'fantasy' (III.iii.299). Thus it is she who finds the voice Desdemona cannot, which dispels the nightmarish unreality: 'I am bound to speak' (184); 'Let me have leave to speak' (195); 'Let heaven and men and devils let them all / All cry shame against me, yet I'll speak' (221–2). And her simple refusal expresses the defiance we have long wished to hear: ''Tis proper I obey him; but not now. / Perchance, Iago, I will ne'er go home' (196–7).

V

Of the three women in the play, two are killed by their husbands after being reviled as whores; the third, Bianca, seems actually to be a whore, and though she survives, it is through no strength of her own, but simply because she is not central enough to be pulled into Iago's plots. We see women defined by men, 'circumstanc'd' (III.iv.201), the object of their 'horrible fancies', fancies which are projections of their own worst fears and failings. Reviled, or adulated and then reviled in proportion to that adulation, they are cursed and killed. The question, how shall the good defend themselves? might be rephrased: how shall women protect themselves against men? And Shakespeare's change of the 'I' of the Willow Song from male to female adds yet another victimized woman.[19] Against the roles in which men cast them, we see the human reality, the reality of women trying to understand their men and to survive. We see that Desdemona can no more be accounted for by the 'lame and impotent conclusion' (II.i.152) of Iago's stereotypes than Emilia can, though it is Othello's tragedy to believe that she can; as it is Iago's strategic error to judge Emilia a 'common thing' (III.iii.302) without moral dimension. We see that woman is not as she is named by man, although it is her tragedy to believe that she is, and that the inadequacy of male definitions is the inadequacy of society's.

In the comedies and romances, and in *Antony and Cleopatra*, women make themselves heard, but part of what is tragic about the tragic world here is that they do not, and they do not because, accepting the restrictive roles assigned them by men, obedient to men's 'fancies', they are mutilated and destroyed. In the world of comedy, Othello and Desdemona would be granted the reprieve of Claudio and Hero, although even in the world of *Much Ado*, Claudio's easy acceptance of slander, so like Othello's, indicates a failure of knowledge and love; Shakespeare provides a better way in Beatrice and Benedick, who represent a love based on self-knowledge and knowledge of one another which is capable of surviving world and time. It is unthinkable that the creator of Beatrice or Cleopatra or Rosalind would perceive in Desdemona the ideal that his critics have seen. But we do not have to leave this play to find an alternative mode of action, since within *Othello* is a woman capable of challenging male prerogatives and assumptions, who might be able to bring about a comic resolution, were the destruction not so far on its course. Shakespeare shows woman, at her best, as capable of a courage which eludes the men and as acceptant of a challenge which, like Emilia's, encompasses 'heaven and men and devils'. Though the men do the killing, it is they who are the more tragically mutilated.

Bianca provides a reflection of what Desdemona is, Emilia a potential of what she might be: an autonomous being capable of speaking from her own centre of self, and finding a language which is strong and clear because it does come from that centre. Desdemona needs more of the one, less of the other. As Desdemona's defencelessness is explicable in terms of a 'feminine' docility, so too are Othello's limitations traceable to the 'manly' ideal of character and conduct involved in his 'occupation'. As with Lear, Hamlet and Antony, the experience of betrayal makes the tragic protagonist doubt his very identity, but unlike the others, Othello assumes that selfhood can be recovered by an act of physical violence and destruction of the loved one. Though we are tempted to cry, with Emilia,

'What should such a fool / Do with so good a wife?' (V.ii.232–3),[20] and though his years and her youth make him the more reprehensible, we must realize that Othello and Desdemona co-operate in their destruction: cut off in tragic incomprehension from one another, they speak two different languages, and she is no more capable of entering into his experience than he is into hers. But by not defying him, Desdemona destroys both of them. She may have an inkling of her complicity in their tragedy when, about to die, she confesses her sins as 'loves I bear you' (V.ii.40).

Othello's investment of his 'manhood' in his 'honesty', in an ideal of honour as reputation that requires Desdemona's death, and in his confusion of her character with her 'chastity', points to an error – not only one of fact, but one involved in the conceptions themselves; not only of Othello, but of society as a whole. Though to the end, Othello is still thinking in such terms, justifying himself as 'an honorable murderer' who 'did all in honor' (V.ii.294–5), 'But why should honor out-live honesty?' (83), Shakespeare is suggesting that woman's virtue need be defined as a more active and positive quality than chastity, the 'preservation of this vessel for my lord' (IV.ii.83); and that the 'honor' for which Othello so readily kills be made of sterner stuff than 'the bubble reputation' (*As You Like It* II.vii.152). The ideal of manly and womanly behaviour that the play finally affirms is something closer to a combination of masculine and feminine than that recognized or represented by Desdemona or Othello: it is the ideal, familiar elsewhere in Shakespeare, that the best of women has something of man in her, and the best of men something of woman.[21]

This is not to imply that the complexities of this tragedy are reducible to a tract on the subject of woman. The sense we are left with is one of woe and wonder, the paradox that we kill what we most love, and that what is grand about these characters, their faith and absolute commitment, is also their doom. But while recognizing and responding to what is splendid in their love, we can question what fatal quality condemns it to death, and whether it need be a *Liebestod*, allied so inevitably to destruction. Perhaps we must finally accept this connection of love and death as an inexorable condition of our lives, man's revulsion from woman accountable, as Arthur Kirsch has suggested in his study of the play, in Freudian terms of man's earliest desire for his mother.[22] But so much of what Freud considered 'inexorable' has been traced, in the past fifty years, to social conditions, and 'essentially' male and female characteristics may not be 'essential', but socially determined. It is equally possible to see man's ambivalence towards woman in terms of his suspicion that he has wronged her: binding her to a double standard in which she has not been consulted, to which she has not consented, he expects her revenge to take the form of sexual betrayal.[23] The social dimension in this play is prominent by virtue of Othello's blackness and the carefully delineated backgrounds, classes and 'occupations' of each of the characters. This man of action, who has never looked within, and his obedient lady are fatally interlocked in the ancient rite of love and death. Though Desdemona comes closer than he does to recognizing the human being and adjusting her ideal accordingly, theirs is not a marriage of true minds, not based on a recognition of persons, and though touching and wondrous, it is fatally flawed; what Heilman calls 'the magical transformation of love' destroys them both. Shakespeare is suggesting, in his radical critique of some of society's most cherished notions, that accepted ideals of manly and womanly behaviour are distortive and destructive of the human reality, and that relations be based on saner and more certain ground than 'this that you call love'.

Notes

1. *Othello* III.iii.449. *The Riverside Shakespeare*, ed. G. Blakemore Evans (Boston, MA: Houghton Mifflin, 1974). All further references to Shakespeare's plays are to this edition.
2. *The Wheel of Fire: Interpretations of Shakespearean Tragedy* (1949; rpt. London: Methuen, 1970), p. 111.
3. *Shakespearean Tragedy* (1904; rpt. Cleveland, OH: World Publ., 1963), p. 147.
4. *Magic in the Web: Action and Language in Othello* (Lexington: University of Kentucky Press, 1965), p. 214.
5. *Shakespeare's Talking Animals: Language and Drama in Society* (Totowa, NJ: Rowman & Littlefield, 1974), p. 133.
6. Heilman discusses Othello's opening speeches in these terms (pp. 139–40). See also F.R. Leavis, 'Diabolic Intellect and the Noble Hero: A Note on *Othello*', *Scrutiny*, 6 (December 1938); and D.A. Traversi, *An Approach to Shakespeare* (Garden City, NY: Doubleday, 1956), pp. 133–5.
7. Heilman, p. 139.
8. 'Reputation' was by no means the only possible conception of honour. In *All's Well*, *Troilus and Cressida*, and *Julius Caesar*, Shakespeare subjects the military ideal of honour as reputation to criticism, and in *1 Henry IV* he opposes the limited, histrionic ideal of Hotspur to the mature, self-defined, and inherent quality represented by Hal. For the variety of views which were available in the Renaissance, see Curtis Watson, *Shakespeare and the Renaissance Concept of Honor* (Princeton, NJ: Princeton University Press, 1960); and Ruth Kelso, 'The Doctrine of the English Gentleman in the Sixteenth Century', *University of Illinois Studies* 14 (April 1929).
9. *Archetypal Patterns in Poetry: Psychological Studies of Imagination* (London: Oxford University Press, 1974), p. 219.
10. Rosalie Colie discusses *Othello* in terms of the 'unmetaphorizing' of Petrarchan conventions: 'In criticizing the artificiality he at the same time exploits in the play, Shakespeare manages . . . to reassess and to reanimate the moral system of the psychological truths at the core of the literary love-tradition, to reveal its problematics and to reaffirm in a fresh and momentous context the beauty of its impossible ideals.' *Shakespeare's Living Art* (Princeton, NJ: Princeton University Press, 1974), p. 167. I would agree that the play offers a dramatization of the values central to Petrarchan love, but I would argue that it is more overwhelmingly negative in emphasis: rather than 'reanimating' and 'reaffirming' these values, it offers a critique which finds them deficient and destructive.
11. Bodkin, p. 222.
12. Traversi, p. 129.
13. *The Stranger in Shakespeare* (New York: Stein & Day, 1972), p. 158. Fiedler claims

Shakespeare shares 'the Moor's paranoia' (p. 165), but his reading is based on a misinterpretation of the women: all three are true, contrary to his claim, and the play as a whole refutes such paranoia, and restores the faith which was lost in *Troilus and Cressida*.

14. *The Second Sex* (New York: Random House, 1974), p. 223.

15. Ibid., p. 725.

16. Heilman, pp. 208–9.

17. Fiedler, p. 148.

18. Cf. de Beauvoir's analysis of women's relationships and their questioning of male pretences and values: 'Woman knows that the masculine code is not hers.... She therefore calls upon other women to help define a set of "local rules," ... a moral code specifically for the female sex' (p. 605). Feeling 'the ambiguity of her position', 'she avoids the snares of over-seriousness and conformism' and can question 'ready-made values' (p. 403).

19. *Othello, A New Variorum Edition*, ed. Horace Howard Furness (New York: Dover, 1963), pp. 276–7.

20. See Carol Neely's excellent article of this name, 'Women and Men in *Othello*: "What should such a fool / Do with so good a woman?"', *Shakespeare Studies* (Spring 1978); to be reprinted in *The Woman's Part: Feminist Criticism of Shakespeare*, ed. Gayle Greene, Carol Neely and Carolyn Lenz, forthcoming (University of Illinois Press). Though her interpretation of Desdemona and her conclusions differ from mine, she, too, sees the tragedy as originating in men's and women's misconception of one another. Her essay contributed considerably to my understanding of the play.

21. Juliet Dusinberre notes that 'Shakespeare believed that for a man to be more than a boy, as for a woman to be more than a child, the masculine and the feminine must marry in his spirit', *Shakespeare and the Nature of Women* (New York: Barnes & Noble, 1975), p. 291; Carolyn Heilbrun sees Shakespeare 'as devoted to the androgynous ideal as anyone who has ever written', *Toward a Recognition of Androgyny* (New York: Knopf, 1973), p. 29; and Virginia Woolf describes Shakespeare's mind as 'the type of the androgynous, of the man-womanly mind', *A Room of One's Own* (New York: Harcourt, 1957), p. 102.

22. 'The Polarization of Erotic Love in Shakespeare's Plays', unpubl. paper read at Shakespeare Association meeting, April 1977, New Orleans.

23. And it does take this form: adultery is often a form of revenge. De Beauvoir's discussion of the causes of jealousy is illuminating: 'Only through adultery can woman prove that she is nobody's chattel.... This is the reason why the husband's jealousy is so quick to awaken.... This is indeed why jealousy can be insatiable', *Second Sex*, p. 213.

4

Shakespeare and Emotional Distance in the Elizabethan Family

Marianne Novy

One of the most startling ideas in Lawrence Stone's *The Family, Sex, and Marriage in England 1500–1800* is the claim that most people in sixteenth- and early-seventeenth-century England 'found it very difficult to establish close emotional ties to any other person'.[1] As he reconstructs it, the Elizabethan family was characterized by 'distance, manipulation, and deference' (p. 117). Stone may overstate his case, but evidence suggests that he is on to something. Some of his harshest critics, like Alan Macfarlane and Randolph Trumbach, point to similar cultural traits in the England they describe in their own work, though they differ with him about origin, time span, and degree.[2] It seems that the Elizabethan aristocracy and middle class strove at least to appear in control of their emotional attachments, though the cost might be suspicion and loneliness.

The world Stone re-creates and the world Shakespeare creates are in sharp contrast. Plays characterized by the 'psychic numbing' (p. 102) Stone attributes to Elizabethan society could never have held the stage for centuries, but beyond this, as C.L. Barber has noted: 'Shakespeare's art is distinguished by the intensity of its investment in the human family.'[3] Are Shakespeare's plays evidence that Stone must be wrong about the Elizabethans?[4] Or was Shakespeare simply ahead of his time in his portrayal of the family?[5] Or is there another kind of relationship between Stone's picture and Shakespeare's?

The relationship I am proposing is not a photographic likeness. It is not enough to say that the warm affectionate families in Shakespeare show that Stone is wrong, or that cold families prove him right. Rather, I would suggest that Stone has identified a cultural ideal of Elizabethan society that generates conflicts pervasive in Shakespeare's plays.

According to Stone, most Elizabethan aristocrats were egocentric. Letters of advice from father to son, a popular genre among the landed classes, 'normally express a thoroughly pessimistic view of human nature, full of canny and worldly-wise hints about how to conduct personal relations which leave little room for generosity, faith, hope, or charity' (p. 96). Diaries, correspondence, and legal records from the fifteenth to the seventeenth centuries show an extraordinary amount of casual violence at all levels of society (p. 93).

The mortality rate for all ages and classes was high (infant mortality did not drop significantly until 1750) and Stone emphasizes practices that can be viewed as treating people as easily replaceable. Aristocrats often used marriage to gain money or power, and remarriage was frequent. Upper-class children were sent out to a succession of wet nurses (who were separated from the children they had borne) and children of all classes lived apart from their parents for the years that they were in fosterage or apprenticeship (pp. 105–14).

What these facts meant emotionally is not easy to say, and some of the evidence could be interpreted differently. If aristocratic fathers told sons not to trust anyone, perhaps sons provoked the advice by trusting people. If sermons warned parents not to love their children too much, and threatened that God might take away a child whose parents were too fond, some parents must have grieved intensely for their children; Stone himself suggests that apparent coldness may have been a defence against the constant possibility of emotional bereavement. He notes too that some people married for emotional reasons, and that Reformation theology and practice placed more emphasis on companionship and love in marriage than had pre-Reformation Catholicism (pp. 135–7).[6]

Nevertheless, Stone's work and that of other historians suggest that there was an ideal personality type valued by many Elizabethans – an ideal that on one hand kept feelings of attachment and grief under strict control, but on the other was more ready to express feelings of anger. The model was primarily a masculine ideal, a point I shall return to later, but because masculinity was more valued than femininity, the emphasis on control could influence women as well, and their deviations from it could be seen as signs of typically feminine weakness. Attempts to follow this model would lead both sexes to difficulties in establishing and maintaining relationships; consequent frustration could fuel the anger expressed; throughout life one might be influenced by an emotional dependence that one constantly denied. If emotional distance was an ideal for self-fashioning – to borrow Stephen Greenblatt's term – it could coexist with hatred and with (denied) love.[7] Thus I do not agree with Stone's suggestion that Elizabethan 'familial emotive ties were so weak that they did not generate the passions which lead to intra-familial murder and mayhem' (p. 95). Strong passions may still exist when they are displaced or controlled. I would emphasize, rather, Stone's admission of exceptions to his generalizations, and push further the implications of those exceptions. In his review, Macfarlane suggests that Elizabethan society included 'some loving parents and some cruel parents, some people bringing their children up in a rigid way, others in a relaxed atmosphere, deep attachment between certain husbands and wives, frail emotional bonds in other cases'.[8] The contrasting elements in this mix would not remain inert; at least some people would notice the differences and would be affected by them. Rather than seeing Elizabethan England as Stone's mass of 'psychic numbing' dotted with exceptions, I would reconstruct a society in conflict about emotions and a constant interplay in the experience of the individual between emotions and the ideal of control – an interplay that we see enacted in Shakespeare's theatre. There attempts at control are constantly played off against underlying emotions; attempts at distance are played off against suggestions of underlying dependence. Analysing almost any speech, we can focus on either emotion or control, much as we can focus on either figure or ground in looking at a painting – except that the more we focus on the amount of control exerted, the more powerful become the hidden emotions, the subtext, that we imagine.

If establishing or admitting emotional ties was difficult for many in Shakespeare's audience partly because of their ideals of control, this ambivalence may have contributed to the appeal of his plays. In the tragedies, the cost of either denying or affirming connections can be mortal; in the comedies, more connections succeed. But in the background of both genres are distances – literal and psychological – between parents and children, and disguises – literal and psychological – that attempt control and dramatize the difficulties of trusting and understanding.

Coriolanus is the tragic hero whose behaviour Shakespeare most explicitly links to a childhood training in ideals of emotional distance. His mother tells us:

> When yet he was but tender-bodied and the only son of my womb ...,
> I, considering how honor would become such a person, that it was no
> better than picture-like to hang by th'wall, if renown made it not stir, was
> pleased to let him seek danger where he was like to find fame. To a cruel
> war I sent him, from whence he returned, his brows bound with oak.
>
> (I.iii.5–6, 9–14)[9]

He tries, as he says, to 'stand / As if a man were author of himself, / And knew no other kin' (V.iii.35–7) to the point of threatening to destroy his own native Rome and his family along with it, but at his mother's pleas he finally relents and takes her hand.[10] The ideal of distance proves impossible to maintain, as Shakespeare suggests throughout the conflict between Coriolanus's emotions and his ideal. Even when he cites the proverbs of emotional control, it is as part of his mother's earlier admonitions:

> You were used
> To say extremities was the trier of spirits:
> That common chances common men could bear;
> ... You were used to load me
> With precepts that would make invincible
> The heart that conned them.

(IV.i.3–5, 9–11)

Coriolanus sounds like Stone's typical aggressive, egocentric aristocrat, moulded by cold child-rearing practices; but unlike Stone, Shakespeare forces us to see the strength of the emotional bonds that remain underneath the cultural ideal; Coriolanus cannot simply keep on killing outside his family, but has to face his feelings towards them; has to face the anger behind his distance, and the dependence behind his anger.

King Lear also is about conflicts between distance and emotion in relations between parent and child. Lear cannot freely express his love for Cordelia, but must set up his intended gift as a reward for her performance in a contest he controls, and then disowns her for insisting on her autonomy and not playing her part properly. While his other daughters treat him cruelly, he strives to control himself and deny his emotional vulnerability; but these attempts break down in his madness. Only Cordelia can save him, and he breaks down again when she is lost for ever; but in Lear's death, as he strains again for a word from her, it is clear that they are inevitably bound to each other. With similar lack of insight, Gloucester dismisses Edmund with 'He hath been out nine year, and away he shall again' (I.i.31–2), and then doubts Edgar's love on the flimsiest of evidence manufactured by Edmund; he underestimates the anger of the one and the love of the other, and the impact that both will have on his life. Edgar, his identity disguised, cares for his father in the blindness that his brother helped to cause. When Edgar reveals himself, Gloucester dies of mingled grief and joy, like Lear showing in his death the strength of his connection to his child.[11]

In one sense, Hamlet's initial manner is already an acknowledgement of his bond to his family; his mourning is an attempt to maintain the tie to the father that death has removed. But in this attempt to cling to his father he seems distant from his mother, and we can trace something of an analogous pattern to the one we have seen in *Coriolanus* and *Lear*. At first Hamlet speaks to his mother only in laconic irony – 'Ay, madam, it is common' (I.ii.74). But later when he speaks to her in her room, it becomes clear how much anger underlies this distance, and how much longing for love underlies the anger.

However, the relevance to *Hamlet* of the emotional distance Stone has described in Elizabethan England is even clearer if we look at the larger structure of the play. *Hamlet* is built around a conflict between an unfeeling society and a hero with strong feelings, which he tries to control – a conflict that parallels both the conflicts I postulated for Elizabethan England: the internal one between defences and emotions and the external one between cooler and more emotional people. The mood of the Danish court sounds much like that of the suspicious Elizabethan court – even Polonius's advice resembles that of the many cynical fathers found by Stone. Hamlet must live among detached, manipulative and suspicious people, and he defends himself from them partly by trying to mask his emotional intensity with emotional distance. He speaks enigmatically from the very beginning – 'A little more than kin and less than kind' (I.ii.65) – and puts on a more elaborate antic disposition after the ghost's revelation widens the gap between him and the rest of the court. He can trust Horatio, but no one else, and it is only after Ophelia's death that he can admit his love for her.

When trust is created in the tragedies, it is a precarious achievement in a perilous world. Othello's relationship with Desdemona breaks down in the context of threats analogous to those Stone suggests – distrust resulting from ideals of emotional control. Living down the stereotype of the passionate African and the unease of the exile, he too is a hero of strong feelings he strives to control. Throughout, the cynical and manipulative world-view has its spokesman in Iago. Emotionally detached from his own wife, he can influence Othello partly because of the basic sense of insecurity and distance which makes it difficult for Othello to believe in the initial success of his love, and partly because of Othello's ideals of coolness.[12] From the beginning he has denied the presence of 'heat' or 'young affects' in his love. When his jealousy shows him his passionate attachment to Desdemona, he believes it is alien to his true character and plans to kill her to restore his self-control: 'I'll not expostulate with her, lest her body and beauty unprovide my mind again' (IV.i.200–02). When he discovers her fidelity, only his own death can restore that control, and his death is equally an attempt to reaffirm their relationship.

In the comedies, the conflicts between emotional distance and control do not require death for their resolution. Thus the distance between parent and child is often presented largely as geographic distance and physical disguise. Parent–child separation and parent–child rejection are kept apart (rather than being combined, as they are in *Othello* and *Lear*). In *The Comedy of Errors*, Antipholus of Ephesus speaks movingly of his separation from his parents, caused by the romance plot conventions of tempest and shipwreck. Here, and in the romances as well, such externally enforced family separation could dramatize the frequent separation of Elizabethan families by death and standard child-rearing practices. Feeling separation as rejection probably alternated with feeling it as beyond human control, like tempest and shipwreck. The reticence that the Antipholus brothers keep in their reunion – they never speak directly to each other –

may show that the ideal of emotional control continues its claims even at the happy ending. At the corresponding point, the Menachmi twins of Shakespeare's source speak to each other with feeling, and we might expect even more eloquence at the father–son reunion not found in the source, but we do not get it.[13] This inarticulacy allows the actors to fill in with gestures, of course, and the audience with imagination; nevertheless, it is interesting that it is the mother who has almost all the words of joy at the resolution, and that her imagery turns on childbirth:

> Thirty-three years have I but gone in travail
> Of you, my sons; and till this present hour
> My heavy burden ne'er delivered.

(V.i.402–4)

The disguises in Shakespeare's comedies can be related to emotional distance in a number of ways. The self-control that masculine disguise imposes on women is an analogue of the control that the masculine ideal imposes on men; the disguise suggests, too, that the women may share in that ideal of control. Rosalind begins *As You Like It* grieving for her banished father, but when she meets him she does not at once reveal the identity behind her disguise. 'He asked me of what parentage I was. I told him, of as good as he; so he laughed and let me go' (III.iv.33–4). For all her warmth, Rosalind maintains some freedom and distance from her father until the last scene. But unlike Edgar's analogous delay in revealing himself, this one has no mortal consequences.

For the lovers in the comedies, disguise can dramatize the difficulties of establishing emotional connections, although it also fosters such connections by giving less risky ones time to develop. Rosalind's disguise may express ambivalence about abandoning herself to her love for Orlando; in many of the comedies, the characters' inability to see through disguise suggests their mixed feelings about forming close ties. Sherman Hawkins has noted the internal obstacles to love in what he calls the comedies of the closed world (*Comedy of Errors, Taming of the Shrew, Love's Labour's Lost, Much Ado about Nothing* and *Twelfth Night*); Orlando's initial inability to speak to Rosalind suggests an internal obstacle in him as well.[14] Proteus, Berowne, Bassanio, Orlando, Claudio and Orsino all make mistakes about the identity of the women they finally marry. These mistakes, and analogous mistakes made by Phebe and Olivia, are, in part, dramatic images of the postures of emotional distance that can remain even when people are falling in love; many of these characters are comically self-centred or fascinated with an idealized image – often unattainable – more than with a human being. Often the degree to which the characters grow is open to question, and the conclusion relies primarily on the literal removal of disguise for the sense of overcoming barriers to relationship.

Most of the conversations between comic lovers involve either literal disguise or hostility. Either alternative externalizes such ambivalence as an audience may have about emotional ties. For an audience with a veneer of defences, Beatrice and Benedick, who begin as mockers of love, consciously cool and rational, or Viola and Rosalind, who in their disguise can never express their love directly, make ideal protagonists; their mockery or concealment of love makes it impossible to dismiss them as pretending to love insincerely. The combination of verbal rapport and concealment in the text permits the audience here, as in the reunions of *Comedy of Errors*, to fill in with whatever depth they can imagine.

The importance of such disguised conversations in mediating emotional distance becomes more evident if we observe the problems of the problem comedies. There the disguised contact that forms the basis for the final marriages is physical, not verbal, and cannot be played out for the audience. Angelo and Mariana don't meet onstage until the final scene of *Measure for Measure*. Angelo and Bertram are more clearly split than the heroes of the earlier comedies between the general coldness of their personalities and the sexual drives that trap them into marriages with women for whom they express no personal warmth. The women love, but the couples can't work out the marriages by themselves; men in authority must impose them.

The romances, like the tragedies, treat difficulties deeper than premarital caution, but present more possibilities for reconciliation. Leontes looks at Hermione's statue and says: 'Does not the stone rebuke me, / For being more stone than it?' (V.iii.37–8). But, as his own heart has lost its coldness to Hermione, the statue comes to life. Here, as in the other romances, the ideal of emotional control breaks down much sooner than in the tragedies; the older characters express emotions of familial attachment more readily, and the young fall in love more quickly. The first half of *The Winter's Tale* provides an anatomy of familial rejection that ties together difficulty in husband–wife and parent–child relations. While Stone, drawing on Freud, suggests that distance from parents in childhood is one of the causes of distance in marriage, causality may work in the other direction as well – Leontes abandons his daughter and loses his son because of his suspicion of his wife. But, on the other hand, Leontes, from the beginning, is able to express his feeling of love for his son, and his grief at his son's death helps him to see his misjudgement of Hermione and mourn for her.

Earlier I suggested that emotional control was more clearly an ideal for men than for women in Elizabethan society. Stone gives largely unexplored hints that patterns and norms of emotional warmth differed for males and females. The parents quoted as sounding distant from children are mostly fathers; furthermore, Stone sees fathers as colder to daughters than to sons, more likely to consider daughters as only a drain on their money. He also provides some evidence that women often wanted more emotional involvement in marriage than did men (p. 105). In this context, the emphasis on distance and manipulativeness in father–son advice letters looks different. Rather than expressing a general norm, it suggests an attempt to initiate the son into standards of coldness required by the conventional adult male.[15]

How much was this a conscious rejection of qualities associated with women? Popular thought often identified women with passion and men with reason, with an emphasis on the necessary subordination of the first to the second; since women, whether nurses or mothers, had primary responsibility for child-rearing, they were associated with everyone's first discovery of emotions.[16] Many documents suggest that Elizabethan men were often suspicious of women, and this suspicion may also be connected with suspicion of feelings of attachment in general.

More historical research needs to be done on how the ideal of emotional distance in the Elizabethan family relates to distrust of women and qualities associated with women – how much it coalesces with emotional distance as a conventional ideal for Elizabethan men. In Shakespeare the connection is often explicit. His characters use language that associates women with expressions of emotional attachment; such language is especially frequent in bereavement. Laertes says of his tears for Ophelia's death: 'When these are gone, / The woman will be out' (IV.vii.187–8). When Sebastian thinks his sister Viola is dead, he says, 'I am yet so near the manners of my mother that, upon the least occasion more, mine eyes will tell tales of me' (II.i.35–7), and Claudius censures Hamlet's mourning by saying: 'Tis unmanly grief' (I.ii.94). When Lear struggles to deny the pain he feels at his daughters' rejection, he cries: 'O, how this mother swells up toward my heart! / Hysterica passio, down, thou climbing sorrow' (II.iv.54–5). Later he prays:

> Touch me with noble anger,
> And let not women's weapons, water drops,
> Stain my man's cheeks.

> (II.iv.271–3)

This pattern of associations often goes beyond words. Most of the rejections of children are rejections of daughters by fathers. Let us recall Leonato and Hero, Old Capulet and Juliet, Brabantio and Desdemona, Cymbeline and Imogen. Furthermore, fathers' rejections of daughters, like husbands' rejections of wives, usually result from suspicion of female sexuality – in one case (Perdita) the daughter is thought to be conceived adulterously; in the others, the fathers object to their daughters' wishes, real or apparent, to love men other than their fathers or their fathers' choices. By contrast, neither mothers nor fathers reject sons because of their sexual behaviour.[17] And on the other hand, verbal attacks on a mother's sexuality may suddenly appear in any threat of rejection from the family, even if the mother herself never appears in the play. Lear says to Regan: 'I would divorce me from thy mother's tomb / Sepulch'ring an adult'ress' (II.iv.126–7); and Isabella to Claudio: 'Heaven shield my mother played my father fair, / For such a warpèd slip of wilderness / Never issued from his blood' (III.i.141–3).

In general, attempts at self-control that inhibit relationships are more central to Shakespeare's male characters than to his female ones. This does not mean that all the women are warm and compassionate while all the men are cold and controlled, as the passage from Isabella's tirade should remind us: but the characters often speak as if such qualities have each an appropriate sex. Almost all Shakespearean tragic heroes and several heroes in the romances and problem plays distrust both female characters and qualities in themselves that they consider female.[18] Yet they do love those characters and possess those qualities. They ultimately find it necessary to express their emotions beyond the cold ideals of their society. They learn, like Lear, that they must weep. Thus the plays implicitly criticize the view of manhood as opposed to feeling. Occasionally the characters themselves hint at different ideals, as Macduff does in his bereavements, when he answers 'Dispute it like a man' with 'I shall do so; / but I must also feel it as a man' (IV.iii.220–21). And in the romances a few of the men learn to reverse the disparagement of female characteristics, and can welcome family reunion with the imagery of childbirth that in *The Comedy of Errors* only a woman could use: Cymbeline says, on finding his children again, 'O, what am I? / A mother to the birth of three? Ne'er mother / Rejoiced deliverance more' (V.v.368–70).

Much of this could be observed by critics whose interest is not primarily historical.[19] But much of the new social history shows that conflicting trends in marriage and the family are not simply a twentieth-century imposition on Shakespeare; it provides a cautionary note for any critic who would look for a psychopathology for Shakespeare in isolation from his society. Stone's view of Elizabethan England is one-sided, as other historians have shown, but he does help us to see one side of a conflict important in Shakespeare's plays. Unfortunately, Stone himself does not see many connections between those plays and the patterns he discusses. He is more inclined to deny connections and make statements like 'Neither Othello, Oedipus, nor Cain were familiar figures in fourteenth-century England any more than they were, so far as is known, in the sixteenth century' (p. 95). He bases this statement on statistics of murders within the family, and in that literal sense it is of course true, though rather uninteresting. But surely Othello, Cain and Oedipus have been meaningful figures to many people who have not killed their wives, brothers or fathers

– familiar to their dreams, if not to their waking moments.

Living out the ideal of emotional control is a matter of degree, not of all or nothing. Under defences, the potential for feeling still remains. Literature, and perhaps especially drama, can permit the vicarious experience of emotions latent but too threatening to acknowledge in everyday life.[20] Eric Bentley has suggested that we go to the theatre to watch 'human beings in living contact with each other' – whether in love or in hate.[21] Art is a protected zone where we can afford a greater range of feelings of sympathy because we don't have to be torn about how far to act on them. At least one of Shakespeare's contemporaries wrote about this very phenomenon. In the forty-fifth sonnet of Sidney's *Astrophel and Stella*, Astrophel tries to break through Stella's emotional distance from him by reminding her how she weeps at literary characters, and pleading:

> Then think, my dear, that you in me do read
> Of lovers' ruin some sad tragedy.
> I am not I, pity the tale of me.

As a communal art form, the theatre lends itself especially to the emergence of submerged attachments. So perhaps the same people who strove to control their own feelings at the loss of their children could drop their defences while watching Lear, could listen to his accusation 'O, you are men of stones. / Had I your tongues and eyes, I'd use them so / That heaven's vault would crack' (V.iii.258–60), and understand his self-reproach 'I might have saved her; now she's gone forever' (V.iii.271). Franz Kafka, another writer preoccupied with family, once declared: 'A book must be the axe for the frozen sea inside us.'[22] I believe that when watching Shakespeare's plays, Elizabethan audiences, like modern ones, could feel frozen seas breaking.[23]

Notes

1. (New York: Harper & Row, 1977), p. 99. Further references to Stone will be indicated by page numbers incorporated within the text. Others who make some similar observations about English Renaissance society include Edward Shorter, *The Making of the Modern Family* (New York: Basic Books, 1975); and Zevedei Barbu, *Problems in Historical Psychology* (London: Routledge & Kegan Paul, 1960).

2. Macfarlane's review appears in *History and Theory* 18 (1979), 103–26; Trumbach's in *Journal of Social History* 13 (1979), 136–42. In *The Origins of English Individualism* (New York: Cambridge University Press, 1978), Macfarlane says that 'the majority of ordinary people in England from at least the thirteenth century were rampant individualists, highly mobile both geographically and socially, economically "rational," market-oriented and acquisitive, ego-centred in kinship and social life' (p. 163), and notes the 'loneliness, insecurity and family tensions which are associated with the English structure' (p. 202). In his review, Trumbach agrees with Stone that the quality of parental attachment improved in the eighteenth century, although he emphasizes that it was not absent earlier (p. 139); in his book, he postulates that the male aggressiveness and female hysteria that he finds more

pronounced before 1750 result from lack of sufficient attachment to a primary mother figure: *The Rise of the Egalitarian Family* (New York: Academic Press, 1978), pp. 230–35. Other critical reviews are E.P. Thompson, 'Happy Families', *New Society*, 20, 8 September 1977, vol. 41, no. 779: 499–501; and Keith Thomas, 'The Changing Family': *Times Literary Supplement* (21 October 1977), 1226–7.

3. C.L. Barber, 'The Family in Shakespeare's Development: Tragedy and Sacredness', in *Representing Shakespeare*, ed. Murray Schwartz and Coppélia Kahn (Baltimore, MD: Johns Hopkins University Press, 1980), p. 188.

4. Stone's dismissal of Shakespeare and other Elizabethan drama and literature is noted in the reviews by Thomas (p. 1226) and Macfarlane (pp. 113–14).

5. Conversation with Alvin B. Kernan, 1975. At this time Stone had written about the Elizabethan family in *The Crisis of the Aristocracy 1558–1641* (Oxford: Clarendon Press, 1965), 'The Massacre of the Innocents', *New York Review* 21 (14 November 1974): 25–31, and 'The Rise of the Nuclear Family in Early Modern England: The Patriarchal Stage', in *The Family in History*, ed. Charles E. Rosenberg (Philadelphia: University of Pennsylvania Press, 1975), pp. 13–57.

6. Macfarlane's review notes also that anthropologists have found no correlation between child mortality rates and parental affection, that Stone omits evidence of grief in the passages from *The Diary of Ralph Josselin* that he cites, and that even fourteenth-century writers sometimes describe marital love and affection (pp. 107, 115).

7. Stephen J. Greenblatt, 'Marlowe and Renaissance Self-Fashioning', in *Two Renaissance Myth-makers: Christopher Marlowe and Ben Jonson*, ed. Alvin B. Kernan, English Institute 1975–76, new series 1 (Baltimore, MD: Johns Hopkins University Press, 1977), pp. 41–69.

8. Macfarlane, review, p. 125.

9. All quotations from the plays are taken from *William Shakespeare: The Complete Works*, gen. ed. Alfred Harbage (Baltimore, MD: Penguin, 1969).

10. Greenblatt contrasts Coriolanus's attempt at self-fashioning with those of Marlowe's heroes on p. 55 of his essay. My view of *Coriolanus* has been much influenced by Janet Adelman's essay '"Anger's My Meat": Feeding, Dependency, and Aggression in *Coriolanus*', in *Representing Shakespeare*, pp. 129–49.

11. See Stanley Cavell, 'The Avoidance of Love', in *Must We Mean What We Say?* (New York: Scribners, 1969), pp. 310–53. I discuss these and other aspects of *Lear* in 'Patriarchy, Mutuality, and Forgiveness in *King Lear*', *Southern Humanities Review* 13 (1979): 281–92.

12. Cf. Stephen J. Greenblatt, 'Improvisation and Power', in *Literature and Society*, ed. Edward W. Said, English Institute 1978, new series 3 (Baltimore, MD: Johns Hopkins University Press, 1980), pp. 78–89.

13. In V.ix of Plautus, *The Twin Menaechmi*, trans. Richard W. Hyde and Edward Weist, in *Anthology of Roman Drama*, ed. Philip Whaley Harsh (New York: Holt, Rinehart & Winston, 1960), p. 46, the following exchange occurs:

> *Menaechmus I*: Oh, welcome, beyond all hope, after all these years!
> *Menaechmus II*: Welcome, dear brother! Sought with such misery and toil, and found with joy at last!

14. Sherman Hawkins, 'The Two Worlds of Shakespearean Comedy', *Shakespeare Studies* 3, ed. J. Leeds Barroll (Cincinnati: J.W. Ford, 1967), pp. 65–9.

15. Trumbach discusses related issues in his review and in *Rise*, pp. 237–85. See also Joseph E. Illick, 'Child-Rearing in Seventeenth Century England and America', in *The History of Childhood*, ed. Lloyd DeMause (New York: Harper, 1975), p. 312. For 'the role of traditional patriarch' as a 'false self', see David Leverenz, *The Language of Puritan Feeling* (New Brunswick: Rutgers University Press, 1980), p. 105.

16. See Dorothy Dinnerstein, *The Mermaid and the Minotaur* (New York: Harper, 1976).

17. For example, when the Duchess of York curses Richard III (IV.iv.195–6) and Volumnia says to Coriolanus: 'This fellow had a Volscian to his mother' (V.iii.178), the rejections are because of the sons' destructiveness, not their sexuality.

18. See Madelon Gohlke, '"I wooed thee with my sword": Shakespeare's Tragic Paradigms', in *Representing Shakespeare*, pp. 170–87.

19. Related points have been made, for example, by Edward Hubler, *The Sense of Shakespeare's Sonnets* (Princeton, NJ: Princeton University Press, 1952), pp. 106–7; and Maynard Mack, 'Engagement and Detachment in Shakespeare's Plays', in *Essays on Shakespeare and Elizabethan Drama in Honor of Hardin Craig*, ed. Richard Hosley (Columbia, MO: University of Missouri Press, 1962), pp. 275–96.

20. See, for example, Simon Lesser, *Fiction and the Unconscious* (Boston, MA: Beacon Press, 1957), pp. 81, 133–4; Norman Holland, *The Dynamics of Literary Response* (New York: Norton, 1975), pp. 92, 98; Cavell, pp. 332–3.

21. Eric Bentley, *Theatre of War*, abridged edn (New York: Viking Compass, 1973), p. 216.

22. Franz Kafka, *Letters to Friends, Family and Editors*, trans. Richard and Clara Winston (New York: Schocken, 1977), p. 16.

23. An earlier version of this essay was presented at the session on 'Marriage and the Family in Shakespeare' at the 1979 MLA convention. I am grateful for comments from participants there, especially Carol Neely, and from Coppélia Kahn and Richard Vann.

5

'The Sign and Semblance of Her Honor': Reading Gender Difference in *Much Ado about Nothing*

Carol Cook

Much Ado about Nothing begins with news of an ending; a rebellious brother has been defeated in battle, and the victorious prince and his retinue are approaching Messina. Don Pedro, Claudio and Benedick return from one kind of conflict to enter another: before they set foot in Messina we hear of a 'merry war', the ongoing 'skirmish of wit', between Benedick and Beatrice (I.i.62–3). Responding to the centrality of sexual conflict in *Much Ado*, critics have sometimes read the play as a struggle in which humane feminine qualities ultimately supersede inadequate masculine values. Barbara Everett has written:

> the play concerns itself with what can only be called the most mundane or 'local' fact in that world of love, in all its forms, that the comedies create: that is, that men and women have a notably different character, different mode of thinking, different system of loyalties, and, partic- ularly, different social place and function. Not only this: but this is the first play, I think, in which the clash of these two worlds is treated with a degree of seriousness, and in which the woman's world dominates.
>
> (p. 320)

John Crick, after describing the limitations of Messina's 'predominately masculine ethos', suggests that Beatrice's 'feminine charity triumphs.... Benedick becomes acceptable to her when he symbolically joins his masculine qualities to her feminine principles by taking up, however reluctantly, her attitude to Claudio ...' (p. 37). Janice Hayes borrows the psychological terms *instrumental* and *expressive* to characterize masculine and feminine modes of behaviour and experience in the play. Contrasting 'the traditionally male sphere of war, honors, and triumph' and 'the private and potentially expressive world of Messina, a world whose functioning is communal and cyclical and whose heirs are women', Hayes sees the Claudio–Hero plot as a ritual action in which Claudio's 'narcissistic instrumentality' is overcome in his symbolic penance at Hero's tomb and his acceptance of an unknown bride (p. 79).

These readings find a resolution to sexual conflict in the play in a thematic movement that privileges the feminine and provides moral closure. In my view, however, whatever conversion or movement the play offers is notably incomplete, for while the sexual conflict points in an illuminating way to the question of gender differences and what is at stake in them, their relation to subjectivity and authority, the play cannot resolve its contradictions from within its own structures of meaning. My reading of *Much Ado* begins by tracing the signifying differences that produce or represent gender in the play, differences especially evident in the cuckold jokes of the opening scene, and suggests that what is at stake in these differences is a masculine prerogative in language, which the play itself sustains. I argue that the play masks, as well as exposes, the mechanisms of masculine power, and that in so far as it avoids what is crucial to its conflicts, the explicitly offered comic resolution is something of an artful dodge.

The pervasive masculine anxiety that characterizes the play's Messina might be read psychoanalytically as castration anxiety; the imagery of horns and wounds in the cuckold jokes points rather insistently in this direction. But 'castration anxiety' is not so much an answer to the play's questions about gender difference as another formulation of them that requires some further explanation, for the phallus and its loss signify only within a larger structure of meanings. *Much Ado* sets up a complex chain of association among the word, the sword and the phallus, marking off language as the domain of masculine privilege and masculine aggression. The masculine, in the world of the play, is the place of speaking and reading subjects, of manipulators and interpreters of signs. The characters are much concerned with self-concealment and the exposure of others, with avoiding objectification by others, the abjection of which the cuckold's horn becomes the fearful sign. To read others in this play is always an act of aggression; to be read is to be emasculated, to be a woman. Masculine privilege is contingent on the legibility of women, and the ambiguous signifying power of women's 'seeming' is the greatest threat to the men of Messina, who engage various defensive strategies against it, from the exchange of tendentious jokes to the symbolic sacrifice of Hero. The play itself is implicated in these strategies, in so far as the characters' plot to recuperate Claudio through the fiction of Hero's death is also the plot of the play: the stability necessary for comic closure requires the exorcism of a disturbingly polysemous image of woman. The strategy is only partially successful, however, for though the 'false knaves', Don John and his henchmen, are ultimately revealed as the manipulators of misreadings, they function as scapegoats, deflecting attention from the unresolved anxieties about language and gender that have been responsible for the play's catastrophe.

I

We can learn a good deal about the place of gender difference in the life and language of *Much Ado*'s Messina by looking at the most persistent theme in the witty discourse of the play's male characters – that of cuckoldry. The cuckold jokes begin when Leonato, asked whether Hero is his daughter, replies: 'Her mother hath many times told me so' (I.i.105), and end with Benedick's closing advice to Don Pedro: 'get thee a wife, get thee a wife! There is no staff more reverent than one tipp'd with horn' (V.iv.122–4) – an absolute equation of marriage with cuckoldry. The tirelessness with which these men return to such jokes suggests an underlying anxiety that is present when the play opens and has not been dispelled by the resolution of the plot's various complications.

The imagery of the play's cuckold jokes reveals much about the anxiety that motivates them. Leonato's casual remark about Hero's mother is a witty circumlocution of the sort that dominates the sophisticated small talk of Messina. In itself it is a trifle, a hackneyed joke that comes automatically to mind and rolls easily off the tongue. We are not to infer that Leonato is harbouring serious doubts about the fidelity of his wife. The very conventionality of the comment, though, points to a larger cultural picture in which men share a sense of vulnerability because they have only a woman's word for the paternity of their children. A man may be a cuckold, it is suggested, and not be aware of his horns.

This anxiety about women's potential power over men is particularly apparent in Benedick's self-consciously misogynistic banter in the first scene, where he airs some of his anti-romantic doctrine for the benefit of Claudio and Don Pedro:

> That a woman conceiv'd me, I thank her; that she brought me up, I likewise give her most humble thanks; but that I will have a rechate winded in my forehead, or hang my bugle in an invisible baldrick, all women shall pardon me. Because I will not do them the wrong to mistrust any, I will do myself the right to trust none; and the fine is (for which I may go the finer), I will live a bachelor.
>
> (238–46)

To submit oneself to a woman by loving and marrying her is to 'have a rechate winded' in one's forehead – a trumpet blast blowing from one's forehead, announcing one's humiliation to the world. Marriage forces a man to 'hang his bugle in an invisible baldrick'. This somewhat obscure metaphor seems to be a concentrated expression of the masculine fears about feminine power in the play. The gloss given for this line in the Riverside edition runs as follows: 'carry my horn not in the usual place on the usual strap (baldrick) but where no strap is seen (because none is present) – on my forehead' (p. 335). As a symbol of man's betrayal and humiliation, the horn displaced from its rightful place to a wrong one must be read, it seems to me, in the light of the play's two metaphoric uses of the word *horn*, for horns are not only signs of cuckoldry but also phallic symbols.[1] What Benedick's metaphor of the invisible baldrick suggests is that marriage emasculates a man and flaunts the evidence of his emasculation by displaying the displaced phallus in his forehead. This theme is sustained in the lines that follow:

> *Bene.* ... Prove that ever I lose more blood with love than I will get again with drinking, pick out mine eyes with a ballad-maker's pen and hang me up at the door of a brothel-house for the sign of blind Cupid.
> *D. Pedro.* Well, if ever thou dost fall from this faith, thou wilt prove a notable argument.
> *Bene.* If I do, hang me in a bottle like a cat and shoot at me; and he that hits me, let him be clapp'd on the shoulder and call'd Adam.
> *D. Pedro.* Well, as time shall try: 'In time the savage bull doth bear the yoke.'
> *Bene.* The savage bull may, but if ever the sensible Benedick bear it, pluck off the bull's horns and set them in my forehead, and let me be vildly painted, and in such great letters as they write 'Here is good horse to hire,' let them signify under my sign, 'Here you may see Benedick the married man.'

> (250–68)

Benedick here offers in succession three versions of his fate if he becomes subjected to a woman, if he 'ever lose[s] more blood with love than [he] will get again with drinking' – a loss of vitality and virility like 'Th' expense of spirit' of sonnet 129, perhaps suggesting also the bleeding wound of castration. What makes these three statements (of what would happen 'if') roughly parallel is their recurrent images of vulnerability, mutilation, and exposure as legible signs. In the first case, loss of eyes suggests the lover's mutilation – and, obliquely, castration – but also enforces the particular humiliation of denying the victim the ability to witness his own condition.[2] Displayed publicly at the site of sexual degradation, the lover is fully objectified, seen but unseeing, subjected to the aggression of others' gazes. That the instrument of blinding is the satiric ballad-maker's pen links the visual objectification through display with a textual objectification through language, as the emasculated cuckold is ridiculed and published in degrading fictions. In the second case, the lover is to be hung 'in a bottle like a cat' and shot at by other men, who compete for the first hit. In his public exposure and vulnerability, the cuckold becomes the target for other men's 'shots', their witty jibes.[3] Finally, Benedick picks up Don Pedro's aphorism about the yoking of the savage bull. The bull's horns are the manifestations of its savagery, its undomesticated masculine power, and by extension an image of virility in general. Should the sensible Benedick ever submit to the yoke, he says, 'pluck off the bull's horns' – that is, turn them from signs of potency to signs of emasculation – 'and set them in my forehead'. The displacement motif here recalls the invisible baldrick, and again the emasculation of the lover is followed by public display – the sign designating the humiliated victim 'Benedick the married man'.

The cuckold joke partakes of all three categories of what Freud calls 'tendentious jokes': the aggressive or hostile joke (the cuckold joke expresses masculine competition), the cynical joke (aimed at the institution of marriage itself), and the obscene or exposing joke. In discussing the last category, Freud makes a number of observations that are pertinent here. 'Smut', he writes, in *Jokes*, or 'the intentional bringing into prominence of sexual facts and relations by speech, is ... originally directed toward women and may be equated with attempts at seduction' (p. 97). Such sexual talk 'is like an exposure of the sexually different person to whom it is directed' (p. 98). If the woman does not respond sexually to the verbal overture – as is often the case at 'the higher social levels', where sexual inhibitions are strongest – 'the sexually exciting speech becomes an aim in itself' and 'becomes hostile and cruel, and ... thus summons to its help against the obstacle the sadistic components of the sexual instinct' (p. 99). Denied its original aim of seduction, the sexual joking will be directed to a new audience: 'The men save up this kind of entertainment, which originally presupposed the presence of a woman who was feeling ashamed, until they are "alone together"' (p. 99). The tendentious joke calls for three participants: 'the one who makes the joke, ... a second who is taken as the object of the hostile or sexual aggressiveness, and a third in whom the joke's aim of producing pleasure is fulfilled' (p. 100).

Freud's diachronic analysis of the origin of 'smut' can be more usefully understood here as an account of the different aims that a joke may simultaneously fulfil. As such, his model turns out to illuminate the cuckold jokes in *Much Ado*. Freud's paradigmatic joke-teller is a man, speaking to a male audience, with women as the silent, absent objects of the jokes. The tendentious jokes work on several levels of direction and indirection. Thus, when Claudio aims a cuckold joke at Benedick for the benefit of Don Pedro ('Tush, fear not, man, we'll tip thy horns with gold ...' [V.iv.44]), the object of the joke is Benedick, imagined as a cuckold and hence as having lost his masculine status in the sexual hierarchy, but at another remove the object is also women, with their fearful power to cuckold men.

The cuckold joke expresses hostility and fear, but the relational structure of the joke-telling situation offers a compensation.[4] Cuckoldry occurs as a triangular relationship that the cuckold joke revises – and perhaps revenges. In the act of cuckolding, which dominates the imaginations of Messina's men, it is the husband who is the silent and absent butt of the joke, while a woman takes the active and powerful role (comparable to that of the teller of a joke), in complicity with a third party in whom, as Freud puts it, the 'aim of producing pleasure is fulfilled'. The telling of cuckold jokes, then, restores the male prerogative: it returns the woman to silence and absence, her absence authorizing the male raconteur to represent her in accordance with particular male fantasies, and produces pleasure through male camaraderie.

Thus Benedick's lines figure emasculation, or the loss of masculine privilege, in two ways: as a literal, physical castration and as a concomitant loss of masculine prerogative in language. In becoming a cuckold, a man relinquishes his role as the teller of jokes, the manipulator, reader and subject of language, and falls instead to the woman's position as the object of jokes, the silent, legible sign. It is the place of the woman to be the object, or referent, of language, a sign to be read and interpreted; silent herself, she becomes a cipher, the target of unconscious fantasies and fears, and is dangerously vulnerable to the representations and misrepresentations of men, as the main plot of *Much Ado* bears out. The woman is therefore doubly threatening, both in her imagined capacity to betray and cuckold men and as an image of what men fear to become: paradoxically, her very vulnerability is threatening.[5]

The social world of *Much Ado*'s Messina seems rather precariously founded on a denial of its most pervasive anxieties, and its potential for violence is triggered when the repressed fear of the feminine, and all that woman represents, is forced into consciousness by Don John's machinations. Messina, the most sophisticated and urbane society in all Shakespeare's comedies, is also the most confined. No moonlit wood or forest of Arden offers escape from Messina's social tensions, and the characters' romantic and sexual roles are not relieved by opportunities for sexual disguise. Social and sexual roles are firmly established, and the inhabitants are acutely conscious of them.

To note the rigidity of this world is not to suggest that Messina lacks charm. Its aristocratic characters demonstrate the most elaborate courtesy; formality does not make their manners less genial, and they move through their elegant social patterns with an almost choreographic grace. Yet beneath their easy charm, their wit and conviviality, the characters are evidently anxious, edgy, afraid of betraying spontaneous emotion, afraid of exposing themselves to one another. Messina is much concerned with its carefully preserved surfaces. The characters talk a good deal about how they dress. We hear about 'cloth o' gold ... down sleeves, side-sleeves, and skirts' (III.iv.19–21); about Benedick's metamorphosis in 'strange disguises' (III.ii.32–3); about 'slops' (III.ii.36), doublets, rabatos, gloves, and vizards; about Dogberry's two gowns; and about 'the deformed thief, fashion' – the rhetorical figure overheard by Messina's night watch, in whose minds 'the thief, Deformed' takes on a remarkably vivid personality and criminal record (III.iii.130–31). Just as the Messinans talk about dress, they talk about talking. They are highly conscious of verbal style. Benedick and Beatrice are known for their 'skirmish of wit' (I.i.63); if they were married 'but a week', Leonato predicts, 'they would talk themselves mad' (II.i.353–4). We hear about the speed of Beatrice's tongue, about 'quips and sentences and paper bullets of the brain', about the 'ill word' that may 'empoison liking', about Don John, who is 'not of many words' (I.i.157).

Entering into the social intercourse of Messina entails dressing well and talking well, and in a way these modes of decorous behaviour serve similar functions. Early in the play, Benedick withdraws from the banter of Don Pedro and Claudio, saying: 'Nay, mock not, mock not. The body of your discourse is sometimes guarded with fragments, and the guards are but slightly basted on neither' (I.i.285–7). Benedick here makes explicit a relation between discourse and dress that continues to be important throughout the play. The discourse of Claudio and Don Pedro (and perhaps of all the major characters except Hero) is guarded – that is, decorated (rhetorically) and also, in the now more common sense of the word, defensive. The characters use their wit to cover their emotional nakedness and to avoid exposure. Discourse in Messina is aggressive and witty; real wounds are dealt in the 'merry war' between Benedick and Beatrice, in which Beatrice 'speaks poiniards, and every word stabs' (II.i.247–8). Because of its capacity to inflict wounds, language – especially wit – is wielded both as weapon and as shield.

The metaphoric language of the play consistently figures speech as phallic and capable of violent penetration. Leonato tells Claudio that his slander, dagger-like, has 'gone through and through' the heart of Hero (V.i.68). When Benedick meets Claudio to avenge that slander (V.i), he tells Claudio and Don Pedro that he wears his wit 'in my scabbard' and will meet Claudio's 'wit in the career and you charge it against me.... [Y]ou break jests as braggarts do their blades ...' (134–5, 185). Margaret compares Benedick's wit to 'fencer's foils', albeit dull ones (V.ii.12) – a lame wit is one that cannot wound. Hero's image for Margaret's jabs at Beatrice – 'there thou prick'st her with a thistle' (III.v.74) – is more benign, but 'prick'st' enforces the phallic association. As Hero's line suggests, phallic language may be appropriated by women – Beatrice speaks poiniards – but remains none the less gendered as masculine. In exchanging quips with Margaret, Benedick describes her wit as a 'greyhound's mouth' that 'catches' (V.ii.11–12), but he claims sword-like phallic wit as a masculine prerogative that women wield only through usurpation:

> *Marg.* Give us the swords; we have bucklers of our own.
> *Bene.* If you use them, Margaret, you must put in the pikes with a vice;
> and they are dangerous weapons for maids.
>
> (V.ii.18–22)

To brandish phallic wit is to defend against others' castrating 'swords' or to deny a castration already accomplished. Or rather, it is both: for both male and female wits in this play use their repartee to disguise a lack or a weakness, a susceptibility or a wound already suffered.

II

The construction of femininity within an economy of representation governed by the phallus – a construction in which women mirror masculine identity by their own lack – obviates the possibility of 'feminine values' or of a feminine alternative to the 'predominately masculine ethos'. Alternatives cannot be generated from within the binary structures by which patriarchy figures gender. The women in *Much Ado* demonstrate in their different ways their entrapment within the contradictions of this system of difference, for ironically it is the docile Hero, rather than her sharp-tongued cousin, who is the primary focus for masculine anxieties. The vocal Beatrice refuses the subjection of femininity, of castration, by placing herself among the men and wielding phallic wit as aggressively as they; it is the often silent Hero who figures the threat of difference for Messinan men.

Like Benedick, Beatrice adopts the role of 'profess'd tyrant' to the opposite sex (I.i.169), satirizing masculine pretensions with agile wit. To Hero, she remarks tartly on paternal authority: 'Yes, faith, it is my cousin's duty to make cursy and say, "Father, as it please you." But for all that, cousin, let him be a handsome fellow, or make another cursy, and say, "Father, as it please me"' (II.i.52–6). And, like Benedick, she makes cynical pronouncements on romantic love and marriage:

> ... wooing, wedding, and repenting, is as a Scotch jig, a measure, and a cinquepace; the first suit is hot and hasty like a Scotch jig, and full as fantastical; the wedding, mannerly-modest, as a measure, full of state and ancientry; and then comes repentance, and with his bad legs falls into the cinquepace faster and faster, till he sink into his grave.
>
> (II.i.73–80)

Beatrice's ironic comments on men and marriage, and her passionate outburst against Claudio in the first scene of Act IV, have led some critics to regard her as the champion of a 'feminine principle' and as a kind of protofeminist.[6] Yet Beatrice's ostentatious flouting of conventional sexual roles is often only a concession to them at another level, and instead of challenging Messina's masculine ethos, she participates in its assumptions and values. In the opening scene, she mocks Benedick's soldiership: 'I pray you, how many hath he killed and eaten in these wars? But how many hath he killed? For indeed, I promised to eat all of his killing' (42–5). On the messenger's remarking that Benedick is a 'good soldier too, lady', she quibbles 'And a good soldier to a lady. But what is he to a lord?' (I.i.53–5). But her insinuation that 'Signior Mountanto' is effeminate does not question the machismo value of soldiership itself.

Beatrice tacitly accepts her culture's devaluation of 'feminine' characteristics – of weakness, dependence, vulnerability – and sees conventionally masculine behaviour as the only defence against them. She usurps the masculine prerogatives of language and phallic wit, speaking poiniards as an escape from feminine silence or inarticulate expression of emotion.

Beatrice's audacious speech might seem a serious violation of Messina's conventions of gender, but it is significant how little she actually threatens Messina's men, who regard her generally as rather a good fellow. Though Benedick professes a hyperbolical terror of 'My Lady Tongue' (II.i.262–75) and Leonato rebukes her mildly ('By my troth, niece, thou wilt never get thee a husband, if thou be so shrewd of thy tongue' [II.i.18–19]), she provokes nothing like the hysterical reactions to the quiet Hero's supposed transgressions against the social and sexual code. When Beatrice retracts a bit on her own impertinence – 'But I beseech your Grace to pardon me. I was born to speak all mirth and no matter' – Don Pedro replies: 'Your silence most offends me, and to be merry best becomes you ...' (II.i.329–32). It is silence and the exposure of vulnerability that are the real threats to Messinan men, painful reminders of the sexual difference that is really a mirror.[7]

Beatrice is as aggressive and as guarded as the men in the play, and for the same reasons: she fears emotional exposure and vulnerability to the opposite sex. As the play begins she already seems to be nursing wounds from some abortive romance with Benedick, to which she alludes cryptically more than once.[8] Beatrice vacillates uneasily between self-exposure and affected indifference; she chafes at times against the constraints of her ironist's role, which consigns her to isolation and detachment when part of her desires love; but recognizing her susceptibility, she clings the more tenaciously to her role. The long first scene of Act II reveals her contradictory impulses. Leonato chides her for being 'so shrewd of [her] tongue' and tells her: 'So, by being too curst, God will send you no horns'. 'Just', she replies, 'if he send me no husband, for the which blessing I am at him upon my knees every morning and evening' (27–9). At Hero's betrothal, however, she speaks in a different key: 'Good Lord, for alliance! Thus goes everyone to the world but I, and I am sunburnt. I may sit in a corner and cry "Heigh-ho for a husband!"' (318–20). If the tone is mock lament here, the sense of exclusion is real; yet each of her tentative gestures of self-exposure is followed by a nervous reassertion of ironic detachment. She alternately challenges others' misreadings of her humorist's mask and encourages them to take her as she appears. When Don Pedro seems too readily to accept her as 'born in a merry hour', she replies: 'No, sure, my lord, my mother cried; but then there was a star danc'd and under that was I born. Cousins, God give you joy!' (334–6).

Chafing at the reductiveness of Don Pedro's image of her as merely 'merry', Beatrice offers a fleeting glimpse of a part of herself and a realm of experience that cannot be given expression in Messina, figured in the labouring mother whose only articulation is an ambiguous cry. But she compulsively banishes the image of the crying mother with that of the dancing star, and quickly turns attention away from herself by congratulating her 'cousins'. She is thus perceived only as 'a pleasant-spirited lady' (341) whose 'merry heart ... keeps on the windy side of care' (314–15). Leonato misses the significance of his own remark when he tells Don Pedro: 'There's little of the melancholy element in her, my lord. She is never sad but when she sleeps, and not ever sad then; for I have heard my daughter say she hath often dreamt of unhappiness and waked herself with laughing' (342–6). Whatever unhappiness haunts Beatrice's dreams, her laughter is a conscious defence against it. She cannot in her waking moments articulate or address the conflicts inherent in her relation to her world. ·

Beatrice is a character of some complexity, a character whose contradictions, manifest in her own words and actions, we read as signs of interiority and ambivalence, as evidence of different levels of motivation. Hero presents another kind of problem. Here the contradictions consist of a tension between the manifest representation of her character (which is quite uncomplicated and one-dimensional) and her latent significance, which is evident in the effects she produces in others. Minimally drawn, with few lines, she is less a character than a cipher, or a mirror to the other characters. She is represented as conventionally feminine; meek, self-effacing, vulnerable, obedient, seen and not heard, she is a face without a voice. In the world of the play Hero's role is to meet or reflect others' expectations of what women are supposed to be (as Beatrice does not) and paradoxically, therefore, to represent a powerful threat.[9]

Hero's status as a character and the mode of her representation are peculiar enough to require special consideration. Crick characterizes Hero as 'nebulous' (p. 36), but he uses the word to dismiss rather than to analyse her. In fact, Hero's nebulousness is significant: she is the 'nothing' that generates so much ado. The pun on *nothing* and *noting* in the play has frequently been remarked, but we might usefully pursue it in this connection. To note can mean to observe (to read) or to make note of (to inscribe); both involve acts of interpretation. A similar ambiguity arises in connection with the word *mark*. Benedick believes that he spies 'some marks of love' in Beatrice once he falls in love with her (II.iii.245–6). In the climactic church scene the friar, 'by noting of the lady' (Hero), has 'marked / A thousand blushing apparitions / To start into her face ...' (IV.i.158–60). Benedick's act of 'marking' is clearly a projection, but the question then arises whether the friar's marking of Hero is not equally so.

Hero's nothing invites noting, her blankness produces marking, and the ambiguity of this action occurs not only in the play but also in the critical commentary. Marilyn French describes Hero this way: 'As a noncharacter, the obedient and silent Hero exemplifies the inlaw [i.e., subordinate] feminine principle at its most acceptable: but like Bianca in *Taming*, she wears the disguise society demands of her, but harbors other thoughts under her impeccable exterior' (p. 133). The equation of Hero with Bianca, a conscious hypocrite who wears a 'disguise' and harbours a subversive will, blurs the distinction towards which French seems to gesture with her initial suggestion that Hero is a 'noncharacter'. Without confronting her conflicting readings as a critical problem, French contradictorily treats Hero sometimes as a character whose hidden depths she can read and sometimes as a symbol that functions as pure surface; but in effect the play itself does the same thing. Ironically, the attempt to read Hero as a psychologically realized character, in this feminist approach to the play, leads French to adopt a notion of Hero's 'seeming' that concurs with the one Claudio takes up in his most misogynistic moment (IV.i). To avoid this difficulty, it seems to me, one must be willing to regard Hero as a kind of cipher or space, which other characters – and perhaps critics as well – fill with readings of their own.

In the opening scene, where the personalities, roles and relations of the characters are largely established, Hero has only one line, seven words, and these are to explain a remark of Beatrice's. Though the actor playing the part has recourse to some non-verbal means of establishing the character for the audience (facial expressions, gestures, placement onstage, etc.), the text itself portrays Hero primarily through the effect she produces on Claudio. Typically, the exchange between Claudio and Benedick about Claudio's 'soft and delicate desires' (303) reveals little about Hero but a good deal about the two speakers. Beside Benedick's energetic irony, Claudio's desires seem a little too delicate, his love a little bloodless. When he tremulously asks whether Benedick does not find Hero 'a modest young lady' (165) and, gathering courage, pronounces her 'the sweetest lady that ever I looked on' (187–8), his adjectives betray more propriety and sentiment than they do passion. When he demonstrates a penchant for romantic hyperbole ('Can the world buy such a jewel?' [181]), which Benedick neatly deflates, his extravagant praise expresses not burning Petrarchan longings but a kind of wistful acquisitiveness.

Benedick greets Claudio's desire to marry with a sardonic lament for the decline of bachelors: 'hath not the world one man but he will wear his cap with suspicion?' (197–9). It becomes clear, however, that Claudio does wear his cap with suspicion – and a good deal of it, too. The cautious reticence of his confession of his love is self-protective: a desire to assess the lady's merit and other men's opinions of it before betraying too ardent a regard for her. He is edgy about the whole business, and wary of his friend's responses. 'Didst thou note the daughter of Signior Leonato? ... Is she not a modest young lady?' he asks Benedick; and he then exhorts him: 'I pray thee tell me truly how thou lik'st her' (161–3, 165, 177–8). Even when he is told what he wants to hear, Claudio has misgivings. When Don Pedro assures him that 'the lady is very well worthy', Claudio responds: 'You speak this to fetch me in, my lord' (221–3). Claudio further reveals his anxieties in the first scene of Act II: anticipating his later behaviour by believing without question Don John's assertion that Don Pedro has won Hero, Claudio gives vent to his sense of betrayal in a brief, telling soliloquy:

> 'Tis certain so. The Prince woos for himself.
> Friendship is constant in all other things
> Save in the office and affairs of love;
> Therefore all hearts in love use their own tongues.
> Let every eye negotiate for itself,
> And trust no agent; for beauty is a witch
> Against whose charms faith melteth into blood.
> This is an accident of hourly proof,
> Which I mistrusted not. Farewell therefore Hero!
>
> (174–82)

Abdicating the use of one's own tongue, Claudio laments bitterly, leaves one vulnerable to treachery; to be represented by another is to be wounded. What is perhaps more revealing, though, is the way in which the speech subtly shifts the blame for the supposed betrayal from its ostensible object, Don Pedro, to the 'witch', female beauty.[10] Though not specifically accused, Hero is subsumed into an archetype of destructive female power – of the sorceress who deprives men of their wills and dissolves the solidarity of masculine bonds into the 'blood' of passion and violence. Like Benedick, Claudio associates love with a loss of blood – not the woman's loss of hymenal blood, but the loss a man suffers from the castrating wound love inflicts. Claudio's references to Hero here take on sexual overtones wholly lacking in his earlier 'noting' of her modesty and sweetness. He perceives her as a sexual being only in her capacity to betray, and then perceives her as a powerful threat, suggesting that in his imagination he has desexualized the Hero he wishes to marry. When he learns that Don Pedro has, in fact, honoured their agreement, and that Hero is to be his, he reverts to his romantic perception of her. The pattern established in this early episode is repeated, as we shall see, in the catastrophe of Acts IV and V.

III

The first three acts of *Much Ado* clearly establish the capabilities and limitations of Messina's aristocratic milieu: its sophisticated, graceful, almost choreographic social forms; its brilliant language and aggressive wit; and the tight rein kept on emotions, making them difficult or dangerous to express. Whether we are more charmed or put off by Messina's genteel artificiality, the violent outburst in the catastrophic church scene comes as a shock (IV.i). We have, of course, seen trouble brewing. Don John's malicious intentions are revealed early (I.iii), and we know from his first attempt at sabotaging Claudio's love that Claudio's distrust of the witchlike powers of female beauty is close to the surface and easily triggered. In a scene paralleling that earlier deception (III.ii), Don John comes to Claudio with his accusation that 'the lady is disloyal' (104). He offers ocular proof, and Claudio, who had earlier resolved to 'let every eye negotiate for itself', swallows the bait: 'If I see anything to-night why I should not marry her, to-morrow in the congregation, where I should wed, there will I shame her' (123–5). It is not so much on Claudio's eye, however, as on his mind's eye that Don John practises deceit. Using subtly sexual language to describe what Claudio will see – 'Go but with me to-night, and you shall see her chamber-window entered' (112–13) – Don John raises the figure of a witchlike, betraying, sexual Hero in Claudio's imagination, and the image of the 'sweet' and 'modest' Hero gives way before it. Claudio believes the ocular proof before he sees anything – 'O mischief strangely thwarting!' he cries (132), as he goes off to spy on her window.

Critics dissatisfied with *Much Ado* have complained that its near-tragic catastrophe violates the comic mood of the rest of the play (see, e.g., Pettet, pp. 132–5; West). The naked emotions that erupt in Act IV among the hitherto highly civil characters are calculated, I think, to be startling. Yet what makes this behaviour almost inevitable has been implicit from the first scene. The witty discourse that gives the play its vitality and the Messinans much of their charm consists mainly of tendentious jokes – covert expressions of aggression or sexual hostility. The polished behaviour, the elegant courtesies and the verbal sophistication of the characters have served through three acts of the play to cover or contain these energies. In the scene at the church, however, once the surface of decorous ritual has been stripped away, the violence of the emotion and the language, especially Claudio's, becomes explicit and shocking.

Though the manner Claudio displays here differs drastically from his reverence for Hero in the scenes of his courtship and betrothal, he is not inconsistent. The self-protective reserve and the conflicted perceptions of Hero underlying his earlier sentimental expressions now motivate his scathing castigation of her. Kerby Neill, writing an 'acquittal' for Claudio, emphasizes Shakespeare's departure from his sources in 'removing all trace of carnality from the hero's love' (97). 'If anything', he argues, 'the bitterness of Claudio's denunciation of Hero shows an abhorrence of . . . carnality. . . . The . . . effect is to idealize Claudio even as he denounces the innocent Hero. He remains a good man, although deceived . . .' (97). Neill, in effect, takes Claudio at his own valuation – claiming that he 'sinned not but in mistaking', as Claudio says of himself (V.i.273–4) – and in so doing accepts implicitly the dualism inherent in Claudio's view of Hero: it is his 'abhorrence of carnality' that allows his romantic idealism to coexist with a powerful misogyny. In the first scene of Act IV the thought that, despite his caution, he was nearly taken advantage of kindles in Claudio a hot, self-righteous resentment. The 'witch' female beauty, he thinks, almost made him the victim of her 'exterior shows'. This time he is well guarded with elaborate language, wittier in his cruelty than he had ever been in jest:

> O Hero! What a Hero hadst thou been,
> If half thy outward graces had been placed
> About thy thoughts and counsels of thy heart!
> But fare thee well, most foul, most fair! farewell;
> Thou pure impiety and impious purity!

> (100–04)

Claudio's radically divided sense of Hero's identity is most fully apparent in this scene. When Leonato suggests that Claudio himself might, in a bridegroom's natural impatience, have 'made defeat of her virginity', Claudio denies it with priggish distaste:

> I know what you would say: If I have known her,
> You will say, she did embrace me as a husband,
> And so extenuate the 'forehand sin.
> No, Leonato,
> I never tempted her with word too large,

But as a brother to his sister, show'd
Bashful sincerity and comely love.

(48–54)

Either Hero must be the unthreatening sexless recipient of Claudio's 'comely' fraternal love, or she becomes the treacherous beauty whose witchlike powers destroy men.[11] But where Claudio had previously responded to alternative possibilities for Hero's identity, he now imagines the dichotomy to be one between her surface and her hidden nature. He is most outraged by what he takes to be her 'seeming':

She's but the sign and semblance of her honor.
Behold how like a maid she blushes here!
O, what authority and show of truth
Can cunning sin cover itself withal!
Comes not that blood as modest evidence
To witness simple virtue? Would you not swear,
All you that see her, that she were a maid,
By these exterior shows? But she is none.
She knows the heat of a luxurious bed;
Her blush is guiltiness, not modesty.

(33–42)

In a sense Claudio is correct in calling Hero 'the sign and semblance of her honor'. Her place in the world of this play is most apparent in this scene, where, nearly silent and finally subsiding into unconsciousness under the onslaught of abuse, she becomes in effect a sign to be read and interpreted by others. Claudio sarcastically rejects her 'authority' to be perceived as she presents herself. He has, he thinks, the clue that allows him to read her true worth and nature. It is particularly the 'blood' visible in Hero's face that is taken to signify the state of her soul. 'Comes not that blood as modest evidence / To witness simple virtue?' he asks, with the ironic jubilance of a reader on to the meaning of a text, the truth that her 'blush is guiltiness, not modesty'. His descriptions of the polarities of Hero's identity become more and more elaborate and literary, and he returns to the significance of her 'blood' in this depiction of opposing female archetypes:

You seem to me as Dian in her orb,
As chaste as is the bud ere it be blown;
But you are more intemperate in your blood
Than Venus, or those pamp'red animals
That rage in savage sensuality.

(57–61)

Having found the key to reading women, Claudio suggests as he exits, he will know how to apply it in the future:

> For thee I'll lock up all the gates of love,
> And on my eyelids shall conjecture hang,
> To turn all beauty into thoughts of harm,
> And never shall it more be gracious.

(105–8)

Leonato, thrown into an anguish of uncertainty by Claudio's outburst, charges his daughter to answer her accusers, but he hardly hears her simple denial. Quickly persuaded when Claudio's claims are seconded by Don Pedro, and by Don John, who hints darkly at the unutterable nature of Hero's crimes ('There is not chastity enough in language / Without offense to utter them' [97–8]), Leonato grasps Claudio's method of reading his child. He believes that her surface has been stripped away to expose the secret foulness of her sexuality; her silence is a horrifying nakedness. When the friar ventures to suggest that her accusers may be mistaken, Leonato rejects the possibility:

> Friar, it cannot be.
> Thou see'st that all the grace that she hath left
> Is that she will not add to her damnation
> A sin of perjury; she not denies it.
> Why seek'st thou then to cover with excuse
> That which appears in proper nakedness?

(170–75)

Leonato also rejects Hero's authority to voice her own nature, which he believes he can read. '[C]ould she here deny / The story that is printed in her blood?' he demands. In her blood he reads the story of 'her foul tainted flesh', and insists that 'Death is the fairest cover for her shame / That may be wish'd for' (121–2, 143, 116–17). Ironically, thinking that they have exposed the 'proper nakedness' of Hero's sin, her accusers expose only themselves.

It is in the wake of this scene of exposure that Benedick and Beatrice reveal their love for each other. Love, and the vulnerability that comes with it, has been a kind of exposure each has dodged through most of the play. Their resolutions to open themselves to love have been followed by physical illness (Benedick's toothache, Beatrice's cold), which, whether real or feigned, suggests the anxiety such exposure produces. Distracted from their anxieties about themselves for a moment by their preoccupation with Claudio's denunciation of Hero, Benedick and Beatrice are able to talk to each other without persiflage. The intimacy of the situation (255–88) quickly leads to revelation, and for a moment we watch what appears to be an alternative to the kind of self-protective emotional display witnessed in Claudio. Benedick initiates it with his sudden, apropos-of-nothing, unprecedentedly literal confession: 'I do love nothing in the world so well as you – is not that strange?' (268–9). And though Beatrice has to be teased out of her evasiveness, she is brought to respond in kind:

> *Beat.* You have stayed me in a happy hour, I was about to protest I loved you.
> *Bene.* And do it with all thy heart.
> *Beat.* I love you with so much of my heart that none is left to protest.
>
> (283–7)

The warmth and simplicity of the language are like nothing we have heard before in the play (as was Claudio's unmasked brutality), and we are apt to watch this exchange with relief. At last the masks seem to be dropped; at last two characters seem to confront each other 'in proper nakedness'. But the intimacy of the moment is volatile, and it leads to something for which we are unprepared. 'Come, bid me do anything for thee', Benedick jubilantly exclaims. And Beatrice quite unexpectedly responds: 'Kill Claudio' (288–9).

Benedick's Claudio-like hyperbole perhaps recalls to Beatrice the whole preceding scene of Hero's rejection and humiliation by the man in whose power she had placed herself, and Beatrice hastily retreats from her emotional surrender. Her demand that Benedick kill Claudio is a double defence, placing Benedick in an impossible position and covering her exposed tenderness with a display of ferocity. She is both magnificent and absurd in her vigorous denunciation of Claudio:

> Is 'a not approv'd in the height a villain, that hath slander'd, scorned, dishonored my kinswoman? O that I were a man! What, bear her in hand until they come to take hands; and then, with public accusation, uncovered slander, unmitigated rancor – O God that I were a man! I would eat his heart in the marketplace!
>
> (301–7)

Beatrice's explosion of moral outrage against Claudio is immensely satisfying, partly because it gives vent to our own frustrated sense of justice (the release of this pent-up emotion is also why we laugh at the scene). Her anger takes in not only Claudio, but men in general – the 'princes and counties' (315), and the fathers, who have united in persecuting Hero and against whom Beatrice is powerless to act.

The critics quoted at the beginning of this essay emphasize particularly this moment in designating Beatrice a champion of the 'feminine principles' needed to correct the evils of Messina's 'predominantly masculine ethos' (Crick, p. 36). John Crick praises her 'feminine charity', her 'generosity and sympathy in a world dominated by ultimately inhumane standards' (37), as Barbara Everett does her 'dogged, loyal, irrational femininity' (p. 327). Although Beatrice's outburst is extremely gratifying – the scene is constructed to make it so – it is important to recognize that her fury imitates what we might call the dogged, brutal, irrational masculinity just displayed by Claudio and Leonato: her rage is generated by her inability to 'be a man with wishing' and to do what men do. She echoes the masculine revenge ethic voiced earlier by Leonato, who, brought finally to consider the possibility of Hero's innocence, had vowed to have his revenge on *somebody* (190–92). Far from proposing an alternative to masculine values, Beatrice regrets their decline and upbraids Benedick for his unmanly reluctance to exchange verbal aggression, which is common coin in Messina, for real violence:

> O that I were a man for his sake! Or that I had any friend who would be a man for my sake! But manhood is melted into cursies, valor into compliment, and men are only turned into tongue, and trim ones too. He is now as valiant as Hercules that only tells a lie, and swears it. I cannot be a man with wishing; and therefore I will die a woman with grieving.
>
> (317–23)

The last line of her tirade raises the question of what might be an adequate 'feminine' alternative to the 'predominately masculine ethos' of Messina. Beatrice longs to take arms against a sea of masculine troubles but, by opposing, would only perpetuate them. The sole alternative that presents itself to her, however, is to follow Hero's model of conventional femininity and 'die a woman' in silent grief.

The friar has proposed a somewhat different way of dealing with the crisis. 'By noting of the lady', he has 'marked' signs of her innocence and produced a plan that he hopes will work changes in Claudio's poisoned imagination by means of a fiction:

> So will it fare with Claudio.
> When he shall hear she died upon his words,
> Th' idea of her life shall sweetly creep
> Into his study of imagination,
> And every lovely organ of her life
> Shall come apparell'd in more precious habit,
> More moving, delicate, and full of life,
> Into the eye and prospect of his soul
> Than when she liv'd indeed. Then shall he mourn,
> If ever love had interest in his liver,
> And wish he had not so accused her.
> No, though he thought his accusation true.
>
> (222–33)

Many critics have seen the friar as the point of moral reference in the play, and also as the instrument of its resolution.[12] His sensible resistance to the false evidence that has fooled Don Pedro and Claudio, his opposition to their outbursts of violent emotion, his attentions to Hero, and his proposal to educate Claudio in Christian forgiveness – all these actions seem to place the religious father outside Messina's masculine ethos, and to confer on him a special moral authority. The tendency to see him in this light, whether we attribute it to indicators in the text (the friar's speech is rhetorically impressive) or to a powerful desire to see moral coherence in Shakespearean comedy, has led otherwise careful critics into a simple error of fact: the friar's plan fails.[13] The plan is specifically a response to Claudio's determination to 'lock up all the gates of love' by hanging 'conjecture' on his eyelids 'To turn all beauty into thoughts of harm'. The friar proposes to change the way Claudio sees, introducing a 'moving' image of Hero 'Into the eye and prospect of his soul' through the fiction of her death. The friar looks to do more than correct Claudio's 'mistake' about Hero's virtue: he hopes that Claudio will change in a way that will induce remorse and love *'though he thought his accusation true'*. Shakespeare dramatized such a conversion much later in *Cymbeline*, when Posthumus, believing himself responsible for Imogen's death, laments his harsh judgement of her in a long soliloquy *before* he learns of her innocence (V.i.1–17).

The proposed resolution does not occur. Not only is Claudio not grief-stricken when we see him next (V.i), he is rather giddy. He shows no shame when Leonato accuses him of killing Hero through his villainy ('My villainy?' he asks indignantly [72]), and he describes the incident flippantly when Benedick arrives: 'We had lik'd to have our two noses snapp'd off with two old men without teeth' (115–16). He then goads Benedick about Beatrice as though nothing had happened since the third scene of Act III. Don Pedro behaves with the same careless good humour, both of them apparently hoping that Hero's 'death' will pass off as merely an unfortunate social awkwardness. It is not until he learns of her innocence that Claudio's feeling changes; the issue is no longer a matter of forgiveness now but only of getting the facts straight. Claudio does not question his behaviour or his assumptions, contending that he 'sinned not but in mistaking', and once in possession of the 'truth' about Hero, he simply reverts to his initial image of her: 'Sweet Hero, now thy image doth appear / In the rare semblance that I lov'd it first' (251–2). The image of the witch is dispelled – and replaced by its opposite – but the sexual dualism that governs Hero's 'image' is not displaced or questioned.

It would perhaps be tendentious to refer this outcome to some moral or tactical failure on the friar's part. The simpler explanation is that the plan to reform Claudio fails because his callousness makes him incapable of responding as predicted. None the less, the friar's well-meaning intervention on Hero's behalf may in some sense undercut its own power to effect changes in the world of the play, and may unconsciously reinforce the assumptions of which Hero is a victim. The friar's plea on behalf of the prostrate Hero reverses but also imitates the speeches of her accusers. Claudio had angrily denied the 'authority' of her 'semblance', and had read her blush as the sign of her guilt. Leonato, too, had insisted on his reading of 'the story that is printed in her blood'. The friar, in opposing these interpretations of what is seen in Hero's face, also emphasizes his authority to speak *for* the silent Hero:

> Trust not my reading, nor my observations,
> Which with experimental seal doth warrant
> The tenure of my book; trust not my age,
> My reverence, calling, nor divinity,
> If this sweet lady lie not guiltless here
> Under some biting error.

(IV.i.165–70)

The friar offers his own reading of Hero's blood:

> I have marked
> A thousand blushing apparitions
> To start into her face, a thousand innocent shames
> In angel whiteness beat away those blushes . . .

(IV.i.158–61)

The friar's plot to counter the 'misprision' of Claudio and Don Pedro parallels in certain respects the plot by which Don John engineers the catastrophe. Don John, though 'not of many words', is a master of representation in the play. Keeping aloof from the action himself, he commissions Borachio to stage the scene in which Claudio will read Hero's guilt. 'I will so fashion the matter that Hero shall be absent', promises Borachio (II.ii.46–7); he then enlists Margaret to represent Hero by dressing in her clothes. The representation succeeds in replacing in Claudio's imagination the image of Hero as chaste Dian with that of her as intemperate Venus. The friar, too, intends to make Hero's absence the occasion for a 'moving' representation of her (IV.i): 'Let her awhile be secretly kept in, / And publish it that she is dead indeed . . .' (203–4). When the fiction of Hero's death reaches Claudio, the friar predicts, her image will present itself to him 'apparell'd in more precious habit, / . . . Than when she liv'd indeed'. Claudio will then see Hero's 'angel whiteness', which the friar believes to represent her true character, 'her maiden truth' (164). Though the friar intends the image to be 'More moving, delicate, and full of life' than her physical presence ('Than when she liv'd indeed'), death is its essential feature: this representation of Hero is cleansed of carnality, of the blood that has been read as the sign of sexuality and guilt; the friar can interpret Hero's blood as the blush of innocence because 'a thousand innocent shames / In angel whiteness beat away those blushes' – leaving her bloodless, white, and corpse-like in her swoon. He will represent her as 'delicate', like the 'soft and delicate desires' that Claudio claims to be 'comely' and asexual; 'every lovely organ of her life' will come to Claudio to be anatomized and read as evidence of chastity, so that the fluid, vital, ambiguous text of her face will be replaced by a petrified monument to her virginity. The displacement is achieved when the penitent Claudio goes in obedience to Leonato, to 'Hang an epitaph upon her tomb' that declares her innocent and glorified by death.

IV

The ghost of Hero's ambiguity continues to haunt the play. In the scenes following Claudio's denunciation, her 'death' has an uncanny force that far exceeds its limited status as a strategic fiction. Like the deformed-thief fashion, the fiction of Hero's death takes on a life of its own, independent of the circumstances for which it was invented. A striking peculiarity of the final act is the way in which the practisers seem taken in by their own device, becoming Hero's mourners and avengers in a plot that exercises a peculiar power over their emotions and imaginations: it is as though they – and somehow the play itself – need Hero to be dead for reasons that have nothing to do with Claudio.

Claudio's outburst against Hero has exposed the potential for cruelty and violence in Messina's masculine order so unequivocally that resolution would seem to depend on some kind of confrontation with the fears and assumptions of which Hero has been a victim. In the fiction of her death, however, the play finds a ritual resolution that reasserts Messina's stability without the need for painful questioning. None the less, the play's attempts to move towards a comic conclusion and to evade what its plot has exposed places a strain on the fifth act, producing a peculiar shiftiness of tone and mode.

As the characters come under the sway of their fiction, they become increasingly enigmatic in a way that seems to mark a shift in the play's mode of representation. Act V begins with Antonio's grieving 'counsel' and Leonato's formal lament:

> I pray thee cease thy counsel,
> Which falls into mine ears as profitless
> As water in a sieve. Give not me counsel,
> Nor let no comforter delight mine ear
> But such a one whose wrongs do suit with mine.
> Bring me a father that so lov'd his child,
> Whose joy of her is overwhelm'd like mine,
> And bid him speak of patience. . . .

(3–10)

Leonato's language, with its past-tense references to Hero, has the emotional impact of a father's lament for his dead child; it carries a weight, a dignity and conviction, which nearly overshadows our own knowledge that the death is a fiction. Somehow this fiction has become the governing reality of the play, a fantasy more real than the 'truth'.

Benedick too, acting on his pledge to Beatrice, challenges Claudio and, like Leonato, becomes formalized and enigmatic as he solemnly maintains Hero's death and appears ready to make it good with his sword: 'You have killed a sweet lady, and her death shall fall heavy on you' (148–9). The characters no longer seem to be in the same play, and the resolution cannot come about until Claudio enters the more formalized dramatic world in which the governing plot is the fiction of Hero's death.

The scene at Hero's 'tomb' (V.iii) marks Claudio's and Don Pedro's entrance into the fictional world created by the other characters. This is the play's most highly formal scene, governed in both its action and its language by the conventions of ritual. Even the few lines of dialogue that are not read from Claudio's prepared text are noticeably conventional in style. Don Pedro's dismissal of the mourners is hardly a return to natural speech:

> Good morrow, masters, put your torches out.
> The wolves have preyed, and look, the gentle day,
> Before the wheels of Phoebus, round about
> Dapples the drowsy east with spots of gray.

> (24–7)

Much of the critical worrying about *Much Ado* and its ending focuses on the question of whether this ritual signifies a change in Claudio sufficient to warrant his good fortune in the next scene, where Hero is restored to him. The question cannot be answered. The entire play has shifted its grounds in a way that makes such assessments impossible, if not irrelevant. Yet the ritual itself witnesses to the survival of the fundamental structures of Messina's masculine ethos – structures that the shift towards ritual has allowed the play to preserve.

As I have argued, the sequence of events in Act V points explicitly to the practical gratuitousness of the fiction and the funeral. Early in the first scene the deception proves ineffectual as a means of softening Claudio, who remains unmoved by the news of Hero's death. Moments later Borachio confesses his crimes and clears Hero's name, leaving no effective reason why the characters cannot produce Hero and reveal her death as a lie. Instead, they complicate the fiction with details about a marriageable niece, and engage Claudio to take part in mourning Hero. Hero's funeral is dramatically necessary as Claudio's ritual of expiation. Were Claudio not assimilable into the circle of Hero's family and friends, Messina would be confronted with a fundamental breakdown of its cultural assumptions, which he reflects. Claudio's submission to the authority of Leonato, his agreement to lead Hero's obsequies and to take an unknown bride, permits the play to reach a kind of comic closure. The question is not whether Claudio is sincere – he is certainly that, in so far as a ritual mode allows for such a distinction. The question is what the ritual and Claudio's participation in it signify.

For the ritual itself is, if anything, a reassertion of Messina's old order in new terms. At this crucial moment Hero's exclusion is the condition on which Claudio's reintegration into Messina's social structure and the play's comic resolution depends. Hero's ambiguous blood has been purged away; she is now only 'glorious fame' (V.iii.8), a name placed unequivocally under the sign of chaste Dian, whose 'virgin knight' (V.iii.13) Hero is declared to be. The ritual exorcizes the threat of Hero's body, whose intactness was so precariously in question, and the ambiguity of her face, which led to violently contradictory readings in Act IV. When Hero becomes a monument, her signifying power is tamed. She is redefined so as to be reappropriated to the patriarchal order as a disembodied ideal, 'the sign and semblance of her honor'. Claudio's placement of the epitaph on her tomb explicitly dramatizes the silencing of the woman's voice, the substitution of the man's: 'Hang thou there upon the tomb, / Praising her when I am dumb' (V.iii.9–10). Claudio's text will always speak for Hero, even after Claudio himself is 'dumb'.

Besides the shift towards ritual, the play engages another strategy in moving towards its comic conclusion. This might be described as a centrifugal process that deflects emphasis from the central characters on to those who constitute the plot's machinery. Claudio's guilt is displaced on to Borachio and ultimately on to Don John, making it possible for Leonato to declare in the last scene that Claudio and Don Pedro are innocent, having accused Hero 'upon the error' perpetrated by others (V.iv.3).

The serviceable Borachio is most immediately behind Hero's undoing. It is he who first discovers Claudio's interest in Hero and relays the information to Don John (I.iii). It is Borachio, again, who concocts the scheme to deceive Claudio with the amorous tableau at Hero's window. Borachio is also, in a sense, responsible for the denouement, as his confession reveals Hero's innocence and Claudio's 'mistake'. Autonomous as Borachio is in inventing and carrying out his plot, it is Don John who is the archvillain and the 'author of all, who is fled and gone' (V.ii.98–9). Don John remains behind the scenes, a shadow himself who causes Claudio to see in shadows the signs of Hero's guilt. Don John's motive is ostensibly resentment towards his legitimate brother; but just as guilt is transferred from Claudio to Borachio to Don John, so Don John's malice, aiming at Don Pedro, glances on Claudio but strikes Hero as its victim. As victim and villain, Hero and Don John serve Messina in the capacities of sacrifice and scapegoat – the one bringing about Messina's atonement through her death, the other carrying off its sins.

The ambiguity of Margaret's role in Borachio's plot has caused some consternation among critics.[14] Logically speaking, Margaret must have known of the accusations against Hero and would inevitably recognize the source of error: that she herself had been mistaken for Hero as she talked with Borachio from Hero's window. Margaret does not disclose any of this, nor does she show any signs of concern or uneasiness during her witty exchange with Benedick in the second scene of Act V. In absolving Claudio and Don Pedro of their 'error' in humiliating Hero, however, Leonato transfers part of the blame to Margaret – 'But Margaret was in some fault for this' – while paradoxically suggesting that she participated 'against her will' (V.iv.1–5). The sequence of Leonato's lines suggests, if somewhat vaguely, that Margaret is being made to bear Claudio's and Don Pedro's guilt, that she is guilty in their place, while at the same time denying her conscious, voluntary complicity. Margaret is, in a sense, Hero's double, wearing her clothes, speaking from her window, answering to her name; and the ambiguity of her innocence or guilt points to an ambiguity about Hero, an ambiguity not 'in' her character but, rather, in others' perceptions of her.[15] The play simultaneously represents Hero as innocent and punishes her as guilty. Margaret both represents and carries off Hero's ambiguous taint.

'If you meet a thief', Dogberry instructs the watch, 'you may suspect him, by virtue of your office, to be no true man; and for such a kind of men, the less you meddle or make them, why the more is for your honesty' (III.iii.50–53). In a passing comment, Freud compares Dogberry's counsel to that of physicians who 'implore us for heaven's sake not to meddle with the evil things that lurk behind a neurosis' (*Enlightenment*, p. 179). Freud finds in Dogberry a convenient figure for avoidance or repression of the unconscious, and does not pursue the comparison with reference to *Much Ado about Nothing*, but perhaps we might take up Freud's analogy in considering Dogberry's function in the play. Despite the admonition not to 'meddle or make with' unsavoury characters, the night watch does 'comprehend' (at least in Dogberry's sense) the 'false knaves' Borachio and Conrade (IV.ii.21). Yet Dogberry and his men do serve the plot as a means of avoiding what might otherwise be the crux of the play: Claudio's intractability in the face of Hero's death. By producing the malefactors and getting their 'villainy ... upon record' (V.i.239–40), Dogberry shifts the play's focus away from this violent and unsettling misogyny and into a more legalistic vein. By providing villains against whom the law can proceed, he allows the play to move toward its comic resolution without meddling further with the tensions that triggered its catastrophe.

Besides functioning as an avoidance mechanism, Dogberry serves in another way to mimic larger processes at work in the play: he participates in and parodies the masculine concern with controlling signification, particularly that which relates to himself. We have seen this masculine anxiety most conspicuously in Benedick's fantastic fear of being marked by, even of becoming, a sign of the cuckold – of losing his status as a subject of language and becoming instead its object, its victim, its fool. Dogberry attempts to impress his authority on others by means of his ponderous language, the inflated diction that leads him from one malapropism to the next. Because he cannot master his own meanings, he is continually over-mastered by a language that eludes his control and undercuts the authority he wishes to exert over it – and through it, over others.

The final scene restores something like the balance of formality and gaiety with which the play opens. Claudio and Don Pedro are absolved in a single line from Leonato, and our attention quickly turns to Benedick's mock-rueful request that the friar 'bind [him], or undo [him]' (V.iv.20) by marrying him to Beatrice. Benedick and Beatrice have left off the dangerous literalness of their mutual self-exposure in Act IV; they resume their roles, knowing full well now how transparent they are, and their playfulness is perfectly winning. The critical consensus seems to be that this union of Benedick and Beatrice answers whatever dissatisfaction we continue to feel over Claudio and Hero, and in a sense this is right: we like these characters and the sense of euphoria their wit produces. But it is another question whether Benedick and Beatrice represent a challenge or an alternative to Messina's limitations. Different as they are in style from Claudio and Hero, Benedick and Beatrice are of a piece with their world; there is no world elsewhere in this play – even their irony cannot create one, for it participates in the assumptions that shape Messina.

In many ways the final scene reiterates what has been problematic from the play's beginning. The four ladies enter masked and remain, in effect, ciphers until called for by their betrothed husbands. (The text indicates no point at which Margaret or Ursula unmasks. Remaining perhaps a little behind Hero and Beatrice on the stage, the effaced women reinforce the status of women as ciphers until named by men.) In revealing herself and giving herself to Claudio, Hero repeats Claudio's dualistic notion of her identity: 'One Hero died defiled; but I do live, / And surely as I live, I am a maid' (V.iv.63–4). Her ritual death has purged Hero of intemperate Venus's sexuality, and she returns as Dian in her orb. Don Pedro's exclamation is telling: 'The former Hero! Hero that is dead!' (65). Hero remains dead in her resurrection, as she is reappropriated to the mode of perception that killed her.

The circularity here is reinforced by the way this final scene repeats the

play's beginning. Having avoided the violent confrontations that threatened to break out after Hero's 'death', the male characters revert to their
verbal aggression, and particularly to their cuckold jokes (V.iv.43–51,
121–2). That the jokes retain their original force indicates that Messina's
masculine ethos survives unchanged. The play began with the defeat of
Don John, and with his defeat it ends, leaving us to wonder, if we care to,
when he will next escape.

The readings of *Much Ado* quoted at the beginning of this essay participate
in the play's drive towards ritual transcendence – a movement invoked and
sanctioned by the friar. To resist this movement, as my reading of the play
does, is manifestly to read against the grain of the play's explicitly offered
resolution: it is to recognize what the play's drive towards comic closure
suppresses but simultaneously exposes. In his repeated exposure of the
limits of his own authority, perhaps Dogberry suggests a way of reading
the play as self-exposure: the play is partly the record of its own
limitations. In presenting Hero as a kind of cipher, *Much Ado* reflects its
patriarchal heritage; yet it is Hero's very blankness that allows the
revealing explosion to occur. The play's explicit representation of
masculine fantasy and delusion trades on, and partakes of, the process it
explores. Or should we say it exposes the process it trades on? The mode
of representation that makes possible the play's main plot – a mode in
which women are ciphers – is implicated in that plot, obliquely revealing
the underlying sexual values and assumptions that motivate the unfolding
of the drama.

Notes

1. *Leon.* So, by being too curst, God will send you no horns.
    Beat. Just, if he send me no husband....

    (II.i.25–7)

The association of cuckoldry with castration and displacement is suggested by the derivation
of the notion of the cuckold's horns, described in the *OED*:

> Cuckolds were fancifully said to wear horns on the brow.... [The origin of this, which
> appears in so many European langs.... is referred to by Dunger (*Germania* XXIX, 39) to
> the practice formerly prevalent of planting or engrafting the spurs of a castrated cock on the
> root of the excised comb, where they grew and became horns, sometimes several inches long.
> He shows that Ger. *hahnreh* or *hahnrei*, 'cuckold', originally meant 'capon'.]

2. In his essay 'The Uncanny', Freud writes: 'A study of dreams, phantasies and myths
has taught us that a morbid anxiety connected with the eyes and with going blind is often
enough a substitute for the dread of castration' (p. 36).
3. Benedick later describes undergoing one of Beatrice's verbal attacks: 'I stood like a
man at a mark, with a whole army shooting at me' (II.i.244–5).
4. Coppélia Kahn, taking her cue from Freud, offers another account of the relation

between cuckoldry and compensation: 'Regarded endopsychically, from the cuckold's point of view, horns are a defense formed through denial, compensation, and upward displacement. They say, "It's not that I can't keep my wife because I don't have enough of a penis. I have two of them, in fact, right up where everyone can see them"' (p. 122). For a related discussion of phallic imagery and compensation fantasies, see Freud's essay 'The Medusa's Head'.

5. The fear of women as castrated and as potentially castrating is a theme to which Freud frequently recurs. In 'The Taboo of Virginity' (1918) he discusses certain beliefs and practices of 'primitive races' that extend in some form into sophisticated culture. The essay begins by examining 'the high value set upon ... virginity' and the extensive taboos related to virginity and defloration, and culminates in a discussion of the male dread of women:

> Wherever primitive man institutes a taboo, there he fears a danger; and it cannot be disputed that the general principle underlying all these regulations and avoidances is a dread of women.... Man fears that his strength will be taken away from him by woman, dreads becoming infected with her femininity and then proving himself a weakling.
>
> (p. 78)

This essay is characteristic of Freud's writings on gender, both in its perspicacity and in its curious reflexiveness. He initially describes the premium placed on female virginity as something difficult to explain, noting only that it is 'but a logical consequence of the exclusive right of possession over a woman which is the essence of monogamy ' He then goes on to 'justify what at first appeared to be a prejudice by referring to our ideas concerning the character of the erotic life in women' (p. 70). It is clear that 'our' ideas are those of male psychoanalysts, shared in an intuitive, less conscious way by all men, both 'savage' and sophisticated. Yet it is not really to these 'ideas' that Freud refers for his explanation but to 'the character of the erotic life in women'; that is, he ceases to distinguish male fantasies and theories about women from female sexuality itself. The elaborate taboos concerning women make sense, Freud suggests, when we recognize them as a response to something real – to women's penis envy and vengeful desire to castrate men: 'Now, upon this penis-envy follows the hostile embitterment displayed by women against men, never entirely absent in the relations between the sexes, the clearest indications of which are to be found in the writings and ambitions of "emancipated women"' (p. 83). Consistently in this essay, Freud refers what is paradoxical in practices and beliefs related to women and to sexuality, not to paradoxes of masculine psychology and patriarchal culture, but to 'the paradoxical reaction of women to defloration ...' (p. 83), thus, in effect, reproducing the very phenomenon (dread of women) he set out to analyse.

6. See Barbara Everett and John Crick. Marilyn French, while noting that Beatrice 'does not break decorum', describes her as 'a Rosalind who has taken a step further into freedom ... a force for anarchy – democracy – in Messina' (p. 131).

7. It could be argued that Beatrice's aggressive tongue serves as a reassuring fetishistic substitute for the phallus: like all fetishes it signifies a denial of female (i.e. the mother's) castration, the denial by which a male child fends off the threat of his own castration. Castrated, the woman mirrors for the male child his own possible fate; the fetish revises the frightening image to figure back a phallically endowed reflection of the male subject. See Freud's 'Fetishism' (1927).

8. For example, Beatrice gives this account of Benedick: 'He set up his bills here in Messina, and challeng'd Cupid at the flight, and my uncle's fool, reading the challenge, subscrib'd for Cupid, and challeng'd him at the burbolt' (I.i.37–40). Was Beatrice the 'fool' who 'subscribed for Cupid'? In her general slander of Benedick she represents him as faithless – 'He wears his faith but as the fashion of his hat; it ever changes with the next block' (I.i.71–2) – and responds to Don Pedro's comment that she has 'lost the heart of Signior Benedick' with 'Indeed, my lord, he lent it me awhile, I gave him use for it, a double heart for his single one. Marry, once before he won it of me with false dice ...' (II.i.274–8).

9. Lynda Boose has pointed out to me that Hero becomes much more apt of speech during the masked-ball scene (II.i) and also in the orchard scene, where she and Ursula trick Beatrice with their stories of Benedick's desperate love for her (III.i). Given a mask or a role to play, Hero improvises well; but her speech serves, as does wit generally in the play, to

disguise or deceive, and in the latter example Hero is explicitly playing a role scripted for her by a man, Don Pedro.

10. In Hayes's reading, Claudio regards Don Pedro as a kind of father figure and fears engaging in Oedipal competition with him (pp. 84–5).

11. Hayes links these lines with 'the incestuous root of Claudio's anxiety . . .' (p. 86).

12. T.W. Craik refers to 'the reasonableness of Friar Francis's plan for Claudio and Hero' (p. 308), measures the other characters against the friar's 'better judgment' (p. 310), and writes, somewhat inaccurately, that 'the effect [of the friar's plan] on Claudio is exactly as Friar Francis prophesied . . .' (p. 312). W.R. Davis agrees that 'the wisdom of the friar's plan is immediately attested' (p. 9). Graham Storey praises 'the Friar's wisdom' and his 'calm sanity [which] admirably "places" Leonato's hysteria' (p. 27). While Storey's argument, which does not deal specifically with gender in the play, places the friar on the side of masculine cool-headedness in the face of 'hysteria', Janice Hayes, who does address questions of gender in the play, places the friar on the side of the 'expressive' qualities she associates with women: 'as the spokesman for Christian grace, the priest is an asexual figure associated with expressive functioning, for the theology of Grace predicates a passive reception of unmerited favor rather than the active pursuit of an earned reward. . . . The resolution of the Claudio–Hero plot is thus contingent upon the intervention of a benign Providence that has placed a man who can function with both his head and his heart in the right place at the right time' (pp. 92, 93).

13. Hayes is ambiguous on this point, acknowledging that 'the play's resolution does not come any more according to the priest's than to Don John's scheming . . .' but arguing that 'ultimately the priest's faith is correct . . .' (p. 93).

14. Allan Gilbert suggests that the peculiar contradictions in Margaret's role result from Shakespeare's having pieced together material from Bandello's story of Timbreo and Fenicia and cantos 5 and 6 of Ariosto's *Orlando furioso*. Gilbert's discussion is both interesting and persuasive, but it leaves room for some account of how Margaret's doubleness affects the play.

15. In *The Interpretation of Dreams* Freud writes: 'The form of a dream or the form in which it is dreamt is used with quite surprising frequency for representing its concealed subject matter' (p. 367). That is, an ambiguity in a dream may have 'no connection at all with the make-up of the dream itself but arises from the material of the dream thoughts and is a constituent of it' (p. 366). This observation may provide a useful analogy for thinking about the ambiguity of Margaret's role – an ambiguity that points, I think, to the dualism that characterizes the play's representation of women.

References

Craik, T.W., '*Much Ado about Nothing*', *Scrutiny* 19 (1953): 297–316.

Crick, John, '*Much Ado about Nothing*', *The Use of English* 17 (1965): 223–7, rpt. in Davis, pp. 33–8.

Davis, Walter R., ed., *Twentieth Century Interpretations of 'Much Ado about Nothing'*, Englewood Cliff, NJ: Prentice, 1969.

Everett, Barbara, '*Much Ado about Nothing*', *Critical Quarterly* 3 (1969): 319–35.

French, Marilyn, *Shakespeare's Division of Experience*, New York: Simon, 1981.

Freud, Sigmund, 'Fetishism', trans. Joan Riviere, in *Sexuality and the Psychology of Love*, pp. 214–19.

———*The Interpretation of Dreams*, trans. James Strachey, New York: Avon, 1965.

———*Jokes and Their Relation to the Unconscious*, trans. and ed. James Strachey, New York: Norton, 1960.

———'The Medusa's Head', trans. James Strachey, in *Sexuality and the Psychology of Love*, pp. 212–13.

———*The Sexual Enlightenment of Children*, ed. Philip Rieff, New York: Macmillan, 1963.

———*Sexuality and the Psychology of Love*, ed. Philip Rieff, New York: Macmillan, 1963.

———'The Taboo of Virginity', trans. Joan Riviere, in *Sexuality and the Psychology of Love*, pp. 70–86.

————'The Uncanny', trans. Alix Strachey, in *Studies in Parapsychology*, ed. Philip Rieff, New York: Macmillan, 1963, pp. 19–60.

Gilbert, Allan H., 'Two Margarets: The Composition of *Much Ado about Nothing*', *Philological Quarterly* 41 (1962): 61–71.

Hayes, Janice, 'Those "soft and delicate desires": *Much Ado* and the Distrust of Women', in *The Woman's Part: Feminist Criticism of Shakespeare*, ed. Carolyn Ruth Swift Lenz, Gayle Greene and Carol Thomas Neely, Chicago: University of Illinois Press, 1980, pp. 79–99.

Kahn, Coppélia, *Man's Estate: Masculine Identity in Shakespeare*, Berkeley: University of California Press, 1981.

Neill, Kerby, 'More Ado about Claudio: An Acquittal for the Slandered Groom', *Shakespeare Quarterly* 3 (1952): 91–107.

Pettet, E.C., *Shakespeare and the Romance Tradition*, London: Staples, 1949.

Shakespeare, William, *Much Ado about Nothing. The Riverside Shakespeare*, ed. G. Blakemore Evans, 2 vols, Boston, MA: Houghton, 1974, 1: 322–62.

Storey, Graham, 'The Success of *Much Ado about Nothing*', in *More Talking about Shakespeare*, ed. John Garrett, London: Longmans; New York: Theatre Art, 1959, pp. 128–43, rpt. in Davis, pp. 18–32.

West, E.J., 'Much Ado about an Unpleasant Play', *Shakespeare Association Bulletin* 22 (1947): 30–34.

6

Hamlet – the *Mona Lisa* of Literature[1]

Jacqueline Rose

It does not seem to have been pointed out that T.S. Eliot's famous concept of the 'objective correlative', which has been so influential in the assessment of literature and its values, was originally put forward in 1919 in the form of a reproach against the character of a woman (Eliot, 1975). The woman in question is Gertrude in Shakespeare's *Hamlet*, and the reproach Eliot makes of her is that she is not good enough aesthetically, that is, *bad* enough psychologically, which means that in relationship to the affect which she generates by her behaviour in the chief character of the drama – Hamlet himself – Gertrude is not deemed a sufficient *cause*.

The question of femininity clearly underpins this central, if not indeed *the* central, concept of Eliot's aesthetic theory, and this is confirmed by the fact that Eliot again uses an image of femininity – and by no means one of the most straightforward in its own representation or in the responses it has produced – to give us the measure of the consequent failure of the play. *Hamlet* the play, Eliot writes, is 'the Mona Lisa of literature' (Eliot, 1975, p. 47), offering up in its essentially enigmatic and undecipherable nature something of that maimed or imperfect quality of appeal which characterizes Leonardo's famous painting. The aesthetic inadequacy of the play is caused by the figure of a woman, and the image of a woman most aptly embodies the consequences of that failure. Femininity thus becomes the stake, not only of the internal, but also of the critical drama generated by the play.

Equally important, however, is the fact that femininity has been at the heart of the psychoanalytic approach to *Hamlet*, from Ernest Jones onwards, a fact which has again been overlooked by those who have arrested their attention at the famous Oedipal saga for which his reading of the play is best known. 'Hamlet was a woman' (Jones, 1949, p. 88) is just one of the statements about *Hamlet* which Jones quotes as indicating the place of the 'feminine' in a drama which has paradoxically been celebrated as the birth of the modern, post-Renaissance, conception of man. In this article, I will try to focus what I see as the centrality of this question of femininity to an aesthetic theory which has crucially influenced a whole tradition of how we conceptualize literary writing, and to the psychoanalytic theory which was being elaborated at exactly the same time, at the point where they converge on the same object – Shakespeare's *Hamlet* – described by Freud as an emblem of 'the secular advance of repression in the emotional life of mankind' (Freud, 1900, p. 264; 4, p. 366).

I

To start with T.S. Eliot's critique of *Hamlet*. T.S. Eliot in fact sees his reading of the play as a move away from psychological approaches to *Hamlet* which concentrate too much on the characters to the exclusion of the play itself· '*Hamlet* the play is the primary problem, and Hamlet the character only secondary' (p. 45). Eliot therefore makes it clear that what he has to say exceeds the fact of the dramatic personae and strikes at the heart of aesthetic form itself. The problem with *Hamlet* is that there is something in the play which is formally or aesthetically unmanageable: 'like the *Sonnets*' (another work by Shakespeare in which a question of sexual ambivalence has always been recognized) '*Hamlet* is full of some stuff that the writer could not drag to light, contemplate, or manipulate into art' (p. 48). Eliot then describes the conditions, as he sees it, of that in which *Hamlet* fails – the successful manipulation of matter into artistic form. It is here that he produces the concept of the 'objective correlative' for the first time:

> The only way of expressing emotion in the form of art is by finding an 'objective correlative'; in other words, a set of objects, a situation, a chain of events which shall be the formula of that *particular* emotion; such that when the external facts ... are given, the emotion is immediately evoked.... The artistic 'inevitability' lies in this complete adequacy of the external to the emotion. (p. 48)

Emotion, or affect, is therefore admissible in art only if it is given an external object to which it can be seen, clearly and automatically to correspond. There must be nothing in that emotion which spills over or exceeds the objective, visible (one could say conscious) facts, no residue or trace of the primitive 'stuff' which may have been the original stimulus for the work of art. This is where *Hamlet* fails: Hamlet (the man) is dominated by an emotion which is inexpressible, because it is in *excess* of the facts as they appear (p. 48). And that excess is occasioned by Gertrude, who precipitates Hamlet into despondency by her 'o'er hasty' marriage to his dead father's brother and successor, who turns out also to have been the agent of the former king's death. For Eliot, Gertrude is not an adequate equivalent for the disgust which she evokes in Hamlet, which 'envelops and exceeds her' (p. 48) and which, because she cannot adequately contain it, runs right across the fabric of the play. Gertrude is therefore disgusting, but not quite disgusting *enough*. Eliot is, however, clear that he is not asking for a stronger woman character on the stage, since he recognizes that it is in the nature of the problem dealt with in this play – a son's feelings towards a guilty mother – that they should be in excess of their objective cause. On this count, Gertrude's inadequacy turns around and becomes wholly appropriate: 'it is just *because* her character is so negative and insignificant that she arouses in Hamlet the feeling which she is incapable of representing' (pp. 48–9).

What is at stake behind this failing of the woman, what she fails to represent, therefore, is precisely unrepresentable – a set of unconscious emotions which, *by definition*, can have no objective outlet, and are therefore incapable of submitting to the formal constraints of art. What we get in *Hamlet* instead is 'buffoonery' – in Hamlet himself the 'buffoonery of an emotion which can find no outlet in action' (p. 49), for the dramatist the 'buffoonery of an emotion which he cannot express in art' (p. 49). Such 'intense', 'ecstatic' (Gertrude uses the word 'ecstasy' to describe Hamlet's madness in the bedchamber scene of the play) and 'terrible' feeling is for Eliot 'doubtless a subject of study for the pathologist', and why Shakespeare attempted to express the 'inexpressibly horrible' we cannot ever know, since we should have finally 'to know something which is by hypothesis unknowable and to understand things which Shakespeare did not understand himself' (p. 49).

Today we can only be struck by the extraordinary resonance of the terms which figure so negatively in Eliot's critique – buffoonery, ecstasy, the excessive and unknowable – all terms in which we have learnt to recognize (since Freud at least) something necessarily present in any act of writing (*Hamlet* included) which only suppresses them – orders them precisely into form – at a cost. Eliot's criticism of *Hamlet* can therefore be turned around. What he sees as the play's weakness becomes its source of fascination, or even strength.

In this context, the fact that it is a woman who is seen as cause of the excess and deficiency in the play, and again a woman who symbolizes its aesthetic failure, starts to look like a repetition. First, of the play itself – Hamlet and his dead father united in the reproach they make of Gertrude for her sexual failing ('O Hamlet what a falling off was there', I.v.47), and *horror* as the exact response to the crime which precedes the play and precipitates its drama ('O horrible! O horrible! most horrible!', I.v.80). Secondly, a repetition of a more fundamental drama of psychic experience itself as described by Freud: the drama of sexual difference in which the woman is seen as the cause of just such a failure in representation, as something deficient, lacking or threatening to the system and identities which are the precondition not only of integrated artistic form but also of so-called normal adult psychic and sexual life. Located by Freud at the point where the woman is first seen to be different (Freud, 1924, 1925), this moment can then have its effects in that familiar mystification or fetishization of femininity which makes of the woman something both perfect and dangerous or obscene (obscene if *not* perfect). And perhaps no image has evoked this process more clearly than that of the *Mona Lisa* itself, which at almost exactly this historical moment (the time of Freud and Eliot alike) started to be taken as the emblem of an inscrutable femininity, cause and destination of the whole of human mystery and its desires:

> The lady smiled in regal calm: her instincts of conquest, of ferocity, all the heredity of the species, the will to seduce and to ensnare, the charm of deceit, the kindness that conceals a cruel purpose all this appeared and disappeared by turns behind the laughing veil and buried itself in the poem of her smile. Good and wicked, cruel and compassionate, graceful and feline she laughed.
>
> (Angelo Conti, cit. Freud, 1910, p. 109)

By choosing an image of a woman to embody the inexpressible and inscrutable content which he identified in Shakespeare's play, Eliot ties the enigma of femininity to the problem of interpretation itself: 'No one has solved the riddle of her smile, no one has read the meaning of her thoughts' (Muther, cit. Freud, 1910, p. 108), 'a presence ... expressive of what in the way of a thousand years men had come to desire' (Walter Pater, cit. Freud, 1910, p. 108). Freud himself picks up the tone in one of his more problematic observations about femininity, when he allows that critics have recognized in the picture:

> the most perfect representation of the contrasts which dominate the erotic life of women; the contrast between reserve and seduction, and between the most devoted tenderness and a sensuality that is ruthlessly demanding – consuming men as if they were alien beings.
>
> (Freud, 1910, p. 108)

What other representation, we might ask, has so clearly produced a set of emotions without 'objective correlative' – that is, in excess of the facts as they appear? T.S. Eliot's reading of *Hamlet* would therefore seem to suggest that what is in fact felt as inscrutable, unmanageable or even horrible (ecstatic in both senses of the term) for an aesthetic theory which will allow into its definition only what can be controlled or managed by art is nothing other than femininity itself.

At the end of Eliot's essay, he refers to Montaigne's 'Apologie of Raymond Sebond' as a possible source for the malaise of the play. Its discourse on the contradictory, unstable and ephemeral nature of man has often been seen as the origin of Hamlet's suicide soliloquy; it also contains an extraordinary passage anticipating Freud, where Montaigne asks whether we do not live in dreaming, dream when we think and work, and whether our waking merely be a form of sleep (Florio, 1885, pp. 219–310). In relation to the woman, however, another smaller essay by Montaigne – 'Of Three Good Women' – is equally striking for the exact reversal which these three women, models of female virtue, represent *vis-à-vis* Gertrude herself in Shakespeare's play, each one choosing self-imposed death at the point where her husband is to die (Florio, 1885, pp. 378–82). The image is close to the protestations of the Player Queen in the Mousetrap scene of *Hamlet* who vows her undying love to her husband; whereupon Gertrude, recognizing perhaps in the Player Queen's claims a rebuke or foil to her own sexual laxness, comments: 'The lady doth protest too much' (III.ii.225) (a familiar cliché now for the sexual 'inconstancy' of females). So what happens, indeed, to the sexuality of the woman, when the husband dies; who is there to hold its potentially dangerous excess within the bounds of a fully social constraint? This could be seen as one of the questions asked by *Hamlet* the play, and generative of its terrible effect.

Before going on to discuss psychoanalytic interpretations of *Hamlet*, it is worth stressing the extent to which Eliot's theory is shot through with sexuality in this way, and its implications for recent literary debate. Taking their cue from psychoanalysis, writers like Roland Barthes (Barthes, 1970, 1971) and Julia Kristeva (1974, 1980) have seen the very stability of the sign as index and precondition for that myth of linguistic cohesion and sexual identity by which we must live but under whose regimen we suffer. Literature then becomes one of the chief arenas in which this struggle is played out. Literary writing which proclaims its integrity, and literary theory which demands that integrity (objectivity/correlation) of writing, merely repeat that moment of repression when language and sexuality were first ordered into place, putting down the unconscious processes which threaten the resolution of the Oedipal drama and of narrative form alike. In this context, Eliot's critical writing, with its stress on the ethical task of writer and critic, becomes nothing less than the most accomplished (and influential) case for the interdependency and centrality of language and sexuality to the proper ordering of literary form. Much recent literary theory can be seen as an attempt to undo the ferocious effects of this particularly harsh type of literary superego – one whose political repressiveness in the case of Eliot became more and more explicit in his later allegiance to Empire, Church and State.

Eliot himself was aware of the areas of psychic danger against which he constantly brushed. He was clear that he was touching on 'perilous' issues which risk 'violating the frontier of consciousness' (Eliot, 1975, p. 92); and when he talks of writing as something 'pleasurable', 'exhausting', 'agitating', as a sudden 'breakdown of strong habitual barriers' (p. 89), the sexuality of the writing process which he seeks to order spills over into the text. And Eliot's conception of that order, what he sees as proper literary form, is finally an Oedipal drama in itself. In his other famous essay 'Tradition and the Individual Talent', which was written in the same year as the '*Hamlet*' essay, Eliot states that the way the artist can avoid his own disordered subjectivity and transmute it into form is by giving himself up to something outside himself and surrendering to the tradition that precedes and surrounds him. Only by capitulating to the world of dead poets can the artist escape his oppressive individuality and enter into historical time: 'Set [the artist] for contrast and comparison among the dead', for 'the most individual parts of his work are those in which the dead poets, his ancestors, assert their immortality most vigorously' (p. 38). Thus, just as in the psychoanalytic account, the son pays his debt to the dead father, symbol of the law, in order fully to enter his history, so in Eliot's reading the artist pays his debt to the dead poets, and can become a poet only by that fact. Eliot's conception of literary tradition and form could therefore be described as a plea for appropriate mourning and for the respecting of literary rites – that mourning whose shameful inadequacy, as the French psychoanalyst Jacques Lacan pointed out in his essay on *Hamlet* (Lacan, 1959), is the trigger and then constant refrain of the play: the old Hamlet cut off in the 'blossom' of his sin, Polonius interred 'hugger mugger', Ophelia buried wrongly – because of her suicide – in sacred ground.

In Eliot's reading of *Hamlet*, therefore, the sexuality of the woman seems to become the scapegoat and cause of the dearth or breakdown of Oedipal resolution which the play ceaselessly enacts, not only at the level of its theme, but also in the disjunctions and difficulties of its aesthetic form. Much has been made, of course, of the aesthetic problem of *Hamlet* by critics other than Eliot, who have pondered on its lack of integration or single-purposiveness, its apparent inability to resolve itself or come to term (it is the longest of Shakespeare's plays), much as they have pondered on all these factors in the character of Hamlet himself.

Hamlet poses a problem for Eliot, therefore, at the level of both matter and form. Femininity is the image of that problem; it seems, in fact, to be the only image through which the problem can be conceptualized or thought. The principal danger: femininity thus becomes the focus for a partly theorized recognition of the psychic and literary disintegration which can erupt at any moment into literary form.

One more example, and perhaps the most graphic, can serve to illustrate how far femininity is implicated in this aesthetic theory – the lines which Eliot uses from Tourneur's *The Revenger's Tragedy* to describe the artist surrendering to his inspiration before ordering it into form:

> And now methinks I could e'en chide myself
> For doating on her beauty, though her death
> Shall be revenged after no common action.
> Does the silkworm expend her yellow labours
> For thee? For thee does she undo herself?
> Are lordships sold to maintain ladyships
> For the poor benefit of a bewildering minute?
> Why doth yon fellow falsify highways,
> And put his life between the judge's lips,
> To refine such a thing – keeps horse and men
> To beat their valours for her?
>
> (Tourneur, cit. Eliot, 1975, p. 42)

For a play that has also been discussed as excessive, and perhaps even more than *Hamlet*, this moment gives the strongest measure of that excess. The speech is made by Vindice, the Revenger, to the skull of his former mistress, who was poisoned by the Duke for resisting his advances. His revenge takes the form of wrapping this skull in the full-bodied attire of the woman and dowsing its mouth with poison so that the Duke will be first seduced and then poisoned in its embrace. In this crazed image, the woman appears at once as purity and lust, victim and destroyer, but the split representation shows how the feminine can serve as a receptacle for a more fundamental horror of sexuality and death. Femininity becomes the place in which man reads his destiny, just as the woman becomes a symptom for the man (Lacan, 1982, p. 168).

Likewise in *Hamlet*, these two themes – of death and sexuality – run their course through the play, both as something which can be assimilated to social constraint and as a threat to constraint and to the social altogether. For *Hamlet* can be seen as a play which turns on mourning and marriage – the former the means whereby death is given its symbolic form and enters back into social life, the latter the means whereby sexuality is brought into the orbit of the law. When *Hamlet* opens, however, what we are given is *too much* of each (perhaps this is the excess) – too much mourning (Hamlet wears black, stands apart, and mourns beyond the natural term) and too much marriage (Gertrude passes from one husband to another too fast). As if it were the case that these two regulators of the furthest edges of social and civil life, if they become overstated, if there is too much of them, tip over into their opposite and start to look like what they are designed to hold off. Eliot's essay on *Hamlet*, and his writing on literature in general, gives us a sense of how these matters, which he recognizes in the play, underpin the space of aesthetic representation itself, and how femininity figures crucially in that conceptualization.

II

If Eliot's aesthetic theories move across into the arena of sexuality, Ernest Jones's psychoanalytic interpretation of *Hamlet* turns out also to be part of an aesthetic concern (Jones, 1949). His intention is to use psychoanalysis to establish the integrity of the literary text, that is, to uncover factors, hidden motives and desires, which will give back to rational understanding what would otherwise pass the limits of literary understanding and appreciation itself: 'The perfect work of art is one where the traits and reactions of the character prove to be harmonious, consistent and intelligible when examined in the different layers of the mind' (p. 49). Jones's reading, therefore, belongs to that psychoanalytic project which restores to rationality or brings to light, placing what was formerly unconscious or unmanageable under the ego's mastery or control. It is a project which has been read directly out of Freud's much-contested statement 'Wo es war, soll Ich werden', translated by Strachey 'Where id was, there ego shall be' (Freud [1933] 1932, p. 80; 2, p. 112). Lacan, for whom the notion of such conscious mastery was only ever a fantasy (the fantasy of the ego itself), retranslates or reverses the statement: 'There where it was, so I must come to be' (Lacan, 1957, p. 524).

For Jones, as for Eliot, therefore, there must be no aesthetic excess, nothing which goes beyond the reaches of what can ultimately be deciphered and known. In this context, psychoanalysis acts as a key which can solve the enigma of the text, take away its surplus by offering us as readers that fully rational understanding which Shakespeare's play – Jones recognizes, like Eliot – places at risk. The chapter of Jones's book which gives the Oedipal reading of *Hamlet*, the one which tends to be included in the anthologies of Shakespeare criticism (for example, Lerner, 1963), is accordingly entitled 'The Psychoanalytic Solution'. Taking his reference from Freud's comments in *The Interpretation of Dreams* (Freud, 1900, pp. 264–6; 4, pp. 364–8), Jones sees Hamlet as a little Oedipus who cannot bring himself to kill Claudius because he stands in the place of his own desire, having murdered Hamlet's father and married his mother. The difference between Oedipus and Hamlet is that Oedipus unknowingly acts out this fantasy, whereas for Hamlet it is repressed into the unconscious, revealing itself in the form of that inhibition or inability to act which has baffled so many critics of the play. It is this repression of the Oedipal drama beneath the surface of the text which leads Freud to say of *Hamlet*, comparing it with Sophocles' drama, that it demonstrates the 'secular advance of repression in the emotional life of mankind' (Freud, 1900, p. 264; 4, p. 366).

But Jones's book and the psychoanalytic engagement with *Hamlet* does not stop there, and it is finally more interesting than this Oedipal reading which, along with Jones's speculations on Hamlet's childhood and Shakespeare's own life, has most often been used to discredit it. For while it is the case that Jones's account seems to fulfil the dream of any explanatory hypothesis by providing an account of factors which would otherwise remain unaccountable, a closer look shows how this same reading infringes the interpretative and sexual boundaries which, like Eliot, it seems to be putting into place.

The relationship of psychoanalysis to *Hamlet* has in fact always been a strange and repetitive one in which Hamlet the character is constantly given the status of a truth, and becomes a pivot for psychoanalysis and its project, just as for Eliot *Hamlet* is the focal point through which he arrives at a more general problem of aesthetic form. For Freud, for instance, Hamlet is not just Oedipus, but also melancholic and hysteric, and both these readings, problematic as they are as diagnoses of literary characters, become interesting because of the way they bring us up against the limits of interpretation and sexual identity alike. The interpretative distinction between rationality and excess, between normality and abnormality, for example, starts to crumble when the melancholic is defined as a madman who also speaks the truth. Freud uses *Hamlet* with this meaning in 'Mourning and Melancholia' written in 1915:

> We only wonder why a man has to be ill before he can be accessible to a truth of this kind. For there can be no doubt that if anyone holds an opinion of himself such as this (an opinion which Hamlet holds of himself and of everyone else) he is ill, whether or not he is speaking the truth or whether he is being more or less unfair to himself. (Freud, 1917, pp. 246–7; 2, p. 255)

Taken in this direction, *Hamlet* illustrates not so much a failure of identity as the precarious distinction on which this notion of identity rests. In 'Psychopathic Characters on the Stage' (Freud, 1942 [1905 or 1906]), Freud includes *Hamlet* in that group of plays which rely for their effect on the neurotic in the spectator, inducing in her or him the neurosis watched onstage, crossing over the boundaries between onstage and offstage and breaking down the habitual barriers of the mind. A particular *type* of drama, this form is none the less effective only through its capacity to implicate us *all*: 'A person who does not lose his reason under certain conditions can have no reason to lose' (Lessing, cit. Freud, 1942 [1905 or 1906], p. 30n). Jones makes a similar point and underscores its fullest social import when he attributes the power of *Hamlet* to the very edge of sanity on which it moves, the way that it confuses the division which 'until our generation (and even now in the juristic sphere) separated the sane and the responsible from the irresponsible insane' (Jones, 1949, p. 70). T.S. Eliot also gave a version of this, but from the other side, when he described poetry in 'Tradition and the Individual Talent' as an escape from emotion and personality, and then added 'but, of course, only those who have personality and emotion can know what it means to want to escape from these things' (Eliot, 1975, p. 43). So instead of safely diagnosing Hamlet, his Oedipal drama, his disturbance, and subjecting them to its mastery and control, the psychoanalytic interpretation turns back on to spectator and critic, implicating the observer in those forms of irrationality and excess which Jones and Eliot, in their different ways, seek to order into place.

Calling Hamlet a hysteric, which both Freud and Jones also do (Freud, 1887–1902, p. 224; Jones, 1949, p. 59), has the same effect in terms of the question of sexual difference, since it immediately raises the question of femininity and upsets the too-tidy Oedipal reading of the play. Freud had originally seen the boy's Oedipal drama as a straightforward desire for the mother and rivalry with the father, just as he first considered the little girl's Oedipal trajectory to be its simple reverse. The discovery of the girl's pre-Oedipal attachment to the mother led him to modify this too-easy picture in which unconscious sexual desires in infancy are simply the precursors in miniature of the boy's and the girl's later fitting sexual and social place (Freud, 1924, 1925, 1931). We could say that psychoanalysis can become of interest to feminism at the point where the little girl's desire for the father can no longer be safely assumed. But equally important is the effect that this upset of the original schema has on how we consider the psychic life of the boy. In a section called 'Matricide' (Jones, 1949, Chapter V, pp. 105–14) which is normally omitted from the anthologies, Jones talks of Hamlet's desire to kill, not the father, but the mother. He takes this from Hamlet's soliloquy before he goes to his mother's bedchamber:

> Let not ever
> The soul of Nero enter this firm bosom;
> Let me be cruel, not unnatural.
> I will speak daggers to her, but use none.

(III.ii.384–7)

and also from Gertrude's own lines 'What wilt thou do? Thou wilt not murder me? Help! Ho!' (III.iv.20–21) (the murder of Polonius is the immediate consequence of this). Thus desire spills over into its opposite, and the woman becomes guilty for the affect which she provokes.

This is still an Oedipal reading of the play, since the violence towards the mother is the effect of the desire for her (a simple passage between the two forms of excess). But the problem of desire starts to trouble the category of identification, involving Jones in a discussion of the femininity in man (not just desire *for* the woman but identification *with* her), a femininity which has been recognized by more than one critic of the play (Jones, 1949, pp. 88, 106).[2] Thus on either side of the psychoanalytic 'solution', we find something which makes of it no solution at all. And Hamlet, 'as patient as the female dove' (V.i.281) (the image of the female dove was objected to by Knight in 1841 as a typographical error: Shakespeare, 1877, I, p. 410n), becomes Renaissance man only to the extent that he reveals a femininity which undermines that fiction. Femininity turns out to be lying behind the Oedipal drama, indicating its impasse or impossibility of resolution, even though Freud did himself talk of its dissolution, as if it suddenly went out of existence altogether. But this observation contradicts the basic analytic premiss of the persistence of unconscious desire.

The point being not whether Hamlet suffers from an excess *of* femininity, but the way that femininity itself functions *as* excess – the excess of this particular interpretative schema (hence, presumably, its exclusion from the summaries and extracts from Jones), and as the vanishing point of the difficulties of the play. And in this, Ernest Jones outbids T.S. Eliot *vis-à-vis* the woman: 'The central mystery [of *Hamlet*] has well been called the Sphinx of modern literature' (pp. 25–6). The femininity of Hamlet is perhaps finally less important than this image of the feminine which Jones blithely projects on to the troubled and troubling aesthetic boundaries of the play.

III

If the bad or dangerous woman is aesthetic trouble, then it should come as no surprise that the opposite of this disturbance – an achieved aesthetic or even creativity itself – then finds its most appropriate image again in femininity, but this time its reverse: the good enough mother herself. As if completing the circuit, André Green turns to D.W. Winnicott's concept of the maternal function as the basis for his book on *Hamlet* (Green, 1982).[3] Femininity now appears as the very principle of the aesthetic process. Shakespeare's Hamlet forecloses the femininity in himself, but by projecting on to the stage the degraded and violent image of a femininity repudiated by his character, Shakespeare manages to preserve in himself that other femininity which is the source of his creative art:

Writing *Hamlet* had been an act of exorcism which enabled its author to give his hero's femininity – cause of his anxieties, self-reproaches and accusations – an acceptable form through the process of aesthetic creation.... By creating *Hamlet*, by giving it representation, Shakespeare, unlike his hero, managed to lift the dissociation between his masculine and feminine elements and to reconcile himself with the femininity in himself. (Green, 1982, p. 256)

The reading comes from Winnicott's paper 'Creativity and its Origins' (Winnicott, 1971), which ends with a discussion of Shakespeare's play. It is a fully psychological reading of the author, but its interest once again lies in the way that femininity moves and slips across the different levels of the text and the analytic process – the enigma and source of the analysis as of the play. More clearly and explicitly for Winnicott than for the other writers discussed so far, it is aesthetic space itself that is conceptualized in terms of sexual difference and the place of femininity within that. Creativity *per se* (the creativity in all of us, so this is not just the creativity of the artist) arises for Winnicott out of a femininity which is that primordial space of being which is created by the mother alone. It is a state of being which is not yet a relationship to the object because there is as yet no self, and it is, as Green defines it, 'au delà de la représentation', the other side of representation, before the coming of the sign (this comes very close to French feminists such as Luce Irigaray on femininity and language).[4] But it is worth noting how the woman appears at the point either where language and aesthetic form start to crumble or else where they have not yet come to be. 'Masculinity does, femininity is' is Winnicott's definition. It took a sceptical analyst in the audience when Winnicott first presented the paper to point to its fully literary and mythical origin; it transpires that Winnicott had been reading Robert Graves's 'Man does, woman is', but the observation from the floor was not included when Winnicott's famous paper was subsequently published in his book (Winnicott, 1971, 1972).[5]

Winnicott's definition, like Green's, and like that of Eliot before them, once again starts to look like a repetition (one might ask what other form of analysis can there be?) which reproduces or repeats the fundamental drama of *Hamlet*, cleaving the image of femininity in two, splitting it between a degradation and an idealization which, far from keeping each other under control (as Green suggests), set each other off, being the reverse sides of one and the same mystification. And like Eliot, Green also gets caught in the other face of the idealization, the inevitable accusation of Gertrude: 'Is the marriage of Gertrude consequence or cause of the murder of Hamlet's father? I incline towards the cause [Je pencherai pour la cause]' (p. 61); and at the end of his book he takes off on a truly wild speculation which makes Gertrude the stake in the battle between the old

Fortinbras and the old Hamlet before the start of the play.

But the fact that *Hamlet* constantly unleashes an anxiety which returns to the question of femininity tells us above all something about the relationship of aesthetic form and sexual difference, about the fantasies they share – fantasies of coherence and identity in which the woman appears repeatedly as both wager and threat. 'Fantasy in its very perversity' (Lacan, 1959, p. 14) is the object of psychoanalytic inter-pretation, but this does not mean that psychoanalysis might not also repeat within its own discourse the fantasies, or even perversions, which it uncovers in other forms of speech.

In Lacan's own essay on *Hamlet* (1959), he puts himself resolutely on the side of the symbolic, reading the play in terms of its dearth of proper mourning and the impossibility for Hamlet of responding to the too-literal summons of the dead father who would otherwise represent for the hero the point of entry into his appropriate symbolic place (the proximity between this essay and Eliot's 'Tradition and the Individual Talent' is truly striking). Lacan therefore places the problem of the play in the symbolic, on the side of the father, we might say; Green in the 'before' of representation, where the mother simply *is*. The difference between them is also another repetition, for it is the difference between the law of the father and the body of the mother, between symbol and affect (one of Green's best-known books in France was an account of the concept of 'affect' in Freud and a critique of Lacan's central premiss that psychic life is regulated by the exigencies of representation and the linguistic sign [Green, 1973]. But it is a difference with more far-reaching implications, which link back to the question of the fantasy of the woman and her guilt with which this essay began. For the concentration on the mother, on her adequacies and inadequacies, was the development in psychoanalytic theory itself which Lacan wanted to redress, precisely because, like *Hamlet*, it makes the mother cause of all good and evil, and her failings responsible for a malaise in all human subjects, that is, in men *and* in women, which stems from their position in the symbolic order of culture itself. The problem of the regulation of subjectivity, of the Oedipal drama and the ordering of language and literary form – the necessity of that regulation and its constant difficulty or failing – is not, to put it at its most simple, the woman's fault.

Finally, therefore, a question remains, one which can be put to André Green when he says that Shakespeare saved his sanity by projecting this crazed repudiation of the feminine on to the stage, using his art to give it 'an acceptable form' (p. 256). To whom is this acceptable? Or rather, what does it mean to us that one of the most elevated and generally esteemed works of our Western literary tradition should enact such a negative representation of femininity, or even such a violent repudiation of the femininity in man? I say 'esteemed' because it is of course the case that Eliot's critique has inflated rather than reduced *Hamlet*'s status. In 'Tradition and the Individual Talent', Eliot says the poet must 'know' the mind of Europe (p. 39); *Hamlet* has more than once been taken as the model for that mind. Western tradition, the mind of Europe, Hamlet himself, each one the symbol of a cultural order in which the woman is given too much and too little of a place. But it is perhaps not finally inappropriate that those who celebrate or seek to uphold that order, with no regard to the image of the woman it encodes, constantly find themselves up against a problem which they call femininity – a reminder of the precarious nature of the certainties on which that order rests.

Notes

1. This essay is based on a talk originally given to the Pembroke Center for Teaching and Research on Women, Brown University; a different version appeared as 'Sexuality in the Reading of Shakespeare: *Hamlet* and *Measure for Measure*', in *Alternative Shakespeares*, edited by John Drakakis (Methuen, 1985). The version published here will be included in a forthcoming collection of articles, *Sexuality in the Field of Vision*, Jacqueline Rose (New Left Books/Verso, 1986).

2. The concept of femininity in relation to Hamlet's character appears again in French, 1982, p. 149; and in Leverenz, 1980.

3. In *Hamlet et HAMLET* (1982), André Green continues the work he began in *Un Oeil en trop (the Tragic Effect)* (1969) on the psychoanalytic concept of representation in relation to dramatic form, and argues that while the explicit themes of *Hamlet* (incest, parricide, madness) have the clearest links with the concerns of psychoanalysis, the play's central preoccupation with theatrical space and performance also falls within the psychoanalytic domain through the concept of psychic representation and fantasy. Green examines the way that theatricality, or show, and femininity are constantly assimilated throughout the play (I.ii.76 ff., II.ii.581 ff., III.i.50 ff.). In the remarks which follow, I concentrate on the concept of femininity which he sets against this negative assimilation in his final section on Shakespeare's creative art (pp. 25–62).

4. See especially Irigaray, 1974, 1977; Montrelay, 1970.

5. Winnicott first presented this paper to the British Psycho-Analytic Society in 1966 under the title 'Split-off Male and Female Elements Found Clinically in Men and Women: Theoretical Inferences' (Winnicott, 1972). It was then included in *Playing and Reality* (Winnicott, 1971). The discussion of sexual difference in the paper as a whole is far more complex and interesting than the final descent (ascent) into mythology which is addressed here, although it is this concept of femininity, with its associated emphasis on mothering, which has recently been imported directly into psychoanalytic readings of Shakespeare (see especially Leverenz, 1980, and the whole anthology in which the article appears, Schwartz and Kahn, 1980).

References

Barthes, Roland (1970) *S/Z* (Paris: Seuil), trans. Richard Miller, *S/Z* (New York: Hill & Wang, 1974).
——— (1971) 'La mythologie aujourd'hui', *Esprit* (April 1971); trans. Stephen Heath,

'Change the Object Itself', in *Image, Music, Text* (London: Fontana, 1977), pp. 165–9.

Eliot, T.S. (1975), *Selected Prose of T.S. Eliot*, ed. Frank Kermode (London: Faber, 1975).

Florio, John (1603) *The Essays of Michael, Lord of Montaigne* (London and New York: Routledge & Sons, 1885).

French, Marilyn (1982) *Shakespeare's Division of Experience* (London: Jonathan Cape).

Freud, Sigmund (1887–1902) *The Origins of Psychoanalysis*, letters to Wilhelm Fliess, Drafts and Notes, ed. Marie Bonaparte, Anna Freud and Ernst Kris (London: Imago, 1954).

—— (1900) *The Interpretation of Dreams. The Standard Edition of the Complete Psychological Works (S.E.)* IV–V (London: Hogarth); Pelican Freud 4.

—— (1910) 'Leonardo da Vinci and a Memory of His Childhood', *S.E.*, XI, pp. 57–137.

—— (1917) (1915) 'Mourning and Melancholia', *S.E.* XIV, pp. 237–58; Pelican Freud 2.

—— (1924) 'The Dissolution of the Oedipus Complex', *S.E.* XIX, pp. 173–9; Pelican Freud 7, pp. 313–22.

—— (1925) 'Some Psychical Consequences of the Anatomical Distinction between the Sexes', *S.E.*, XIX, pp. 243–58; Pelican Freud 7, pp. 323–43.

—— (1931) 'Female Sexuality', *S.E.* XXI, pp. 223–43; Pelican Freud 7, pp. 367–92.

—— (1933) (1932) The Dissection of the Psychical Personality', *New Introductory Lectures, S.E.* XXII, pp. 57–80; Pelican Freud 2, pp. 88–112.

—— (1942) (1905 or 1906) 'Psychopathic Characters on the Stage', *S.E.* VII, pp. 303–10.

Green, André (1969) *Un Oeil en trop* (Paris: Minuit); trans. Alan Sheridan, *The Tragic Effect: Oedipus Complex and Tragedy* (Cambridge University Press, 1979).

—— (1973) *Le discours vivant, le concept psychanalytique de l'affect* (Paris: Presses Universitaires de France).

—— (1982) *Hamlet et HAMLET, une interprétation psychanalytique de la représentation* (Paris: Balland).

Irigary, Luce (1974) *Speculum de l'autre femme* (Paris: Minuit); trans. Gillian C. Gill, *Speculum of the Other Woman* (Ithaca, NY: Cornell University Press, 1985).

—— (1977) 'Women's Exile: An Interview with Luce Irigaray', *Ideology and Consciousness* 1: 24–39.

Jones, Ernest (1949), *Hamlet and Oedipus* (New York: Norton, Anchor edn, 1954).

Kristeva, Julia (1974) *La révolution du langage poétique* (Paris: Seuil).

—— (1980) *Desire in Language, A Semiotic Approach to Literature and Art*, ed. Leon S. Roudiez trans. Thomas Gora, Alice Jardine and Leon S. Roudiez, (Oxford: Blackwell).

Lacan, Lacques (1957) 'L'instance de la lettre dans l'inconscient ou la raison depuis Freud in *Ecrits* (Paris: Seuil, 1966), pp. 493–528; trans. Alan Sheridan, 'The Agency of the Letter in the Unconscious', in *Ecrits, a Selection* (London: Tavistock, 1977), pp. 146–78.

—— (1957–8) 'Les formations de l'inconscient', *Bulletin de Psychologie* II: 1–15.

—— (1958) 'Propos directifs pour un Congrès sur la sexualité féminine', in *Ecrits* (Paris: Seuil, 1966), pp. 725–36; trans. Jacqueline Rose, 'Guiding Remarks for a Congress on Feminine Sexuality', in Juliet Mitchell and Jacqueline Rose, eds, *Feminine Sexuality: Jacques Lacan and the école freudienne* (London: Macmillan, 1982), pp. 86–98.

—— (1959) 'Desire and the Interpretation of Desire in *Hamlet*', in Shoshana Felman, ed., *Literature and Psychoanalysis, The Question of Reading: Otherwise*, Yale French Studies 55/56, 1977, pp. 11–52.

—— (1975) 'Séminaire du 21 January 1975', *Ornicar?* 3, 1975: 104–10: trans. in *Feminine Sexuality*, pp. 162–71.

Lerner, Laurence (1963) *Shakespeare's Tragedies, an Anthology of Modern Criticism* (Harmondsworth: Penguin).

Leverenz, David (1980) 'The Woman in *Hamlet*: An Interpersonal View', in Murray M. Schwarz and Coppélia Kahn, eds, *Representing Shakespeare: New Psychoanalytic Essays* (Baltimore, MD and London: Johns Hopkins University Press).

Montrelay, Michele (1970) 'Recherches sur la féminine', *Critique* 26: 654–74; revised 'Inquiry into Femininity', trans. and introduced by Parveen Adams, *m/f* 1: 65–101.

Schwartz, Murray M. and Coppélia Kahn (1980) *Representing Shakespeare, New Psychoanalytic Essays* (Baltimore, MD and London: Johns Hopkins University Press).

Shakespeare, William (1877) *Hamlet*, Variorum Edition, ed. H.H. Furness, 15th edn (Philadelphia, PA: Lippincott).

—— (1882) *Hamlet*, Arden Edition, ed. H. Jenkins (London: Methuen).

Winnicott, D.W. (1972) (1966) 'Split-off Male and Female Elements Found Clinically in Men and Women: Theoretical Inferences', *Psychoanalytic Forum* 4, J. Linden, ed. (New York: International University Press).

—— (1971) *Playing and Reality* (London: Tavistock).

7

Jewels, Statues, and Corpses: Containment of Female Erotic Power in Shakespeare's Plays

Valerie Traub

In recent years many feminist, psychoanalytic and New Historical critics have exposed the existence and analysed the possible meanings of a masculine anxiety towards female power in Shakespeare's plays. Although they approach the problem from different orientations, together these critics have created a body of criticism that analyses the psychological motivations and historical contexts for such fear. Violence against women in Shakespeare's tragedies, says Madelon Gohlke, obscures 'deeper patterns of conflict in which women as lovers, and perhaps more importantly as mothers, are perceived as radically untrustworthy'.[1] Murray Schwartz analyses 'Shakespeare's recurrent preoccupation with betrayal and with feminine powers to create and destroy *suddenly*, and ... the repeated desire of [Shakespeare's] male characters both to be that all-powerful woman and to control the means of nurturance themselves'.[2] Janet Adelman psychoanalyses this fear of maternal power by focusing on the pre-Oedipal relation of mother and son, and also examines the threat women pose to male bonding and masculine identity.[3] Edward Snow explores the workings of sexual repression in *Othello* which culminate in a 'repetition and undoing' of sexual consummation.[4] Stephen Greenblatt argues that such repression and anxiety stem from a Renaissance Christian ethic which posits even marital sexuality as sinful.[5] And, more recently, Carol Cook reveals how the plays expose, yet paradoxically mask, 'mechanisms of masculine power' that work to defend against the powers men ascribe to women.[6]

Through close attention to language, metaphor and symbol,[7] these critics not only persuasively demonstrate that masculine anxieties towards female power are, indeed, expressed in the plays, they also analyse the psychosexual and political dynamics within male–female relationships that produce such fears. In general, these analyses attempt to negotiate between the historical fact of women's oppression and the psychological power accredited to women by men. Asserting that a certain mobility and mutability of power characterize gender relationships both within the plays and in Elizabethan social life, these critics view women neither as wholly *victims* of patriarchal relations nor as the *cause* of male sexual anxieties. Political and social constraints are imposed, at least in part, because men credit women with enormous emotional power; this, however, in no way denies the material oppression of Renaissance women.

This essay derives from, and is indebted to, the work of these critics. Their insights into the threat posed by female autonomy, maternal power, and sexuality provide a point of departure for my own study of the specifically erotic component of masculine anxieties about women. I draw heavily from the work of four critics (Snow, Greenblatt, Cook and Schwartz), offering as my contribution an analysis of the progression of a particular dramatic strategy. As my title suggests, I argue that in certain plays – namely *Hamlet* (1600–01), *Othello* (1604) and *The Winter's Tale* (1610–11) – male anxiety towards female erotic power is channelled into a strategy of containment. Through this strategy, the threat of female erotic power is psychically contained by means of a metaphoric and dramatic transformation of women into jewels, statues and corpses.

It is by now a commonplace that Shakespeare was preoccupied with the uncontrollability of women's sexuality; witness the many plots concerning the need to prove female chastity, the threat of adultery, and, even when female fidelity is not a major theme of the play, the many references to cuckoldry in songs, jokes, and passing remarks. As Cook points out in her essay on *Much Ado about Nothing*, references to cuckoldry stem from men's anxiety, their shared 'sense of vulnerability because they have only a woman's word for the paternity of their children'.[8] But Cook's analysis also emphasizes that through cuckold jokes, the male prerogative of power in language is restored; through the vilification of women upon which cuckold jokes depend, feminine presence is reduced to silence and absence.[9]

This masculine imposition of silence, and more particularly of stasis, on women is connected, I believe, with a fear of chaos associated with the sexual act. Hamlet, Othello and Leontes all express a longing for stasis, for a reprieve from the excitations and anxieties of erotic life; and, in response to their fear that such security and calm are not forthcoming, they metaphorically displace their own desire for stasis on to the women with whom they are most intimate. The result: the fetishization of the dead, virginal Ophelia, the sexualized death of Desdemona, and the transformation of Hermione into a living but static form, a statue.[10]

I am not, of course, suggesting literal causes of female characters' deaths but, rather, metaphoric displacements which take various forms according to the requirements of genre; the specific strategy of objectification is modified as Shakespeare's art uncovers, releases, and then reorganizes masculine anxieties into new modes of expression. According to Joel Fineman: 'plays are not only a means of representative expression but as such constitute strategies of psychological defense, defending, that is, against the very fantasies they represent'.[11] My attempt, then, is *not* to explicate *Hamlet*, *Othello*, or *The Winter's Tale* but, rather, to analyse the multiple deployments of a recurring anxiety and the means by which the playwright and his characters exorcize or assuage it.

I

In *Hamlet*, Gertrude's adultery and incest – the uncontrollability, in short, of her sexuality – are, in Hamlet's mind, projected outward to encompass the potential of such contamination in all liaisons between men and women. Gertrude's adultery turns all women into prostitutes and all men into potential cuckolds.[12] Hamlet's entire world is contracted into 'an unweeded garden / That's grown to seed, things rank and gross in nature / Possess it merely'.[13] In this vile yet seductive garden, sexually threatening women poison vulnerable and unwitting men. Thus, women, through their erotic power, adjudicate life and death – a connection nicely summed up by the 'Mousetrap' player who reads the speech inserted by Hamlet in the play performed to 'catch the conscience of the King': 'A second time I kill my husband dead, / When second husband kisses me in bed' (II.ii.605; III.ii.184–5).

The threat posed by Gertrude's sexuality is paranoiacally projected on to Ophelia, whom Hamlet exhorts: 'Get thee to a nunn'ry, why wouldst thou be a breeder of sinners? ... I could accuse me of such things that it were better my mother had not borne me' (III.i.120–23). As the culmination of this speech makes clear, those 'things' of which Hamlet could accuse himself are less the pride, ambition and knavery that he mentions than his suspicion that he, like his father before him, will be cuckolded: 'Get thee to a nunn'ry, farewell. Or if thou wilt needs marry, marry a fool, for wise men know well enough what monsters you make of them' (III.i.136–9). As the pun on nunnery and brothel makes clear, Hamlet is not concerned with Ophelia's ability to contaminate other men; trapped as he is within the boundaries of the Oedipal relation, Hamlet's paranoia extends only to himself and his beloved father.[14] And women make men into monsters, the Elizabethan euphemism for cuckolds, because they deceive. Hamlet rages:

> I have heard of your paintings, well enough. God hath given you one face, and you make yourselves another. You jig and amble, and you lisp, you

nickname God's creatures and make your wantonness your ignorance.
Go to, I'll no more on't, it hath made me mad. I say we will have no moe
marriage.

(III.i.141–7)

No more marriage because all marriage is madness and whoredom –
degrading to both parties, but especially to the man, who never knows who
else has slept between his sheets. And not only is marriage likened to
whoredom, but Hamlet himself becomes a whore as he, unable to carry out
the revenge thrust upon him by his father's Ghost, 'Must like a whore
unpack [his] heart with words / And fall a-cursing like a very drab, / A
stallion' [male prostitute] (II.iii.585–7).

However potent Hamlet's fear of cuckoldry, one senses something else
behind his vituperation of Ophelia: an anxiety associated with the sexual
act itself. The language with which Hamlet describes sexuality is riddled
throughout with metaphors of contagion and disease; his mother's hidden
adultery and incest are imagined as an 'ulcerous place' that 'infects
unseen' (III.iv.147–9). For Hamlet, who early asks, 'And shall I couple
hell?' II.v.93) – the phraseology of which suggests the possibility of
coupling *with* hell – *all* sex is unnatural.

Hamlet's sexual nausea finds its antecedent in his father's Ghost, who
characterizes Gertrude thus: 'But virtue, as it never will be moved, /
Though lewdness court it in a shape of heaven / So lust, though to a radiant
angel link'd, / Will sate itself in a celestial bed / And prey on garbage'
(I.v.53–7).[15] Here the sexually dualistic ideology that divides women into
lustful whores and radiant angels collapses upon itself, revealing the fear
upon which it is based: women are imagined as either angels or whores as
a psychological defence against the uncomfortable suspicion that underneath, the angel *is* a whore. The collapse of this defensive structure
unleashes precisely the masculine aggression it was originally built to
contain. Even the Ghost's ostensible protection of Gertrude from Hamlet's
wrath is sexually sadistic: 'Taint not thy mind, nor let thy soul contrive /
Against thy mother aught. Leave her to heaven, / And to those thorns that
in her bosom lodge / To prick and sting her' (I.v.85–8). Gertrude's
conscience is imagined as an aggressive phallus, pricking and stinging her
female breasts, in a repossession, replication, and reprojection of the action
that simultaneously effeminized King Hamlet, and deprived him of his life
and wife: 'The serpent that did sting they father's life / Now wears his
crown' (I.v.38–9), crown symbolizing both his kingship and his wife's
genitalia.

Identified as Hamlet is with his father, it is small wonder that Ophelia
merges, in his mind, with Gertrude, and that violence towards both women
becomes his only recourse. Although Hamlet's violence remains verbal

rather than physical, Ophelia's death is as much an outcome of his rage as it is an expression of her grief, madness, or self-destruction.[16] Since she is killed off before she can deceive or defile Hamlet, it is clear that only in death can Ophelia-as-whore regain the other half of her dichotomized being: chaste virgin. Contaminated in life by the taint of Gertrude's adultery, Ophelia reclaims sexual desirability only as a dead, but perpetual, virgin.

In our first view of Ophelia, Laertes warns his sister of the unlikelihood of Hamlet's fulfilling her expectations of betrothal:

> Then weigh what loss your honor may sustain
> If with too credent ear you list his songs,
> Or lose your heart, or your chaste treasure open
> To his unmast'red importunity.
> Fear it, Ophelia, fear it, my dear sister,
> And keep you in the rear of your affection,
> Out of the shot and danger of desire.
> The chariest maid is prodigal enough
> If she unmask her beauty to the moon.
> Virtue itself scapes not calumnious strokes.
> The canker galls the infants of the spring
> Too oft before their buttons be disclos'd,
> And in the morn and liquid dew of youth
> Contagious blastments are most imminent.
>
> (I.iii.29–42)

As imagined by Laertes, Ophelia's genitalia are a 'chaste treasure', a 'button', that must be clasped shut against the 'unmast'red importunity', the 'contagious blastments', the 'shot and danger' of masculine desire. Laertes's language interweaves Hamlet's equation of sexuality and disease (canker, contagion) with his own view of sexuality as masculine aggression (importunity, shot and danger, strokes, blastments). Ophelia's reply, "Tis in my memory lock'd, / And you yourself shall keep the key of it' (I.iii.85–6), suggests not only that Laertes's advice is 'lock'd' in her memory, but also that Laertes alone possesses the key to her properly immured 'chaste treasure'.

As if to underscore the importance of Laertes's warning, in the next scene Ophelia is interrogated by Polonius, who is similarly concerned with the status of his daughter's chastity. His accusation 'you yourself / Have of your audience been most free and bounteous' (I.iii.93–4) links Ophelia's personhood (her audience) with the sign of her femaleness (her genitalia) through the reiteration of Laertes's metaphors of closed and open space. To be 'free and bounteous' with one's person is to risk opening one's 'chaste treasure'. When Claudius later asks Polonius to repeat the advice he gave to Ophelia regarding Hamlet's advances, Polonius replies: 'That she should lock herself from his resort' (II.ii.143). The message of father and son is clear: the proper female sexuality is closed, contained, 'lock'd'.[17]

In the graveyard scene – the last scene in which her presence is required – Ophelia's dead, virginal body is fetishized by Hamlet and Laertes alike. As Ophelia's funeral procession reaches her newly dug grave, Laertes exclaims: 'Lay her i' th' earth, / And from her fair and unpolluted flesh / May violets spring!' (V.i.239–40). Soon thereafter he leaps on top of her casket: 'Hold off the earth a while, / Till I have caught her once more in mine arms' (V.i.249–50). Such passion, of course, incites Hamlet to claim his place as chief mourner: 'Dost thou come here to whine? / To outface me with leaping in her grave?' (V.i.277–8).

Critics largely focus on the grave as a site of masculine competition, neglecting to mention that Ophelia's grave becomes the only 'bed' upon which Hamlet is able to express his sexual desire.[18] And yet, it is neither the right to mourn Ophelia, nor the right to enjoy her sexual body (that is, her dynamic, self-expressive sexuality), that is actually being contested; rather, Laertes and Hamlet fight over the right to appropriate Ophelia's chastity. Fetishized to the extent that it is utterly divorced from the rest of her being, Ophelia's chastity embodies, as it were, a masculine fantasy of a 'female essence' wonderfully devoid of that which makes women so problematic: change, movement, inconstancy, unpredictability – in short, life. The conflict between Hamlet and Laertes is over the right (and rite) of sexual possession, and occurs only after Ophelia's transformation into a fully possessible object. The earlier punning of the gravedigger seems eerily premonitory as he responds to Hamlet's query regarding who is to be buried in the newly turned grave: 'One that was a woman, but, rest her soul, she's dead' (V.i.135). No longer a woman, Ophelia is no longer likely to incite sexual anxiety; she is, however, a likely object to figure in sexual fantasies of masculine prowess. In addition to masculine competition, then, the conflict between Hamlet and Laertes suggests an underlying necrophiliac fantasy. As a sexualized yet chaste corpse, Ophelia not only signifies the connection between sexuality and death previously explored in *Romeo and Juliet*, but also suggests that sexuality is finally safely engaged in only with the dead. Earlier, Hamlet spoke of his own death as 'a consummation / Devoutly to be wish'd' (III.i.62–3), narcissistically linking his own death with sexual intercourse, and imagining both as the perfection of his desire.[19] Here, the fear shared by Hamlet and Laertes of a dynamic, expressive female sexuality culminates in the imposition of stasis on that which threatens to bring sexual (and for Hamlet, metaphysical) chaos, and in the desire, having acquired a fully immobile object, to possess her fully.

In *Othello*, as both Greenblatt and Snow brilliantly argue, the need to suppress the anxieties that female sexuality engenders is tragically manipulated into the murder of the woman who elicits these anxieties. As critics have noted, Othello is both emotionally vulnerable to Desdemona and ambivalent about women in general,[20] and it is precisely because his anxieties are multivalent and mutually reinforcing that Othello is susceptible to Iago's seduction. Like Brabantio's premonition of Desdemona's elopement – 'This accident is not unlike my dream, / Belief of it oppresses me already' (I.i.142–3) – and Hamlet's suspicion of Gertrude's crimes – 'O, my prophetic soul!' (I.v.40) – Othello's belief in woman's power of deception lies just under the surface of his idolization. Othello himself exclaims in reaction to Iago's intimations: 'Think my lord! By heaven, *he echoes me*, / As if there were some monster in his thought / Too hideous to be shown' (III.iii.94–6; emphasis mine), suggesting that Iago echoes not merely Othello's words, but his thoughts. Indeed, having betrayed her father, Desdemona is suspect to all men except the similarly manipulated Cassio. Warns Brabantio: 'Look to her, Moor, if thou hast eyes to see: / She has deceived her father and may thee' (I.iii.292–3). And Iago voices the same refrain: 'She did deceive her father, marrying you' (III.iii.210).

That a woman may 'seem' to be one thing and yet 'be' another comes to signify, in the masculine mind of *Othello*, woman's very existence. Whereas usually women are presumed to be either virgins or whores, in *Othello* the split within each woman between 'seeming' and 'being' suggests that women are simultaneously 'seeming' to be virgins and 'being' actual whores. In *Hamlet*, we have seen that the breakdown of the carefully contrived sexual dichotomy (wherein virgin and whore are mutually exclusive terms) unleashes Hamlet's aggression towards Gertrude and Ophelia. Importantly, however, Hamlet's suspicions never obtain the status of existential Truth; they never assume irrevocable judgement. Gertrude, though an adulteress, may be redeemed if she avoids the marriage bed. And Ophelia's madness and death rectify her virginity, as Laertes testifies: 'Lay her i' th' earth / And from her fair and unpolluted flesh / May violets spring! I tell thee, churlish priest, / A minist'ring angel shall my sister be / When thou liest howling' (V.i.238–41).

The price of such redemption, however, is a complete capitulation to masculine terms as well as the resurrection of the faulty structure of sexual dualism. Hamlet explicitly instructs his mother to re-form her being in the shape of a virgin:

> *Hamlet*:   Confess yourself to heaven,
> Repent what's past, avoid what is to come,
> And do not spread compost on the weeds
> To make them ranker. . . .
> *Queen*:   O Hamlet, thou hast cleft my heart in twain.
> *Hamlet*:   O throw away the worser part of it,

And live the purer with the other half.
Goodnight, but go not to my uncle's bed
Assume a virtue if you have it not.

(III.iv.149–58)

In order to allay masculine suspicions and anxieties – in order not to 'be' a whore – Gertrude must throw away her 'worser' part, her sexuality, and assume married chastity, an appropriate response to Hamlet's call for 'no moe marriage'.

Such redemption, equivocal though it may be, is not offered in *Othello* because here suspicion quickly takes on the irrevocable status of Truth, and female deception becomes not a hideous impossibility but a damned certainty. Bemoans Othello: 'O curse of marriage, / That we can call these delicate creatures ours, / And not their appetites!' (III.iii.272–4). As the ambiguous syntax of the first line shows, marriage is not only cursed by women's sexual appetites and deception, marriage is itself a curse. Unlike Hamlet, for whom women's deception is cause for the abolition of marriage, for Othello women's inconstancy comes to signify the *very foundation* of the marriage relation, its source and hidden origin.

Paradoxically, the need to discipline women is both the 'cause' and the 'cure' that Shakespeare offers throughout *Othello*. To discipline an erring wife is entirely appropriate within the play's ethos. For Desdemona to have ventured beyond the bounds of patriarchal dictates would have been automatic evidence of guilt. Though her tarnished reputation is burnished by the end of the play, the play's ethos itself determines the impossibility of her innocence outside of that ethos. In one moment Desdemona is vindicated *and* reinserted securely within masculine control.[21]

In his confession to the Venetian senators – 'I do confess the vices of my blood' (I.ii.123) – Othello dismisses consummation as an aspect of his desire, declaring himself to be impotent:

Vouch with me, heaven, I therefore beg it not
To please the palate of my appetite;
Nor to comply with heat – the young affects
In me defunct – and proper satisfaction;
But to be free and bounteous to her mind.

(I.iii.261–5)

The halting measure of the first four lines contrasts sharply to the lyrical expansion of the final line, suggesting that sexual matters evoke in Othello an anxiety that is abated only by idealizing speeches that lift, as it were, sexuality from the earth and into the heavens that would 'vouch' for him. Prior to consummation, the image of a 'free and bounteous' Desdemona helps Othello to cerebralize and desexualize their relationship. Equally comforting is Brabantio's early description of his daughter: 'A maiden, never bold; / Of spirit so still and quiet that her motion / Blush'd at herself' (I.iii.94–6). After consummation, however, Desdemona's 'fruitfulness and liberal heart' are signs of a 'hot and moist' sexuality which must be 'sequester[ed] from liberty' (III.iv.38–40). At this point Othello shares with Hamlet, Laertes, Polonius and Brabantio the sense that women's sexuality should be locked up.

Desdemona's sexuality generates anxiety in Othello, suggest Greenblatt and Snow, largely because Othello unconsciously perceives his relation with Desdemona to be adulterous. For Snow, Othello's fear of adultery masks a more basic castration anxiety, a fear of 'thralldom to the demands of an unsatisfiable sexual appetite in woman', brought on by the consummation of his marriage.[22] Othello's murder of Desdemona, then, is a ritualistic effort to repeat and undo his own sexual complicity.

> Othello manages to have it both ways in [his] necrophiliac fantasy. This 'death' will quiet rather than arouse her, purify rather than pollute her. . . . 'Killing' Desdemona . . . is a way of extinguishing what threatens to turn her from a passive object of desire into an actively dangerous lover; at the same time it is a displaced means of killing the feelings that threaten to engulf his own inner being.[23]

For Greenblatt, Othello's guilt and anxiety stem from Iago's manipulation of the Christian doctrine of sexuality that posits even marital sexuality as sinful. Importantly, both Greenblatt and Snow argue that Othello's insecurity is merely the extreme expression of a common masculine anxiety: says Snow of Othello's internalized racial and sexual self-hatred, 'Othello's Moorishness merely forces him to live out with psychotic intensity the metaphors of self-contempt that every civilized white man can be brought to experience in his sexual relations with a woman'.[24]

Whereas I agree in essentials with both Greenblatt and Snow, I would emphasize that Othello's anxieties stem also from fear of the chaos he associates with the sexual act. As is perhaps befitting in a military officer who makes crucial decisions regarding war and peace, life and death, Othello's subjectivity is predicated upon an absolute dichotomy between chaos and stasis. He characterizes all relations – within himself and between self and other – by means of these terms. Othello associates romantic love with calm and 'content[ment]' and, as the following quote makes clear, the loss of that love with chaos: 'Excellent wretch! Perdition catch my soul / But I do love thee; and when I love thee not / Chaos is come again' (III.iii.91–3). However, throughout the play Othello also equates Desdemona's sexuality with chaos and violence. A disjuncture thus exists within Othello's psyche between romantic love (associated with stasis and calm) and sexuality (associated with chaos and violence). Such hostilities, brought to a head by his marriage, between the psychic structures necessary to his sense of self and those related to his sexuality must ultimately be reconciled if Othello is not to go mad. The means for such reintegration? Employing violence to achieve stasis.

The equation between Desdemona's sexuality and stormy violence is first forged by the unwitting victim. Before the Senate and her angry father, Desdemona frankly declares her prospective sexual union with Othello: 'That I did love the Moor to live with him, / My downright violence and storm of fortunes / May trumpet to the world' (I.iii.248–50).[25] The syntax of her speech equates her sexual desire to 'downright violence' that may be 'trumpeted' to the world by her 'storm of fortunes', as well as characterizes her sexuality as a 'storm of fortunes': a storm that may trumpet *itself* to the world – as Desdemona is doing at that moment.

Othello also likens Desdemona's sexuality to a storm, but to him the equation is far more troubling. After their first night together and upon their victorious reunion in Cyprus, Othello holds forth:

> It gives me wonder great as my content
> To see you here before me. O my soul's joy!
> If after every tempest come such calms,
> May the winds blow till they have waken'd death,
> And let the labouring bark climb hills of seas
> Olympus-high and duck again as low
> As hell's from heaven. If it were now to die,
> 'Twere now to be most happy; for I fear
> My soul hath her content so absolute
> That not another comfort like to this
> Succeeds in unknown fate. . . .
> I cannot speak enough of this content;
> It stops me here; it is too much of joy.
> And this, and this, the greatest discords be   [*They kiss*]
> That e'er our hearts shall make!
>
> (II.i.181–97)

Othello's 'content' is permeated throughout with a sense of dangers barely escaped, his longing for stasis more complex than a desire for land after a sea battle. Or, more precisely, for Othello the consummation of sexuality *is* a sea battle after which he is quite ready to die (pun intended) – but not to rise up again; rather, to escape the turbulence of future storms. For Othello, as was true of Hamlet, sexual gratification is linked to death; and his speech concludes with a conjunction of discord (violence) and sex. As Greenblatt states:

> The calmness Othello speaks of may express gratified desire, but, as the repeated invocation of death suggests, it may equally express the longing

for a final *release* from desire, from the dangerous violence, the sense of
extremes, the laborious climbing and falling out of control that is
experienced in the tempest.[26]

As in his earlier speech before the Senate, Othello's consciousness of
sexuality causes him to falter, to halt, so that he swallows his words just
when he asserts that he cannot refrain from speaking: 'I cannot speak
enough of this content; / It stops me here'.

Othello's 'content' does indeed stop him, for his desire for calm fixates
his gaze on that which threatens to disrupt his tranquillity, Desdemona's
sexuality. The myopia of that gaze works counter to its own best interest,
for Othello never again achieves a 'content so absolute': 'I had been happy
if the general camp, / Pioneers and all, had tasted her sweet body, / So I
had nothing known. O, now for ever / Farewell the tranquil mind! farewell
content!' (III.iii.349–52). As the ambiguous syntax suggests, as much as
Othello wishes he had remained ignorant of Desdemona's betrayal, he also
regrets having 'tasted her sweet body', a regret explicitly linked to his loss
of repose.

And having 'tasted her sweet body', Othello is, as Iago suggests, 'eaten
up with passion' (III.iii.395). The love that promised calm and repose
actually sparks sexual excitation and desire, and with it the fear of
complete chaos: 'Get me some poison, Iago – this night. I'll not
expostulate with her, lest her body and beauty unprovide my mind again
– this night, Iago' (IV.i.200–02). The only protection against 'unprovision'
is to project on to the loved one the tranquillity that she is supposed to (but
because of sexuality, fails to) create.[27] Paradoxically, that imposition of
stasis can be achieved only through violent means, imaginatively linked for
Othello with the tempestuous sea that he seeks to escape:

> Like to the Pontic sea,
> Whose icy current and compulsive course
> Ne'er feels retiring ebb, but keeps due on
> To the Propontic and the Hellespont;
> Even so my bloody thoughts, with violent pace,
> Shall ne'er look back, ne'er ebb to humble love,
> Till that a capable and wide revenge
> Swallow them up.
>
> (III.iii.456–64)

The imposition of calm on Desdemona is explicitly offered as a remedy
for the 'hot and moist' palms of her excessively sexual body (III.iv.39). Just
prior to the murder, Desdemona's moistness and heat are replaced in
Othello's imagination by the cool, dry, immobile image of 'monumental
alabaster' (V.ii.5).[28] Once dead, Desdemona is compared to 'another world /

Of one entire and perfect chrysolite' for which Othello would not have sold her, if only she had been true (V.ii.146–7). Having realized his error, Othello compares himself to a 'base Indian' who 'threw a pearl away / Richer than all his tribe' (V.ii.347–8). Despite the value such idealization appears to ascribe, the comparison of Desdemona to jewels is part of Othello's strategy for containing her erotic power.[29] By imaginatively transforming Desdemona into a jewel – hard, cold, static, silent, yet also adored and desired – Othello is able to maintain both his distance from and his idealization of her. By reducing a warm, living body to a static yet idealized object, he hopes to master the situation that threatens him, just as Hamlet defends against the image of Gertrude's incest by projecting Claudius as a 'cutpurse' who stole the queen, a 'precious diadem' (III.iv.99–100).

The equation of women and jewels, of course, predates *Othello*. Indeed, the poetic catalogue of feminine attributes is a standard Petrarchan convention. I would argue, however, that the equation of female body parts with precious gems – the body metaphorically revealed, undressed and dismembered through the poet-lover's voyeuristic gaze – is a crucial strategy in the attempt both to construct a modern masculine subjectivity and to exert control over a situation in which the poet-lover's power is limited and secondary. In the context of patriarchal discourse, every representation is an appropriation of power. In so far as masculine subjectivity is developed and asserted through conflict with a feminine 'Other', the poet-lover masters his lady by inscribing her in a text, constructing and dismembering her, part by body part.

This strategy of mastery is, I believe, operative in *Othello*. However, the intensely insecure and ambivalent Othello cannot wholly depend upon metaphorical objectification. Instead, he must fulfil the promise, only nascent in Petrarchanism, of fully containing the love-object. In Othello's defensive strategy, what is idealized becomes sacramentalized, and objectification finds its final expression as religious sacrifice. As Othello assumes the role of priest – invulnerable, omnipotent, and supremely justified – his strategies of idealization and objectification are conjoined and elevated in a powerful synthesis, sacramentalized murder.

'Peace, and be still' becomes the one cry of the increasingly urgent and obsessive Othello (V.ii.46), as he seeks to quiet the woman whose 'bold motion' is stilled, but only temporarily, in sleep. Kissing the slumbering Desdemona, Othello murmurs: 'One more, one more. / Be thus when thou art dead, and I will kill thee / And love thee after' (V.ii.17–19). Like Hamlet, who idealizes *and* sexualizes Ophelia's corpse, Othello may safely sexualize Desdemona only posthumously, after she is permanently immobilized and sacramentally elevated.

The anxieties of which *Othello* is a particularly vehement testament are to be found throughout the Shakespearean canon. Othello's strategies of containment, for example, form a part of the subplot of the earlier play, *Much Ado about Nothing* (1598–9). In fact, it is as if Shakespeare split the subplot of *Much Ado about Nothing* into two parts, and then followed each trajectory to its ultimate destination in *Othello* (1604) and *The Winter's Tale* (1610–11). The fraught courtship of Claudio and Hero is replicated in Othello's marriage to Desdemona, while Hero's semblance of death for restorative purposes is, even in the failure of its ritual resolution, reproduced in *The Winter's Tale*.[30] Like Othello, Claudio first idealizes the object of his affection, using similar metaphors – 'Can the world buy such a jewel?' (I.i.181) – and Claudio's readiness to suspect Hero's infidelity matches Othello's susceptibility to Iago's allegations. Like Ophelia and Desdemona, Hero is divided into virgin and whore, a 'Dian ... / As chaste as is the bud ere it be blown' and an 'intemperate Venus' or animal that 'rage[s] in savage sensuality' (IV.i.57–61). The flip side of Claudio's romantic idealism is his intense misogyny, and both stem from a fear of female erotic power.

The tragic brutality of *Othello*, however, seems to have operated as a kind of exorcism for the playwright. Although fear of women's sexual power dominates later plays, particularly *King Lear* (1605) and *Macbeth* (1606), never again are the strategies employed to combat those fears so vitriolic and vituperative – or so horrifyingly final. Rather, Lear and Macbeth are themselves victimized by the sexual power wielded by commanding and evil women. With *The Winter's Tale*, however, Shakespeare returns to his previous paradigm, as if in an effort to moderate both its ferocity and its efficacy.

Leontes, too, experiences Othello's anxiety about betrayal by a woman to whom he has become vulnerable; and he, too, commits Othello's error. But after suffering sufficiently, he is given another chance. According to most critics, this romance reintroduces the possibility of mutuality in the Shakespearean canon; and, in so far as the second generation is allowed to renegotiate the terms of heterosexual alliance, and generational continuity succeeds over filial rupture, *The Winter's Tale* does amend the tragic vision of *Hamlet* and *Othello*.[31] In addition, the communal vitality and playfulness of Bohemia, and Hermione's magical reappearance as a living statue, broaden the previously contracted and paranoid world of Leontes's Sicilia. However, to my mind, as much as such reformations relieve psychic stress, they do not resolve the primary conflict posed by the fear of woman's sexual betrayal. What is commonly accepted as the play's essential reparative act – Hermione's transformation, first into a statue and then into a woman – is inspired none the less by the threat Hermione's sexuality poses to Leontes.

The Winter's Tale retraces the pattern of sexual anxiety in *Hamlet* and

Othello. All the men in Leontes's court depend upon sexual dualism to mediate their relations with women. Polixenes's narration of the kings' shared boyhood ambivalently projects women as simultaneously sacred and sexually seductive. 'O my most sacred lady, / Temptations have since then been born to's; for / In those unfledg'd days was my wife a girl, / Your precious self had then not cross'd the eyes / Of my young playfellow' (I.ii.76–80). Underneath the idealized appellations is the unconsciously felt danger of the temptation. Leontes's ostensible compliment to Hermione in the story of their betrothal – 'Why, that was when / Three crabbed months had sour'd themselves to death, / Ere I could make thee open thy white hand, / And clap thyself my love' (I.ii.101–4) – replicates three of Hamlet's and Othello's most potent associations: the link between love and death, the image of women's sexuality as an opening, and the use of hands as an erotic emblem. Although here Hermione's open hand is a positive image, just a few lines later it becomes a prostitute's 'paddling palm'; and her 'free face' that derives a 'liberty / From heartiness' signifies whorish behaviour (I.ii.112–15).[32] As Leontes's metaphors make clear, Hermione's sexuality has become too open and 'too hot, too hot!' (I.ii.108).

In a reworking of Hamlet's and Othello's objectification of women, Leontes imagines Hermione as a 'medal, hanging about [Polixenes's] neck' (I.ii.307–8), a medal representing, even more explicitly than jewels, the power and prestige of the male. In a powerful reversal of Othello's moral absolutism – 'My life upon her faith!' (I.iii.295) – Leontes bases everything upon his fantasy of Hermione's infidelity: 'is this nothing? / Why then the world, and all that's in't, is nothing. / The covering sky is nothing. Bohemia nothing, / My wife is nothing, and nothing have these nothings, / If this be nothing' (I.ii.292–6). Paranoia and projection become the order of the day, as even Antigonus, in his ambivalent effort to defend the honour of his queen, projects Leontes's accusations on to his daughters:

> Be she honour-flaw'd,
> I have three daughters: the eldest is eleven;
> The second and the third, nine and some five:
> If this prove true, they'll pay for't. By mine honour
> I'll geld 'em all; fourteen they shall not see
> To bring false generations.

> (II.i.143–8)

In its explicit clarity, Antigonus's verbal violence invites a comparison to Leontes's increasingly vituperative, yet confused, sexual disgust:

> And many a man there is (even at this present,
> Now while I speak this) holds his wife by th'arm,
> That little thinks she has been sluic'd in's absence

And his pond fish'd by his next neighbour, by
Sir Smile, his neighbour: nay, there's comfort in't,
Whiles other men have gates, and those gates open'd
As mine, against their will.

                                                          (I.ii.192–8)

As Schwartz points out, Leontes not only rages against cuckoldry, but his ambiguous syntax suggests that he does so through a confused identification with the woman: 'The genital violation of the woman-as-property is equivalent to homosexual assault.'[33] Thus, both Hermione's and Leontes's 'gates' are 'open'd' in what must be for Leontes a doubly terrifying loss of sexual control.[34]

Regardless of the psychoanalytic cause of Leontes's anxiety, what is crucial is that Leontes psychically kills Hermione, as he ambivalently admits years after her 'death': 'She I kill'd! I did so: but thou strik'st me / Sorely, to say I did' (V.i.16–18). Confining Hermione to prison is not sufficient, only the fantasy of her death brings Leontes psychic calm: 'say that she were gone, / Given to the fire, a moiety of my rest / Might come to me again' (II.iii.6–9). Like Othello, Leontes imagines Hermione's death to be a sacrifice: 'Given to the fire', Hermione is an offering made in hopes of reconstituting his sacred feminine ideal.

In contrast to Ophelia and Desdemona, of course, Hermione is not literally killed, nor does Leontes himself turn her into a statue. Indeed, it is Paulina who, after Hermione faints at the news of her son's death, fabricates the fiction of her death; and she acts to help, not hinder, her beloved friend and queen. And Leontes quickly (almost too quickly?) repents: 'Apollo, pardon / My great profaneness 'gainst thine oracle! / I'll reconcile me to Polixenes, / New woo my queen' (III.ii.154–6). Why, then, is Hermione whisked off to seclusion? Why the sixteen-year delay in reconciliation? Why the seemingly superfluous, albeit spectacular, transformation of Hermione into a statue? Exigencies of plot, of course, require that time pass: Perdita and Florizel must meet, woo and marry, and Leontes must demonstrate devotion to his dead wife. For 'tyranny [to] / Tremble at patience' (III.ii.31–2), Hermione's patience must be given dramatic form. I would argue that, in addition, Leontes must experience a reprieve from the exigencies of sexual life before he can re-enter marriage with any degree of psychic comfort, and, most importantly, that Hermione's 'unmanageable' sexuality must be metaphorically contained and psychically disarmed.

Thus, the strategy of containment begun in the subplots of *Much Ado about Nothing* and *Hamlet*, and given its most extreme form in *Othello*, completes its progression in *The Winter's Tale*. Out of his own anxieties, Leontes creates the myth of Hermione's adultery, and the projection of

those anxieties leads to her metaphoric death. That death is reversed only
when another symbolic form of stasis and control is imposed: Hermione's
transformation into a statue. Hermione's 'dead likeness' (V.iii.15)
re-presents her living body through the illusion of preserved feminine
integrity. '[W]arm' but not hot (V.iii.109), Hermione is chastened (made
chaste), her erotic power severely curtailed. Upon her revivification,
Hermione is granted one speech of eight lines, and this speech a maternal
blessing and query directed towards her daughter. Her silence towards
Leontes bespeaks a submissiveness most unlike her previous animation.
Rather than being a victory for the wronged heroine, the final scene works
as wish fulfilment for Leontes, who not only regains his virtuous wife and
loses his burden of guilt, but also reassumes his kingly command of all
social relations, represented by his deft matchmaking and integration of the
two remaining isolated figures, Paulina and Camillo. This wish fulfilment
enables Leontes to come to terms with his specific anxieties *vis-à-vis*
Hermione's alleged adultery with Polixenes, but it does not substantially
alter the relation of Hermione to Leontes within the marriage structure. The
conflicts ostensibly resolved by the 'new marriage' still lurk in the
background, temporarily abated, but able to create instability at any time.
Had Hermione exceeded the bounds of patriarchal dictates, she never
would have been revivified. Cook's comments on *Much Ado about Nothing*
are equally true of *The Winter's Tale*: 'the play masks, as well as exposes,
the mechanisms of masculine power and ... in so far as it avoids what is
crucial to its conflicts, the explicitly offered comic [or romance] resolution
is something of an artful dodge'.[35]

II

Many feminist critics would argue that Leontes's repentance, Hermione's
forgiveness, and Paulina's unifying role illustrate a victory of feminine
over masculine values. Juliet Dusinberre, Marilyn French and Irene Dash
argue that because of such an assertion of 'feminine values', Shakespeare
can be appropriated to feminist ends.[36] Other feminists – for instance,
Madelon Gohlke – credit Shakespeare with expressing 'feminine values',
but at the same time charge him with participating in and thereby
perpetuating patriarchal gender distinctions.[37]
    The rejection of such a 'feminist Shakespeare' is most aptly argued by
Kathleen McLuskie and Carol Cook. Asserting the historical specificity of
the plays' 'narrative, poetic, and theatrical strategies', and the way that
these strategies position and manipulate the audience to understand the
play from a particular point of view, McLuskie argues that feminist
criticism must subvert rather than assimilate the 'patriarchal Bard'.[38]

Alternatively, Cook maintains that the phallogocentric bias of all patriarchal discourse, including Shakespeare's, precludes the possibility of
positive 'feminine values':

> The construction of femininity within an economy of representation
> governed by the phallus – a construction in which women mirror
> masculine identity by their own lack – obviates the possibility of
> 'feminine values' or of a feminine alternative to the 'predominately
> masculine ethos'. Alternatives cannot be generated from within the
> binary structures by which patriarchy figures gender.[39]

In other words, in so far as 'feminine values' exist, they are merely the
figuration of the reduced 'Other' of full, masculine presence.[40]

Although my conclusion is similar to that of McLuskie and Cook, I must
distinguish between our methods. McLuskie charges feminist psychoanalytic criticism with 'mimetic essentialism' – that is, with accepting a
mimetic model of the relation between ideas and drama, and believing in
an ahistorical, essential masculinity and femininity. I believe, however, that
a politicized and historically attuned psychoanalysis is a valuable tool for
exploring those anxieties and attitudes towards women which have
endured through time. Interestingly, the weakness in Cook's argument
seems to be precisely such ahistoricism. Cook's analysis poses patriarchy
as a monolithic, transhistorical entity that can be transformed only with the
destruction of phallogocentrism. I, however, see patriarchy as a profoundly
historical, hegemonic ideology, continually contested from without and
conflicted from within.[41] The risk of taking Cook's position is subscribing
to a certain brand of cultural determinism. However delimited and
inscribed by patriarchal codes our resistances, rebellions, and women's
movements and communities may be, their very existence argues that
alternatives can be generated from within 'the binary structures by which
patriarchy figures gender'.

I would like here to shift the critical emphasis away from the structural
oppositions that figure gender distinctions, and towards the psychological
anxieties generated by those structures. The cause of masculine fears may
lie in the pre-Oedipal bond between mother and son, and in the fact that
men's first and most intense dependency is upon their mothers, whom they
must renounce in favour of paternal identification.[42] The transformation of
such gender arrangements, as Nancy Chodorow's and Dorothy Dinnerstein's defences of gender-shared child-rearing argue, could significantly
alter definitions of maleness and femaleness, transform the masculine
ethos, *and* begin to deconstruct the binary structures of patriarchal
dominance.[43]

My analysis of the dramatic strategies of *Hamlet*, *Othello*, and *The
Winter's Tale* suggests to me the following hypothesis: the genres of

Shakespearean tragedy and, to a lesser extent, romance disallow the affirmation of 'femaleness',[44] precisely because the masculine anxieties upon which these genres are based circumscribe and delimit the entire dramatic action. With the arguable exception of Cleopatra's Egypt, within these genres we never step outside the masculine ethos.[45] Although Shakespeare may assert the necessity of nurturance, mutuality and relatedness, this in itself does little to offset the vilification of female erotic power. While dramatically exploring masculine anxieties, and even presenting the tragedy of masculinist values, Shakespeare none the less perpetuates defensive structures of dominance instituted by men. A reconciliation with any of the wronged heroines of *Hamlet, Othello* or *The Winter's Tale* is imaginable only *within* the territory of masculine prerogatives. Once dead, Ophelia becomes an angel, a status as imbued with masculine anxiety as was her previous degradation. Gertrude is granted the possibility of redemption, but only at the cost of her sexuality. Desdemona is declared innocent after death, but exists thereafter only as a jewel in the masculine imagination – the tragedy being less the murder of her innocence than the justification her guilt would have given to such violence. Hermione is reunited with her husband, but the anxieties that incited him to impose stasis upon her are still immanent – indeed, inherent – in their relationship. In so far as Shakespeare's theatre serves as a projective or transitional space in which to articulate and thereby assuage psychic concerns, the dramatization of *Hamlet, Othello*, and *The Winter's Tale* may act as a temporary exorcism of masculine anxieties. However, the metaphoric displacement of sexually threatening women into jewels, statues and corpses attests that these plays contain rather than affirm female erotic power.

The point – evident, I hope, by now – is not moral condemnation of male treatment of women in Shakespeare's plays, nor condemnation of the Bard himself. Such blanket judgements reduce the complexity of the social systems that constitute males and females as gendered sexual subjects. Masculine anxieties towards female erotic power (like feminine anxieties about masculine sexuality) find that source not in individual psyches only, nor only in vast social structures, but in the intersection and interplay of the two. By analysing the expression of sexual anxieties within Shakespearean drama, perhaps at this late date we can begin to exorcize them.

Notes

1. Madelon Gohlke, '"I wooed thee with my sword": Shakespeare's Tragic Paradigms', in *Representing Shakespeare*, ed. Murray M. Schwartz and Coppélia Kahn (Baltimore, MD: Johns Hopkins University Press, 1980), p. 180.

2. Murray M. Schwartz, 'Shakespeare through Contemporary Psychoanalysis', in

Representing Shakespeare, p. 29. See also Schwartz's articles: 'Leontes' Jealousy in *The Winter's Tale*', *American Imago* 30 (1973): 250–73; and '*The Winter's Tale*: Loss and Transformation', *American Imago* 32 (1975): 145–99.

3. Janet Adelman, '"Born of Woman": Fantasies of Maternal Power in *Macbeth*', in *Cannibals, Witches, and Divorce*, ed. Marjorie Garber (Baltimore, MD: Johns Hopkins University Press, 1987), pp. 90–121 and 'Male Bonding in Shakespeare's Comedies', in *Shakespeare's 'Rough Magic'*, ed. Coppélia Kahn and Peter Erickson (Newark: University of Delaware Press, 1985), pp. 73–103.

4. Edward Snow, 'Sexual Anxiety and the Male Order of Things in *Othello*', *English Literary Renaissance* 10 (1980): 384–412.

5. Stephen Greenblatt, *Renaissance Self-Fashioning* (Chicago: University of Chicago Press, 1980).

6. Carol Cook, '"The Sign and Semblance of Her Honor": Reading Gender Difference in *Much Ado about Nothing*', this volume, p. 75.

7. Snow, for example, explains his method in the following way: 'When we look for what resists dramatic foregrounding and listen for what language betrays about its speaker, then much of what is so emphatically declared and ostentatiously displayed in the world of [*Othello*] ... begins to take on the appearance of a neurotic defense symptomatic of the "cause" it exists to conceal' (pp. 387–8). Gohlke supports a psychoanalytic strategy of reading metaphor in feminist terms: 'A serious feminist critic ... cannot proceed very far without becoming paranoid unless she abandons a strictly intentionalist position. To argue sexism as a conscious conspiracy becomes both foolish and absurd. To pursue the implications of metaphor, on the other hand, in terms of plot, character, and possibly even genre, is to adopt a psychoanalytic strategy that deepens the context of feminist interpretation and reveals the possibility at least of a feminist psycho-history' (p. 170).

8. Cook, p. 77.

9. Cook agrees that cuckold jokes may be read psychoanalytically as castration anxiety, but points out that '"castration anxiety" is not so much an answer to the play's questions about gender difference as another formulation of them that requires some further explanation, for the phallus and its loss signify only within a larger structure of meanings' (p. 76). Cook's politicization of psychoanalysis and of the fears it is meant to address is, I think, crucial to an analysis of gender relations.

10. Cook associates such objectification of women with their role in language: 'It is the place of the woman to be the object, or referent, of language, a sign to be read and interpreted: silent herself, she becomes a cipher, the target of unconscious fantasies and fears, and is dangerously vulnerable to the representations and misrepresentations of men' (p. 80). Such an analysis suggests that woman's object-status occurs upon her entrance into language. Patriarchal language relations are always already there, and language thus operates as an a priori determinant. While it is valuable in that it poses the difficulty of operating within patriarchal discourse, to my mind this analysis ultimately closes off the possibility of women seizing and manipulating language and other gendered institutions.

11. Joel Fineman, 'Fratricide and Cuckoldry: Shakespeare's Doubles', in *Representing Shakespeare*, p. 73.

12. It also turns all *sons* into bastards. At least part of Hamlet's anxiety is about his own legitimacy.

13. *Hamlet* I.ii.135–7. All Shakespeare quotations are from *The Riverside Shakespeare*, ed. G. Blakemore Evans *et al.* (Boston, MA: Houghton Mifflin, 1974) and will be cited hereafter parenthetically in the text.

14. For analysis of Hamlet's Oedipal conflict, see Ernest Jones, *Hamlet and Oedipus* (Garden City, NY: Doubleday, 1954). I find the most persuasive evidence of Oedipal conflict in the ambiguous syntax of the following lines spoken by Hamlet: 'How stand I then, / That have a father kill'd, a mother stain'd' (IV.iv.56–7). Unlike Prince Hamlet, who is concerned almost exclusively with his own condition, the soldier Othello extends his paranoia into a concern for his brothers: 'Yet she must die, else she'll betray more men' (V.ii.6). Here, male bonding rather than masculine competition overshadows the heterosexual relation.

15. My interpretation depends on reading both 'lust' and 'radiant angel' as referring to Gertrude. '[R]adiant angel' is equally compelling as King Hamlet's self-characterization. I

suggest that the passage should be read both ways, as a fine example of Shakespeare's overdetermined use of language.

16. Gohlke also sees Hamlet as deflecting the violence he feels towards his mother on to Ophelia and, like me, sees Ophelia's madness and death as a direct outcome of his rage: 'It is not his mother whom Hamlet kills (Claudius takes care of that) but Ophelia. Only when she is dead, moreover, is he free to say clearly that he loved her' (p. 173). Gohlke, however, does not pursue the psychological implications of Hamlet's inability to love the living Ophelia.

17. Perhaps the image of a locked female sexuality is a holdover from the medieval chastity belt.

18. The grave in *Hamlet* is symbolically and geographically analogous to the marriage bed in *Othello*. A comparison of both the grave and marriage bed to the tomb of *Romeo and Juliet* extends the implications of each. The tomb is characterized by the friar as the earth's womb, to which all humankind must return (II.iii.9–12). The implication of all three plays is that women, because of their procreative capacities, are to be blamed for male mortality. Apparently, women grant less the gift of life than the curse of death: men are condemned to live only to die.

19. The OED defines 'consummation' as 'the completion of marriage by sexual intercourse' for as early as 1530. Other early meanings include (a) 'That act of completing, accomplishing, fulfilling, finishing, or ending', (b) 'Completion, conclusion, as an event or condition; end; *death*', (c) 'The action of perfecting; the condition of full and perfect development, *perfection*, acme', and (d) 'A condition in which desires, aims, and tendencies are fulfilled; crowning or fitting end; *goal*'. It seems to me that all of these definitions serve to expand the resonances of Hamlet's desire. (Emphasis added.)

20. See Gohlke, Greenblatt, and Snow.

21. Snow makes a similar point: 'Even Emilia's moving, ethically resonant assertion of Desdemona's chastity after the murder only makes it more difficult to bring into focus the pernicious effects of chastity itself, as a doctrine men impose upon women. That Othello turns out to have been mistaken merely lets the law itself off the hook' (pp. 386–7). He sums up: 'The tragedy of the play, then, is the inability of Desdemona to escape or triumph over restraints and Oedipal prohibitions that domesticate woman to the conventional male order of things' (p. 407).

22. Snow, p. 407.

23. Snow, p. 394.

24. Snow, p. 400.

25. Snow and Greenblatt both mention Desdemona's sexual frankness. (See Snow, p. 406). Whereas I agree with Greenblatt's psychological schema, the weight of his analysis comes perilously close to blaming the victim: 'Desdemona's frank acceptance of pleasure and submission to Othello's pleasure is, I would argue, as much as Iago's slander the cause of her death, for it awakens the deep current of sexual anxiety in Othello, anxiety that with Iago's help expresses itself in quite orthodox fashion as the perception of adultery' (p. 250).

26. Greenblatt, p. 243.

27. Gohlke also sees Othello's murder as 'a desperate attempt to control'. However, in place of Desdemona's erotic power, she posits Othello's fear of victimization, 'Desdemona's power to hurt', as the focus of Othello's anxiety. At any rate, in Gohlke's analysis of the plays, love is possible only through death: 'If murder may be a loving act, love may be a murdering act, and consummation of such a love is possible only through the death of both parties' (p. 175).

28. Greenblatt remarks that Othello turns 'Desdemona into a being incapable of pleasure, a piece of "monumental alabaster", so that he will at last be able to love her without the taint of adultery' (p. 251).

29. Making a similar point, Snow points out that Othello's 'apparent moment of insight and repentance perpetuates (and invites us to become complicit in) the definition of Desdemona as a valuable object, a private possession that was his either to keep or dispose of' (p. 386).

30. The bond between Hermione and Leontes is restored in much the way as is the bond between *Much Ado*'s Hero and Claudio. In both plays, the woman is hidden away, presumed

to be dead, and then re-offered in a ritual marriage ceremony; in both plays, the attempted rejuvenation of an emotional bond fails. As Cook points out, the friar hides Hero in order to motivate Claudio's repentance even 'though [Claudio] *thought his accusation true*' (p. 93). Yet, as with Leontes, Claudio's feelings change only after Hero's innocence has been re-established – and immediately his old, idealized image of woman replaces the tarnished one.

31. Most psychoanalytic interpretations of *The Winter's Tale* agree that it enacts a reparative vision. See, for instance, Richard Wheeler: '[T]he ending of *The Winter's Tale* is centered emotionally in the protagonist's recovery of lost relations of mutuality and trust. . . . Essential to the comic achievement that takes *The Winter's Tale* beyond the catastrophic world of tragedy is the movement towards a reciprocal, mutually creative relation between a vigorously rendered manhood and a comparably complete realization of essential womanly power' (Wheeler, '"Since first we were dissevered": Trust and Autonomy in Shakespearean Tragedy and Romance', in *Representing Shakespeare*, pp. 164–6). For Schwartz, 'the great work of [Shakespeare's later] drama ... was the reconstitution of symbolic (cultural) continuity after he had seen through his own defensive actions (false autonomy, untested idealization, hierarchy as enforced power) in the mature tragedies. I mean that he saw through these illusions in a double sense: he used them as ways of structuring motives (he saw by means of them), and he saw them through, exhausted their possibilities in love and aggression.... [T]he re-creation of masculine identity and cultural continuity in the romances depends on restored trust in feminine capacities *and* the restoration of paternal design of the relationships within which women exist' (Schwartz, 'Shakespeare through Contemporary Psychoanalysis', pp. 26, 30). Adelman points out that the marriage of Perdita and Florizel 'enacts in a safely displaced way the necessarily disrupted homosexual union of the parents', and she sees the restoration of Hermione in the context of the simultaneous recovery of Polixenes: '[H]omosexual and heterosexual bonds are ruptured and recovered together. Hermione can return only when the lost bond with Polixenes is recovered' ('Male Bonding', p. 92).

32. That hands are cathected with erotic energy is also evident as the angry Polixenes interrupts the young lovers, Florizel and Perdita, just when they clasp hands.

33. Schwartz, 'Leontes' Jealousy in *The Winter's Tale*', p. 267.

34. Interestingly enough, Polixenes repeats this image in his threat to Perdita: 'If ever henceforth thou / These rural latches to his entrance open, / Or hoop his body more with thy embraces, / I will devise a death as cruel for thee / As thou are tender to't' (IV.iv.438–42).

35. Cook, p. 76.

36. See Juliet Dusinberre, *Shakespeare and the Nature of Women* (New York: Barnes & Noble, 1975); Marilyn French, *Shakespeare's Division of Experience* (New York: Ballantine Books, 1981); and Irene Dash, *Wooing, Wedding, and Power: Women in Shakespeare's Plays* (New York: Columbia University Press, 1981).

37. '[W]hile Shakespeare may be said to affirm the values of feeling and vulnerability associated with femininity, he does not in dramatic terms dispel the anxiety surrounding the figure of the feminized male' (Gohlke, pp. 179–81).

38. Kathleen McLuskie, 'The Patriarchal Bard: Feminist Criticism and Shakespeare: *King Lear* and *Measure for Measure*', in *Political Shakespeare*, ed. Jonathan Dollimore and Alan Sinfield (Ithaca, NY: Cornell University Press, 1985), pp. 88–108.

39. Cook, p. 82. For explanations of the term 'phallogocentrism', see the work of Jacques Derrida, Jacques Lacan, Barbara Johnson, Shoshana Felman, and Gayatri Spivak. Briefly, the term refers to the central position of both phallus and logos in Western civilization, as well as their mutually reinforcing relation in determining Western concepts of presence, rationality, and value.

40. I could extrapolate from Cook's analysis the following denial of Paulina's role as spokeswoman for feminist concerns in *The Winter's Tale*: although she is an untiring advocate of Hermione's innocence, Paulina herself is inscribed by those patriarchal codes, represented by the Oracle (of manly honour, feminine chastity, religious piety and filial bonds), that Leontes rejects in his solipsistic assumption of supreme power. Paulina's defence of the identity of Hermione's child colludes with patriarchal imperatives:

Behold my lords,
Although the print be little, the whole matter
A copy of the father: eye, nose, lip;
The trick of's frown; his forehead nay, the valley,
The pretty dimples of his chin and cheek; his smiles;
The very mold and frame of hand, nail, finger.

(II.iii.97–102)

Paulina resists tyranny, yes; she does not, however, do so as a feminist. As the monarchal and personal state of Sicilia is reformed, Paulina is subsumed by patriarchal prerogatives as she is mechanically married off to Camillo, her masculine counterpart.

41. By referring to a force external to patriarchy, I am suggesting that various communities of women, particularly lesbian separatists, have successfully – if temporarily – disengaged themselves from patriarchal values and structures, including the material, emotional, sexual and spiritual.

42. In Snow's analysis of *Othello* and Schwartz's analysis of *The Winter's Tale*, male fantasies of maternal betrayal or engulfment are seen to be crucial determinants of misogyny. To base an argument on infant psychology need not open this interpretation to charges of transhistoricism, universalism or essentialism, because throughout history women have acted as primary nurturers of infants, whether as biological mothers or as hired or enslaved nurses.

43. See Nancy Chodorow, *The Reproduction of Mothering* (Berkeley: University of California Press, 1978); and Dorothy Dinnerstein, *The Mermaid and the Minotaur* (New York: Harper & Row, 1976)

44. I use 'femaleness' instead of 'femininity' in order to eschew traditional associations of what it means to be a gendered female. However, female*ness* also implies a kind of essentialism that I do not intend, since what it means to be female can be theorized only in the context of social inscriptions.

45. Cook, of course, would not see Cleopatra's Egypt as existing outside a masculine ethos. My own view is that in *Antony and Cleopatra* Shakespeare ambivalently dramatizes the conflict between masculine and feminine values. In addition, I would suggest that in *As You Like It* and, to a lesser degree, *Twelfth Night* Shakespeare temporarily upsets the masculinist world-view. The 'feminism' of these plays, however, is qualified, as each comic heroine is recalled from the 'green land' and, through marriage, reinserted into a restored patriarchal order. The critical question is whether the comic disruption of order serves as a method of containment, a psychic 'letting off of steam' which thereby conserves existing social hierarchies, or whether the release and resultant anarchy of manifold possibilities are subversive in effect, if not in intent.

8

Topical Ideology: Witches, Amazons, and Shakespeare's Joan of Arc[1]

Gabriele Bernhard Jackson

> Glory is like a circle in the water,
> Which never ceaseth to enlarge itself
> Till by broad spreading it disperse to nought.
> With Henry's death the English circle ends;
> Dispersed are the glories it included.
> *1 Henry VI* I.ii.133–7[2]

This wonderfully evocative description of the everything that is nothing, an exact emblem of the rise and disintegration, in Shakespeare's first tetralogy, of one new centre of power after another, is assigned to Joan of Arc, the character whom most critics agree in calling a coarse caricature, an exemplar of authorial chauvinism both national and sexual, or at best a foil to set off the chivalric English heroes of *1 Henry VI*. Her portrait, says Geoffrey Bullough in his compilation of Shakespeare's sources, 'goes far beyond anything found in Hall or Holinshed or in the Burgundian chronicler Monstrelet'.[3] Bullough ruefully lauds Shakespeare's mastery in discrediting the entire French cause through Joan; many subsequent critics have shared Bullough's admiration, although not his compunction, over the skill with which Shakespeare delineated an 'epitome of disorder and rebellion' to pit against the 'epitome of order and loyalty', the English hero Talbot: 'She is absolutely corrupt from beginning to end,' rejoices the author of one book on Shakespeare's history plays.[4] When the play was presented in 1591 or 1592, English troops were once again in France, once again supporting a claim to the French crown, a claim by another Henry – their religious ally Henry of Navarre. 'A play recalling the gallant deeds of the English in France at an earlier period . . . would be topical,' Bullough rightly says.[5]

The portrait of Joan, by this calculus of relation between drama and social context, takes its place among 'English attempts to blacken the reputation of Joan of Arc'[6] – an easy task in the Elizabethan period, when women 'who refuse[d] the place of silent subjection' could, like Shake-speare's Joan in Act V, be carted to execution as witches.[7] By this reckoning, the character of Joan of Arc becomes a regrettable sign of the times.

Neither the content nor the form of Joan's words about glory easily supports such a reading. Joan's image of the circle in the water is not only the most poetically resonant statement in the play, it is also specifically borne out by the action. The eloquence of her recognition that all human achievement is writ in water, one of the play's thematic pressure points, sorts ill with a lampooned character 'coarse and crude in language and sensibility'.[8] Yet *1 Henry VI* does contrast English chivalry, especially in the figure of heroic Talbot, with the pragmatism of the French, especially Joan; and Act V does dispel both Joan's power and her pretensions to divine aid in a series of progressively less dignified scenes.[9]

First she vainly offers diabolical spirits her blood and sexual favours in exchange for continued French success; subsequently captured, she rejects her old father to claim exalted birth; finally, faced with the prospect of death by burning, she claims to be pregnant, shifting her allegation of paternity from one French leader to another in response to her captors' insistence that each of these is a man whose child should not be allowed to live.

Perhaps it is a reflection as much on accepted critical standards of aesthetic unity as on the gullibility of individual critics that several have read this last scene as Joan's admission of sexual activity with the whole French camp. Ridiculous as such a reading is, it does at least integrate Act V with what precedes, undercutting Joan's claims to virginity just as her conjuring undercuts her claims to divinity. Such an interpretation of Act V makes it synchronic with previous acts in meaning; only the revelation of that meaning is postponed. Similarly, Joan's claims to divine mission, which she never mentions again after her introductory speeches in Act I, become in such an interpretation synchronic with the action which follows them. In the long central section of the drama, according to such a unified interpretation, Joan's prior assertion of godliness struggles against Talbot's repeated assertions of diabolism until Act V vindicates Talbot. The unstated premiss of this kind of reading is that temporally multiple suggestions of meaning collapse finally into an integrated pattern that transcends the temporal process of dramatic presentation. In this final pattern, all suggested assignments of value are reconciled and each plot line or character is allotted its proper plus or minus sign *sub specie unitatis*. The individual incident or dramatic effect has no more final autonomy than a number in a column for addition has in the sum below the line. These assumptions are very clear in Riggs's influential 1971 summation of Joan's character: 'Beneath these postures, Joan is generically an imposter. . . .

Hence the scenes in which she is exposed and burnt as a witch, like the stripping of Duessa in *The Faerie Queene*, serve a formal expository purpose that supersedes any need for a controlled, sequacious plot.'[10]

Now of course the typical Shakespearean play does have a very powerful sense of ending, partly brought about by a 'formal expository' resolution of difficult issues. I want to emphasize, however, that it is equally typical of Shakespeare to present unexplained and suggestive discontinuities. One might remember the complete reversal of Theseus' attitude to the lovers in *Midsummer Night's Dream*: having backed up Hermia's coercive father in Act I by citing the unalterable law of Athens, Theseus reappears in Act IV (after a two-act absence) to overrule the same father and the same law with no explanation whatever. A more subtle version of this kind of turnabout occurs when Othello, calmly superior in Act I to the accusation that he has used sorcery in his relationship with Desdemona, informs her in Act III that the handkerchief which was his first gift to her is a magical talisman. In these instances, the critic's expectation of unity forces interpretative strategy back on unspoken motivations and implicit character development, raising such questions as whether Othello deliberately lied to the senate in Act I, or when exactly he gave Desdemona the handkerchief. I want to propose that these are unsuitable strategies and questions for a phenomenon that has little to do with unity of character and much to do with the way in which a character is perceived by the audience at a particular moment of dramatic time. I would argue that in Act I Othello had not given Desdemona a magic handkerchief as his first gift, but in Act III he had. It is a matter of the character's consonance with the key into which the movement of the play has modulated.

This is not the place to make a detailed case for such an interpretative approach, or to try to identify for these examples the reasons – external to a concept of character as coherent selfhood – that direct a change in Shakespeare's presentation. Applying such an approach to the problem of Joan's significance, however, permits us to recognize and give individual value to the phases of her portrayal, which, not untypically for Shakespeare, is partially continuous and partially disjunct. The changing presentation allows Joan to perform in one play inconsistent ideological functions that go much beyond discrediting the French cause or setting off by contrast the glories of English chivalry in its dying moments.[11] As Bullough long ago suggested, the play's ideology is topical, but in what way and to what end cannot be answered as simply as he or some of the play's subsequent critics have believed.[12] To characterize its main military hero, Talbot, the play alludes specifically to the contemporaneous French expedition led by Essex, as John Munro first suggested, but it incorporates far more ideologically ambiguous detail than has been recognized. Similarly, for its presentation of Talbot's national and sexual opposites, the

three Frenchwomen who are the play's only female characters, it draws
heavily on the current controversy about the nature of women and on the
interrelated types of the Amazon, the warrior woman, the cross-dressing
woman, and the witch, all figures that – for a variety of reasons – were
objects of fascination both in England and on the Continent at the end of
the sixteenth century.

It is now generally accepted that the play dates from 1591/92, when
English troops under Essex had been sent to France for the particular
purpose of besieging Rouen; the play unhistorically dramatizes that city's
recapture from the French. Actually, Rouen had never been retaken; nor
was it after this hopeful piece of stagecraft. But the parallel does not remain
general and wishful. The play explicitly links Talbot to the current effort
through a neatly turned compliment to Queen Elizabeth which has, oddly,
been deflected by critics to Essex alone. Bearing away the fallen Talbot and
his son, the English messenger declares: 'from their ashes shall be rear'd
/ A phoenix that shall make all France afeard' (IV.vii.92–3). The phoenix
was one of Elizabeth's emblems; Shakespeare uses it again in *Henry VIII*.
She had not up to this time fulfilled the messenger's prediction. early
military success against French forces in Scotland had been completely
cancelled by a disastrous occupation of Le Havre in 1563. The vaunting
compliment can refer only to the most recent French expedition. Its leader
– the dashing young popular favourite Essex – would be an eminently
suitable candidate for the role of Talbot redivivus.[13] In 1591 the becalmed
campaign was serving as backdrop for his exploits, one of them mimicked
by another of the play's departures from its sources. Encamped before
Rouen, 'Essex sent a challenge to the Governor of the town daring him to
fight either a duel or a tournament', which was, not surprisingly,
declined.[14] In *1 Henry VI*, Talbot similarly challenges Joan and her
supporters as they stand victorious on the walls of Rouen (II.ii.56 ff.).[15] He
is contemptuously rebuffed by Joan in one of those moments when English
chivalry confronts French pragmatism: 'Belike your lordship takes us then
for fools, / To try if that our own be ours or no' (III.ii.62–3). A critic guided
by the play's obvious national sympathies could plausibly feel that Joan's
reply, however momentarily amusing, lacks magnanimity.

A closer look at the topical link between Talbot and Essex, however,
suggests a more complicated ideological situation. Both the expedition and
its leadership were controversial. Henry IV had broken his promise of
reinforcements for a first set of troops, sent in 1589, and Elizabeth sent the
second army with misgivings, putting the hot-headed Essex in command
with a reluctance well justified by the results. 'Where he is or what he doth
or what he is to do,' she wrote angrily to her other officers, 'we are
ignorant'.[16] Halfway through the expedition she ordered her uncontrollable
deputy home, although he talked her into sending him back. A likely

rescripting of this sequence of events appears in Act III, where Talbot interrupts his conquests to go and visit his sovereign 'with submissive loyalty of heart' (III.iv.10) and receives acclaim, reward, and a commission to return to battle (III.iv.16–27; IV.i.68–73). In the second of these scenes, Talbot strips a coward of his undeserved Order of the Garter and makes a long speech about the value of 'the sacred name of knight' (IV.i.33ff.) – another touchy subject after Essex's temporary recall, for he had just knighted twenty-four of his do-nothing soldiers. Lord Treasurer Burghley kept this news from Her Majesty as long as he could; Elizabeth was notoriously stingy with new titles – holding, in fact, rather the attitude expressed by Shakespeare's Talbot. She had wanted to deny Essex the privilege of dubbing knights, and remarked caustically on hearing of the twenty-four newcomers to fame unsupplemented by fortune: 'his lordship had done well to have built his almshouses before he had made his knights'.[17]

Are these portions of Talbot's behaviour and speech, then, aligned with the latest news from France in order to celebrate Essex?[18] Or do they obliquely defend him by rewriting his indiscretions in more acceptable terms, sympathetically dramatizing the 'real' meaning of his grand gestures? Or do Talbot's loyal actions, on the contrary, undercut the play's apparent endorsement of Essex by showing how a truly great champion acts? The answers are not all clear.[19] What is evident is that the play situates itself in an area of controversy easily identifiable by its audience, an area of growing ideological conflict in which a 'war party' contested, if it did not openly confront, the Queen's favoured policy of negotiation, delay, and minimal expenditure. Far from playing down the controversial aspects of Essex's command, the drama singles them out for re-enactment, but presents them in such a manner that either side could claim the play for its own. In light of the play's tendency to go both ways, Joan's sardonic reply to Talbot's challenge acquires an integrity of its own, sounding surprisingly like the voice of Her caustic Majesty Queen Elizabeth. Is the play, then, lauding chivalry or correcting it? Is it pro-war or not? This irritable reaching after fact and reason that Keats found so uncharacteristic of Shakespeare is not soothed by the parallels between Talbot and Essex, or by the tone of Joan's voice. The coexistence of ideologically opposed elements is typical of the play's dramatic nature, and foreshadows the mature Shakespeare.

Critical examination of the play's three women has not proceeded on this assumption. The perceived dominance of patrilineal and patriarchal ideology in Shakespeare's era and in the play's action has been the basis of most interpretations, whether feminist or masculinist.[20] The three women have been seen as a trio of temptresses,[21] of threats to male, and particularly English, hegemony and to the chivalric ideal,[22] as incarnations

of what Marilyn French calls the 'outlaw feminine principle'.[23] This kind
of negative reading, like the purely positive reading of the play's military
expedition, has support in the action. All three women are in different ways
unconventionally strong, and all three threaten the English with losses.
Coppélia Kahn's claim that Shakespeare is here exposing, but not sharing
in, male anxieties about women is surely counsel of desperation.[24]
Fortunately, it is not the only alternative to pathological or paternalistic
Shakespeare. Like the positive militaristic reading, with which it is closely
connected, the negative misogynist one neglects both the play's topicality
and the historical moment's ideological complexity.

The nature of women had long been under discussion in Western Europe
in a semi-playful controversy that became especially active in sixteenth-
century England. Contributors to this controversy buttressed or undercut
female claims to virtue by citing *exempla*, worthy or unworthy women
chosen from history, the Bible, and legend. As Linda Woodbridge's
account of this literary subgenre in England points out: 'The formal
controversy did not always appear full-blown, in carefully developed
treatises; it was sometimes sketched in cameo, with the names of a few

FIGURE 1 Two Amazons. From Sir John Mandeville, *The Voiage and Travaile of syr J. Maundevile*, 1568 (STC 17250), sig. G8v. Reprinted by courtesy of Special Collections, the Van Pelt Library, University of Pennsylvania.

FIGURE 2 Boadicea. From Raphael Holinshed, *The Firste Volume of the Chronicles of England*, 1578 (STC 13568A), 'The Historie of England', p. 61. Reprinted by courtesy of Special Collections, the Van Pelt Library, University of Pennsylvania.

FIGURE 3 Woada and her daughters. From Raphael Holinshed, *The Firste Volume of the Chronicles of England*, 1578 (STC 13568A), 'The Historie of Scotland', p. 45. Reprinted by courtesy of Special Collections, the Van Pelt Library, University of Pennsylvania.

FIGURE 4 Flora (left) and 'armed Pallas' as joint patrons of Thucydides' history. Their foothold on the queen's initials suggests that they may be intended for aspects of her. From R.B. McKerrow and F.S. Ferguson, *Title-page Borders used in England & Scotland 1485–1640* (London, 1932 [for 1931]), plate 74. Reprinted by courtesy of Special Collections, the Van Pelt Library, University of Pennsylvania, and the publisher.

exemplary women stamped on it like a generic signature.'[25] The 1560s had seen a spate of plays about individual *exempla* in the controversy. By the time *1 Henry VI* appeared, the controversy had already been naturalized into narrative fiction by George Pettie's *A petite pallace of ... pleasure* (1576), and Lyly's bestselling *Euphues* (1578). In these fictional contexts, the old techniques 'could be used to characterize, to comment on the action, even to advance the plot'.[26] *1 Henry VI* incorporates just such a cameo controversy. The play's three women are surrounded by allusions to legendary females which problematize their evaluation. The Countess of Auvergne compares herself to Tomyris, a bloody warrior queen, and is connected by verbal echo with the Queen of Sheba – two entirely opposite figures.[27] Margaret of Anjou is cast in her lover's description of his situation as Helen of Troy (V.v.103 ff.), a woman claimed by both attackers and defenders in the controversy. Joan appears amidst a tangle of contradictory allusions: she is among other identifications a Sibyl, an Amazon, Deborah, Helen the mother of Constantine, and Astraea's daughter to the French, but Hecate and Circe to the English. Of the women alluded to in *1 Henry VI*, eleven appear as *exempla* in the formal controversy. The genre itself was tolerant of, not to say dependent upon, divergent evaluations of the same phenomenon; a number of its *exempla*, like Helen of Troy, appeared regularly on both sides, and some writers handily produced treatises both pro and con. It would come as no surprise to readers of the controversy that one man's Sibyl is another man's Hecate.

1 Henry VI should be classed with what Woodbridge calls the 'second flurry of plays centering on prominent *exempla* of the formal controversy', which 'appeared in the late 1580s and 1590s'.[28] Its deployment of these stock figures is as germane to its ideology as its structural alignment of the female characters, but whereas the play's structure points in the direction of synthesis, of the synchronic or temporally transcendent reading, the *exempla* point towards differentiation, the temporally disjunctive reading.

Joan is evaluated by the French choice of *exempla* at the beginning and by the English choice at the end. At all times before Act V, however, because of the armour she is described as wearing and the military leadership she exercises, she is an example of what the Elizabethans called a virago, a woman strong beyond the conventional expectations for her sex, and thus said to be of a masculine spirit.[29] The increasing fascination of such women is evident in the proliferation of Amazons, female warriors, and cross-dressing ladies in the English fiction and drama of the late sixteenth century.

The Amazon and the warrior woman were already established as two of the most valued positive *exempla* of the controversy over women. Joan is identified with both immediately on her entry into the play's action: 'thou art an Amazon', exclaims the Dauphin, 'And fightest with the sword of Deborah' (I.ii.104–5). The power of this combination reaches beyond the arena of the formal debate. Spenser had just used it in *The Faerie Queene*, published 1590, in praise of 'the brave atchievements' of women (3.4.1.3): those 'warlike feates ... Of bold Penthesilee', the Amazon who aided the Trojans, or the blow with which 'stout Debora strake / Proud Siscra' (3.4.2.4–5, 7–8).[30] For him these two fighters define Britomart, his female knight in armour, who in turn defines Queen Elizabeth, 'whose lignage from this lady I derive along' (3.4.3.9). Both Amazons and women warriors already had some degree of British resonance because the Trojans who received Penthesilea's help were the supposed ancestors of the British, while a proud chapter in legendary English history recounted Queen Boadicea's defence of her country against Roman invasion. The evocation of heroines related to England is continued by Joan's association with Saint Helen, the mother of Constantine; though not a warrior, this finder of the remains of the True Cross was by popular tradition British.[31] The Dauphin's welcome to Joan is thus calculated to arouse the most unsuitably positive and even possessive associations in an Elizabethan audience.

Elizabethan literature, of course, contained many other Amazons besides Penthesilea; the race had a long and honourable history, derived from such respected authorities as Plutarch, Ovid, and Apollonius of Rhodes.[32] In the sixteenth century Amazons became a topic of current relevance when exploration of the Americas and Africa began bringing reports of Amazonian tribes sighted or credibly heard of.[33] Within a brief period after *1 Henry VI*, both Ralegh (1596) and Hakluyt (1599) would specify the Amazons' exact location. Perhaps because of their increased timeliness, Amazons were also about to become a vogue onstage; they would appear in at least fourteen dramatic productions from 1592 to 1640.[34]

Elizabethan stage Amazons are all either neutral or positive, an evaluative convention generally in line with their ever more frequent mention in Elizabethan non-dramatic literature. On the other hand, *The Faerie Queene* contains an evil Amazon alongside its positive allusions. For the Amazon figure was inherently double: although 'models of female magnanimity and courage' who appeared regularly in lists of the nine female worthies and were venerated both individually and as a race, Amazons were also acknowledged to be, at times, cruel tormentors of men.[35] From the very beginning, then, Joan's ideological function is complicated to the point of self-contradiction: she seems both French and English, both a type of Penthesilea who helps her countrymen in battle and an unspecified Amazon who may embody threats to men – in fact, a representative of the full complexity of late-Elizabethan perception of the strong woman.

These contradictions continue for as long as Joan appears in the role of woman warrior. Although she triumphs over the English, and so must be negative, she carries with her a long positive tradition reaching back to Plato's assertions that women could and should be trained for martial exercise, and to the figure of the armed goddess Minerva. These classical references, as well as invocations of the Old Testament Deborah and Judith, figured repeatedly in the formal defences of women. Female military heroism under special circumstances carried the prestigious sanction of Elyot, More and Hoby, and Joan's actions conform to the pattern they approved as well as to the current literary conventions defining a praiseworthy female warrior. She fights in defence of her country, 'particularly under siege', and converts the Duke of Burgundy to her cause with a simile that likens France to a dying child (III.iii.47–9) – defence of her children being a recognized motivation of the virtuous woman fighter.[36] Like Spenser's Britomart and countless others, she deflates male boasts and engages in a validating duel with a would-be lover.

As Spenser's connection of Britomart with Queen Elizabeth suggests, the tradition of the woman warrior acquired particular contemporaneous relevance from her existence. The maiden warrior-goddess Minerva provided an irresistible parallel with the virginal defender of Protestantism, who even before the year of the Armada was called 'for power in armes, / And vertues of the minde Minervaes mate' by Peele in *The Arraignment of Paris* (1584).[37] Deborah, a magistrate as well as her country's saviour in war, was also adopted immediately into the growing iconology of Elizabeth: the coronation pageant contained a Deborah, and the name was frequently used thereafter for the queen.[38] Not unexpectedly, Spenser identifies the Trojan-orientated Penthesilea as an analogue of his Belphoebe, the avowed representation of Queen Elizabeth.[39]

In light of these accumulated associations, a Minerva-like French leader who is a Deborah and Amazon, and is also called 'Astraea's daughter' (I.vi.4) at a time when Astraea, goddess of justice, was another *alter ego* of Elizabeth, must be reckoned one of the more peculiar phenomena of the Elizabethan stage.[40] But it is likely that Joan was more than peculiar: she was probably sensational. For the odd fact is that despite all the outpouring of Elizabethan literature both cultivated and popular on the subject of Amazons and warrior women, there seems to be only one rather obscure woodcut of real – as opposed to allegorical – armed women to be found in the English printed books, pamphlets, broadsides, and pictorial narrative strips of the entire era; nor had any such personage (as far as I have yet discovered) ever appeared on the stage.[41] Two Amazons that illustrate Mandeville's *Travels* are clad with impeccable feminine respectability (Fig. 1, p. 147). The coronation Deborah (1559), despite the pageant verses' reference to 'the dint of sworde', was equipped with Parliament robes, not with a deadly weapon, as in Spenser's fantasy.[42] Holinshed's

Boadicea (1577) had a wide skirt and long hair (Fig. 2, p. 148). What is more, there seem to be no pictures of women in men's clothing of any kind. It looks as though there was an unspoken taboo on such representations – a taboo just beginning to be breached occasionally in the 1570s, when Holinshed included in his *History of Scotland* an illustration of Woada's daughters (Fig. 3, p. 148). In the 1560s come the first mentions of real Elizabethan women wearing articles of real male apparel, though not armour or weapons, a fashion that was soon to grow into a fad. It is not until the 1580s that a very few cross-dressing ladies appear onstage, and not until after *1 Henry VI* that Amazons, women warriors, and girls in male disguise become a triple dramatic vogue. In 1591/92, dressing Joan in armour was a stunning *coup de théâtre*.

It had perhaps been anticipated. Outside the world of the stage lived a connoisseur of theatrical effect as daring as Shakespeare. In 1588, on the eve of the expected Spanish invasion, Queen Elizabeth visited her soldiers in the camp at Tilbury 'habited like an Amazonian Queene, Buskind and plumed, having a golden Truncheon, Gantlet, and Gorget', according to Heywood's later description.[43] Leonel Sharp, afterwards James I's chaplain and in 1588 'waiting upon the Earl of *Leicester* at *Tilbury* Camp', reported as eyewitness that 'the Queen rode through all the Squadrons of her armie, as Armed *Pallas*'[44] – a figure whose iconographic conventions of plumed helmet, spear and shield (Fig. 4, p. 149) coincided with descriptions of Amazon queens.[45] This was the occasion of her famous speech: 'I know I have the bodie, but of a weak and feeble woman, but I have the heart and Stomach of a King, ... and think foul scorn that ... any Prince of Europe should dare to invade the borders of my Realm.... I my self will take up arms, I my self will be your General.'[46] Whether or not Elizabeth actually wore armour, her review of the troops was a grand gesture of virago-ship, which combined visual uniqueness with enactment of time-honoured conventions identifying the woman warrior. It is probably the shadowy double behind the sudden appearance in the French camp of Joan, the puzzlingly Astraea-connected Amazonian, to lead her army against the invaders of her country.[47]

This probability does not make life any easier for the critic of *1 Henry VI*. One could simplify the situation by seeing Joan as a sarcastic version of such a figure, an anti-Elizabeth, a parodic non-virgin whose soldiership (finally) fails. Perhaps that was the point, or one of the points. But such close mirroring is hard to control. It is difficult to keep doubles separate. An obviously parodic presentation of a figure so suggestive might slide over into parody (dare one breathe it?) of the queen herself.[48] At the same time, the strong honorific associations of the Amazon–Deborah–Elizabeth combination exert their own pull in the opposite direction from parody. If Joan, parodied, functions as inferior foil for English chivalry, Joan honoured also functions as its superior. It seems likely, then, that Joan in armour is as fair and foul as the traditional double-potentialled Amazon, and that what she says or does is as likely to undercut 'the glorious deeds of the English in France' as to set off their splendour. She is a powerful warrior and a powerful enemy, but also an inverted image of both. Lest this interpretation seem an implausibly modern critical recourse to ambiguity, we should take notice of one elaborate European visual representation in the Elizabethan period of women in armour, Bruegel's *Dulle Griet* or Mad Meg. As described by Natalie Davis in her account of the sociological phenomenon she calls 'women on top', the painting sends a similar double message. It 'makes a huge, armed, unseeing woman, Mad Meg, the emblem of fiery destruction ... and disorder. Bruegel's painting cuts in more than one way, however.... Nearby other armed women are beating grotesque animals from Hell.'[49] This visual oxymoron sorts well with the double-valanced Amazon figure which is the period's prototype of the powerful and active woman.

Amazon, goddess, or queen, the numinous representative of a strength which, in its very transcendence of social convention, becomes salvific is from another perspective a potential subverter of established order and belief, an overturner of values. Nowhere is this clearer than in the disparity between Elizabethan or Jacobean fictions of cross-dressing women and accounts of real ones from the same period. Both attest to the fascination of the time with gender subversion, as does the cross-dressing phenomenon itself. Fiction could delight in Mary Ambree (1584), who avenged her lover's death in battle by putting on armour to lead the English troops; or in Long Meg of Westminster, said to have lived in Henry VIII's reign: she came from the country to work in a London tavern, dressed in men's clothes, fought and defeated obstreperous males, and went with the soldiers to Boulogne, where she achieved victory over the champion of the French and was honoured by the king.[50] Long Meg's story was told in two ballads, a play, and several reprintings of her pamphlet life, all between 1590 and about 1650. And no wonder; for when Long Meg had overcome the (Spanish) aggressor Sir James and humiliated him in the tavern by revealing her womanhood, she 'sat in state like her Majesty'.[51] Once again the warrior woman is assimilated to that modern numinous exemplar, Queen Elizabeth. But during the same period, women who really do participate in the growing fashion for wearing men's clothes, including ultimately weapons, are complained against with mounting sarcasm and hysteria. It is one thing to embody, in the encapsulated realm of fiction or of royalty, transcendence of social constraint – quite another to undermine on the street the customs around which society is organized.[52]

If Joan's initial presentation plays with the numinous aura and royal superiority of the virago, her portrayal in the play's middle section brings to the fore a special form of the virago's potential for subversion.[53] Uncommitted to convention, Joan is also uncommitted to the ethical stereotypes that structure the consciousness of other characters. This is her most threatening and most appealing function. It can be clearly seen in her comment after her eloquent speech has persuaded Burgundy to return to the French: 'Done like a Frenchman! [*Aside.*] – turn and turn again' (III.iii.85). Although this is a topical throwaway for the audience, its effect is very like that of early asides by Richard III, or of Falstaff playing first Henry IV and then Hal. It is characteristic of her persistent demystification of cherished idealisms, an ideological iconoclasm that does not spare her own achievements once she has finished with her original claim to divine aid.

Joan's speech constantly invites scepticism at the very moments when values are in need of affirmation, as when Rouen is captured, when Burgundy is about to desert, when Talbot falls. We should recall her sardonic response to Talbot's chivalric challenge – modelled, it is worth remembering, on Essex's conception of chivalry. Her conversion of Burgundy uses a different mode but achieves a similar shift of perspective, suddenly presenting an audience that enjoys 'the gallant deeds of the English in France' with a point of view that sees 'the cities and the towns defac'd / By wasting ruin of the cruel foe' (III.iii.45–6) and forces them to look at the enemy 'As looks the mother on her lowly babe / When death doth close his tender dying eyes' (III.iii.47–8). This clash of perspectives becomes extreme, and reaches beyond momentary effect, when the issue is the meaning of death itself. After the messenger who is searching for Talbot has recited the hero's titles of honour, performing unawares the eulogistic function of a traditional funeral oration, Joan observes: 'Here is a silly-stately style indeed! / ... / Him that thou magnifiest with all these titles, / Stinking and fly-blown lies here at our feet' (IV.vii.72–6). Like the cross-dressing woman she is, Joan perceives as futile convention what representatives of the status quo perceive as a visible sign of inner nature, be it formulaic titles or formulaic clothing. If her view is allowed, honour's a mere scutcheon, as her fellow-subversive Falstaff later agrees. Like Falstaff, Joan must be neutralized on behalf of stable values, but like his, her point of view is too compelling to be forgotten even when her circle in the water disperses in the humiliations of the fifth act. Although Talbot is the play's ostensible hero and nobility's decay its subject, it is Joan who expresses most forcefully both the vanity of all ideologies and an unorthodox *consolatio*. Like the cross-dressing festival ladies of misrule,[54] Joan offers relief from idealistic codes of behaviour – and thus from the need to mourn their demise.

The need to neutralize the virago, however, even the admired virago, is as pervasive in the period's writing as the evident fascination with her;

indeed, it is probably a tribute to the force that fascination exerted. This hypothesis helps in understanding some oddities in the presentation of the period's literary Amazons and warrior women.

Two sets of stage Amazons have no lines at all, nor any action relevant to the plot. Three more are actually men in disguise.[55] But by far the most popular strategy for neutralizing the manly woman was to feminize her. Hippolyta in both Shakespeare and Beaumont and Fletcher is a bride, while in an Elizabethan translation from the French, she is said to have become so eager to serve Theseus that she licked his wounded shoulder with her tongue.[56] Less crude and more congenial was the ancient story that when Penthesilea had been slain by Achilles, her helmet fell off and revealed her beauty, causing Achilles to fall in love with her – sadly, luckily, too late. Amplified by the addition of a flood of golden hair loosed from the fallen helmet, the incident enriched Spanish and Italian romance and made its way to Elizabethan England, where at least six Amazonians, including Britomart, met with a version of this accident – all of them deliciously powerless to hide from admiring male gaze their quintessential femininity.[57] Holinshed's Boadicea, with her long tresses, and Mandeville's two gowned Amazons present the same feminized picture. Britomart, who sleeps 'Al in her snow-white smocke, with locks unbownd' (3.1.63.7), having overcome her opposite number, the wicked Amazon, immediately changes all the rules of Amazon-land and 'The liberty of women did repeale, / Which they had long usurpt; ... them restoring / To mens subjection' (5.7.42.5–7). Even robust Long Meg, who looses her hair voluntarily to embarrass her vanquished opponent, returns from her French conquests to recant; having married a soldier who 'had heard of her manhood' and 'was determined to try her' in a combat with staves, she silently accepts 'three or four blows' and then, 'in submission, fell down on her knees, desiring him to pardon her, "For," said she, "... it behoves me to be obedient to you; and it shall never be said, ... Long Meg is her husband's master; and, therefore, use me as you please."'[58] The strength of her subversive attraction can be measured by the violence with which she is reintegrated into conservative ideology. She is too powerful to be wedded in another key.

We may anticipate, then, what those in Shakespeare's audience familiar with the conventions defining the woman warrior must also have anticipated: that the more free play Joan's attractive force is permitted, the more completely she will have to be feminized at the end of the play. Her scenes in Act V should be read in the light of this expectation, in full acceptance of their radical difference from her earlier behaviour. Her conjuring, once established, assigns her to an overwhelmingly female class of malefactors: informed estimates place the proportion of women executed as witches at about 93 per cent.[59] Her rejection of her father reduces to female vanity the serious social claim implicit in her male clothing, for, as a number of recent writers point out, cross-dressing attacks the concept of natural hierarchy on which, for the Elizabethans, social class is built.[60] Her terrified snatching at subterfuges in the face of death would count as peculiarly female behaviour; and when, finally, she claims to be pregnant, naming everyone and anyone as a lover, her feminization becomes irreversible. She has lost her helmet for ever. Her captors' harsh reactions to her pleas are the equivalent of Long Meg's beating: Warwick's sadistically merciful directions – 'And hark ye, sirs; because she is a maid, / Spare for no faggots, let there be enow' (V.iv.55–6) – are followed by York's unequivocal 'Strumpet, . . . / Use no entreaty, for it is in vain' (84–5).

The witch is Joan's last topical role. Executions for witchcraft in England reached peaks in the 1580s and 1590s, high points on a long curve that Belsey considers 'coterminous with the crisis in the definition of women and the meaning of the family'; she notes that in the last two decades of the sixteenth century 'the divorce debate was also reaching a climax'.[61] These events coincide with the beginnings of the vogue for Amazons and women warriors onstage, and with the early phases of the fad for cross-dressing. But of all that twenty-year span, 1591 was the year of the witch in England. It brought to London the pamphlet *Newes from Scotland*, a full account of the spectacular treason-cum-sorcery trials King James had supervised there in the winter of 1590–91, in which large numbers of his subjects were accused of having made a mass pact with the devil in order to raise storms against the ship bringing the King and his bride from Denmark.[62] The pamphlet had political overtones, as did the trials. King James, described to the English by the tract as 'the greatest enemie the Devil hath on earth', was, after all, an aspirant to their throne.[63]

It is not at all clear, however, that James's 'forwardness', as the English ambassador called it in a letter to Burghley,[64] elicited the kind of acclaim that could help us read Joan's treatment by York and Warwick as pro-Jamesian political doctrine. There are indications that his self-interested zeal may have worked the other way. A woman whom, for political reasons, he particularly wanted disembowelled was acquitted. Moreover, it appears that popular opinion in Scotland did not support the political aspects of the prosecution.[65] Perhaps still more serious, 'the picture of himself as the principal target for witches' might easily look foolish, to say no worse, in a more sophisticated country that had never been as harsh or consistent in its punishment of witches as the continent, where James had first acquired his demonological ideas. As Larner says: 'there was a possibility that his new-found interest in witchcraft . . . could . . . damage his image, especially in England'.[66] Although England executed witches, it did not burn or torture them, and one wonders what an English audience made of James's vindictiveness or of Warwick's call for plenty of faggots and extra barrels of pitch for Joan's stake (V.iv.56–7).[67] Furthermore, it was absolutely standard practice in both England and Scotland to put off a witch's execution if she was pregnant, as was the woman whose grisly punishment James unsuccessfully urged. Although Joan is only pretending, her captors are at best playing cat and mouse with her as they condemn her supposed child to death anew each time she assigns it a different father. Joan is the butt of the brutal joke here, but it is unlikely that York and Warwick come off unscathed by the negative associations of their total violation of English custom: 'we will have no bastards live. . . . It dies and if it had a thousand lives. . . . Strumpet, thy words condemn thy brat and thee' (V.iv.70, 75, 84).

It is altogether difficult to be sure how an Elizabethan audience might have reacted to Joan's punishment. Opinion on witches in 1591 was by no means monolithic. Scepticism about witch-trials was gathering force; on the Continent Montaigne had commented as recently as 1588: 'After all, it is putting a very high price on one's conjectures to have a man roasted alive because of them',[68] and at home Reginald Scot had even earlier published his 600-page attack (1584) on 'those same monsterous lies, which have abused all Christendome' and been the undoing of 'these poore women'.[69] Scot's book was clearly labelled as subversive when it was (appropriately) burnt by the hangman. Later, James attacked Scot by name in his own tract *Daemonologie*. This makes it all the more interesting that the portrayal of Joan divides into a subversively Scot-like main section and a Jamesian demonological coda. In the long middle section of the play already discussed, her triumphs are based simply on boldness, common sense, and resourcefulness. Comically, this supposed witch is the most down-to-earth pragmatist in the play: 'had your watch been good / This sudden mischief never could have fallen' (II.i.58–9). In consequence, Talbot's repeated insistence that she is a witch sounds not dissimilar to the deluded allegations recounted by Reginald Scot. Joan herself, unlike Talbot and the French leaders, never falls back on metaphysical notions about her opponent. Whereas her companions suggest that Talbot is 'a fiend of hell' or a favourite of the heavens (II.i.46–7), Joan simply expresses realistic respect for his prowess and invents several plans to evade it. Her successes are well served by Scot's commentary: 'it is more strange, that we will imagine that to be possible to be doone by a witch, which to nature and sense is impossible; . . . [for in other legal cases] the judge dooth not attend or regard what the accused man saith; or yet would doo: but what is prooved to have beene committed, and naturallie falleth in mans power and will to doo'.[70] Yet in Act V, Joan appears as a witch engaged in a diabolical compact, a demonological feature never very important in English witch-trials but topically responsive to James's recent proceedings.

The presentation of Joan as witch is almost as diverse in its implications as her Amazonian image, of which it is a kind of transformation. The common folk belief in witches with beards, like the tradition of the Amazon's armour, renders visible the concept of a woman who 'exceeds her sex' (I.ii.90).[71] Hall calls her 'This wytch or manly woman',[72] as if the two were so close that he could hardly decide between them. A comment by Belsey illuminates this aspect of Joan's witchhood:

> The demonization of women who subvert the meaning of femininity is contradictory in its implications. It places them beyond meaning, beyond the limits of what is intelligible. At the same time it endows them with a (supernatural) power which it is precisely the project of patriarchy to deny. On the stage such figures are seen as simultaneously dazzling and dangerous.[73]

Joan's dazzle is, of course, neutralized by her fifth-act humiliations, but her danger persists in her final curse on England. Quickly, she is taken off to be neutralized more thoroughly at the stake. Her helplessness *vis-à-vis* her male captors may serve to remind us that despite folk belief, there were no Elizabethan pictures of witches with beards, or any other kind of power-laden sexual ambiguity.[74] Joan's fate enacts that annihilation fantasized for the cross-dressing woman by the anonymous author of a Jacobean pamphlet: 'Let . . . the powerful Statute of apparell [the sumptuary law] but lift up his Battle-Axe, so as every one may bee knowne by the true badge of their bloud, . . . and then these *Chymera's* of deformitie will bee sent backe to hell, and there burne to Cynders in the flames of their owne malice.'[75] Yet in a final twist of meaning, as we have seen, the terms of Joan's reintegration into conservative ideology recognizably damage her captors' own ideological sanction.

In my reading of *1 Henry VI*, the disjunctive presentation of Joan that shows her first as numinous, then as practically and subversively powerful, and finally as feminized and demonized is determined by Shakespeare's progressive exploitation of the varied ideological potential inherent in the topically relevant figure of the virago. Each of her phases reflects differently upon the chivalric, patriarchal males in the play, especially Talbot, who also have topical referents outside the drama. At no stage is the allocation of value clear-cut.

Neither is the definition of dominant ideology clear-cut in the play's social context. To bring detailed topical considerations into an assessment of the ideology of *1 Henry VI* is to come upon some truisms worth restating: that there is probably more than one opinion on any crucial issue at any time in any society, and that it is often hard to sort out the relationship between views and power. If the queen considers a French expedition disadvantageous but her subordinate succeeds in continuing it, is the dominant ideology war or peace? If pamphleteers complain that women are becoming moral monsters by cross-dressing, but a fad for Amazons arises and women cross-dress more than ever, what is the ideological situation? This kind of uncertainty complicates the concept of subversion, which I have invoked from time to time in my analysis.

Given the multiple uncertainties within the play's milieu and the uncertainties the play itself generates, it becomes strikingly evident that *1 Henry VI*, like so much of Shakespeare's later work, locates itself in areas of ideological discomfort. It uses culturally powerful images ambiguously, providing material for different members of a diverse audience to receive the drama in very different ways. Although one must agree with the critical judgement that in this play 'the individual consciousness never engages in an *agon* with its milieu, and never asks the great questions',[76] the presence of Joan does provide a form of *agon*, if a less profound one than in the great tragedies. Even the ending, with its strategies of neutralization, cannot disqualify the questions raised.

Finally, once the ways in which disturbing ideological positions are neutralized by the play have been made clear, it seems well to point out that the theatre is an illusionistic medium, and that to neutralize onstage is not necessarily to neutralize in reality. In fact, it is possible that maintaining the illusion that an ideological tendency can be reliably neutralized may help to enable toleration of threatening ideas.[77]

Notes

1. This essay was first presented at the 1986 World Shakespeare Conference in Berlin and, in another form, at the Northeast Modern Language Association on 3 April 1987. It shares a common concern about Joan's ideological ambiguity with Leah Marcus, 'Elizabeth', in *Puzzling Shakespeare: Local Reading and Its Discontents* (Berkeley: University of California Press, 1988, pp. 51–105), but we arrive at different conclusions. Professor Marcus was kind enough to allow me to read her work while I was completing this essay.

2. Citations are from *The First Part of King Henry VI*, ed. Andrew S. Cairncross, *The Arden Shakespeare* (London, 1962).

3. Geoffrey Bullough, *Narrative and Dramatic Sources of Shakespeare* (New York, 1960), III, 41.

4. Robert B. Pierce, *Shakespeare's Historic Plays: The Family and the State* (Columbus, OH, 1971), pp. 46–7. In the same spirit, Don M. Ricks identifies the tone she sets as 'treachery, depravity, and insolence' in *Shakespeare's Emergent Form: A Study of the Structures of the Henry VI Plays* (Logan, UT, 1968), p. 45. So common is the critical view of Joan as a moral write-off that she is sometimes assigned reprehensible behaviour that does not even occur in the text, as when Catherine Belsey remarks that she 'puts heart into the enemy by her rhetoric', in *The Subject of Tragedy. Identity and Difference in Renaissance Drama* (New York, 1985), p. 183. At the very least she is presumed to be the butt of continuous irony (e.g. by David Bevington in 'The Domineering Female in *1 Henry VI*', *Shakespeare Studies* 2 [1966]: 51–8 and John Wilders in *The Lost Garden: A View of Shakespeare's English and Roman History Plays* [Totowa, NJ, 1978], p. 36). A signal exception is H.M. Richmond in *Shakespeare's Political Plays* (New York, 1967), who allows her 'heroic power' and even some 'magnetism'; he also goes quite against the current of critical commentary by alluding to 'her subtlety and finesse' (p. 23), but

he agrees on 'the harshness of the portrait' (p. 22).

5. Bullough, pp. 24–5.

6. Lisa Jardine, *Still Harping on Daughters: Women and Drama in the Age of Shakespeare* (Sussex, 1983), p. 124.

7. Belsey, p. 184.

8. Marilyn French, *Shakespeare's Division of Experience* (New York, 1981), p. 47.

9. See David Riggs, who admirably elucidates the play's structure in *Shakespeare's Heroical Histories: Henry VI and Its Literary Tradition* (Cambridge, MA, 1971), pp. 100 ff. On the play's ideology we disagree.

10. Riggs, p. 107. Riggs's view has been more recently affirmed by Norman Rabkin, *Shakespeare and the Problem of Meaning* (Chicago, 1981), pp. 88–9 and n. 39. Ricks and David Sundelson also make explicit, in slightly different ways, a criterion of integration to explain the last act: 'her final degeneration in Act V is but a spectacular demonstration of the unsaintliness which has been implicit in her words and behavior all along. There is nothing contradictory, therefore, about the two views of Joan as Pucelle and as "Puzzel" [whore]' (Ricks, p. 46); 'Shakespeare himself seems unable to tolerate any uncertainty about the source of Joan's potency. He resolves the matter with a scene in which she conjures … thus confirming Talbot's explanation' (David Sundelson, *Shakespeare's Restorations of the Father* [New Brunswick, NJ, 1983], p. 20).

11. See, e.g., Rabkin, pp. 86–7.

12. Detailed proposals of the play's topicality have been made by T.W. Baldwin, *On the Literary Genetics of Shakespeare's Plays 1592–1594* (Urbana, IL, 1959), pp. 324–40. Less extended suggestions of parallels have come from J. Dover Wilson in the introduction to his edition of *The First Part of King Henry VI* (Cambridge, 1952), pp. xviii–xix; Emrys Jones, *The Origins of Shakespeare* (Oxford, 1977), pp. 119–26; John Munro in *TLS*, 11 October, 1947; Hereward T. Price, *Construction in Shakespeare*, University of Michigan Contributions in Modern Philology No. 17 (Ann Arbor, MI, 1951), pp. 25–6; and Ernest William Talbert, *Elizabethan Drama and Shakespeare's Early Plays: An Essay in Historical Criticism* (Chapel Hill, NC, 1963). Leah Marcus offers a most thorough treatment of many of the play's topical allusions that takes full account of their complexity in 'Elizabeth' (see note 1 above).

13. John Munro first interpreted the lines about the phoenix as a reference to Essex. J. Dover Wilson follows suit in his introduction to the play, where he also suggests that 'Talbot was intended to stand as in some sort the forerunner of Essex' (p. xix). T.W. Baldwin, in his study of the play's 'literary genetics', is dubious about Munro's identification, but agrees that the allusion is to the English armies in France 1589 and following' (p. 334). E.W. Talbert similarly cites Munro and also accepts the play's connection with the Essex expedition (pp. 163–4 and p. 163 n. 6).

14. J.E. Neale, *Queen Elizabeth I* (Garden City, NY, 1957), p. 337.

15. J. Dover Wilson sees the parallel between Talbot's and Essex's challenges, but interprets it simply as a reminiscence of Essex's gallantry (p. xix). He considers the play 'an outlet for the growing sense of exasperation, anger, and even despair which was felt in London at the impending failure of an invasion of France' (p. xvi).

16. Neale, p. 335.

17. Ibid., p. 336. Elizabeth called the campaign 'rather a jest than a victory' and ordered Essex home for good in January 1592 (ibid., p. 337).

18. That a steady stream of ephemera carried bulletins from France to English readers is evident from the entries in the Stationers' Register. The diversity of possible attitudes to the expedition is perhaps suggested by the contrasting titles of two such pieces: an obviously enthusiastic 'ballad of the noble departinge of the right honorable the Erle of ESSEX lieutenant generall of her maiesties forces in Ffraunce and all his gallant companie' (23 July 1591) and a possibly more ominous-sounding 'letter sent from a gentleman of accoumpte concerninge the true estate of the Englishe forces now in Ffraunce under the conduct of the right honorable the Erle of ESSEX' (6 September 1591).

19. The well-known compliment to Essex in *Henry V,* V Cho. 30–34, is also ambiguous in light of the sentence that follows it (34–5). That this passage refers to Essex has been generally accepted, but the identification has been challenged by W.D. Smith. See G.

Blakemore Evans, 'Chronology and Sources', *The Riverside Shakespeare*, ed. G. Blakemore Evans (Boston, MA, 1974), p. 53.

20. E.g. Marilyn French (n. 8 above), following L.C. Knights and Northrop Frye, calls the play a search for legitimacy (p. 43). She believes that legitimacy is presented as a strictly masculine principle – 'Shakespeare's women can never attain legitimacy' – although, somewhat confusingly, she also claims that it can contain 'the inlaw feminine principle' (p. 49).

21. Bevington (n. 4 above), pp. 51–8.

22. Riggs (n. 9 above).

23. French (n. 8 above), p. 51.

24. Coppélia Kahn, *Man's Estate: Masculine Identity in Shakespeare* (Berkeley, CA, 1981), p. 55 and p. 55 n. 11.

25. Linda Woodbridge, *Women and the English Renaissance: Literature and the Nature of Womankind 1540–1620* (Urbana, IL, 1984), p. 61. Shakespeare's interest in this controversy is evident not only in his frequent allusions to its *exempla* (Woodbridge cites references, pp. 126–8, and there are many more) but in his use of at least ten of them as characters in his works, four as protagonists. His is an impressive roster even in a period when plays about the controversy's *exempla* were a growth industry (Woodbridge, pp. 126ff.). The four protagonists are Venus, Lucrece, Cressida and Cleopatra; the other characters, Volumnia in *Coriolanus*, Portia in *Julius Caesar* and Portia in *The Merchant of Venice* (carefully identified, as Woodbridge notes on p. 127, with 'Cato's daughter, Brutus' Portia'), Octavia, Helen of Troy, and Hippolyta (Thisbe should also be mentioned). The maligned and repudiated Mariana in *Measure for Measure*, too, may be a relative of Mariamne, Herod's defamed second wife, another favourite of the controversialists.

26. Woodbridge, pp. 61–2, 66.

27. Cairncross, 2.3.7–10n.; and Bevington.

28. Woodbridge, p. 126. Woodbridge's account of the controversy is invaluable. I cannot agree with her, however, that the plays written in and after the later 1580s were probably not influenced by it; her own evidence (and there is more she does not cite) seems to point overwhelmingly the other way. She observes that 'the drama had many other potential sources', which is true but does not account for the upsurge in plays devoted specifically to *exempla* from the controversy, and she points out that dramatists often treated these *exempla* differently from controversialists – but this objection assumes that to influence is to produce a copy.

29. The term was almost entirely positive and denoted either physical or spiritual prowess. For the virago's 'manly soul', see Simon Shepherd, *Amazons and Warrior Women: Varieties of Feminism in Seventeenth-Century Drama* (Sussex, 1981), pp. 34–5. Various contemporary allusions to the Queen invoked the pun *virgo/virago*, and her 'masculine' spirit was frequently remarked upon with admiration. See Winfried Schleiner, '*Divina virago*: Queen Elizabeth as an Amazon', *Studies in Philology* 75, 2 (1978): 163–80. I am grateful to Louis Montrose for calling this extremely useful article to my attention.

30. All citations from *The Faerie Queene* will be identified by book, canto, stanza, and line numbers in my text; these refer to Edmund Spenser, *The Faerie Queene*, ed. R.E. Neil Dodge (Cambridge, MA, 1936). Spenser was mistaken; Yael, not Deborah, struck Sisera.

31. I am indebted to F.J. Levy for calling my attention to this fact.

32. Ironically – or as a calculated symbolic counterstatement to the Maid? – Henry VI's Paris coronation pageant included 'la sage Hippolyte' and her sister Menalippe, as well as Penthesilea and Lampeto, as female worthies. See Robert Withington, *English Pageantry: An Historical Outline*, vol. 1 (Cambridge, MA, 1918), pp. 138–9, n. 4. Celeste Turner Wright calls attention to Henry's coronation pageant in 'The Amazons in Elizabethan Literature', *Studies in Philology* 37 (July 1940): 437 n. 41 (n.b.: because of a numbering error in this volume, Wright's article begins on the *second* occurrence of p. 437).

33. See Abby Wettan Kleinbaum, 'The Confrontation', in *The War Against the Amazons* (New York, 1983). I appreciate being directed to this book by Daniel Traister, Curator of Rare Books at the University of Pennsylvania.

34. Schleiner (see n. 29 above) also identifies as 'Amazons' the female characters in a mock tournament of 1579, presented for the Queen and the Duke of Alençon's representative

(p. 179), although her quotation from her source refers only to 'ladies' (pp. 163–4, n. 3). *Tamburlaine* mentions Amazon armies, but they do not appear. Greene's *Alphonsus*, an obvious offspring of *Tamburlaine*, may have preceded *I Henry VI* in presenting visible Amazons as well as a warrior maiden, but this play has never been satisfactorily dated. Rabkin believes it was 'probably written 1587', but does not give his reasons (introduction to Robert Greene, 'Friar Bacon and Friar Bungay', *Drama of the English Renaissance. I: The Tudor Period*, ed. Russell A. Fraser and Norman Rabkin [New York, 1976], p. 357). The play's general derivative quality suggests, however, that Iphigina is more likely to be a daughter of Joan than the reverse. The other productions I know of containing Amazons are 'A Masque of the Amazons . . . played March 3, 1592' (Henslowe's diary, quoted in William Painter, *The Palace of Pleasure*, ed. Joseph Jacobs, 3 vols [London, 1890], I, 1xxxi); 'field pastimes with martiall and heroicall exploits' staged for Prince Henry's christening in 1594 (John Nichols, *Progresses, Public Processions, &c. of Queen Elizabeth*, 3 vols [London, 1823], III, 355); *Midsummer Night's Dream*, 1595; Marston's *Antonio and Mellida*, 1602; *Timon of Athens*, ?1605–9; Jonson's *Masque of Queens*, 1609; Beaumont and Fletcher's *Two Noble Kinsmen*, ?1613, *The Sea Voyage*, 1622, and *Double Marriage*, 1647; the anonymous *Swetnam, the Woman-Hater*, 1620; Heywood's *Iron Age*, 1632; Shirley's dramatization of the *Arcadia*, 1640; and Davenant's *Salmacida Spolia*, 1640. There is a discussion of Fletcher's *Sea Voyage* and some Amazon dramas 1635–85 in chapter 11 of Jean Elisabeth Gagen, *The New Woman: Her Emergence in English Drama, 1600–1730* (New York, 1954).

For many of these titles and the beginnings of all my information about Amazons, I have relied on the encyclopedic Wright (n. 32 above). Her non-chronological organization assumes, however, that the degree of interest in Amazons and writers' attitudes towards them remained stable throughout the period from which she takes her examples (some undated). Her evidence suggests otherwise.

35. Wright, pp. 442–3, 449–54. Wright's data are difficult to get around in chronologically, but it looks as though doubts about the Amazons – including scepticism about their existence – may have increased in England after 1600, although the Amazonian vogue lasted right up to the Civil War.

Although there are Elizabethan accounts of the Amazons' ruthless origins and habits, I do not agree with Shepherd (n. 29 above) that the period's overriding feeling was 'Elizabethan distress about Amazons' (p. 14), in support of which view he instances Radigund and the egregious misogynist Knox. Shepherd wants to extrapolate Spenser's opposition between Radigund and Britomart into a pervasive Elizabethan distinction between Amazons and warrior women: 'Against the warrior ideal there is the Amazon' (p. 13). This schema will not hold up in the face of a mass of evidence for Elizabethan Amazon-enthusiasm. Shepherd's own evidence for the Elizabethan period is slender and largely extrapolated from Stuart texts. Although he does say that the negative meaning of Amazon 'coexists with the virtuous usage' (p. 14), this concession, in itself inadequate, is forgotten in his subsequent loosely supported account.

Nor can I agree with Louis Adrian Montrose's implication in his otherwise insightful and imaginative '"Shaping Fantasies': Figurations of Gender and Power in Elizabethan Culture', *Representations* 1, 2 (Spring 1983): 61–94, that English Renaissance texts about Amazons generally express 'a mixture of fascination and horror' (p. 66). The passages he quotes detail the Amazons' origins and/or customs; others of this type are often flat in tone and delivered without comment, like Mandeville's (1499, rpt. 1568), while some mention no horrors at all. Even the Amazon-shy Spenser compliments the supposed South American tribe: 'Joy on those warlike women, which so long / Can from all men so rich a kingdome hold!' (*F.Q.* 4.11.22.1–2). Although Montrose calls attention to the association sometimes made between Amazons and the destruction of male children, and in some travel books between Amazons and cannibalism, in an equal number of accounts they produce male children for neighbouring tribes and are thought of as desirable breeding stock. By far the greatest number of Amazon allusions, moreover, refer to specific Amazons and appear in a positive context. Penthesilea, the hands-down favourite, is always treated with admiration and respect, as is Hippolyta.

My observations are based on the following Tudor texts: Agrippa, trans. Clapham, *The Nobilitie of Woman Kynde*, 1542 (STC 203), p. 360v; Anghiera (Peter Martyr), trans. Eden,

Decades of the Newe World, 1555, ed. Arber, *The First Three English Books on America*, 1885, pp. 69, 177, 189; Richard Barckley, *The Felicitie of Man*, 1598 (STC 1381), III, 266–8; Bocaccio, *De Claris Mulieribus*, 1534–47, ed. Wright, EETS (London, 1943), pp. 39–42, 66–7, 103–5 and *Tragedies*, trans. Lydgate, 1554 (STC 3178), I, 12; Quintus Curtius, trans. Brende, *History of ... Alexander*, 1553 (STC 6142), pp. Pii–Piii; Anthony Gibson, trans. *A Womans Woorth*, 1599 (STC 11831), pp. 5, 37v; Richard Madox, *An Elizabethan in 1582: The Diary of Richard Madox ...* ed. Elizabeth Story Donno, Hakluyt Society second series No. 47 (London, 1977), p. 183; Sir John Mandeville, *The Voyage and Travel ...*, 1568 (STC 17250), pp. Gviii verso; Ortuñez de Calahorra, trans. T[yler], *The Mirrour of ... Knighthood*, 1578 (STC 18859), 26.91v, 55.219; Hieronimus Osorius, trans. Blandie, *The Five Books of Civill and Christian Nobilitie*, 1576 (STC 18886), II, 25v; Ovid, trans. Turberville, *Heroycall Epistles*, 1567 (STC 18940.5), p. 23; William Painter, *The Palace of Pleasure*, 1575, ed. Joseph Jacobs, 3 vols (London, 1890), II, 159–61; Sir Walter Ralegh, *The Discoverie of ... Guiana*, 1596 (STC 20636), pp. 23–4 and *History of the World*, 1614 (STC 20637), I.4.195–6; William Shakespeare, *King John*, 1594–6, ed. Herschel Baker, in Evans; Sir Philip Sidney, *The Countess of Pembrokes Arcadia*, 1590, ed. Robertson (Oxford 1973), pp. 21, 36; Edmund Spenser, *The Faerie Queene*, I–III, 1590, IV–VI, 1596 (see n. 30); Andre Thevet, *The New Found World*, trans. 1568 (STC 23950), pp. 101–74 (*recte* 103); William Warner, *Albion's England*, 1586 (STC 15759), pp. 25–6; and two accounts of Spanish voyages known in England, those of Francesco Orellana and Gonzalo Pizarro, *Expeditions into the Valley of the Amazons*, trans. and ed. Clements R. Markham, Hakluyt Society (New York, n.d.), pp. 13, 26, 34, 36. I have also found useful Kleinbaum's chapters 'The Net of Fantasy' and 'The Confrontation'.

36. Woodbridge, p. 21.

37. Cited by both Wright and Shepherd.

38. Wright, p. 455.

39. He makes this identification in 1590, just a year and a half after the Armada crisis (see discussion below, in text). Penthesilea was frequently used as a comparison for Elizabeth, especially around this time (see Schleiner [n. 29 above], pp. 170–73). The Amazon analogy was still current in 1633, when Phineas Fletcher likened his 'warlike Maid, / *Parthenia*', a recognizable variant of Elizabeth, to Hippolyta in *The Purple Island* 10.27–40 (STC 11082), pp. 141–4.

40. In 'Elizabeth', Leah Marcus also comments on some of Joan's symbolic identities.

41. For information on woodcuts I am most grateful to Ruth Luborsky, who is currently completing a catalogue of all woodcut-illustrated printed English documents in the period, keyed to the STC. For pictorial narratives, I have consulted David Kunzle, *The Early Comic Strip: Narrative Strips and Picture Stories in the European Broadsheet from 1450–1895* (Berkeley, CA, 1983). I have examined the engraved representations in Arthur M. Hind, *Engraving in England in the Sixteenth and Seventeenth Centuries*, 3 vols (vol. III ed. Margery Corbett and Michael Norton) (Cambridge, 1952–64); in Ronald B. McKerrow, *Printers' and Publishers' Devices 1485–1640 in England and Scotland* (London, 1913); in Ronald B. McKerrow and F.S. Ferguson, *Title-page Borders Used in England & Scotland 1485–1640* (London 1932 [for 1931] [*sic*]); and in Margery Corbett and Ronald Lightbown, *The Comely Frontispiece: the emblematic title-page in England, 1550–1660* (London, 1979).

42. Nichols (n. 34 above), II, pp. 53–4.

43. Quoted from Thomas Heywood's *Exemplary Lives*, 1640, by Shepherd (n. 29 above), p. 22.

44. Leonel Sharp, Letter to George Villiers, Duke of Buckingham, n.d. [1623–5], *Cabala, Mysteries of State, in Letters of the great Ministers of K. James and K. Charles* (1654), p. 259.

45. Stow in his *Annals* (1615) calls the Queen at Tilbury 'Bellona-like' (quoted by Miller Christy, 'Queen Elizabeth's Visit to Tilbury in 1588', *EHR* 34 [1919], 58), and an anonymous poem of 1600 appeals to her as 'Thou that ... bearest harnesse, speare, and shielde' (Schleiner [n. 29 above], p. 174). Schleiner, who does not mention the Sharp letter, calls Heywood's 1640 description 'probably only theatrical imagination' (p. 176). Heywood was drawing on his own dramatic spectacle, created in 1633 when he brought his two-part

stage biography of the Queen to its climax with a final Tilbury scene: 'Enter ... Queen ELIZABETH, completely armed'. See Thomas Heywood, *The Second Part of If You Know Not Me, You Know No Bodie* (1633), in *Thomas Heywood's Dramatic Works*, ed. J. Payne Collier (London, 1853), II, 156; for the date, see editorial note [xxiii]. (The 1606 version of the play does not contain this stage direction, but may of course have used the same costume.)

I do not know where Paul Johnson gets his circumstantial description of a white velvet dress, etc., in *Elizabeth I: A Study in Power and Intellect* (London, 1974), p. 320, which Montrose (n. 35 above) follows, p. 77. The description is not in any of the sources Johnson cites in his footnote. Susan Frye casts doubt on the reliability of Sharp's account (which includes the speech) in her wonderfully thorough 'The Myth of Elizabeth at Tilbury', *The Sixteenth Century Journal* XXIII, 1 (1992): 95–114. In her view, the 'myth' of armour arose in the early seventeenth century. She does not, however, to my mind, decisively discredit the several evocations of martial accoutrements in poetry contemporaneous with the event (pp. 105–6). Comparing the Sharp speech with two versions of a different purported speech by Elizabeth on this occasion (pp. 101–5), Frye comments: 'Elizabeth I may have delivered both speeches, or neither' (p. 104). Probably neither Elizabeth's clothing nor her speech can be settled definitively.

46. Sharp, p. 260. J.E. Neale, 'Sayings of Queen Elizabeth', *History* n.s. 10 (October 1925): 212–33, considers this speech substantially authentic (pp. 226–7). Sharp, who recounted it soon after 1623, could have received a copy of it in 1588; he relates that at Tilbury he had been 'commanded to re-deliver' the oration to 'all the Armie together, to keep a Publique Fast' (Sharp, p. 259) after Elizabeth's departure.

For evidence that Elizabeth's rhetorical self-presentations may have implied androgyny, see Leah S. Marcus, 'Shakespeare's Comic Heroines, Elizabeth I, and the Political Uses of Androgyny', in *Women in the Middle Ages and the Renaissance*, ed. Mary Beth Rose (Syracuse, NY, 1986).

47. In 'Elizabeth', Leah Marcus notes numerous similarities between Joan and the queen, including the proposed celebration of a saint's day commemorating each woman and the identity in name between two of Joan's supposed lovers and two of Elizabeth's suitors.

48. Leah Marcus, in 'Elizabeth', does interpret Joan as a figure of parody that embodies 'suppressed cultural anxieties' about Elizabeth.

49. Natalie Zemon Davis, 'Women on Top', *Society and Culture in Early Modern France* (Stanford, CA, 1975), p. 129.

50. 'The Life of Long Meg of Westminster', *The Old Book Collector's Miscellany*, ed. Charles Hindley, vol. II (London, 1872). See also Shepherd (n. 29 above), pp. 70–71. The outlines of Long Meg's story exhibit striking similarities with the outlines of Joan's; according to Hall, Joan too came from the country and 'was a greate space a chamberleyn in a commen hostrey' (Bullough, p. 56) before going off to lead the army against the English champion and being honoured by the Dauphin.

51. Hindley, p. xii, quoted by Shepherd, p. 73. The ballad of Mary Ambree is given in Thomas Percy, *Reliques*, vol. III (1823), pp. 46–51 (series 2, Bk. 2, no. 19). She was a well-known figure, mentioned by Fletcher and Ben Jonson (Percy, p. 46). Long Meg was even more familiar; she is referred to by Lyly, Nashe, Harvey, Deloney, Taylor, Dekker, Jonson, Beaumont and Fletcher, Middleton, and William Gamage's collection of epigrams (see Hindley and Shepherd).

All modern critics who discuss Long Meg give a wrong date of 1582 for the first pamphlet account of her life. This edition's title page and colophon are forged from an unrelated book published 1582; the rest of the text is *c.* 1650. See William A. Jackson, ed. *Records of the Court of the Stationers' Company 1602–1640* (London, 1957), pp. 112–13 and n. 6 (this information is incorporated in the STC's revised vol. II, ed. Katharine Pantzer). The earliest mention I know of Meg's story is the 18 August 1590 entry in the *Stationers' Register* for her life, followed on 27 August the same year by an entry for a ballad about her. On 14 March 1594/95, another ballad is entered. The first extant life would thus become one printed in 1620 (STC 17782.5), followed by further editions in 1635 and 1636 (STC 17783, 17783.3). After these would come the '1582' (*recte c.* 1650). Hindley, who reprints the 1635 edition, includes in his introduction another reprint, which he believes to be an abridged version (n.d.) of the supposed 1582 text. It does seem to be Elizabethan, for it contains the casual reference to 'Her Majesty'; later, this phrase was economically altered by the printer to 'she sat in her Majesty' (1635; I have not seen the 1620 edition). Thus the life in Hindley's introduction may be the version registered in 1590; if so, it is our earliest text.

52. Lawrence Stone believes that female cross-dressing was a reflection of the Jacobean court's homosexuality, and that 'The playwrights noticed what was happening and gave it further circulation'; see *The Crisis of the Aristocracy 1558–1641* (Oxford, 1966), pp. 666–7. Given the early beginnings of both real and fictional cross-dressing, however, behaviour at the Jacobean court comes much too late to be an explanation.

53. There is contemporaneous evidence for the possibility of regarding Joan as a heroine. Gabriel Harvey in his commonplace book set her between Alexander and her shepherd-analogue David (Shepherd, p. 35). By the 1620s, she was publicly entered among warlike and valorous women in Thomas Heywood's *Gynaikeion* (Jardine [n. 6 above], p. 137 n. 66) and admitted to membership in the long-running formal controversy in Christopher Newstead's *An Apology for Women*, a positive *exemplum* after all (Woodbridge [n. 25 above], p. 80).

54. Davis (n. 50 above), pp. 138–9.

55. The Amazon army in Greene's *Alphonsus* stands by silently while its non-Amazon leader fights the Amazons in the masque of Shakespeare's *Timon* sing and dance. Since these are early manifestations of the Amazon vogue in drama, their extraneousness probably reflects their initial use as spectacle rather than integrated content. Marston's *Antonio and Mellida*, the anonymous *Swetnam the Woman-Hater*, and Shirley's dramatization of the *Arcadia*, which fall into the later part of the period, contain men disguised as Amazons.

56. Anthony Gibson, trans. *A Womans Woorth* (1599), cited by Wright (n. 32 above), p. 437.

57. Ortuñez's Claridiana (trans. 1585), Spenser's Britomart and Radigund (although the latter's loss of helmet releases no golden hair), Ariosto's Bradamante (trans. 1591), Tasso's Clorinda (trans. 1600), and Phineas Fletcher's Hippolyta (*The Purple Island*, 1633). See Wright, p. 441, and Shepherd, pp. 9–10. Mary Ambree (1584) removes her helmet to astonish the besieging forces; Shepherd says she 'was forced to reveal her true gender to avoid being killed' (p. 222 n. 2), but the tone of the ballad is triumphant. Nevertheless, Ambree does share in the woman warrior's climactic feminization.

58. Hindley (n. 51 above), p. xx; quoted in a slightly different form by Shepherd, pp. 71–2.

59. Belsey (n. 4 above), p. 185. Christina Larner gives the proportion of females among those put on trial for witchcraft in England at close to 95–100% in *Witchcraft and Religion: the Politics of Popular Belief*, ed. Alan Macfarlane (New York, 1984), p. 85. Belsey's figure is taken from earlier work by Larner.

60. Cf. Mary Beth Rose's comment that cross-dressing women are 'obscuring ... the badge of their social status as well, and thereby endangering critically the predictable orderliness of social relations' ('Women in Men's Clothing: Apparel and Social Stability in *The Roaring Girl*', *English Literary Renaissance* 14 [1984]: 374).

61. Belsey, p. 185. Overall, Belsey is concerned with an extended period of 'crisis' lasting from 1542 to 1736, when the last statute against witchcraft was repealed.

62. This tract, with its new emphasis on the spectacular pact with the devil, which had not previously been a factor in Scottish witch-trials and was never very important in English ones (Larner, pp. 4, 8, 80–81, 88), seems to have evoked a little spate of conjuring dramas in the early 1590s, including *Dr Faustus* and possibly *Friar Bacon and Friar Bungay* (written between 1589 and 1592).

63. Larner, pp. 69, 9–10, 12.

64. Ibid., p. 12.

65. Ibid., pp. 12–13.

66. Ibid., pp. 14, 4, 10–11, 15.

67. Warwick does say 'That so her torture may be shortened' (V.iv.58), but it seems at best a mixed recommendation. As for the usual English treatment of witchcraft, although it sounds sufficiently grim to us, it was 'fairly far down the scale' of intensity compared with that of other countries, sufficiently different to be often called 'unique' by recent

investigators, although Larner is not willing to go that far (pp. 70–71).

68. Michel de Montaigne, in *Witchcraft in Europe 1100–1700: A Documentary History*, ed. Alan C. Kors and Edward Peters (Philadelphia, 1972), p. 337.

69. Reginald Scot, Kors and Peters, pp. 327, 326.

70. Scot, Kors and Peters, pp. 318–19.

71. This phrase and its variants (sometimes in Latin) were regularly applied to Queen Elizabeth. James's eulogistic inscription on her monument identifies her, typically, as '*super sexum*' (see Schleiner [n. 29 above], pp. 172–3).

On witches' beards, Belsey (p. 186) cites Keith Thomas's *Religion and the Decline of Magic*, p. 678. Thomas Alfred Spalding, *Elizabethan Demonology* (London, 1880), p. 99, instances *The Honest Man's Fortune*, *The Honest Whore*, and *The Merry Wives of Windsor* – besides, of course, *Macbeth*, to which both Belsey and Spalding refer.

72. Bullough, p. 61.

73. Belsey, p. 185.

74. For information on pictures of witches, I am again indebted to Ruth Luborsky. Many illustrations are also reproduced in Kors and Peters, including some of witches with animal heads and limbs, but none with transsexual characteristics.

75. *Hic Mulier*, C1v, cited by Rose (n. 61 above), p. 375.

76. Ronald S. Berman, 'Shakespeare's Conscious Histories', *Dalhousie Review* 41, 4 (Winter 1961–2): 486.

77. The research for this essay has relied greatly on the knowledgeable and generous help of Georgiana Ziegler, at the time of its preparation curator of the Furness Collection at the University of Pennsylvania, to whom I owe much gratitude.

9

'Miranda, Where's Your Sister?':
Reading Shakespeare's *The Tempest*

Ann Thompson

These are Prospero's first words in *The Tempest, or The Enchanted Island*, the adaptation of Shakespeare's play created for the most part by William Davenant, with some input from John Dryden, in 1667. They act as a clear signal to a knowing audience or reader that this is not the original. Davenant's Miranda does indeed have a younger sister, Dorinda, and the two are described in the *Dramatis Personae* as 'Daughters to Prospero, that never saw Man'. Dorinda is balanced, and ultimately partnered, by another new character, Hippolito, heir to the dukedom of Mantua, 'one that never saw Woman'. In the insistent pattern of parallels and repetitions which characterizes Davenant's version, Ariel has a female consort, Milcha, and even Caliban has a twin sister named after their mother, Sycorax, whom he proposes as a bride for Trinculo.[1] This proliferation of female roles can presumably be attributed in part to the need to provide employment for actresses on the Restoration stage.

In contrast, women are notably absent from Shakespeare's *Tempest*. Miranda at one point stresses her isolation and lack of female companionship by saying 'I do not know / One of my sex, no woman's face remember, / Save from my glass, mine own' (III.i.48–50),[2] though at the beginning of the play she had claimed at least a vague recollection: 'Had I not / Four or five women once that tended me?' (I.ii.46–7). Apart from Miranda herself, the only females mentioned in the First Folio's list of the 'Names of the Actors' are Iris, Ceres, Juno and the Nymphs, all of whom are 'spirits' explicitly impersonated by Ariel and his 'fellows'. While Ariel is clearly a male spirit, he is also required to impersonate a 'nymph of the sea' (I.ii.301) and a half-female harpy (stage direction at III.ii.52), indicating a degree of ambiguity about his gender. The part has often been performed by women or by androgynous youths. Conversely, the part of Miranda would in actuality have been performed by a boy actor on Shakespeare's stage.

Miranda, in Shakespeare's play, has no sister and apparently no mother.

It is odd that she does not even inquire about the fate of the latter, though she might have been prompted to do so by Prospero's reply to her question 'Sir, are not you my father?' In his only reference to his wife Prospero says 'Thy mother was a piece of virtue, and / She said thou wast my daughter' (I.ii.56–7). This is apparently all that needs to be said about her. Some fifty lines later, Miranda demonstrates that she has fully internalized the patriarchal assumption that a woman's main function is to provide a legitimate succession when asked to comment on the wickedness of Prospero's brother: 'I should sin / To think but nobly of my grandmother: / Good wombs have borne bad sons' (I.ii.117–19).

The worldly cynicism of such standard jokes was formerly thought inappropriate to the innocent Miranda, and they were often omitted from performances from the late eighteenth century to the early twentieth century; Davenant's Miranda more explicitly denies that she had a mother when she remarks with a coy naivety to Dorinda that she thinks Prospero 'found us when we both were little, and grew within the ground' (I.ii.332–3). In Shakespeare's version, Miranda's destined spouse, Ferdinand, is also motherless, and *his* sister's absence is curiously stressed: although the distance from Naples to North Africa is not enormous, Alonso insists that Claribel is 'so far from Italy removed / I ne'er again shall see her' (II.i.108–9), and Antonio expresses her remoteness even more extravagantly:

> She that is Queen of Tunis; she that dwells
> Ten leagues beyond man's life; she that from Naples
> Can have no note unless the sun were post –
> The man'i'th'moon's too slow – till newborn chins
> Be rough and razorable;

                                                                        II.i.244–8

Claribel had to wait until 1949 for the female poet H.D. to make her visible and give her a voice.[3] Shakespeare's Caliban has no sister and his mother, Sycorax, is long dead by the time the play's events take place. Sycorax also has a North African connection, having been banished by the Algerians, who apparently spared her life because she was pregnant. Her power is at least recognized by Prospero, Ariel and Caliban, though she is vilified by the two former characters as a 'hag' and a 'foul witch'. Oddly, Shakespeare draws on the lines Ovid gave another notorious female enchantress, Medea, for Prospero's big 'conjuring' speech, 'Ye elves of hills, brooks, standing lakes, and groves' (V.i.33 ff.), but Medea herself is not mentioned.

The fact that I have chosen nevertheless to discuss *The Tempest* in the context of this book [*Feminist Criticism: Theory and Practice*, ed. Susan Sellers] may seem perverse, but my choice is a deliberate one and relates precisely to the *absence* of female characters. I want to ask what feminist criticism can do in the face of a male-authored canonical text which seems to exclude women to this extent. Much early feminist criticism consisted merely in privileging female characters and identifying with their view-points, especially if they could be claimed to be in any way subversive or protofeminist. This is clearly impossible in *The Tempest*: even nineteenth-century female critics, who on the whole participated enthusiastically in the trend of aggrandizing and romanticizing Shakespeare's heroines, could not find a great deal to say for Miranda. Anna Jameson wrote in *Shakespeare's Heroines* (first published in 1833) that in Ophelia and Miranda Shakespeare had created two beings in whom 'the feminine character appears resolved into its very elementary principles – as modesty, grace, tenderness', but added that by the same token Miranda 'resembles nothing on earth';[4] and Mrs M.L. Elliott remarked in *Shakespeare's Garden of Girls* (1885) that Miranda was too ethereal and thus tended to be more popular with male than with female readers.[5] Anyone who has taught the play recently will know that these seem very moderate views compared to the opinions of twentieth-century female students, who find Miranda an extremely feeble heroine and scorn to identify with her. Perhaps, then, *The Tempest* can be used as something of a test case for discovering what else a feminist approach may offer beyond this character-based level.

Faced with a comparable problem in relation to *King Lear*, where modern readers hesitate to identify with either the stereotype of the bad woman represented by Goneril and Regan or with the stereotype of the good woman represented by Cordelia, Kathleen McLuskie writes:

> Feminist criticism need not restrict itself to privileging the woman's part or to special pleading on behalf of female characters. It can be equally well served by making a text reveal the conditions in which a particular ideology of femininity functions and by both revealing and subverting the hold which such an ideology has for readers both female and male.[6]

I shall attempt in the remainder of this essay to explore the 'ideology of femininity' at work in *The Tempest*, both through a reading of the play and through a survey of some of the most influential ways in which it is currently being reproduced in literary criticism.

Despite her small and comparatively passive role, the text claims that Miranda is nevertheless crucial to the play. Explaining the storm, Prospero tells her: 'I have done nothing but in care of thee' (I.ii.16). A feminist critic might ask in what sense this is true, and whether Miranda's gender is significant: would the play have worked in the same way if Prospero had had a son? How does sexuality, and especially female sexuality, function in this narrative? Reading the play with an explicit focus on issues of gender, one is immediately struck by its obsession with themes of chastity and fertility, which occur in its figurative language as well as in its literal events. These themes are often specifically associated with female sexuality. In the first, rather startling metaphor of this kind, Gonzalo imagines the very ship which seems to founder in the opening scene as being 'as leaky as an unstanched wench' (I.i.47–8), a phrase interpreted as alluding either to a sexually aroused (insatiable) woman or to one menstruating 'without the use of absorbent padding', as the Oxford editor puts it. In his long narrative speech to Miranda in the second scene, Prospero uses a metaphor of birth to describe Antonio's treachery – 'my trust, / Like a good parent, did beget of him / A falsehood' (I.ii.93–5), and seems almost to claim that he gave a kind of second birth to Miranda in his sufferings on the voyage to the island:

> When I have decked the sea with drops full salt,
> Under my burden groaned, which raised in me
> An undergoing stomach to bear up
> Against what should ensue.
>
> I.ii.155–8

This scene also introduces the literal contrast between the chaste Miranda and the 'earthy and abhorred' Sycorax who arrived on the island pregnant (by the devil himself, according to Prospero at I.ii.319) and there 'littered' or 'whelped' her subhuman son. It is notable that the acknowledged, if evil, power of Sycorax is effectively undermined by the bestial stupidity of her son, rather as the power of Tamora is defused in *Titus Andronicus* and that of the Queen in *Cymbeline*. As in the earlier plays, the son of the witch like woman is a rapist (or would-be rapist); Caliban is accused of attempting to rape Miranda, and he does not deny the charge:

> O ho, O ho! Would't had been done!
> Thou didst prevent me – I had peopled else
> This isle with Calibans.
>
> I.ii.348–50

He later promises Stephano that Miranda, seen as one of the spoils of victory, will 'bring thee forth brave brood' (III.ii.103). It is perhaps not surprising, therefore, that Ferdinand's 'prime request' to Miranda on first seeing her is 'If you be maid or no' (I.ii.428), a topic to which he returns twenty lines later, ignoring Prospero's intervention in the dialogue.

Miranda's chastity apparently has a quasi-mystical power. She herself swears 'by my modesty, / The jewel in my dower' (III.i.53–4), and tells Ferdinand: 'I am your wife if you will marry me; / If not, I'll die your maid' (III.i.83–4). Prospero warns Ferdinand in what seem to be unnecessarily harsh terms against breaking her 'virgin-knot before / All sanctimonious ceremonies' (IV.i.15–16), threatening dire consequences:

No sweet aspersion shall the heavens let fall
To make this contract grow; but barren hate,
Sour-eyed disdain, and discords shall bestrew
The union of your bed with weeds so loathly
That you shall hate it both. Therefore take heed,
As Hymen's lamps shall light you.

IV.i.18–23

Ferdinand's reply is comparably graphic:

As I hope
For quiet days, fair issue, and long life,
With such love as 'tis now, the murkiest den,
The most opportune place, the strong'st suggestion
Our worser genius can, shall never melt
Mine honour into lust, to take away
The edge of that day's celebration
When I shall think or Phoebus' steeds are foundered,
Or night kept chained below.

IV.i.23–31

Ostensibly reassuring, such language seems to suggest that the minds of both men are dwelling in morbid detail on the possibilities of completing Caliban's attempted violation: the image of Miranda as a rape victim interferes disturbingly with the image of Miranda as a chaste and fertile wife. The masque which Prospero organizes for the entertainment of the young couple in this scene explicitly banishes lust in the form of Venus and Cupid, and emphasizes the blessed fertility of honourable marriage. And yet, reading as a woman, I continue to get the feeling that the play protests too much on this score.

The speakers in the masque promise rewards for premarital chastity. As Ceres sings:

Earth's increase, foison plenty,
Barns and garners never empty,
Vines with clust'ring bunches growing,
Plants with goodly burden bowing,
Spring come to you at the farthest,
In the very end of harvest!

IV.i.110–15

This language echoes that of the earlier scene in which Gonzalo speculates on what he would do, 'Had I plantation of this isle' (II.i.141), to make nature bring forth 'all foison, all abundance' (II.i.161), in a utopian vision which is at the same time colonialist in so far as the 'commonwealth' is subject to his royal command. Sebastian jokes that he will 'carry this island home in his pocket and give it his son for an apple', to which Antonio replies: 'And sowing the kernels of it in the sea, bring forth more islands' (II.i.88–91), similarly invoking a picture of benign exploitation and a fantasy of magical male fecundity.

The play at times takes the power of the sea to give birth, or rebirth, quite seriously: later in II.i.249 Antonio refers to all the courtiers as 'sea-swallowed, though some cast again', a metaphor repeated by Ariel when, disguised as a harpy, he tells the 'men of sin' that Destiny 'the never-surfeited sea / Hath caused to belch up you' (III.iii.55–6). These are both parodies of birth: birth from the mouth rather than from the uterus. A cruder version of what the body can throw forth arises at II.ii.101–2, when Stephano sees Trinculo, hiding under Caliban's cloak, as the 'seige' or excrement of the 'mooncalf'. More seriously, in his Medea-inspired speech, Prospero claims the power to resurrect the dead: 'Graves at my command / Have waked their sleepers, oped, and let 'em forth (V.i.48–9), though Ferdinand asserts elsewhere that it is Miranda who 'quickens what's dead' (III.i.6). At the end of the play, after Ferdinand's apparent death 'mudded in that oozy bed' of the sea (V.i.151), he rhetorically attributes his 'second life' to Prospero (V.i.195), although it is Miranda's literal fertility which will, as Gonzalo explains, permit Prospero's 'issue' to become kings of Naples (V.i.205–6).

How, then, can a feminist interpret this pattern of references? What is going on in this text which seems, on the one hand, to deny the importance – and even in some cases the presence – of female characters, but which simultaneously attributes enormous power to female chastity and fertility? One noticeable feature of the handling of these themes is the insistence on male control: Prospero must control Miranda's sexuality before he hands her over to Ferdinand. Alonso, her father, formerly controlled Claribel's sexuality, but the play is ambivalent about his decision (a willing version of Desdemona's father Brabantio?) to 'lose' or 'loose' her to an African rather than to a European suitor (II.i.123),[7] and she herself is said to have been 'Weighed between loathness and obedience' in the matter (II.i.128). Men are seen as capable of controlling the fertility of nature, and Prospero even controls Ceres, the goddess of harvests, in so far as the play makes it clear that she is represented in the masque by his servant Ariel (IV.i.167). Recent criticism of *The Tempest* suggests two theoretical frameworks for discussing this question of control, the psychoanalytical and the political, both of which can be utilized in a feminist approach.

The traditional reading of *The Tempest* prevalent in the nineteenth century and earlier twentieth century interpreted Prospero's control of its events and characters as entirely benign; he was often seen as the representative of Art itself, or even identified with Shakespeare as author.

Freudian and post-Freudian psychoanalytic studies of the play have undermined this view, exposing the darker side of the 'family romance' by suggesting that Prospero's control might be more problematic and that his concern with his daughter's sexuality might indicate an incestuous desire for her. In David Sundelson's essay '"So rare a wonder'd father": Prospero's *Tempest'*, the play is fraught with anxieties and uncertainties on this level which are only partially resolved by its endorsement of what he calls both Prospero's and the play's 'paternal narcissism: the prevailing sense that there is no worthiness like a father's, no accomplishment or power, and that Prospero is the father *par excellence'*.[8] Coppélia Kahn, writing on 'The Providential Tempest and the Shakespearean Family', agrees in seeing the play as a 'fantasy of omnipotence' in which Prospero, coming from Milan to the island, 'went from child-like, self-absorbed dependency to paternal omnipotence, skipping the steps of maturation in between'. Miranda, like Marina in *Pericles* and Perdita in *The Winter's Tale*, doubles the roles of mother and daughter, uniting chastity and fertility in a non-threatening way. Yet, in so far as Kahn claims that 'Prospero's identity is based entirely on his role as father, and his family is never united or complete' – indeed he is left at the end in a state of social and sexual isolation – the 'romance' is still a narrative of imperfect wish fulfilment representing the universally ambivalent desire we all have both to escape from our families and to continue to be nurtured by them.[9] Both these readings lay stress on the tensions that arise in the play and the sheer struggle involved in asserting the supposedly natural harmony of patriarchal control: it appears that an 'unstanched wench' constitutes a serious threat to this order.

Stephen Orgel has pointed out a danger in the tendency of psychoanalytic readings to treat the play as a case-history, either of the author or of the characters, overlooking the extent to which the reader, playing the role of analyst, is a collaborator in the resultant fantasy. He further notices that while psychoanalysis evokes an unchanging, essential human nature, the theoretical framework does change:

> Recent psychoanalytic theory has replaced Freud's central Oedipal myth with a drama in which the loss of the seducing mother is the crucial trauma. As men, we used to want reassurance that we could successfully compete with or replace or supersede our fathers; now we want to know that our lost mothers will return. (p. 52)[10]

In consequence, his essay, called 'Prospero's Wife', transfers the centre of interest from the present, dominant father to the absent mother, a strategy comparable to the one employed by Coppélia Kahn in her essay on 'The Absent Mother in *King Lear'*.[11] It is, as Orgel acknowledges, a problematic strategy in so far as it deals not with the text itself but with the gaps and blanks that Shakespeare has chosen not to fill in. Indeed, he begins his study with the defensive statement 'This essay is not a reading of *The Tempest*', and worries about the possible parallels with such currently unfashionable texts as Mary Cowden Clarke's *The Girlhood of Shakespeare's Heroines*. Nevertheless, his work is highly suggestive for feminist critics in its willingness to explore a whole network of feminine allusions and absences, ranging from the obvious one of his title to more obscure issues such as the puzzling references to 'widow Dido' at II.i.70–90, Dido being a 'model at once of heroic fidelity to a murdered husband and [of] the destructive potential of erotic passion' (p. 51). He also challenges the traditional view of *The Tempest* as a happy courtship comedy, remarking that while the play does move towards marriage, the relationships are 'ignorant at best, characteristically tense, and potentially tragic'. He sees this as typical of the author:

> relationships between men and women interest Shakespeare intensely, but not, on the whole, as husbands and wives. The wooing process tends to be what it is here: not so much a prelude to marriage and a family as a process of self-definition. (p. 56)

Current political approaches to *The Tempest* often have links with psychoanalytic approaches. Orgel exemplifies one such link as he moves from his discussion of the missing wife, by way of speculations about Shakespeare's own family experiences, to an analysis of power and authority in the play in terms of the ways these issues were conceived in Jacobean England. He points out that in setting up the contest for the island between Caliban, who claims his inheritance from his mother, and Prospero, whose authority is self-created, Shakespeare is representing positions which were available – indeed, normative – at the time. Further, in his edition of *The Tempest*, Orgel goes on to consider the real-life significance of political marriages like the one in the play where Prospero goes to considerable trouble to marry his daughter to the son of his chief enemy, thereby staging a counter-usurpation of Naples by Milan.

The fact that *The Tempest* was performed at court in 1613 during the wedding festivities of King James's daughter Elizabeth and Frederick the Elector Palatine gives a further resonance to such speculations. This historical circumstance is the starting point for Lorie Jerrell Leininger's feminist reading, 'The Miranda Trap: Sexism and Racism in Shakespeare's *Tempest*'.[12] She imagines the sixteen-year-old princess as the real-life equivalent of Miranda: beautiful, loving, chaste and above all obedient to her all-powerful father. Miranda's role as the dependent female is crucial to the play's dynamics of power in so far as Caliban's enslavement is justified by his attempt to rape her: 'Prospero needs Miranda as sexual bait, and then needs to protect her from the threat which is inescapable given his hierarchical world' (p. 289). Shakespeare's play allows Miranda no way out of this situation, but Leininger invents an epilogue for a modern Miranda who refuses to participate in the play's assumptions that Prospero is infallible, that Caliban is a 'natural' slave, and that a daughter is a 'foot' in a family organism of which the father is the head.

Most political readings of *The Tempest*, however, centre on the issue of colonialism. This is the focus of Francis Barker and Peter Hulme's essay '"Nymphs and Reapers Heavily Vanish": The Discursive Con-texts of *The Tempest*',[13] and of Paul Brown's essay '"This thing of darkness I acknowledge mine": *The Tempest* and the Discourse of Colonialism'.[14] Both employ the technique of intertextuality to relate the play to nascent seventeenth-century European colonialism, reassessing the 'sources' in the context of New World voyage materials and arguing that anxiety and ambivalence result from the struggle to create a self-justifying, colonialist discourse. We are encouraged in these readings to be deeply suspicious of Prospero and to sympathize with Caliban as the representative of an exploited Third World. Brown draws on Freudian theory to point out an analogy between the political operations of colonialism and the modes of psychic repression, and he uses the Freudian concept of 'dreamwork' to discuss the way in which Prospero's discourse subordinates that of the other inhabitants of the island, as, for example, when he imposes his memory of earlier events on both Caliban and Ariel in I.ii.

An explicitly feminist version of this kind of reading, and one which is moreover undertaken from a Third World viewpoint, is performed by the Indian critic Ania Loomba as the final chapter of her book *Gender, Race, Renaissance Drama*.[15] Loomba is critical of the tendency of 'alternative' readings of *The Tempest* to seize upon Caliban as a symbol of exploitation and potential rebellion, and points out that some anti-colonialist or anti-racist readings have been unthinkingly sexist: the specific repression of Miranda has been neglected. Setting out to delineate the limits of the text's supposed 'radical ambivalence', she discusses the myth of the black rapist, the significance of Sycorax as 'Prospero's other', and the contradictory position of Miranda as typical of that of all white women in the colonial adventure: the nature of her participation confirms her subordination to white men.

Both psychoanalytic and political theoretical approaches nevertheless deny some of the pleasures experienced by earlier generations of audiences and readers who were apparently able to identify more readily with the viewpoint of Prospero as white male patriarch and colonizer. Today, white male critics in Britain and the United States understandably feel uncomfortable and guilty about participating in these attitudes. Reading the play as a woman and as a feminist, it is possible to feel good about delineating and rejecting its idealization of patriarchy, and one can go beyond the play to consider the conscious and unconscious sexism of its critical and stage history. Reading as a white British person, my conscience is less clear: women as well as men benefited (and still benefit) from the kind of colonialism idealized in *The Tempest*.

The current situation as I have sketched it above seems to leave two major questions unanswered (and unanswerable within the scope of this essay): first, is it possible for a staging of *The Tempest* to convey anything approaching a feminist reading of the text (without rewriting it or adding something like Leininger's epilogue); and secondly, what kind of pleasure can a woman and a feminist take in this text beyond the rather grim one of mapping its various patterns of exploitation? Must a feminist reading necessarily be a negative one?

Notes

1. Maximilian E. Novak and George Robert Guffey, eds, *The Works of John Dryden* (vol. X, Berkeley, CA. and London: University of California Press, 1970). I would like to thank Andrew Gurr for drawing my attention to the line which forms my title.

2. References and quotations from *The Tempest* are from the Oxford Shakespeare text, ed. Stephen Orgel (Oxford and New York: Oxford University Press, 1987).

3. See *By Avon River* (New York: Macmillan, 1949). For a discussion of H.D.'s transformation of *The Tempest* in this experimental work, see Susan Stanford Friedman, 'Remembering Shakespeare Differently: H.D.'s *By Avon River*', in Marianne Novy, ed., *Women's Revisions of Shakespeare* (Urbana and Chicago: University of Illinois Press, 1990), pp. 143–64.

4. *Shakespeare's Heroines*, 1897 reprint (London: George Bell & Sons), pp. 134, 149.

5. *Shakespeare's Garden of Girls*, published anonymously (London: Remington & Co., 1885), p. 265.

6. 'The Patriarchal Bard: Feminist Criticism and Shakespeare: *King Lear* and *Measure for Measure*', in Jonathan Dollimore and Alan Sinfield, eds, *Political Shakespeare* (Manchester: Manchester University Press, 1985), pp. 88–108.

7. The First Folio's spelling, 'loose', was the normal spelling of 'lose', but most modern editors, with the exception of Stephen Orgel, print 'loose', presumably because it carries an undertone of greater sensuality.

8. In Murray M. Schwartz and Coppélia Kahn, eds, *Representing Shakespeare: New Psychoanalytic Essays* (Baltimore, MD and London: Johns Hopkins University Press, 1980), pp. 33–53.

9. In Schwartz and Kahn, *Representing Shakespeare*, pp. 217–43. Passages cited are on p. 238 and p. 240.

10. 'Prospero's Wife', in Margaret W. Ferguson, Maureen Quilligan and Nancy J. Vickers, eds, *Rewriting the Renaissance: The Discourses of Sexual Difference in Early Modern Europe* (Chicago and London: University of Chicago Press, 1986), pp. 50–64. This essay was first published in *Representations* 8 (1984): 1–13.

11. In Ferguson, Quilligan and Vickers, *Rewriting the Renaissance*, pp. 33–49.

12. In Carolyn Ruth Swift Lenz, Gayle Greene and Carol Thomas Neely, eds, *The Woman's Part* (Urbana and Chicago: University of Illinois Press, 1980), pp. 285–94.

13. In John Drakakis, ed., *Alternative Shakespeares* (London and New York: Methuen, 1985), pp. 191–205.

14. In Dollimore and Sinfield, *Political Shakespeare*, pp. 48–71.

15. Manchester: Manchester University Press, 1989, pp. 142–58.

10

The Two Antonios and Same-Sex Love in *Twelfth Night* and *The Merchant of Venice*

Joseph Pequigney

I

The comic Antonios have more in common than a name. The earlier and more prominent one is the title character of *The Merchant of Venice*, written in 1596/97, whose friend is the suitor and winner of Portia, Bassanio. The other, created some five years later for *Twelfth Night*, is the sea captain whose companion is Viola's twin and Olivia's husband-to-be, Sebastian. Each Antonio loves his friend more than anyone or anything else, is emotionally dependent on him, proves willing to risk his very life on the friend's account, and provides him with funds, with painful consequences to himself. Neither shows romantic or other interest in a woman. The friends, however, do otherwise, both choosing wedlock and appearing with a wife or fiancée in, among other scenes, the last, where Antonio appears too, but ladyless. Of major concern here will be whether or not the striking resemblances between the Antonios include that of sexual orientation.

The Shakespeare professoriat has a long history of avoiding the topic of homosexuality, and the critics and scholars who have written on these comedies fall into three categories: those – the largest group – who have given this topic no thought; those who are doctrinaire in denying the topic pertinence; and those – a relatively small but recently growing number, many of them feminists – who ascribe homosexuality to both the Antonios.[1] The second group always and the third ordinarily are assertive of positions that they think are self-evident and require – or admit of – no proof, so that disagreement rules in the commentary. Moreover, the critics who postulate homoerotic Antonios also maintain that the homoerotic impulses are suppressed; that the love returned by the other is non-erotic; and that the characters are finally ostracized and marginalized.

My argument will generate different answers to the above questions, and will find others germane, as how the stories of love between men are thematized in congruence with the peculiar conception of the Christian ethic that saturates *The Merchant of Venice* and with the psychological/ bisexual pattern that pervades *Twelfth Night*. Starting with Antonio the sea captain in *Twelfth Night* and Sebastian, I will proceed by examining: the discourse of Antonio; the treatment of the actions and characters of the two male intimates and the rendition of their shared history; scenes in which they do not appear but which serve to shed light on their behaviour; and a series of analogous love-experiences inscribed in the plot. My endeavour will be to *secure* the homoerotic character of the friendship by attempting to settle the question through textual analysis and argumentation, in the hope of removing it from current vagaries, distortions and prejudice. The procedure will be hermeneutic in so far as I am able to discover norms for determining which friends in other Shakespearean plays are represented as homosexual. Then my discussion of the merchant Antonio and his friend Bassanio will utilize those norms.

II

That the Antonio of *Twelfth Night* is passionately in love with his friend 'his words [that] do from such passion fly'[2] will amply demonstrate. The openly amorous language habitual to him whenever he speaks to or about Sebastian – and rarely does his attention turn to anything else – is the foremost clue to the erotic nature of their friendship. In their first scene, when Sebastian initially proposes that they separate, Antonio says: 'If you will not murder me for my love, let me be your servant' (II.i.31), that is, accompany you as a 'servant', a word that can also mean 'lover'; and the love that ascribes the cruel power to slay to the beloved is romantic, smacking of Petrarchan love. Then in soliloquy at the end of the scene, despite his 'many enemies' in Illyria, Antonio resolves to go there in pursuit of Sebastian, for 'I do adore thee so, / That danger shall seem sport, and I will go' (II.i.44–7). Such 'adoration', especially as prompting the adorer to risk his all happily and carelessly only to be with the other, must stem from passion. Later catching up with Sebastian, Antonio explains: 'My desire, / More sharp than filed steel, did spur me forth' (III.iii.4–5). This impelling 'desire' is sensual: the very word would connote libido even apart from the intensifying metaphor of the flesh-cutting metal spur. Afterwards, under the mistaken impression that Sebastian has refused to return money given him, an offended and irate Antonio gives even fuller utterance to his idolization of the youth, with stress on his physical beauty: 'And to his image [that is, his external appearance], which methought did promise / Most venerable worth, did I devotion.' But the devotion was apparently misplaced: 'O how vile an idol proves this god', the youth deified and adored, who has 'done good feature [that is, his handsome looks] shame', for 'Virtue is beauty' and 'the beauteous evil' [that is, rascally beauties, such as this one] 'are empty trunks, o'er-flourish'd by the devil' (III.iv.371–9). Then in the last act Antonio tells of 'My love without retention or restraint', where 'without restraint' is particularly suggestive, and says: 'A witchcraft drew me hither' – that is, he was pulled into this city of enemies by erotic enchantment. The only real parallel in Shakespeare for such eroticized speech about a fair youth occurs in the sonnets.

Not his words only but also his correlated actions reflect Antonio's avid devotion to the master-mistress of *his* passion. So unacceptable is separation from Sebastian that despite the danger to himself in a hostile Illyria, Antonio follows him there and, finding him, leaves to make overnight accommodations. This second separation is followed by a second reunion at the end of the play. The companions had long since been inseparable, in fact ever since their first meeting: 'for three months ... No int'rim, not a minute's vacancy / Both day and night did [they] keep company' (V.i.92–4). And Antonio will see to it that they 'keep company' this night also as he goes off to arrange for their dining and sleeping together at the Elephant, an inn. 'There,' he says, 'shall you have me' (III.iii.42).

Before going he hands a purse to Sebastian, who asks 'Why I your purse?' He may chance upon 'some toy' he wishes to buy, Antonio replies, and 'your store is not for idle markets, sir' (III.iii.43–6). A kind and generous gesture, to be sure, but the intent behind it is less simple than the reply suggests. In the next adjacent scene, and some few lines later, Olivia, doting on Cesario, asks Maria: 'How shall I feast him? What bestow on him? / For *youth is bought more oft than begg'd or borrow'd*' (III.iv.2–3; emphasis added). This observation clearly has retrospective reference to the purse, indicating that it is given with the ulterior motive of pleasing, if not purchasing, the desired youth.

In I.ii Viola appears for the only time dressed as a girl, and she, like her twin, is also with a sea captain. She plans to part from him too, and while she remarks his 'fair and outward character', and believes him to have a 'mind that suits' with it (I.ii.49–51), their pending separation is depicted as casual and unemotional, over against the strong feelings the corresponding separation elicits in Sebastian (II.i.39) and *his* sea captain. These two, it is true, have been longer and closer together, but the calm parting of the unattached female and the appealing male, where attraction might have been more expected, is tellingly juxtaposed with the emotionally charged parting of the characters who are both male.

To turn now to Sebastian's part in their story: for months he has continuously remained with an adoring older man who is frankly desirous of him, who showered him with 'kindnesses' (III.iv.360), and who, moreover, saved him from death at sea and nursed him back to health. It is the classic homoerotic relationship, wherein the mature lover serves as guide and mentor to the young beloved. Sebastian comes to depend on Antonio both emotionally and in practical matters: emotionally when he can scarcely hold back tears, the shedding of which he regards as effeminate ('the manners of my mother' [II.i.39]) at his proposed parting from Antonio; and practically in looking to him for advice when he is perplexed by Olivia's unaccountable conduct: 'Where's Antonio then? . . . His counsel now might do me golden service' (IV.iii.4–8).

For making the original decision to go off alone Sebastian gives the curious reason that he is afraid his own bad luck may rub off on his friend ('the malignancy of my fate might perhaps distemper yours' [II.i.4–5]). The motivation is flimsy – both dramatically (although dictated by the plot) and also in his mind – for he quickly relents when Antonio finds him and thereafter says nothing more about wanting to withdraw. Sebastian's change of heart is anticipated by the melancholy leave-taking, and is more in character than the initial decision, for everywhere else he shows himself obliging, compliant alike to the wishes of Olivia and of Antonio, as a boy who cannot say no.

When he is initially about to depart, Sebastian makes the curious admission that as a companion to Antonio he had always gone by another name, calling himself Roderigo. Why he should do so goes unexplained in both the comedy and the commentary. The alias may be demystified if it is seen as a means to hide his identity, his true name and family connections, during a drawn-out sexual liaison with a stranger in strange lands. When his twin Viola, in male disguise, correspondingly goes by an assumed name, Cesario, she gets caught up in novel, and homoerotic, sexual situations. Isn't this an intimation of something analogous happening – as it does – to Roderigo? Then, too, the given name Sebastian recalls the martyr traditionally pictured as a handsome youth – a kind of Christian Adonis – with a nearly nude body pierced by arrows. Our Sebastian is not a martyr, of course, although he once came close to death by drowning; yet like the saint, he is a young male beauty and, again like him, passive, the target of Olivia's as well as Antonio's desires.[3]

And what will happen to the male friends after one of them is startlingly claimed by a lady for her husband? The virtually unanimous opinion of critics, in the words of one of them, is that 'Poor Antonio is left out in the cold.' Stephen Greenblatt's judgement rests on dubious textual grounds, and is connected with his sense of 'the disquieting intensity of Antonio's passion for Sebastian'.[4] Disquieting to whom? Not to Sebastian or Antonio, nor to any other character, and not to the playwright when one looks closely at what he actually wrote. When, near the end of *Twelfth Night*, Sebastian makes his last entry, he speaks to his fiancée Olivia fondly ('sweet one') and apologetically (for hurting her kinsman), but he has far more ardent words for his comrade – whom he at first sought to quit, has since been frantically seeking, and now to his great relief finds: 'Antonio! O my dear Antonio, / How have the hours rack'd and tortur'd me, / Since I have lost thee!' (V.i.216–18). This, the most impassioned speech Sebastian delivers, is hardly the prelude to a rejection; and, further, with his late dramatic change of fortune, the sole reason he gives for the separation disappears. The expectation is set up that in taking a wife Sebastian will not and need not suffer the 'rack and torture' of losing his male lover. Not the rejected 'poor Antonio' of the commentary, he is instead the 'dear Antonio' here and hereafter of lucky Sebastian.[5] Does this imply a *ménage à trois* at Olivia's house? That's anybody's guess, but a guess about nothing, for once they leave the stage the characters vanish into thin air.

From the data amassed above I gather that Sebastian has a personality endowed with a homoerotic component that has been awakened and activated under a peculiar and propitious set of circumstances. These include his continuous and clearly agreeable association, during a lengthy sojourn in the freedom of pseudonymity, with a saviour, benefactor, fervid admirer, and would-be lover. Inasmuch as he proves capable of erotically responding to man and woman, Sebastian would be bisexual, while Antonio, who is depicted with desire confined to a male object, would appear to be homosexual.

Sebastian's amorous involvement with members of both sexes falls into a broader configuration of the plot and derives substantiation from different dramatic situations. Bisexual experiences are not the exception but the rule in *Twelfth Night*, and they are vital to the course of love leading to wedlock for the three principal lovers other than Sebastian: Orsino, Olivia, and Viola.

Near the close of the play, Orsino asks Cesario for his/her hand. He proposes marriage to someone he knows and has come to love only as a male servant, seen only in masculine clothes, whose feminine name he never once utters, and whom in the scene he twice addresses as 'boy' (V.i.127, 264) – even at the proposal itself – and refers to as late as his final speech as being still a 'man' (385). Early on, despite the cross-dressing, he does perceive Viola's true gender, noting her girlish lip and voice and 'all' as 'semblative to a woman's part' (I.iv.30–34). The response, though, may do less to establish his heterosexual credentials than to symptomatize homoerotic proclivities, for according to Freud, 'what excited a man's love' in ancient Greece (and still may do so) 'was not the *masculine* character of a boy, but his physical resemblance to a woman as well as his feminine mental qualities', with the 'sexual object' being 'someone who combines the characters of both sexes' and 'a kind of reflection of the

subject's own bisexual nature'.[6] This theory seems clearly borne out by
Orsino; and, further, his capacity to love the youth Cesario and the girl
Viola is crucial to the happy ending for them both. His attraction to Olivia,
where he is heterosexually straight, like the other would-be wooers Sir
Andrew Aguecheek and Malvolio, is a disaster. The love for Cesario could
not have changed instantaneously with the revelation of his femaleness; if
it is erotic, then it would have been erotic before; what does change is that
marriage suddenly becomes possible, hence the immediate proposal. This
love that commences as homoerotic and conducts Orsino into nuptual
heterosexuality is an unbroken curve, a bisexual continuity.

Olivia ends up engaged to marry a perfect stranger, Sebastian, and not
the one she fell madly in love with and thought she had become betrothed
to, who all along had been a male-impersonating girl. If she misses the tell-
tale signs of femaleness that Orsino picks up on, that is because it is in her
erotic interest to fantasize Cesario as virile, yet the feminine subtext,
however ignored, remains legible. In Sebastian's last speech to her, coming
just after the confusion of identity has been straightened out, he says,
almost tauntingly,

> So comes it, lady, you have been mistook.
> But nature to her bias drew in that.
> You would have been contracted to a maid;
> Nor are you therein, by my life, deceiv'd:
> You are betroth'd both to a maid and man.

> (V.i.257–61)

She has been 'mistook' in two related senses: 'mistaken' in taking Cesario
for a male, and 'taken amiss' in being captivated by a female (cf. II.ii.34).
But in 'that' matter of being 'mistook', nature 'drew' 'to her bias' or
described a curved course (like the curve of a bowling ball that the noun
denotes), and this homoerotic swerving or lesbian deviation from the
heterosexual straight and narrow cannot be considered unnatural, since it
is effected by nature herself. 'Would' in the third line above, indicative of
a contrary-to-fact condition, may also connote 'would like [to]', a
condition of wishing. That 'you are betroth'd both to a maid and man' is
not a deception but precisely right: to 'both' twins, the maid who elicited
your love and whom you thought you were contracting to marry, and the
man who accidentally and unbeknownst to anyone substituted for her, and
to whom you are in fact engaged.[7] The line (261) may also bear this
alternate reading: Sebastian could be referring only to himself, as a maiden
man, a girl/boy, a master (to Olivia)-mistress (to Antonio).[8]

Like Orsino, Olivia goes through a homoerotic phase that lasts through
and beyond betrothal; both have experiences that evince their bisexuality.
Nor do they ever pass beyond it, for it is the *sine qua non* of their

psychological development – his away from a fruitless doting on her, hers away from fixation on a dead brother – and it has a crucial, integral, and unerasable part in both their love stories, that of Orsino with Cesario/Viola and that of Olivia with Cesario/Sebastian.[9]

Viola works a variation on this bisexual theme. In imitating her brother as his 'glass' (III.iv.389–93), she combines both sexes: 'I am all the daughters of my father's house, / And all the brothers too' (I.iv.121–2). From the fourth scene on, however, she plays a brother rather than a daughter, being masculine in name, dress, behaviour, and the awareness of the other characters; not until the late recognition scene between the twins is she called Viola, and nobody else ever uses her real name. As Cesario she enters into a male friendship with Orsino, having man-to-'man' talks with him, mainly about women and love; and spontaneously responding to the beauty of Olivia ('Tis beauty truly blent' [I.v.142–6, 255]), she throws herself headlong into the assignment of courting her. Partly because she is in love and knows how she would like to be wooed, she succeeds with the proud and disdainful lady, even reducing her to amorous desperation. She proves herself a better man at wooing than Orsino is, with his go-betweens, or than her brother, with the strain of passivity in his nature, could ever be. Sebastian could never have done what was necessary to win Olivia, and his only chance was for his sister to perform this masculine role for him. Her Cesario makes a lasting impression.

Sebastian turns out to be the most extreme exemplar of this recurring theme of bisexuality, for he is not only attracted to, but also able and willing sexually to enjoy, both a man and a woman – and in his case a man and a woman who are, and with obvious passion, enamoured of him. While he remains heterosexually virginal, he is unlike the virgins Viola and Olivia or Orsino in that he entertains homosexual impulses that are fully conscious and indulged. Antonio awakens those impulses, initiates him into interpersonal sexuality, and perhaps thereby prepares him to receive the sudden, surprising advances of the Illyrian lady. The reason for Antonio's portrayal as homosexual is that a liaison with him opens space for Sebastian in the diverse bisexual fictions that make up *Twelfth Night*.[10]

These fictions have a dimension of metadrama, and nowhere else does Shakespeare more elaborately play with his theatre's convention of boys in the opposite-sex roles. In this comedy five actors play three male characters and two who are female, including the one disguised most of the time as male, that are love-related in the following pairs: a man (Orsino) and a pseudo-boy (Cesario); a cross-dressed (Viola) and another young woman (Olivia); male with female (both Sebastian with Olivia and Orsino with Viola); and two men (Sebastian and Antonio). The first two pairs are sexually ambiguous, the next two move towards heterosexual unions, and the last is homosexual. It is in this last relationship that the dramatic representation becomes most transparent to what was actually happening on the Elizabethan stage, since the lovers are both males, and so were the players who took the roles.

III

As *The Merchant of Venice* opens, the other Antonio is sad, and says he does not know why. That 'why' (I.i.1) never receives an explicit answer. When the pair Salerio/Solanio probe for the causes, one suggests: 'Why then you are in love' (I.i.46). The response is an evasive 'Fie, fie!' which registers a mild embarrassment at the very idea, and which is received by the others as a negation that closes the subject.

Solanio had clearly meant 'in love' erotically and heterosexually, which Antonio never is. His 'fie, fie' rules out that, but not the kind of love he holds for Bassanio. He had known something about his friend's wife-seeking plans even before the opening speech, and that the pending loss of him was the cause of the initial sadness is implicit in the description of his behaviour when Bassanio was setting out for Belmont. Then, 'with affection wondrous sensible', an eye 'big with tears', face averted and hand held behind him, Antonio 'wrung Bassanio's hand, and so they parted'. The listener adds: 'I think he only loves the world for him' (II.viii.46–50), a choral comment amply justified by Antonio's actions.

He seldom verbalizes his love, and we hear more about it from others' mouths than from his own. He makes his fullest statement on the subject in the courtroom as he expects to be put to the knife by Shylock; he again bids Bassanio farewell and now asks him to tell his 'honorable wife' 'how I lov'd you' and to 'bid her judge / Whether Bassanio had not once a love' (IV.i.269–73). Here the word 'love' may signify 'an experience of love', as I suspect it does. But it may also or instead mean 'lover', in which case the usage, of one man as the 'love' of another, is rare, and with the exception of the sonnets does not occur elsewhere in Shakespeare or, I believe, in the period.

The word 'lover' as 'friend', without erotic connotation, was quite common, however. It is used twice with reference to Antonio, by Lorenzo to Portia – 'How dear a lover of my lord your husband' – and then by her some ten lines later (III.iv.7, 17) in an important and often misconstrued speech. She makes it after having wed Bassanio and sent him off to Venice with ducats galore to redeem Antonio. Her insight, first into male friendship, and then into the deep affinity between that friendship and the erotic love of man and woman, is remarkable. She explains:

                    in companions
That do converse and waste the time together,
Whose souls do bear an egall yoke of love,
There must be needs a like proportion
Of lineaments, of manners, and of spirit;
Which makes me think that this Antonio
Being the bosom lover of my lord,
Must be like my lord.

                                                        (III.iv.11–18)

As opposed to the idea that opposites attract, the true basis of liking here
is likeness – moral, spiritual, and even physical. 'Lineaments' is a curious
word: it brings bodily features or physical but asexual compatibility of
some sort into this conception of friendship, but it does not specify physical
beauty. Her husband and his 'bosom lover' are necessarily so close that
Portia can be confident that in knowing the one she thereby gains
knowledge of the other whom she has never met. She continues:

                    If it be so,
How little is the cost I have bestowed
In purchasing the semblance of my soul
From out the state of hellish cruelty!

                                                        (18–21)

While 'my soul' could figuratively allude to Bassanio, as most annotators
surmise, a literal reading seems to me far preferable and impossible to
dismiss. Antonio is the 'semblance' of Portia's soul because the love each
has for Bassanio ensures that their souls or selves, in resembling his, must
thereby resemble each other.[11] Portia postulates a kind of spiritual homol-
ogy between the male–male and male–female loves, and sees them as now
composing a triangle, although one without discord among its members.
The insight enunciated here has, as will be seen, telling implications for the
comic resolution at the close.

Antonio expresses his love primarily through deeds. His pledge to
Bassanio that 'My purse, my person, my extremest means / Lie all
unlock'd to your occasions' (I.i.137–9) is amply carried out in what
follows, as he not only risks his fortune and life by signing the bond but
is content to give up both for his friend: 'pray God Bassanio come / To see
me pay his debt, and then I care not' (III.iii.35–6), and in a last message
to him the sole request is that 'I might but see you at my death', and even
then only if love and not 'my letter' should 'persuade you to come'
(III.ii.318–20).

Bassanio's love – along with Portia's urging – does persuade him to
come, and he speaks of his devotion early on: 'to you Antonio / I owe the
most in money and in love' (I.i.130–31). Later he asserts that 'life itself,

my wife, and all the world, / Are not with me esteem'd above thy life. / I would lose all ... to deliver you' (IV.i.280–83). Even though this Antonio may love Bassanio exclusively, emotionally, and to the point of willingness to die for him, and even though Bassanio may return the love along with gratitude and to the extent of valuing his friend higher than everything else, their love is very different from that between Antonio and Sebastian in *Twelfth Night*.

Neither of the Venetian friends ever makes reference to physical beauty in the other, or even speaks in amorous terms to or about the other, and neither has any reason to employ an alias. Neither do they ever lodge together, let alone keeping exclusively to themselves for months on end without let-up. Both Antonios put their lives in jeopardy on account of the friend and provide him with funds, the one knowing he will lose him thereby, and the other seeking to hang on to him. Both save their friends: one from ruinous debt and deprivation of a desirable marriage, and the other from drowning, although the latter, upon nursing Sebastian back to health, cannot bear to relinquish him, while the merchant, however sorrowfully, does accept Bassanio's departure. While they have little to do with women, and most of that with women in disguise, the one Antonio belongs to the commercial life of Venice, the other chooses a life at sea on manned ships, except that lately he has been roaming on land with the fair young 'Roderigo'. As to the friends, the acquiescence that is so salient in Sebastian is a trait not shared by the enterprising, risk-taking Bassanio, and his name does not conjure up any associations of youthful comeliness and pierced flesh such as 'Sebastian' can evoke. Moreover, male friendship in *The Merchant of Venice* is furnished with no comparable scenes and no plot rich in situational analogues of the kind that corroborate and thematize bisexuality and homoeroticism in *Twelfth Night*. Even cross-dressing works differently in the two comedies: Portia and Nerissa adopt male disguise to participate in a legal action, as distinct from Viola, whose disguise involves her in varied eroticized actions.

As the above contrasts make plain, the profusion of detail that establishes and supports the homoerotic character of the liaison between Antonio and Sebastian in *Twelfth Night* is not to be found in *The Merchant of Venice*, wherein there is almost nothing to suggest a sexual dimension in the amity of Antonio and Bassanio. This Antonio is not, then, like the other, 'in love', and his love for his friend is philia instead of eros.

Such love was expounded by Aristotle and Cicero, and consciously cultivated and idealized in the Renaissance. But commentators as a rule have had trouble distinguishing between, on the one hand, the homoeroticism in the depiction of Antonio and Sebastian in *Twelfth Night* or of the male lovers of the sonnets and, on the other hand, the non-libidinal mutuality exemplified by Antonio and Bassanio, and of which Hamlet and

Horatio are but two of the many other exemplars in Shakespearean drama. The term 'same-sex love' in my title does not translate *homosexual* but is meant to be more comprehensive, more akin to Eve Sedgwick's notion of 'male homosocial desire', comprising the male bond in which the sexual body takes part and the one in which it does not,[12] as well as affinities between those bonds, as, for example, the affective attachment to the other and psychic need of him common to both Antonios.

To eliminate the reigning misguidance in the commentary that has another poor Antonio ending up relegated to the outer cold,[13] it is imperative to re-examine the episode of the rings, which begins near the middle of *The Merchant of Venice* and becomes dominant towards the end.

Portia, overjoyed when Bassanio wins the lottery and herself, gives him a ring with the injunction that discarding it would 'presage the ruin of your love, / And be my vantage to exclaim on you'. He receives it with the pledge that he would relinquish it only with his life (III.ii.173–4, 183–4). The compact is so solemn that any violation of it should have dire consequences, but in this comedy the breaking of contracts, when higher principles intervene, is commendable – as witness what happens to the bond.

Portia's own motives for reclaiming the ring, in her role as Balthasar and as a reward for 'his' legal brilliance and triumph, are never directly disclosed; but they are implicitly contained in a statement made to Nerissa when she resolves likewise to get her husband's ring, which he too had sworn 'to keep forever'. Portia remarks 'We shall have old swearing / That they did give the rings away to men; / And we'll outface them, and outswear them too' (IV.ii.15–17). Gratiano has just delivered Bassanio's ring when she says this, but she is not bothered; to the contrary, she is in high spirits and anticipates with relish the scene that will ensue at Belmont when both husbands return ringless and tender tall excuses the wives have fun disputing. Portia's words here and her behaviour in the final scene, the jocund one she forecasts, imply that her intention in seeking the ring is to play a practical joke, and certainly that is a part of it, if not all.

Bassanio surrenders the ring only when Balthasar has left and Antonio requests that he do so: 'Let his deservings and my love withal / Be valued 'gainst your wife's commandment' (IV.i.446–7). Another too had urged the very same course – that wife herself in disguise. Portia and Antonio, the two to whom he is most deeply committed and who most have earned the audience's trust, both press him, one cryptically (IV.i.440–44) and the other openly, to give away the ring. It is more than dramatic irony, it is intuition born of really knowing Portia that causes Bassanio to say to her afterwards at Belmont: 'Had you been there, I think you would have begg'd / The ring of me to give the worthy doctor' (V.i.221–2). How right he is: she was there and did so.

Before Portia, Bassanio rather desperately defends parting with the ring, but he does refer to the decision as a 'fault' and asks her to 'forgive me this enforced wrong' (V.i.186, 240). If *enforced*, the wrong is unavoidable, and one might regard him as having been in an impossible dilemma, wrong to and wrong not to let go of the ring. However, he extends the apology (a) still ignorant of Balthasar's true identity, and (b) under Portia's relentless and wittily disingenuous verbal assaults, which he takes at face value, before learning what we have known all along: that she has been teasing him. If she has a serious purpose as well, it materializes when and by the manner in which she gives him the ring once again.

For these actions of Portia and Bassanio to be fully understood they must be viewed in the larger context of the play's religion and morality. A Christian–Jewish opposition is fundamental to *The Merchant of Venice*, with Judaism exemplified almost singly by Shylock, the villain, and Christianity by most of the other characters, and particularly by the three kindred spirits Antonio, Portia, and Bassanio. The religion treated herein is hardly theological – outside Portia's 'quality of mercy' speech, God and salvation are rarely mentioned, Christ never. Apart from the exegetical dispute between Antonio and Shylock over the Genesis account of Jacob and Laban's sheep (I.iii.66–90) and the allusion to the Lord's Prayer at IV.i.196–8, religion is hardly scriptural either. Instead religion is pretty much restricted to right conduct. The Christian ethic does not derive from the New Testament so much as from Portia's father, who devised the inscription on the winning lead casket, and it may be reformulated as a beatitude: blessed is he who chooses to 'give and hazard all he hath' (II.vii.9, 16; II.ix.21). Shylock's actions – and that they are presented as characteristically Hebrew is truly disquieting – go counter to this principle: he will give and hazard nothing. This is his business as well as his personal ethic. As a moneylender he takes security to eliminate risk, in contrast to Antonio, who deals in the hazardous – hence laudable – enterprise of overseas trading. To make money by venture capital is commendable, by banking reprehensible. When Jessica elopes with some of Shylock's wealth and, with her Christian husband, squanders it, that not only serves the miser right, but her prodigality is a seal of her conversion. The ring from Leah may have sentimental value for Shylock, but it sears him to let go of any material possession. He wishes his own daughter dead, and his ducats and jewels restored with the corpse (III.i.108–13, 80–82). He ends up with nothing except what Christian mercy vouchsafes him. It is better to give than to receive in this moral universe, in no small part because those who give abundantly receive abundantly. This paradox does not conflict with the commandment that valorizes, along with loving one's neighbour, loving oneself. It is when self-interest, especially with regard to affluence, is prioritized and exclusory that it becomes Shylockian. The comic version of Christian charity entails rich mundane rewards. Justice prevails in the here and now, with no reference to any hereafter. The graspers and hoarders lose; the givers gamble and win.

Bassanio gambles everything on the lottery. Like the others who play, he risks having to remain wifeless, but in addition he risks utter financial ruin. Again, in the courtroom he 'would lose all' he had gained by his victory, along with his life, to deliver Antonio. This proposal reveals a frame of mind in which Bassanio is detached enough from his new acquisitions to be able to forgo them for a higher imperative, and it places him, in terms of bountifulness, in a class with Antonio and Portia. He follows their advice and manifests feeling the opposite of Shylock's in resigning the ring. Here he rightly takes another chance. He again complies with the give-and-hazard code of conduct. This code – operative in both the pound-of-flesh and casket-test plots, and linking them, as also in the ring episode – is everywhere sanctioned and always rewarded in the comedy.[14]

Each of the instances of giving and/or hazarding proves beneficial to Bassanio. In the first he wins Portia and her fortune; in the second his projected self-sacrifice is obviated when Portia/Balthasar comes to the rescue of Antonio; in the third the ring is returned with interest, that of a renewed and abiding friendship with Antonio.

Portia is at once the prize of the lottery and put at risk by it, hazarding out of filial obedience her nuptial happiness. The results are not simply a matter of luck, however, for the winner must prove to be perspicacious and right-minded, as Bassanio does in choosing the lead casket. Then Portia gives him all she has – herself, her wealth, her mansion, her servants – with the one regret that she does not have immensely more to give (III.ii.152–7). Nor is this exuberant wish to lavish favours on him frustrated. The next benefit she finds to confer is to liberate his friend. Then she gets the ring back in order to give it to him a second time, and this time through and with Antonio.

Antonio is the referent of the title because, besides being the protagonist to Shylock's antagonist, he gives and hazards the most. All his wealth is risked in foreign trade and then seemingly lost, and without distressing him; he lets go of Bassanio, on account of whom alone he loves the world; and most crucially, he ventures the pound of flesh and is ready to lay down his life for his friend – than which 'greater love hath no man' (John 15:13): 'Grieve not that I am fall'n to this for you', and 'your friend ... repents not that he pays your debt' (IV.i.262, 274–5).

Upon such sacrifices the Bard himself throws recompense. The moral law peculiar to this comedy coincides with the law common to all Shakespearean comedies, according to both of which felicity and, in cases of suffering, equitable to superabundant compensation await the virtuous, be they lovers, spouses, siblings, rulers, servants, or friends, and this

Antonio is no exception. He joins the others – 'precious winners all', as
their counterparts are called in *The Winter's Tale* (V.iii.131) – at Belmont.
Having there been introduced to Portia, and then having witnessed the
altercations over the missing rings, he interjects: 'I am th'unhappy subject
of these quarrels'; to which Portia replies 'Sir, grieve not you; you are
welcome notwithstanding' (V.i.238–9). He is not the cause of the quarrels
– as she knows very well – and he is 'unhappy' in the sense of
'unfortunate' as well as 'grieved'. His sadness here is more specifically
focused and momentary than that of the opening scene. When Bassanio
seeks reconciliation with Portia by asking her pardon, Antonio chimes in:

I once did lend my body for his wealth . . .
    I dare be bound again,
My soul upon the forfeit, that your lord
Will never more break faith advisedly.

                                  (V.i.247–53)

Having earlier staked his flesh on something of monetary value, now he
stakes his very soul on something of moral value, Bassanio's fidelity to
Portia; and he thereby assumes, as guarantor, a part in their marriage vows.
Portia accepts him as such: 'Then you shall be his surety: give him this,
/ And bid him keep it better than the other' (254–5). The way she returns
the ring is particularly compelling. She does so not directly but by
symbolic indirection from wife through friend to husband. This gesture, in
accord with the accompanying words, does not signify the rejection of
Antonio but, to the contrary, his incorporation into the marriage. He is
permanently and more closely than ever bound to his friend. Hence he is
no longer sad; his brush with unhappiness in this scene reminds us of his
earlier melancholy, and underscores his change of heart. He greets a further
reward with astonishment: at Portia's news that his ships have come in he
is 'struck dumb'. When he says to her in his last speech, 'Sweet lady, you
have given me life [by saving mine] and living [by informing me of my
safe cargoes]', he expresses gratitude to a benefactress and seems, further,
to acknowledge a second friend, as might have been expected when he and
she and Bassanio are 'semblances' of one another's souls.

    Why the nearly universal assent to the mistaken critical view that both
Antonios at the finish are excluded and unhappy? Since the Shakespearean
text does not lend support to this view – quite the reverse – it must be
imported and imposed by readers. Could so many of them actually have
entertained, at whatever level of consciousness, the bourgeois attitude that
confirmed bachelors deserve to suffer loneliness and lovelessness for
failing to marry and have children? Such an attitude will explain why even
an Antonio guiltless of inversion would still be blameworthy, and so would
get his just deserts at the play's end. Then if the Antonio is an invert to

boot, the fear and aversion of homophobia may come into play. It adds antipathy towards immoral and 'unnatural' sexuality to the bias against bachelorhood. It would seem that readers who can predicate homoerotic impulses of the Antonios would be free of such prejudice. Not necessarily, however, when the judgement can be facilitated and encouraged by the certainty that a penalty lies in store for the deviant characters. Some feminist critics give homophobia a special twist when they admire Portia's invention of the ring trick as a device to protect her marriage from the threat to it mounted by the husband's friend's homosexuality. With such misapprehensions and obscurantism bedevilling the comedies, some effort at objectivity is clearly called for.[15]

Homosexuality may not inform the bonding of Antonio and Bassanio, but the topic is none the less introduced into *The Merchant of Venice* in the bantering of Portia and Nerissa with Bassanio and Gratiano over the rings. Their talk is bawdy, as befits the occasion wherein the young couples have been reunited and are sooner or later this day to consummate their marriages (cf. V.i.300–03). Putting into effect the original scheme to 'outwit' and 'outswear' their husbands, the women harp on adultery: each wife feigns suspicion that the rings have been presented to other women; the wives vow that if ever given the opportunity they will lie with the doctor and clerk who have the rings; and upon returning the rings, the women come up with the story that they got them from the doctor and clerk with whom they spent the previous night. The men's quips, by contrast, are about homosexuality. Gratiano first calls it up in a sadistic form with his jealous threat to 'mar the young clerk's pen[is]' (V.i.237). Then, once the truth about Balthasar and his aid comes out and the pressure is lifted, the relieved husbands enter into the fun with gusto. Bassanio says to Portia: 'Sweet doctor, you shall be my bedfellow; / When I am absent then lie with my wife', and Gratiano anticipates 'couching with the doctor's clerk' (V.i.284–5, 305). These jests might be considered cruel if the Antonio in whose hearing they are made had harboured homosexual passion, and for one who does the jesting too; however, they can remind us of those two 'bedfellows' in *Twelfth Night*, Antonio and Sebastian, who so often had 'couched' together.

Finally, the comedy concludes with a bawdy pun. From now on Gratiano's only concern will be 'keeping safe Nerissa's ring', and he here expresses what had all along been tacit: that each woman's giving of her ring was symbolically the giving of her pudenda, a round of flesh. The humour is broad and easy-going, as Shakespeare and his audiences liked it, and the attitudes towards all the varieties of sexualities, including the male–male type, are relaxed. Only once does someone get out of line, and it is when Gratiano wisecracks about being cuckolded and Portia calls him down: 'Speak not so grossly' (V.i.265–6).

She does not, however, find the joking about men going to bed together 'gross' *or* disquieting.

IV

The distinction I have drawn between the amorous reciprocal love of Antonio and Sebastian in *Twelfth Night* and the amicable love between Antonio and Bassanio in *The Merchant of Venice* is quite unusual, not to be found in the critical discourse of those who deny sexuality to either of the loves or of those who affirm sexual love in both the Antonios. No less unusual is my conclusion that each Antonio at the close of his comedy is permanently reunited with his friend, and included in the community composed of reconciled, loving, and admirable members, with neither one being or deserving to be omitted or self-excluded with the likes of a Shylock or a Malvolio. The conclusions depend for their persuasiveness to a degree on the method used in reaching them. Textual analysis has been fundamental throughout, and it generates supportive evidence. The evidence for securing the homoerotic character of relations between Antonio and Sebastian falls into the categories outlined at the outset as follows: (1) diction, with initial emphasis on the amorous language of Antonio; (2) character, including modes of conduct, the personalities they manifest, and the individual histories as reported and dramatized; (3) scenes that illuminate the thesis with circumstantiality comparable to that of the two companions, and these may be subsumed under: (4) the structure of incidents that make up the main plot. These categories, while initially tailored to *Twelfth Night*, turn out to have a broader applicability; it may be suggested by their close correlation with the principal parts of comedy and tragedy – plot, character, diction – distinguished by Aristotle in the *Poetics*. My next point has been to turn these components of one play into criteria for determining whether or not homoeroticism enters into the friendship of Antonio with Bassanio in another, and the criteria produce a negative result. They may further serve as a test for detecting sexuality in male bonding in other Shakespearean plays. The failure of expositors until now to differentiate the two Antonios in terms of erotic desire may stem in part from their neglecting to invent an adequate method of inquiry.

Notes

1. See e.g. Janet Adelman, 'Male Bonding in Shakespeare's Comedies', in *Shakespeare's 'Rough Magic': Renaissance Essays in Honor of C. L. Barber*, ed. Peter Erickson and Coppélia Kahn (Newark, NJ, 1985), p. 88; Lawrence Danson, *The Harmonies of* 'The Merchant of Venice' (New Haven, CT, 1978), pp. 34–5, 40; Leslie A. Fiedler, *The Stranger*

in Shakespeare (New York, 1972), p. 132; Stephen Greenblatt, *Shakespearean Negotiations: The Circulation of Social Energy in Renaissance England* (Berkeley, CA, 1988), p. 91; Nancy K. Hayles, 'Sexual Disguise in "As You Like It" and "Twelfth Night"', *Shakespeare Survey* 32 (1979): 71, 72n; Coppélia Kahn, 'The Cuckoo's Note: Male Friendship and Cuckoldry in *The Merchant of Venice*', in *Shakespeare's 'Rough Magic'*, pp. 106, 110–11; Richard A. Levin, *Love and Society in Shakespearean Comedy* (Newark, NJ, 1985), p. 142; W. Thomas MacCary, *Friends and Lovers: The Phenomenology of Desire in Shakespearean Comedy* (New York, 1985), pp. 167, 183; Kenneth Muir, *Shakespeare's Comic Sequence* (Liverpool, 1979), p. 60; Stephen Orgel, 'Nobody's Perfect: Or Why Did the English Stage Take Boys for Women?', *South Atlantic Quarterly* 88 (1989): 27–8.

2. III.iv.382. Quotations from the plays are from The New Arden Shakespeare editions: *Twelfth Night*, ed. J. M. Lothian and T. W. Craik (London, 1975); *The Merchant of Venice*, ed. John Russell Brown (Cambridge, MA, 1975). Some punctuation has been silently altered.

3. Sebastian is also the name Julia takes when she poses as a male in *The Two Gentlemen of Verona*. As MacCary, thinking also of Rosalind as Ganymede, puts it: 'These names certainly carry associations with pederasty' (p. 186). Well, so does Viola's Cesario. Julius Caesar, for his sexual relations with King Nicomedes of Bithynia, was sometimes mocked and greeted as 'queen'. The incident, recorded by Suetonius (*De vita Caesarum* I.49.1–4), was used by Dante, who lets a reference to it identify the sin of the purgatorial sodomites (*Purgatorio*, 26.76–9). Portia's alias Balthasar has no such homoerotic associations, but that is because in male disguise she performs a lawyer's and not a lover's role.

4. Greenblatt, pp. 93, 91; cf. Adelman, pp. 88–9, Hayles, pp. 71–2n.

5. If I were to direct the play, I would want Olivia, Sebastian (in the middle), and Antonio to leave the stage together, arm in arm. But the difficulty is that Antonio throughout the scene is under guard, and at the end has yet to be set free. That could be taken care of by a mere wave of the Duke's hand. Such a gesture, though without an authorizing stage direction, is in line with the script. Everything points to Antonio's imminent release. Orsino already admires him, heaping praise on him for his skill and success as a victorious opponent once in a naval battle (V.i.56–7); then he not only went to rescue Cesario, who will be Orsino's wife, but also saved the life and became the friend of her twin, who is to be Orsino's brother-in-law. Enmity cannot survive these emergent relationships – or not without exerting a destructive effect.

6. *Three Essays on the Theory of Sexuality, The Standard Edition of the Complete Psychological Works*, ed. James Strachy (London, 1953–74), VII, 144.

7. Greenblatt's reading of the passage is the mirror opposite of mine. For him the swerving connotes heterosexuality, which is '*licit* sexuality' and 'the *only* craving the play *can* represent as *capable of finding satisfaction*', while to be homosexually matched, instead of '*correctly* paired', is 'to follow an *unnaturally* straight line'. To make the licit, natural, and superior equivalent to 'bent' and the illicit, unnatural, and inferior equivalent to 'straight' is to skew ordinary geometrical symbolism and is even suspect as English. He then follows those annotators who give 'male virgin' as the signified of 'maid' at line 261, even though the same word is used two lines before with its more customary meaning (pp. 67–8, 71; emphasis added). For all his dazzling new-historical detours through tabloid French anecdotes and antiquated anatomy, Greenblatt comes back to a conventional and conservative interpretation of *Twelfth Night*.

8. Stephen Orgel seemingly reads the line this way; and he sees Antonio and Sebastian as 'an overtly homosexual couple' whose presence in the play 'acknowledges ... that men *do* fall in love with other men' ('Nobody's Perfect: Or Why Did the English Stage Take Boys for Women?', *South Atlantic Quarterly* 88 [1989]: 27–8).

9. A few critics can grant a homosexual ingredient in the affectionate or passionate responses of some or all of the principal characters – Olivia, Orsino, Viola, Sebastian – because they regard them as passing through a temporary phase of adolescent sexual confusion on the way to heterosexual maturity (Coppélia Kahn, *Man's Estate: Masculine Identity in Shakespeare* [Berkeley, CA, 1981], p. 211; and see Helene Moglen, 'Disguise and Development: The Self and Society in *Twelfth Night*', *Literature and Society* 23 [1973]: 13–23). Nothing to worry about, it's all a normal part of growing up. But Orsino's attraction

to Cesario postdates rather than antedates his heterosexual infatuation with Olivia. The heterosexual male characters who are presented as untinged by homoerotic feelings and as sexually not unready for marriage, however deficient in other respects, are these specimens: the pre-Cesario Orsino, Malvolio, Sir Andrew Aguecheek – all three of whom seek to wed Olivia – and Sir Toby Belch. No, the play does not lend itself to such attempts to domesticate its treatment of homoerotic desire.

10. Adelman also discusses, though in somewhat different terms, the aspect of the play that I call its bisexuality, and her sense of the way it operates is close to mine (pp. 86–91). Moreover, she explicates some of Antonio's speeches in demonstrating the homosexual nature of his love and is one of the few critics to recognize that Sebastian's response to him is erotic. I have some disagreements with her, yet find her insights into *Twelfth Night* fresh and penetrating.

11. Danson reads Portia's speech in this way also (pp. 48–9); in other respects as well his reading corresponds with mine, notably in the recognition that Bassanio does the right thing in giving up the ring (pp. 192–3, 195) and that Antonio is not excluded at the end, the ring episode resulting in 'the reaffirmation of Antonio's loyalty to both Bassanio and Portia' (pp. 40, 36).

12. *Between Men: English Literature and Male Homosocial Desire* (New York, 1985), pp. 1–2, 25.

13. Adelman, pp. 79–80; Anne Barton in *The Riverside Shakespeare*, ed. G. Blakemore Evans *et al.* (Boston, MA, 1974), p. 253; Kahn, 'Cuckoo's Note', pp. 106–7, 110–11; Fiedler, pp. 135–6; Leonard Tennenhouse, 'The Counterfeit Order of *The Merchant of Venice*', in *Representing Shakespeare: New Psychoanalytic Essays, ed. Murray M. Schwartz* and Coppélia Kahn (Baltimore, MD, 1980), pp. 63, 66.

14. John Russell Brown makes thematic sense of the play in much the way I do. For him the 'central theme [is] love's wealth': not only 'how this wealth is gained and possessed by giving freely and joyously' but also 'how destructive the opposing possessiveness can become'. He perceives, as well, that to 'give and hazard' is a guiding principle of several of the characters (*Shakespeare and His Comedies* [London, 1957], pp. 70, 74, 62, 67).

15. In the interpretation of one feminist critic, 'men, if they are to marry, must renounce their friendships with other men – must even, perhaps, betray them'. The ring plot 'portrays tug-of-war in which women and men compete – for the affections of men'; and a 'strong shrewd woman like Portia' must 'combat the continuing appeal of [homoerotic] ties between men'. She does so by getting back the ring in order 'to teach [her] husband a lesson' about the primacy of marriage over male friendship, put him to a test, and even plot against him for 'erring' in proposing to sacrifice wife and all to deliver Antonio. The contest between Portia and Antonio lasts until he 'offers to sacrifice himself once again', when Portia and marriage triumph over Antonio – the title character! – and ward off an inviting 'homo-erotic attachment' (Kahn, 'Cuckoo's Note', pp. 106–7, 109–11; cf. Adelman, p. 80; Richard Wheeler, 'The *Sonnets*, *The Merchant of Venice*, and *Othello*', in *Shakespeare's 'Rough Magic'*, pp. 194, 197, 200; and see Danson, p. 40).

The message here unearthed is a forbidding one: this 'feminist' Portia uses the ring for entrapment and plays on her husband's 'fears of cuckoldry' in the interest of removing a male rival and gaining full and exclusive possession of him. Maybe shrewd, she is certainly turned into a shrew, one as possessive, if not quite as ruthless, as Shylock. The notion that homosexuality is a temptation to married men, and so poses a danger to marriages, has no more validity as social than as exegetical commentary.

11

Love in Venice

Catherine Belsey

I

Love in Venice generally has a poor record. For Othello and Desdemona, as three centuries later for Merton Densher and Kate Croy, things work out badly. Love in Venice withholds happiness from Henri and Villanelle, the protagonists of Jeanette Winterson's novel *The Passion*. It is fatal, of course, to Thomas Mann's Gustav Aschenbach. And Jessica, the twentieth-century heroine of Erica Jong's *Serenissima*, goes to Venice to play her namesake, and has the misfortune to fall in love with Shakespeare.[1] Though the nature of their tragedies changes with cultural history, Venice is generally no place for lovers.

In the circumstances, this essay, which is about *The Merchant of Venice*, should perhaps have been called 'Love in Belmont'. Belmont, after all, is so evidently the location in the play of happy love. Belmont is a fairytale castle, where three suitors come for the hand of the princess, and undergo a test arranged by her father in order to distinguish between true love on the one hand and self-love and greed on the other. It is a refuge for eloping lovers, who flee the precarious world of capital and interest and trade, to find a haven of hospitality, music, poetry, old love stories retold in the night – and the infinite wealth (without origins) which makes all this possible. Belmont is the conventional critical *other* of Venice, its defining romantic opposite. Belmont, it is widely agreed, is feminine, lyrical, aristocratic – and vanishing – while Venice represents the new world of men, market forces and racial tensions.

And yet it is the relationship between Venice and Belmont which generates the romantic plot of the play. Portia's princely suitors are in the event an irrelevance: true love turns out to rely on credit. And when Portia takes an active hand in the affairs of capital, true love undergoes, I want to argue, a radical transformation which has continuing repercussions for us now.

It is surely perverse in a volume on Politics and Shakespeare to talk about *The Merchant of Venice* without discussing Shylock, who has quite properly come for twentieth-century criticism, particularly since the Second World War, to represent the crucial issue of this puzzling and in many ways disturbing play. The history of anti-Semitism in our own epoch demands that this question be accorded full attention. If I say nothing about it, that is not because I regard it as less than central, but only because I have nothing of value to add to the existing debate.[2] And meanwhile, the play also presents a sexual politics which is beginning to be the focus of feminist criticism and the cultural history of gender.[3] This essay is offered as a contribution to that discussion.

A reading of the sexual politics of the play might begin where interest in Shylock ends, in Act V. The action of the play seems to have been completed already: the conflict, for better or worse, is over. Act V constitutes a coda to the main plot, a festival, set in Belmont, of love and concord and sexuality, combining elements of poetry and comedy, just as weddings do. Although it has no part in the main events of the play, Act V is conventionally held to complete its 'harmonies', to dissipate tension and reconcile differences.[4] The classic analysis is surely C.L. Barber's:

> No other comedy, until the late romances, ends with so full an expression
> of harmony as that which we get in the opening of the final scene of *The*
> *Merchant of Venice*. And no other final scene is so completely without
> irony about the joys it celebrates.[5]

It is true that Act V *alludes to* harmony in Lorenzo's account of the music of the spheres. But it also reminds us that we cannot hear the celestial concord 'whilst this muddy vesture of decay / Doth grossly close it in' (V.i.64–5), and this way of talking about the body might seem, if not ironic, at least incongruous in an unqualified celebration of the joy of love. So too, perhaps, is the choice of love stories the newly married Lorenzo and Jessica invoke so lyrically: Troilus and Cressida, Pyramus and Thisbe, Dido, Medea (V.i.1–14). Nor does the text select from their tragic narratives moments of reciprocal happiness. On the contrary, Troilus is represented on the walls of Troy, sighing his soul towards the Greek camp and the absent Cressida. Thisbe is fearful and dismayed, Dido already deserted. Medea, gathering enchanted herbs, has not yet murdered her children in revenge for Jason's infidelity, but the text hints at her demonic powers and begins her characterization as a witch.[6]

The stories of Troilus and Cressida, Dido and Aeneas, and Pyramus and Thisbe are also represented on the walls of the temple of Venus in Chaucer's *Parliament of Fowls* (lines 289–91).[7] The temple, with its near-naked goddess lying on a bed of gold in the scented half-light, is surely a perfect allegory of desire. But desire is predicated on deprivation: love's acolytes in the temple include pale-faced Patience and bitter Jealousy; two young people kneel to the goddess crying for help; the altar-candles flicker, fanned by lovers' sighs. The stories painted on the walls tell more of sorrow than of joy. Happy love, as Denis de Rougemont repeatedly reminds us, so that the phrase becomes a kind of refrain running through *Love in the Western World*, happy love has no history.[8] In Chaucer's poem the parliament of the birds, to which the account of the temple of Venus is no more than a prelude, would have no story at all if Nature simply prevailed, and the fowls unproblematically chose their mates and flew away. But the narrative is sustained by the courtly eagles, all three in love with the same mistress, so that two at least are doomed to despair, and all three compelled to wait in hope and fear and longing.

'The moon shines bright. In such a night as this . . .'. The rhythms and the internal rhymes, in conjunction with the climatic conditions – 'When the sweet wind did gently kiss the trees' (*The Merchant of Venice* V.i.1–2) – all serve to contain and dissipate what is most distressing in Shakespeare's classical and Italian narratives transmuted into medieval romance. The effect is thrilling to the degree that pleasure is infused with danger. It is also profoundly nostalgic in that it looks back to a world, fast disappearing in the late sixteenth century, where love was seen as anarchic, destructive and dangerous. In the play this world is no longer dominant. Love in *The Merchant of Venice* means marriage, concord, consent and partnership. It means mutual compatibility and sympathy and support. But the older understanding of love leaves traces in the text, with the effect that desire is only imperfectly domesticated, and in consequence the extent to which Venice is superimposed on Belmont becomes visible to the audience.

II

Desire, as characterized in Western culture, is dangerous. It depends on lack: you desire what you don't have; desire fulfilled is desire suspended. Psychoanalytically, desire can be satisfied only at the level of the imaginary, in that it insists upon absolute recognition from the other.[9] Lacan distinguishes desire from demand, the appeal for love which can be formulated – and met. Desire is the residue of demand, the unutterable within or beyond it. Lacan calls it the 'want-to-be' ('manque-à-être') that demand 'hollows within itself'. Because love cannot be fully present in the signifier, desire is brought to light precisely by the signifying chain itself, the otherness of language, in which it can never be met, since language too lacks being.[10]

Western literature presents desire as immoderate, disproportionate, unstable, thrilling precisely because it is hazardous. Villanelle, Jeanette Winterson's web-footed, cross-dressed Venetian croupier heroine, consistently associates desire with gambling, gambling with passion. Both are compulsive and urgent; both risk the possibility of loss. 'Somewhere between fear and sex passion is.'[11] Gustav Aschenbach is paradoxically elated by the discovery of disease in Venice because he senses a correspondence between the concealed, physical threat to the population and the dangerous secret of his own emotional condition.

Desire is perilous because it annihilates the speaking, knowing, mastering subject, the choosing, commanding self so precious to the Free West. Lovers are conventionally speechless (what can they say that would do justice to desire?). They are uncertain, irrational, out of control; transformed, transported, other than they are. Gustav Aschenbach, the rational, disciplined writer, knows that he ought to warn the Polish family about the pestilence and then leave Venice, but he also knows that passion will prevent him from doing either. 'It would restore him, would give him back himself once more; but he who is beside himself revolts at the idea of self-possession.'[12] For these reasons, desire also undermines the *idea* of the self, calling in question the dualism on which it is founded, deconstructing the opposition between mind and body, as each manifests itself in the province of the other.

We know from endless accounts of burning, freezing Petrarchan lovers, still pursuing, still disdained, wrecked and racked by love neglected, that the Renaissance took full account of the element of danger in desire.[13] And we know it too from the efforts of Astrophil to resist his destruction, from the ambivalence of Antony towards his strong Egyptian fetters, and from countless tragedies of love in the period – most particularly, perhaps, the work of Middleton. Passion turns women to whores; it renders men effeminate, incapable of manly pursuits; it threatens identity, arousing fears that subjectivity itself is unstable.[14]

Bassanio is able to solve the riddle of the caskets not only because he sees through outward show, but also because he alone among the suitors recognizes the appropriate emblem of desire: 'thou meagre lead / Which rather threaten'st than dost promise aught, / Thy paleness moves me more than eloquence . . .' (III.ii.104–6).[15] The Prince of Aragon thinks of his own desert, and the silver casket acts as a mirror for his narcissism, revealing the portrait of a blinking idiot (II.ix.30–32, 50, 53). Morocco resolves to take his own desert for granted (II.vii.31–4), and thinks of Portia's value: 'never so rich a gem / Was set in worse than gold' (II.vii.54–5). The golden casket contains death, the destiny of those who serve Mammon. Only Bassanio is motivated by desire and knows that lovers give and hazard all they have. His choice vindicates Portia's conviction: 'If you do love me, you will find me out' (III.ii.41).

Even in his triumph Bassanio displays all the symptoms of passion: he is bereft of words; only his blood speaks in his veins, reducing subjectivity to sensation. Turmoil within the subject confounds the familiar system of differences: 'Where every something being blent together / Turns to a wild of nothing save of joy / Expressed and not expressed'. And in case it should all be too easy from now on, he willingly accepts the new hazard that Portia has set him: 'when this ring / Parts from this finger, then parts life from hence' (III.ii.175–84). Even Portia's picture, which is no more than her 'shadow', is full of metaphorical dangers. Her parted lips are sweet friends *sundered*; her hair is a spider's web, 'A golden mesh t'untrap the hearts of men / Faster than gnats in cobwebs'. And in a strange, baroque conceit, Bassanio argues that the rendering of her eyes should surely have blinded the painter: 'having made one, / Methinks it should have power to steal both his / And leave itself unfurnished' (III.ii.118–29).

III

Riddles too are traditionally dangerous because they exploit the duplicity of the signifier, the secret alterity that subsists in meaning. They prevaricate, explicitly deferring and obscuring the truth. Riddles demonstrate that meaning is neither single nor transparent, that words can be used to conceal it. They show that language itself seduces and betrays those who believe themselves to be in command of it, who imagine it to be an instrument for their use, at their disposal. Riddles equivocate: Portia is what many men desire; but so is death. His own portrait is what Aragon deserves precisely because he supposes that he deserves Portia.

'What has one voice, and goes on four legs in the morning, two legs in the afternoon, and three legs in the evening?' The Sphinx posed her riddle to the Thebans, and each time they got it wrong, she devoured one of them. In the play suitors who fail to solve the riddle of the caskets undertake never to marry. Penalties of this kind are common. Riddles are posed by the wise to isolate the foolish. Solomon delighted in them. They feature prominently in the Book of Proverbs. The riddle for Portia's hand has the sacred character of a trial by ordeal. As Nerissa explains:

> Your father was ever virtuous, and holy men at their death have good inspirations; therefore the lottery that he hath devised in these three chests of gold, silver, and lead, whereof who chooses his meaning chooses you, will no doubt never be chosen by any rightly but one who you shall rightly love.
>
> (I.ii.27–32)

Traditionally riddles are no joke. It is only the Enlightenment regulation of language, with its insistence on the plain style, affirming the transparency of the signifier, that relegates riddles to the nursery,[16] along with ogres and fairies and all the remaining apparatus of the uncanny.

In folk-tales riddles are a common way of exalting the humble and meek. The youngest of three brothers or the poorest of three candidates has only ingenuity or virtue to draw on. Success depends on quick wits or the help of a grateful friend. One of the commonest situations in folk-tales is a contest for the hand of the princess, and the motif of winning a bride by solving a riddle goes back to the Greek romances, and reappears in the Middle Ages.[17] Bruno Bettelheim proposes a broadly Freudian interpretation of this recurrent phenomenon:

> Solving the riddle posed by a particular woman stands for the riddle of woman in general, and since marriage usually follows the right solution, it does not seem farfetched that the riddle to be solved is a sexual one: whoever understands the secret which the other sex presents has gained his maturity.[18]

In a broadly Lacanian reformulation of this proposition it could be argued that the riddle for the hand of the princess is a riddle about the nature of desire, and that the text of *The Merchant of Venice* comes close to making this explicit. In the presumed source in the *Gesta Romanorum*, where the protagonist, interestingly, is a woman, the inscription on the lead vessel is providential: 'Who so chooseth mee, shall finde that God hath disposed for him.'[19] Shakespeare's change locates the meaning of the lead casket firmly in the realm of the secular and the sexual.

Moreover, riddles could be said to enact at the level of the signifier something of the character of desire. Both entail uncertainty, enigma. Both are dangerous. Riddles tease, torment, elude, challenge and frustrate. Once the answer is known the riddle ceases to fascinate, just as desire evaporates once the *otherness* of the other is mastered. Both riddles and desire depend on a sense of the unpresentable within the process of representation, though desire imagines a metaphysical presence, a real existence elsewhere, while riddles refer to the unpresented, the meaning which is not there but can be found, and found nowhere else but there.[20] In this sense the wooing of Portia displays a perfect appropriateness, a ceremonial decorum which endows it with all the traditional impersonality of the Anglican marriage service itself (this man ... this woman, making a formal undertaking).[21]

IV

The riddle for Portia's hand is posed, appropriately enough, by a dead father, and solved by the romantic hero. Portia, who also has immoderate desires, cannot act on them but waits, a sacrificial virgin, for the happy outcome of the ordeal (III.ii.111–14, 57). The news from Venice, however, changes everything. Antonio's predicament also poses a riddle: how can he fulfil his contract without losing his life? This time, Bassanio stands helplessly by while Portia and Nerissa turn to men, and Portia-as-Balthasar finds the equivocation which releases her husband's friend: flesh is not blood. An apparently archetypal and yet vanishing order is radically challenged by cross-dressed women who travel from Belmont to Venice and, uniquely in Shakespearean comedy, intervene not only in the public world of history, but specifically in the supremely masculine and political world of law, with the effect of challenging the economic arrangements of the commercial capital of the world.

And then in the final episode of the play it is the women who produce a series of equivocations which constitute yet another riddle, this time concerning the meaning of gender difference within a new kind of marriage, where a wife is a partner and a companion. The exchanges in Act V between Lorenzo and Jessica about old tales of love and death and the unheard music of the spheres are interrupted by the voice of Portia (V.i.110, 113), and her first words to them constitute a riddle to which, of course, the audience knows the answer: 'We have been praying for our husbands' welfare, / Which speed (we hope) the better for our words' (V.i.114–15). The remainder of the play (almost 180 lines of it) consists largely of a series of increasingly bawdy puns and doubles entendres about rings, and this festival of plurality at the level of the signifier poses a riddle about sexual identity which presumably pleases the audience, but entirely baffles Bassanio.

George Puttenham discusses riddles in his handbook for vernacular writers, *The Arte of English Poesie*, printed in 1589. For Puttenham, with his clear humanist and Renaissance commitments, riddles are already becoming childish, though it is possible to see more in them than children might.

My mother had an old woman in her nurserie, who in the winter nights would put us forth many pretty riddles, whereof this is one:

I have a thing and rough it is
And in the midst a hole Iwis:
There came a yong man with his ginne,
And he put it a handfull in.

The good old Gentlewoman would tell us that were children how it was meant by a furd gloove. Some other naughtie body would peradventure have construed it not half so mannerly.[22]

Evidently for Puttenham riddles are engaging, harmless equivocations or ambiguities (unless they're unduly lewd), and the answer can be deduced from the terms of the puzzle itself, though it is not necessarily the first solution a grown-up might think of.[23]

But Puttenham also identifies another category of equivocation, this time profoundly disturbing, to which Steven Mullaney has drawn attention. This is the kind that seduces and betrays Macbeth, because it lies like truth, making it impossible to tell where truth resides. Puttenham calls this figure *amphibology*, and he condemns it roundly as a threat to order. Amphibologies are frequently without evident human or social origin: they emanate from oracles, pagan prophets – or witches, of course. And they particularly constitute the figure of insurrection, misleading the people in times of rebellion:

as that of Iacke Straw, & Iacke Cade in Richard the seconds time, and in our time by a seditious fellow in Norffolke calling himself Captaine Ket and others in other places of the Realme lead altogether by certaine propheticall rymes, which might be constred two or three wayes as well as that one whereunto the rebelles applied it.[24]

Amphibologies depend on an indeterminacy of meaning which only events can resolve. Puttenham has no patience with them because they have unexpected consequences, and because he associates them with challenges to the social order.

It is difficult to identify with any confidence a clear formal distinction between Puttenham's amphibologies and his riddles. Both depend on ambiguity; both prevaricate and equivocate. Both use words to conceal what is meant, paradoxically bringing out into the open the hidden alterity of meaning. The difference seems to lie in the question of mastery. Riddles promise closure: the old woman in the nursery has the answer, and the children can expect to be told if they have guessed correctly. Like Macbeth, however, Captain Ket has to wait until experience reveals the truth. The proof of the pudding is deferred until it is too late to be any use. Amphibologies mislead. Riddles install the knowing subject: amphibologies undermine the subject's power to know and consequently to control events.

The riddles posed by Portia and Nerissa in the rings episode of *The Merchant of Venice* mostly concern the sex of the lawyer. 'In faith, I gave it to the judge's clerk. / Would he were gelt that had it for my part', Graziano stoutly affirms (V.i.143–4). The clerk *is* 'gelt', of course, to the extent that in the Renaissance, as in a different way for Freud, women are incomplete men,[25] and the pleasure for the audience lies in identifying a meaning which is not available to the speaker.

> *Nerissa*: The clerk will ne'er wear hair on's face that had it.
> *Graziano*: He will an if he live to be a man.
> *Nerissa*: Ay, if a woman live to be a man.
> *Graziano*: Now by this hand, I gave it to a youth ...
>
> (V.i.158–61)

All these utterances are true. By a radical transgression of the differences that hold meaning in place, the youth and the woman are the same person, though Nerissa and the woman she speaks of are not the same. The speed of the exchanges requires some agility on the part of the audience, though not, perhaps, the degree of mobility needed to follow the dizzying series of shifts in the meanings Portia attributes to the 'doctor':

> Since he hath got the jewel that I loved,
> And that which you did swear to keep for me,
> I will become as liberal as you.
> I'll not deny him anything I have,
> No, not my body nor my husband's bed:
> Know him I shall, I am well sure of it.
> Lie not a night from home. Watch me like Argus.
> If you do not, if I be left alone,
> Now by mine honour, which is yet mine own,
> I'll have that doctor for my bedfellow.
>
> (V.i.224–33)

Here Bassanio once again confronts three apparently exclusive options. First, the doctor is a woman (but not Portia, whose honour is still her own), and the woman has taken the 'jewel' that Bassanio promised, by marrying her, to keep for Portia herself. Second, the doctor is a man, and Portia is willing to share her bed with him. And finally the doctor is Portia, her bedfellow when she is alone. Each of the options contains part of the answer. No wonder Bassanio is baffled, and Portia has to spell out the truth for him (V.i.269–70).

The full answer to the riddle of the rings is that Portia has more than one identity. There is a sense in which the multiple meanings here recapitulate the action of the play. Portia has always been other than she is. The fairytale princess, a sacrificial virgin, as she characterized herself, was not only 'an unlessoned girl' but also (and in the same speech) 'the lord / Of this fair mansion, master of my servants, / Queen o'er myself' (III.ii.159, 167–9). Evidently to be an heiress is already to disrupt the rules of gender. But her marriage in conjunction with her Venetian journey (and the deferred consummation confirms them as inextricable) invests her with a new kind of polysemy. The equivocations and doubles entendres of Act V celebrate a sexual indeterminacy, which is not in-difference but multiplicity.

In this sense the episode of the rings surely resembles Puttenham's category of amphibology rather than his concept of the riddle. The answer cannot be deduced from the terms of the puzzle itself. At one level, of course, the solution to the ambiguities and equivocations of the scene is readily available: the doctor and his clerk are also women. That knowledge sustains all the puns and resolves all the contradictions, and thus ensures for the audience the pleasure of mastering a succession of rapidly shifting meanings. This pleasure may help to account for the feeling of harmony which so many critics derive from Act V. But there is another sense in which the implications of the episode are more elusive. The double act between Portia and Nerissa takes their performance beyond the realm of the individual, endowing it with a representative quality, and the reference back through the text, which the episode invites, suggests a more metaphysical question: what, in a world where Belmont encounters the values of Venice, does it mean to be a wife?

Portia claims the ring in return for rescuing Bassanio's friend and thus, indirectly, Bassanio himself. Like Britomart, the lady becomes a warrior, and the equal of her man. 'If you had known,' she says to Bassanio, 'half her worthiness that gave the ring ...' (V.i.199–200). The role of desire is fully acknowledged in the casket scene, and the importance of sexual difference is repeatedly affirmed in the bawdy double meanings of Act V. This is evident in the final pun, delivered, appropriately, by Graziano: 'Well, while I live I'll fear no other thing / So sore, as keeping safe Nerissa's ring' (V.i.306–7), though Stephen Orgel points out that an element of indeterminacy remains even here. Anatomical rings may be masculine as well as feminine, and the preceding lines are: 'But were the day come, I should wish it dark / Till I were couching with the doctor's clerk.' But the other non-sexual, non-differential 'half' of Portia's worthiness as a wife is made apparent in her performance as Bassanio's fellow-warrior, partner and friend. The solution to the riddle of the rings is thus a utopian vision of the new possibilities of marriage. The riddle does not originate with Portia and Nerissa, nor even entirely with their author, for all his familiar human wisdom. On the contrary, it is the effect of a specific cultural moment when the meaning of marriage is unstable, contested, and open to radical reconstruction.[26] The riddle is also deeply socially disruptive in its fundamental challenge to the patriarchal order.

In the episode of the rings happy love acquires a history by super-imposing a similitude on the existing difference. The otherness which is the condition of desire is brought into conjunction with a comradeship which assumes a parallel, a likeness of values and dispositions. The gap that lies

between these two 'halves' of what constitutes conjugal worth is dramatized both in the disjunction between the two parts of Act V and in the
multiple identity that is required of Portia.

V

If the term 'wife' absorbs the meaning of 'friend', what place in the
signifying chain, what specific difference, is left for the meaning of
friendship? We can, of course, reduce the metaphysical burden of
Antonio's apparently unmotivated melancholy to disappointed homoerotic
desire. This is a possible reading, and not one that I wish to discredit.[27]
Certainly the play constructs a symmetry between Antonio and Portia. It
is Antonio who assures Bassanio: 'My purse, my person, my extremest
means / Lie all unlocked to your occasions' (I.i.138–9), but it might equally
have been Portia who said it (see III.ii.304–5). And certainly in Acts IV and
V this symmetry turns into the contest between two kinds of obligation
which is evident in the episode of the rings. But my view is that the play
here presents to the audience the implications of a contest for meaning,
including the meaning of sexuality, which throws into relief something of
the distance between the culture of Renaissance England and our own.

In court in Act IV Bassanio declares:

> Antonio, I am married to a wife
> Which is as dear to me as life itself,
> But life itself, my wife, and all the world
> Are not with me esteemed above thy life.
> I would lose all, ay, sacrifice them all
> Here to this devil, to deliver you.

(IV.i.279–84)

Bassanio's priorities are surely shocking to a modern audience. Men are
not supposed to prefer their friends to their wives. On the contrary, in our
normative society, while adolescent sexuality is allowed to include
homosocial or even homoerotic desire, this phase is supposed to be left
behind by adults, who 'naturally' privilege heterosexual marriage. (At least
one recent reading of The Merchant of Venice takes this pattern of 'normal'
development for granted.[28])

But Bassanio's position is not without a Renaissance pedigree. In Sir
Thomas Elyot's The Governour (1531) Titus and Gysippus grow up
together and are inseparable until Gysippus falls in love and decides to
marry. But when Titus meets his friend's proposed bride, to his own horror,
he instantly falls in love with her too. Overcome by the double anguish of
desire and disloyalty, Titus takes to his bed. At last Gysippus prises the

secret out of him, and once he knows the truth he is easily able to resolve the problem. The friends agree to substitute Titus for Gysippus on the wedding day. Thus friendship is preserved. Gysippus is publicly embarrassed, and has to leave town for a time, but otherwise all is well, and Elyot triumphantly cites the story as an 'example in the affectes of friendshippe'.[29] The values here resemble those of Chaucer's *Knight's Tale*, where love tragically destroys chivalric friendship. The relationship between Palamon and Arcite is heroic; love, on the other hand, is high folly, according to Theseus, and the text does nothing to counteract this view (lines 1798–9). According to Geron's aphoristic assessment of the priorities in Lyly's *Endimion*:

> Love is but an eye-worme, which onely tickleth the heade with hopes, and wishes: friendshippe the image of eternitie, in which there is nothing moveable, nothing mischeevous.... Time draweth wrinckles in a fayre face, but addeth fresh colours to a faste friende, which neither heate, nor cold, nor miserie, nor place, nor destiny, can alter or diminish.
>
> (III.iv.123–36)[30]

Eumenides accepts this evaluation, chooses friendship, and is rewarded with love too.

When Damon is falsely accused of spying in the play by Richard Edwards, his friend Pithias volunteers to take his place in prison and to be executed if Damon fails to return in time. The hangman finds this remarkable:

> Here is a mad man I tell thee, I have a wyfe whom I love well,
> And if iche would die for her, chould iche weare in Hell:
> Wylt thou doo more for a man, then I woulde for a woman(?)

And Pithias replies firmly: 'Yea, that I wyll' (lines 1076–80).[31] It is not clear how seriously we are invited to take the values of the hangman, but it is evident that Pithias is right about the supreme obligations of friendship in this most pedagogic of plays, written in the 1560s by the Master of the Chapel Royal for the Children to perform. Even as late as *The Two Noble Kinsmen* in 1613 the conflicting claims of marriage and friendship are matter for debate – this time between women. Hippolyta reflects without rancour on the affections of Theseus, divided between herself and his friend Pirithous:

> Their knot of love,
> Tied, weaved, entangled, with so true, so long,
> And with a finger of so deep a cunning,
> May be outworn, never undone. I think
> Theseus cannot be umpire to himself,

> Cleaving his conscience into twain and doing
> Each side like justice, which he loves best.
>
> (I.iii.41–7)

Hippolyta finally concludes that Theseus prefers her (I.iii.95–7), but not before Emilia has put the case for friendship between members of the same sex as the stronger force: 'the true love 'tween maid and maid may be / More than in sex dividual' (I.iii.81–2). In the end Hippolyta and Emilia agree to differ.

Both *The Governour* and *Endimion* are cited by Bullough as possible sources of *The Two Gentlemen of Verona*, where Valentine offers his beloved Silvia to his friend Proteus.[32] Bullough finds Valentine's gesture 'Quixotic', as presumably most twentieth-century commentators would.[33] And indeed the play has so enlisted our sympathy for Julia that we cannot want Proteus to accept his friend's generosity. Elsewhere too Shakespeare's texts tend to opt, however uneasily, for the nuclear couple. Othello, who should prefer his wife, tragically listens to his friend. More specifically, in *Much Ado about Nothing*, which is chronologically closer to *The Merchant of Venice*, Beatrice's imperative to Benedick on behalf of her cousin also foregrounds the conflicting obligations of lovers and friends. The loyalty of Beatrice to Hero is absolute, and at the moment when Benedick declares his love for Beatrice, her immediate concern is Hero's honour. Beatrice's challenge necessarily threatens the loyalty of Benedick to Claudio.

> *Benedick*: Come, bid me do anything for thee.
> *Beatrice*: Kill Claudio.
> *Benedick*: Ha! Not for the wide world.
>
> (IV.i.289–91)

Whether or not Benedick's moment of recoil is played as comedy, the play goes on in the event to realign him explicitly as Beatrice's 'friend' (IV.i.319) and thus as Claudio's enemy. Later the text reverts to this issue when, in the course of a series of teasing exchanges, an instance of the verbal friction characteristic of desire,[34] Beatrice sets up an opposition between Benedick's friendship and his 'heart'. But this time she opts for friendship with Benedick even at the price of love:

> *Benedick*: … I love thee against my will.
> *Beatrice*: In spite of your heart, I think. Alas, poor heart. If you spite it for my sake I will spite it for yours, for I will never love that which my friend hates.
>
> (V.ii.61–4)[35]

This *is* comedy. The play's treatment of the issue is more complex:

Beatrice's challenge to Benedick to fight for her evokes classical myth and medieval romance, rather than the new model of marriage. At the same time, we are invited to understand that Benedick qualifies as a husband to the degree that he is prepared to sacrifice his friend. It is no surprise, therefore, that in *The Merchant of Venice* Bassanio's declaration that his friend comes first does not go unchallenged. At once Balthasar, uniquely in the court scene, draws the attention of the audience to his/her other identity: 'Your wife would give you little thanks for that / If she were by to hear you make the offer'(IV.i.285–6). When Bassanio surrenders the ring to Balthasar, it is in response to Antonio's persuasion, and the conflict of obligations is made explicit:

> My Lord Bassanio, let him have the ring.
> Let his deservings and my love withal
> Be valued 'gainst your wife's commandëment.

> (IV.i.446–8)

Bassanio subsequently excuses himself to Portia in the vocabulary of chivalry:

> Even he that had held up the very life
> Of my dear friend. What should I say, sweet lady?
> I was enforced to send it after him.
> I was beset with shame and courtesy.
> My honour would not let ingratitude
> So much besmear it.

> (V.i.214–19)

And here, perhaps, is a pointer to the residual meaning of friendship in the period. Georges Duby gives a graphic account of the life of chivalry among the 'youth' of twelfth-century France. These men constituted a substantial proportion of the audience – and therefore, no doubt, much of the motive – for the new romantic love stories and troubadour poems of the period. A version of their image survives in ideal form in the nostalgic culture of late-sixteenth-century England, most obviously in texts like *The Faerie Queene*, in response to the Queen's enthusiastic cultivation of the heroic and courtly ideal.

Duby's 'youths' were fully grown knights who were not yet fathers. This stage of life might last, it appears, for upwards of twenty years. During this period the 'youth', often accompanied by a slightly more experienced 'youth', or as one of a group of fast friends who loved each other like brothers, roamed in pursuit of adventure and, more specifically, in quest of a wife. The eldest son could expect in due course to inherit his father's property. But in a world where the patrimony was expected

to provide a living for the couple as well as a marriage settlement for
the wife, younger sons had usually little to hope for outside a career in
the Church, unless they could locate an heiress, secure her father's
approval and marry her.

Since the life of the 'youth' was violent and dangerous, whole male
lineages were in practice eliminated, and rich women were not as rare as
might be expected, though only a tiny minority of the 'youth' could hope
to secure one. In the meantime, groups of men, officially celibate, lived and
fought together. We may assume that in such circumstances the virtue of
loyalty was paramount: at least in their idealized, literary form, the knights
were conventionally bosom friends and inseparable companions. Once
married, and a father, the knight gave priority to his own establishment,
though he might well retain some of his former comrades in his household,
and indeed help them to find suitable brides.[36]

Duby's account gives no indication of a conflict between love and
friendship. In a chivalric culture love endangers friendship when it
becomes rivalry, as *The Knight's Tale* shows, but wives do not supplant
friends: their role is quite different. The new model of marriage in the
sixteenth century, however, identified wives precisely as friends, and the
texts of the period bring to light some of the uncertainties and anxieties
which attend the process of redefinition. Antonio is sad because he is in
mourning for friendship. Of course, Portia does it nicely. She gives the ring
to Antonio to give back to Bassanio, so that Antonio feels included. But he
knows from the beginning of the play that things will never be the same
again.

And what about the place of homoerotic desire? Perhaps we shall never
know. Eve Kosofsky Sedgwick is surely right to urge that 'the sexual
context of that period is too far irrecoverable for us to be able to
disentangle boasts, confessions, undertones, overtones, jokes, the unthinkable, the taken-for-granted, the unmentionable-but-often-done-anyway,
etc.'.[37] It seems unlikely that medieval knights were as chaste as the
chivalric code required. On the other hand, while sodomy was consistently
identified as an abominable crime, homosexual acts were very rarely
prosecuted in England in the Middle Ages or the Renaissance.[38] In practice
the whole issue seems to have generated relatively little anxiety. Stephen
Orgel, in a brilliant contribution to the cultural history of the sixteenth
century, argues that homosexual acts were perceived as less dangerous to
men than heterosexual love, because it was association with women which
was effeminating.[39]

A single example may indicate the difficulty we have in construing the
meanings of a vanished culture. In *The Two Noble Kinsmen* the relationship
between Palamon and Arcite is treated in remarkable detail. They love each
other; they lighten each other's imprisonment. Arcite declares, apparently

without embarrassment, that since imprisonment will prevent them from marrying, 'We are one another's wife, ever begetting / New births of love' (II.ii.80–81). At the same time, it is clear that their explicit sexual preferences are heterosexual. The whole plot depends on this. And besides, the text makes clear that they admire each other greatly for their former heterosexual conquests (III.iii.30–42).

Possibly our difficulty resides in the plurality of the word 'love'? Palamon loves Arcite; Arcite loves Palamon; but both Palamon and Arcite love Emilia. Perhaps it is not only our difficulty: Palamon explicitly distinguishes between love and desire, in order to be sure that his cousin is really his rival. 'You love her then?' 'Who would not?' 'And desire her?' (II.ii.159–61). It could be argued, then, that the play sets up its own system of differences: that while love might or might not be sexual, desire is erotic in this text. It could be argued, were it not for Palamon's final words to the dying Arcite, which surely deconstruct any such opposition:

> O cousin,
> That we should things desire which do cost us
> The loss of our desire! That nought could buy
> Dear love, but loss of dear love.

(V.vi.109–12)

Here heterosexual passion and homosocial friendship are defined in exactly the same terms: both are dear love; both are desire. It remains for the audience to determine whether Palamon's words are best understood as conflating difference (one love, one desire, at the price of its similitude) or as turning to account the difference within the signifier (one love, one desire, at the cost of its distinguishing, differentiating other).

VI

A tentative history of our own cultural moment emerges from all this. Our more carefully regulated meanings impose narrow limits on the range of possibilities available to us. Since Freud we have learned that all intense emotion is 'really' sexual; since the Enlightenment we have known how to classify and evaluate deviance; and since *The Merchant of Venice* we have known that marriage, which includes every imaginable adult relationship, ought to be enough for anyone.

I wonder . . .

Notes

1. I owe this reference to Kristina Engler.
2. For an account of the debate (and selective bibliography), see Walter Cohen, *Drama of a Nation: Public Theater in Renaissance England and Spain* (Ithaca, NY, 1985), pp. 196–7. See also Cohen's own analysis, pp. 195–211; Thomas Moisan, '"Which is the Merchant here? and Which the Jew": Subversion and Recuperation in *The Merchant of Venice*', in *Shakespeare Reproduced: The Text in History and Ideology*, ed. Jean E. Howard and Marion F. O'Connor (New York, 1987), pp. 188–206; Kiernan Ryan, *Shakespeare* (London, 1989), pp. 14–24; and John Drakakis, '*The Merchant of Venice*, or Christian Patriarchy and its Discontents', in *Mortal Shakespeare: Radical Readings*, ed. Manuel Barbeito (Santiago de Compostela, 1989), pp. 69–93.
3. See, for example, Linda Bamber, *Comic Women, Tragic Men: A Study of Gender and Genre in Shakespeare* (Stanford, CA, 1982), pp. 109–33; Keith Geary, 'The Nature of Portia's Victory: Turning to Men in *The Merchant of Venice*', *Shakespeare Survey* 37 (1984): 55–68; Lars Engle, '"Thrift is Blessing": Exchange and Explanation in *The Merchant of Venice*', *Shakespeare Quarterly* 37 (1986): 20–37; Karen Newman, 'Portia's Ring: Unruly Women and Structures of Exchange in *The Merchant of Venice*', *Shakespeare Quarterly* 38 (1987): 19–33; Jean Howard, 'Crossdressing, the Theatre, and Gender Struggle in Early Modern England', *Shakespeare Quarterly* 39 (1988): 418–40.
4. See, for example, Lawrence Danson, *The Harmonies of 'The Merchant of Venice'* (New Haven, CT, 1978), pp. 170–95.
5. C. L. Barber, *Shakespeare's Festive Comedy: A Study of Dramatic Form and its Relation to Social Custom* (Princeton, NJ, 1959), p. 187.
6. The specific reference is to Ovid, *Metamorphoses* vii, 162 ff. Medea treats Aeson with rejuvenating herbs. When the daughters of Pelias subsequently ask for her help, she deliberately offers them inefficacious herbs and thus causes them to bring about his death. I owe this point to Michael Comber. See also Jonathan Bate, 'Ovid and the Mature Tragedies: Metamorphosis in *Othello* and *King Lear*', *Shakespeare Survey* 41 (1989): 133–44 (134–5).
7. Geoffrey Chaucer, *Works*, ed. F. N. Robinson (London, 1957).
8. Denis de Rougemont, *Love in the Western World*, trans. Montgomery Belgion (Princeton, NJ, 1983), p. 15 and *passim*.
9. Jean Laplanche and J.-B. Pontalis, 'Wish (Desire)', in *The Language of Psycho-analysis*, trans. Donald Nicholson-Smith (London, 1973), pp. 481–3. Cf. Jacques Lacan, *Écrits: A Selection*, trans. Alan Sheridan (London, 1977), p. 58.
10. Lacan, *Écrits*, pp. 263, 265.
11. Jeanette Winterson, *The Passion* (London, 1988), p. 62. Cf. pp. 55, 66.
12. Thomas Mann, *Death in Venice, Tristan, Tonio Kröger* (London, 1955), p. 74.
13. See Scott Wilson, 'Racked on the Tyrant's Bed: The Politics of Pleasure and Pain and the Elizabethan Sonnet Sequences', *Textual Practice* 3 (1989): 234–49.
14. Laura Levine, 'Men in Women's Clothing: Antitheatricality and Effeminization from 1579–1642', *Criticism* 28 (1986): 121–43; Stephen Orgel, 'Nobody's Perfect: Or Why Did the English Stage Take Boys for Women?', *South Atlantic Quarterly* 88 (1989): 7–29.
15. Freud argues that Bassanio's choice (which is really a choice between three women) betrays an acknowledgement of ineluctable death, masked as the choice of a desirable woman (Sigmund Freud, 'The Theme of the Three Caskets', *Complete Psychological Works*, *SE* 12, ed. James Strachey [London, 1958], pp. 291–301). Sarah Kofman, developing Freud's argument, sees the episode as a representation of the 'ambivalence' (or duplicity) of love: the wish for love is superimposed on the awareness of death, but the imagery prevents the complete success of the process, so that the audience is satisfied at the level of fantasy but also at the level of the intellect (Sarah Kofman, 'Conversions: *The Merchant of Venice* Under the Sign of Saturn', in *Literary Theory Today*, ed. Peter Collier and Helga Geyer-Ryan [Cambridge, 1990], pp. 142–66).
16. Mark Bryant, *Dictionary of Riddles* (London, 1990), p. 51.
17. Stith Thompson, *The Folktale* (Berkeley, CA, 1977), pp. 153–8.

18. Bruno Bettelheim, *The Uses of Enchantment: The Meaning and Importance of Fairy Tales* (London, 1978), p. 128.

19. John Russell Brown, ed., *The Merchant of Venice* (London, 1959), p. 173.

20. Wyatt exploits the parallel in his riddles of forbidden desire. See, for example, 'A ladye gave ne a gyfte she had not' . . . and 'What wourde is that that chaungeth not?', in *The Collected Poems of Sir Thomas Wyatt*, ed. Kenneth Muir and Patricia Thomson (Liverpool, 1969), pp. 238, 36.

21. The view that Bassanio is no more than a fortune-hunter who desires Portia only, or primarily, for her money seems to me anachronistic, probably filtered by Victorian fiction, where love and money are commonly opposed.

22. George Puttenham, *The Arte of English Poesie*, ed. G. D. Willcock and A. Walker (Cambridge, 1936), p. 188.

23. William Dodd identifies a structural analogy between riddle and comedy, which also sets a puzzle and finally solves it, though not in the most obvious way. See *Misura per misura: la transparenza della commedia* (Milan, 1979), pp. 203 ff.

24. Puttenham, *Arte*, pp. 260–61. Steven Mullaney, 'Lying Like Truth: Riddle, Representation and Treason in Renaissance England', *ELH* 47 (1980): 32–47.

25. Stephen Greenblatt, 'Fiction and Friction', in *Shakespearean Negotiations: The Circulation of Social Energy in Renaissance England* (Oxford, 1988), pp. 66–93.

26. See Catherine Belsey, 'Disrupting Sexual Difference: Meaning and Gender in the Comedies', in *Alternative Shakespeares*, ed. John Drakakis (London, 1985), pp. 166–90; *The Subject of Tragedy: Identity and Difference in Renaissance Drama* (London, 1985), pp. 129–221. Eighty years later it would be possible for a good woman to propose that it would be 'nobler' to be her husband's friend than his wife (John Dryden, *Troilus and Cressida* II.i.143–5, *Works*, vol. 13, ed. Maximillian E. Novak [Berkeley, CA, 1984]). I owe this point to M. C. Bradbrook.

27. This has been a recurrent interpretation of the play at least since Tillyard toyed with the idea in 1966. See Danson, *Harmonies*, pp. 34–40.

28. W. Thomas MacCary, *Friends and Lovers: The Phenomenology of Desire in Shakespearean Comedy* (New York, 1985), especially pp. 167–8.

29. Sir Thomas Elyot, *The Governour* (London, 1907), p. 183.

30. John Lyly, *Endimion*, in *The Complete Works*, ed. R. Warwick Bond (Oxford, 1902), 3 vols, vol. 3. Cf. Elyot, *The Governour*, II.xi, and Montaigne, 'Of Friendship', cited in Eugene Waith, ed., *The Two Noble Kinsmen* (Oxford, 1989), p. 50.

31. Richard Edwards, *Damon and Pythias* (Oxford, 1957).

32. Geoffrey Bullough, *Narrative and Dramatic Sources of Shakespeare*, vol. I. (London, 1957), pp. 203–17.

33. Bullough, *Sources*, vol. I, p. 203.

34. Greenblatt, 'Fiction and Friction', pp. 88–91.

35. I owe this point to A. D. Nuttall.

36. Georges Duby, 'Youth in Aristocratic Society', in *The Chivalrous Society*, trans. Cynthia Postan (London, 1977), pp. 112–22. I owe this connection to Mary Beth Rose, *The Expense of Spirit: Love and Sexuality in English Renaissance Drama* (Ithaca, NY, 1988), pp. 178–235, though she reads the texts with a rather different emphasis.

37. Eve Kosofsky Sedgwick, *Between Men: English Literature and Male Homosocial Desire* (New York, 1985), p. 35.

38. For a discussion of the available evidence, see David F. Greenberg, *The Construction of Homosexuality* (Chicago, 1988).

39. Orgel, 'Nobody's Perfect'.

12

The Shakespearean Editor as Shrew-Tamer

Leah Marcus

I

We all know how Shakespeare's uncomfortable play *The Taming of the Shrew* ends. Kate makes a long and eloquent speech of submission to Petruchio in which she argues for the subordination of wives on legal, biological and ethical grounds, finally offering to place her hand beneath her husband's foot if that will 'do him ease'. Petruchio responds with gusto 'Why, there's a wench!'[1] and after a bit more repartee, the company scatters, commenting on the miracle of Kate's taming, even though, at least as we like to read and teach the play nowadays, it is by no means clear that Kate is thoroughly converted to the system of patriarchal hegemony she advocates. Whether she is or not, there is a strong illusion of reality surrounding her speech at the end of the play: we are invited to forget that the taming of Kate by Petruchio started out as a mere play within a play performed for the delectation of one Christopher Sly, drunken tinker turned temporary aristocrat.

In actual productions of the play within the last fifteen years in London or New York, Stratford or New Haven, however, Christopher Sly is harder to forget. As often as not in recent stagings, he remains onstage and alert until almost the end of the taming plot, calling for the clown figure to come back onstage, commenting on the action, and even intervening to stop it when some of the characters appear about to be hauled off to prison.[2] When he finally does drift into sleep around the beginning of Act V, the Lord orders him carried back to his original place and he becomes once more a drunken tinker lying in a stupor before an alehouse. Sly awakens, somewhat dazed, and concludes that the taming play he has watched has been a vivid dream, the bravest and best he has ever had. The reality of the taming plot in this version is severely undercut: it has remained 'only' a play – or even a dream – throughout. Moreover, Sly's final lines compromise Kate's message even further. He lurches off, vowing to tame his own termagant wife at home now that his dream has taught him how to do it. He is unlikely to succeed, we can confidently predict, given his staggering condition and his obvious characterological distance from the charismatic stage figure Petruchio. Instead of convincing us that the inner play's wife-taming scenario is a possible one in reality, Sly's vow turns it into the wish-fulfilment fantasy of a habitual drunkard who is as likely to be punished by his wife for this night out as he has been for past transgressions. Shrew-taming becomes the compensatory fantasy of a socially underprivileged male.

It is not difficult to imagine why the Christopher Sly ending is gaining increasing popularity in theatrical productions of *The Taming of the Shrew*: it softens some of the brutality of the taming scenes, which can then be viewed as tailored to the uncultivated tastes of Sly; it distances late-twentieth-century audiences from some of the most unacceptable implications of Kate's pronouncements on male sovereignty. But on what authority do directors tack the Sly episodes on to the written text as we all know it from our standard editions? To attempt to answer that question is to enter a labyrinth in which any stable sense we may have of the identity of Shakespeare and his work very quickly begins to dissolve. By examining the textual and performance history of *The Taming of the Shrew* we will gain a fresh sense of the provisionality, even the fragility, of our standard text.

II

The easy and traditional answer to the question 'On what authority?' is 'On no authority whatsoever'. The scenes of Sly's intervention in the action and eventual return to the alehouse are, as most recent editors of the play agree, 'not Shakespeare', and therefore inadmissible into the canonical text of the play and usually relegated to an appendix. These episodes featuring Sly come from *The Taming of a Shrew*, a play generally regarded by editors as artistically inferior to *The Taming of the Shrew* but viewed in its own time, for copyright purposes at least, as the same play as *The Shrew*. *The Taming of a Shrew* (or *A Shrew*, as it is termed to differentiate it from *The Shrew*) was published in a 1594 quarto and again in 1596 and 1607. *The Shrew* appeared in print for the first time in the 1623 First Folio of Shakespeare's works without having been entered separately in the Stationers' Register; it was reprinted in quarto form in 1631 by the printer who owned the copyright to *A Shrew*.[3] So far as we know, the earlier printed version of *A Shrew* was not republished after 1607. It was, however, closely associated with other early quarto versions of Shakespeare plays: it was, according to its 1594 title page, 'sundry times acted by the Right honorable the Earle of Pembrook his servants', a company with which Shakespeare may have been briefly associated; it was sent to the printer around the same time as the quarto versions of *Henry VI Parts 2 and 3* and *Titus Andronicus*, very likely because by 1594 the Earl of Pembroke's Men had become indigent and dissolved. A play called by Henslowe 'the tamynge of A shrowe' was performed at Newington Butts in 1594 by the Lord Chamberlain's Men, a company with which Shakespeare was probably already associated by the end of that year, if not earlier; other plays performed alongside it included *Titus Andronicus* and some version of *Hamlet*.[4] At the very least, *The Taming of a Shrew* was closely connected with other early plays now accepted by textual revisionists as Shakespearean.

Nevertheless, beginning with Edmond Malone in the late eighteenth century, an enormous amount of editorial energy has gone into proving – over and over again and by various ingenious strategies – that no part of *The Taming of a Shrew* can be Shakespeare. Whether consciously or not, recent editors have suppressed the degree of visibility *A Shrew* has had in the textual history of *The Shrew*. Modern editors, when they consider *A Shrew* at all, tend to state that of all Shakespeare's previous editors, only Alexander Pope admitted the Christopher Sly episodes and conclusion to his text of *The Taming of the Shrew*. That significantly understates the matter: not only Pope, but, following him, Thomas Hanmer, Lewis Theobald, Samuel Johnson, William Warburton, and Edward Capell all included some or all of the Sly materials in their editions as 'Shakespeare'. The eighteenth-century pattern was broken by Malone, who argued that *A Shrew* was not Shakespeare, but Shakespeare's source play for *The Shrew*.[5] Since Malone's edition of Shakespeare in the late eighteenth century, *The Taming of the Shrew* in printed versions has looked much as we know it in our standard editions today – with Sly dropping out early on and the taming plot opening out into 'reality' at the end. In every generation there have been a few hardy souls who have argued that *A Shrew* is indeed Shakespeare – an early apprentice version of the play that later became *The Shrew*. From time to time there have also been hardy souls who have argued that their preferred text, *The Shrew*, or at least most of it, was also not written by Shakespeare. During the twentieth century, however, opinion has rigidified significantly. *The Shrew* has been generally accepted as canonical and *A Shrew* moved further and further from Shakespeare. Instead of being regarded as the source play for *The Shrew*, as it was by most editors until the 1920s, it now has lost even that status, and is generally considered instead a 'vamped-up' copy – a 'bad quarto' of the 'original' play, *The Taming of the Shrew*. Yet, curiously, *A Shrew* is not included among the other 'bad quartos' in Michael J.B. Allen and Kenneth Muir's handsome facsimile edition of *Shakespeare's Plays in Quarto*, on the grounds that its text is anomalous, 'longer and more coherent than the texts of the other bad quartos'.[6] What gets called 'Shakespeare' in the case of *A Shrew* and *The Shrew* is protean and malleable, shifting over the years along with literary fashions, along with social mores, and especially – this is the part that interests me the most – along with shifting views of male violence and female subordination. 'Shakespeare' is a historical construction, grounded in historical data, to be sure, but data so scanty that they can be reconfigured rather easily to support one or another hypothesis about what constitutes a genuine text.

III

In *The Taming of the Shrew* we are dealing with a particularly tricky form of marginality: what might Shakespeare have written or helped to write when he was not yet sounding like 'Shakespeare'? Even though the early history of *A Shrew* so closely parallels that of *Titus Andronicus*, which now has a secure place in the canon, and that of the quarto versions of *Henry VI Parts 2 and 3*, which are now accepted as Shakespeare by revisionist critics, *A Shrew* remains in a curious limbo. It is too regular and original to be a 'bad quarto', yet somehow too derivative and uncouth to be acceptable Shakespeare. There are, I would suggest, good reasons why twentieth-century editors and critics have been particularly reluctant to associate *The Taming of a Shrew* with Shakespeare, either as source play or as Shakespeare's early version of the standard text. For traditional editors, *A Shrew* has been less acceptable than *The Shrew* at least in part because of an affinity between shrew-taming as valorized in *The Taming of the Shrew* and what editors have traditionally liked to do with texts. As an essay by Gary Taylor has recently pointed out, the editing of Shakespeare has traditionally been a gendered activity, with the editor almost always male and the text implicitly female.[7] Good texts are not supposed to be wild and unruly; to the extent that they appear so, it is the editor's job to tame them into meaning, ironing out uncouthness and grotesqueries as a way of showing the essential elevation and refinement of 'gentle Shakespeare's' creation once the disfigurements introduced by ignorant actors, copyists and printers have been carefully cleared away. In *The Shrew*, shrew-taming is explicitly associated with humanist pedagogy: Petruchio's subduing and refinement of Kate operates parallel to the purported efforts of Bianca's tutors to teach the two sisters Vergil and the art of the lute. By learning to speak the pedagogue's language of social and familial order, Kate shows herself to be a better student of standard humanist doctrine than her sister.[8] In *A Shrew*, as we shall see, the taming process is considerably less efficacious. To accept *A Shrew* as Shakespeare would be, from the standpoint of traditional editorial practice, to leave the shrew (and the text) in disorder. It would also be to lose a convenient mechanism by which the forcible suppression of female insurgency is naturalized as reality and truth.

But even for reader-critics whose views are markedly less traditional, *A Shrew* has usually been kept safely on the margins, at considerable distance from the 'genuine' play, perhaps because if allowed to come into close proximity with the 'correct' text, it would undermine yet another version of 'gentle Shakespeare' – his time-honoured reputation for unusual benignity, at least by the standards of his day, in his understanding of and sympathy for women. To the extent that they have considered *A Shrew* at all, modern editors and critics have regularly fragmented it, citing it piecemeal in order to demonstrate the superior artistry and the superior humanity of the 'authentic' version. They regularly excerpt parts of Kate's speech of submission from *A Shrew*, which argues for wifely obedience on the basis of Eve's responsibility for the Fall, in order to demonstrate the vastly decreased misogyny of Kate's arguments in Shakespeare's 'authentic' version. Just as regularly, they identify as defects features of *A Shrew* which, if analysed instead as alternate versions of the text, might make the canonical *Shrew* sound less than humane by comparison.[9] In all modern editions of the authorized text, *A Shrew* is treated not as an artistic structure with its own patterns of meaning and its own dramatic logic, but as a heap of shards thrown together by ignorant actors with no capacity for coherence. As we shall see, there has long been a radical disjunction between what passes as genuine Shakespeare in the printed text of the play and what is accepted as Shakespeare in performance, with performance traditions sometimes running a good half-century ahead of editorial practice. If that pattern holds, then *A Shrew*, with its heavy undercutting, through the return of Christopher Sly, of Kate's long sermon at the end about proper female subordination, may be on the verge of becoming 'Shakespeare', just as it was during most of the eighteenth century and just as, since then, other suspect plays like *Titus Andronicus*, *King John* and the *Henry VI* plays and their quartos have gradually been brought into the canon.

Recent post-structuralist theory positing the fundamental indeterminacy of all literary texts has shaken up most of the interpretative categories by which editors have been able to assert confidently in the matter of *A Shrew* and *The Shrew* that the latter is 'Shakespeare' while the former is not. In the case of *King Lear*, many editors and bibliographers are now willing to accept the argument of Steven Urkowitz, Michael Warren and Gary Taylor that there are not one but two authoritative versions of that play – the 1608 quarto version and the 1623 folio. Both are printed in the New Oxford Shakespeare and in Warren's *The Complete King Lear, 1608–1623* (Berkeley, 1989). Little by little, the status of the 'bad quartos' of

Shakespeare is rising.[10] Instead of damning them in the language of the First Folio itself as 'stolne and surreptitious copies',[11] we are beginning to regard them as valuable records of performance with their own logic and artistic merits, their own 'local' identities, their own distinctive claim to critical attention. It is time to extend that attention to *A Shrew* and its undercutting of patriarchal authority.

IV

What happens if, instead of regarding *A Shrew* as *ipso facto* a foul corruption of the 'true' play, we regard it as a text in its own right, a text in which difference does not have to be read as debasement? The differences are many and striking. *A Shrew* is shorter and often simpler; the verse has many borrowings from Marlowe and is often metrically irregular, although that is occasionally true of *The Shrew* as well. More strikingly, *A Shrew* has a different setting (Athens) and different names for all the main characters except Kate. Petruchio is named Ferando. In *A Shrew*, the subplot to the taming play is quite different: Kate has two sisters instead of one, and each has her own suitor, so that the rivalry of *The Shrew* for the hand of Bianca is absent. The taming plot itself is much like that of the play as we know it, except that the incidents are arranged somewhat differently, the characters are less vividly and fully drawn, Kate's motivation in accepting Petruchio is clearer, and Petruchio's in taming Kate is less clear. Editors have traditionally disparaged *A Shrew* on the grounds that its portrayal of motivation is murky, failing to notice that their generalization applies only to the male characters, not to Kate herself.[12] In *A Shrew* Kate tells the audience in an aside that she will play along with her tamer: 'But yet I will consent and marry him, / For I methinks have lived too long a maid, / And match him too, or else his manhood's good.'[13] That aside does not exist in *The Shrew*.

Some of the most profoundly patriarchal language of *The Shrew* is not present in *A Shrew*. Petruchio/Ferando never states that his only motive in wiving is financial, nor does he refer to Kate as one of his possessions – goods, chattels, household stuff, 'My horse, my ox, my ass, my anything' (III.ii.221). Indeed, *A Shrew* is remarkable for the absence of such language – none of Petruchio's most demeaning speeches in regard to female weakness and impotence exists in *A Shrew*. In *A Shrew*, as he carries Kate off after the wedding, Petruchio/Ferando even suggests that if she humours him for the present, he will do her recompense later on: 'Come, Kate, stand not on terms, we will away; / This is my day; to-morrow thou shalt rule, / And I will do whatever thou commands' (p. 32, ll.87–9). In *A Shrew*, Petruchio/Ferando's method of taming by opposites is less elaborate and cleverly psychological than in *The Shrew*, or at least less clearly articulated as such by him; on the other hand, in *A Shrew*, Kate has less far down to go in order to appear properly tame – a proper 'household Kate' – and Petruchio/Ferando clearly considers some of her most flamboyant gestures of subservience to be excessive. Kate's speech of submission in *A Shrew* is very different from the parallel passage in *The Shrew*. Although the very few editors who have discussed it have, following the traditional pattern of debasing *A Shrew* in order to exalt *The Shrew*, found it *more* unredeemedly sexist than the authorized Shakespearean version, I would characterize it as offering a different kind of patriarchal argument, one that was less up to date in sixteenth-century terms. Whether we regard it as more or less misogynist will depend on our evaluation of different modes of patriarchy.

Kate's speech in *A Shrew* can be described as a restatement of traditional misogyny on religious grounds. Much of it is taken up with platitudes about the creation: God made the world out of chaos, a 'gulf of gulfs, a body bodiless' before it was shaped by his framing hand (p. 62, l. 124). After the six days' work, he fashioned Adam, and out of his rib created woman:

> Then to His image did He make a man,
> Old Adam, and from his side asleep
> A rib was taken, of which the Lord did make
> The woe of man, so termed by Adam then
> 'Wo-man', for that by her came sin to us;
> And for her sin was Adam doomed to die. (p. 62, ll. 130–35)

This interestingly inaccurate view of the Fall blames woman, as usual, for the plight of humankind – she is named a 'woe' by Adam before she has even had a chance to act – but it is not echoed by other elements of the play, nor does it limit the woman's sphere of action as the alternative speech in *The Shrew* does. By contrast, Kate's rationale for obedience in *The Shrew* is given a political rather than a religious base: she advocates wifely obedience in terms of a theory of sovereignty by which the household is modelled on the kingdom and wifely disobedience becomes a form of 'petty treason' against her 'king' and husband. 'Thy husband is thy lord, thy life, thy keeper, / Thy head, thy sovereign' (V.ii.146–7); 'thy lord, thy king, thy governor' (V.ii.138) – an authority against whom disobedience or even peevishness is (according to the doctrine of petty treason) the same crime as that of a rebellious subject against a monarch:

> Such duty as the subject owes the prince,
> Even such a woman oweth to her husband.
> And when she is froward, peevish, sullen, sour,

And not obedient to his honest will,
What is she but a foul contending rebel
And graceless traitor to her loving lord? (V.ii.155–60)

The machinery of state lying behind this appeal for submission is rather more awesome and immediate than the diffuse and generalized appeal for order in *A Shrew*. We will note, too, that in the two speeches, the meaning of obedience is startlingly different. In *A Shrew*, Kate appeals to wives to obey because their husbands need their assistance: 'Obey them, love them, keep, and nourish them, / If they by any means do want our helps' (p. 62, ll.137–8). In *The Shrew*, the rationale is precisely reversed: women are presented as helpless, passive creatures of the household, who lie 'warm at home, secure and safe' while their hardy lords and masters venture out into the maelstrom for their benefit (V.ii.151). Kate's vision of a housewife lying safe and protected at home sounds so familiar to us that we may fail to recognize its relative newness in the Renaissance. *The Shrew*'s image of the wife as a private possession of the husband to be tucked away at home was – in England at least – only beginning to emerge as the most desirable family model for haut-bourgeois households.[14]

To be sure, Kate's final gesture of submission is more extreme in *A Shrew* than in the version we are accustomed to. In *The Shrew*, she commands the wives:

Then vail your stomachs, for it is no boot,
And place your hands below your husband's foot.
In token of which duty, if he please,
My hand is ready, may it do him ease.

(V.ii.176–9)

Petruchio's response 'Why, there's a wench!' registers his approval of her extravagant gesture of submission and also, perhaps, an element of condescension. In *A Shrew*, Kate makes the same gesture, but its symbolic rationale is not articulated (and this is one of the things editors have traditionally pointed to as an indication that *A Shrew* is a borrowed and derivative text). In *A Shrew*, Kate's act becomes a piece of deliberate excess, which her husband stops instead of approving:

Laying our hands under their feet to tread,
If that by that we might procure their ease;
And for a precedent I'll first begin
And lay my hand under my husband's feet.

(p. 63, ll.139–42)

The stage direction calls for her actually to lay her hand beneath his foot. Petruchio/Ferando responds 'Enough, sweet, the wager thou hast won; /

And they, I am sure, cannot deny the same' (p. 63, ll. 143–4), which makes her masochistic gesture something acknowledged as excessive – performed to help her husband win the bet. It is possible, of course, to make the same interpretation of her meaning in *The Shrew*, but we have to create it ourselves by reading between the lines. In *A Shrew* it is unequivocally articulated in the text.

The reaction of the other characters is also strongly contrasted in the two versions of the play. In *The Shrew*, Kate's speech silences the other women; only the men speak thereafter. In *A Shrew*, Emelia (Bianca) makes it clear that she finds Kate's speech ridiculous. After Kate and Petruchio/Ferando exit at the end, Bianca/Emelia asks Polidor (Lucentio): 'How now, Polidor, in a dump? What say'st thou, man?' He retorts: 'I say thou art a shrew', to which she replies: 'That's better than a sheep'. He responds, as though with a shrug: 'Well, since 'tis done, let it go! Come, let's in', and they exit (p. 63, ll. 157–61). In this version Kate's sister is not only not silenced, it looks very much as though she has won. When she and her new spouse exit, Sly returns, and Kate's message of submission is compromised even further – contained within a series of dramatic events, rather like a nest of boxes, which narrows down its applicability and ideological impact to almost nothing.

Perhaps the most fascinating differences between *A Shrew* and *The Shrew* are metadramatic: a play is a much more limited entity in *A Shrew*, much more exalted and powerful in *The Shrew*. To imagine Shakespeare in connection with *A Shrew* is to associate The Bard with a very lowly profession. The actors in *A Shrew* are humble, ill-educated itinerants. They enter bearing packs on their backs, and one of them is so ignorant that he has not mastered the classical generic terms of his trade. When the Lord asks them what they can perform for him, Sander, the actor-clown, answers: '*Marry, my lord, you may have a tragical, or a comodity, or what you will*', and the other actor fiercely corrects him: '*A comedy, thou should'st say; souns, thou'lt shame us all*' (p. 3, ll. 59–61). In *A Shrew*, the actors and Sly inhabit the same world of hardship, and they are able to give him the entertainment he wants: he remains awake enjoying it almost to the end. In *The Shrew*, by contrast, the actors are allied with the Lord and his household against Sly. They are urbane and well educated, at home in the world of humanist discourse rather than alien from it. In this version, unlike the other one, Sly has never seen a play. The butt of the 'comodity' joke is not an actor, but Christopher Sly himself, who queries, when offered a 'pleasant comedy', 'Is not a comonty a Christmas gambold or a tumbling trick?' (Induction ii.132–3). And of course the play itself is far above him: he wearies of it by the end of the first scene: ''Tis a very excellent piece of work, madam lady. Would 'twere done!' and is never heard from again (I.i.243).

In *The Shrew*, and in that version only, dramatic and pictorial art are valued for their verisimilitude: Sly is presented with sexually explicit pictures of Adonis, Cytherea, and Io 'beguilèd' and ravished by Jove, 'As lively painted as the deed was done' (Induction ii.52). The Lord praises one of the actors for a similar verisimilitude in a previous role: 'that part / Was aptly fitted and naturally performed' (Induction i.82–3). The same claim is made at least implicitly by the taming play itself: instead of being bounded by the reappearance of Sly, it has become independent of his narrow vision and attained, at the end, the status of 'nature' rather than performance. In *The Shrew*, the Induction is also more clearly localized than its counterpart in *A Shrew*, with numerous evocations of Shakespeare's own early neighbourhood in Warwickshire. In the nineteenth century, Bardolators liked to search out Slys in the Stratford area as a way of pointing to the wonderful realism of Shakespeare's art – drawn to the very life.[15]

The Shrew's more compelling aura of reality is one of the salient characteristics for which that version has been preferred over the cruder and more farcical *A Shrew*. We will note, however, that in *The Shrew* the rising status of the actors in terms of their ability to claim a kind of truth for their art is bought at the price of woman's power and autonomy, since there is nothing to qualify the 'truth' of female subordination they offer up at the end. If we imagine the play as a relatively bounded economy, then the actors triumph by putting women down, 'realizing' womanly weakness in both senses of the term through their staging of Kate's submission. In *A Shrew*, the actors are lower and stay low; the women are brought less low. John Harington's *The Metamorphosis of Ajax* (1596) referred to *A Shrew* in a way that suggested he (and other readers of the quarto) found the play's message of shrew-taming in that version to be fatally and ruefully compromised by Sly's fantasy at the end: 'For the shrewd wife, reade the booke of taming a shrew, which hath made a number of us so perfect, that now every one can rule a shrew in our countrey, save he that hath her.'[16]

V

Given the significant ideological difference between the two versions of the play, it is relatively easy to see why modern editors and critics have been at such pains to distance the two texts from each other, or at least to go along with earlier editorial decisions to keep them apart. With the passage of the centuries, the gulf between the two has widened. In the Renaissance, as we have noted, the two *Shrews* were regarded as one in terms of copyright; in the early eighteenth century they were considered an earlier and later draft by Shakespeare. Beginning with Malone, *A Shrew* was less frequently considered early Shakespeare, more frequently identified as Shakespeare's source for *The Shrew*. In all these hypotheses *A Shrew* comes out as the earlier play, and I have made a case for that view as well. The shifts from *A Shrew* to *The Shrew* can be seen as the articulation of 'modern' ideas (for the Renaissance, at least) about women's place within the household and within the absolutist state; the name of Shakespeare thus becomes identified with the rise of individualism and the development of the haut-bourgeois family model. Similarly, the status of the actors rises considerably from *A Shrew* to *The Shrew*, running parallel to the rising status and prosperity that theatrical historians associate with the profession during Shakespeare's time, and with Shakespeare's own career in particular.[17]

During the late seventeenth and eighteenth centuries, the cultural need to naturalize the story of the play was so intense that in Garrick's highly popular afterpiece *Catherine and Petruchio*, *The Taming of the Shrew* was whittled down to the taming story *tout seul*, a sentimentalized version of *The Shrew* with no Sly, no subplots, and a softened conclusion in which Petruchio and Kate share in the delivery of the final speech. John Lacy's *Sauny the Scot, or The Taming of the Shrew* (1667) similarly omitted the frame entirely. The Sly material was not discarded, however; it formed the basis of two farces, both called *The Cobler of Preston*, by Charles Johnson and Christopher Bullock respectively, both published in 1716. On the eighteenth-century stage, it would seem, the Sly plot and the taming plot were kept strictly separate so that neither could compromise the 'reality' of the other. As Samuel Johnson noted scoffingly in his edition of Shakespeare, the story of the shrew and her tamer was printed as fact in *The Tatler*, passed off as a notable 'transaction in Lincolnshire'.[18] During the same century Kate's speech was split off from the play and published separately (with a few added lines) as a wholesome sermon on wifely duty. Eighteenth-century readers and playgoers seemingly wanted the taming story to be true, although some women readers even then found Kate's submission excessive. However, they didn't much care whether or not the story was really Shakespeare.[19]

Garrick's *Catherine and Petruchio* continued to be popular on the stage until almost the end of the nineteenth century. But during the same period there was a growing thirst for 'authentic' Shakespeare on the part of both editors and theatregoers. The name of the exalted Bard had to be reattached to the taming story. *The Shrew* in its Folio version had been absent from the stage for two hundred years. It was revived, with the Induction but without the Sly interruptions and conclusion, in England in the 1840s, in America in the 1880s. Thereafter the 'authentic' text of *The Shrew* gradually won the stage over from *Catherine and Petruchio*. In Victorian productions most directors took great care to keep Christopher Sly and the

Induction from undercutting the taming story. Critics and audiences of the Victorian productions of *The Shrew* seem generally to have liked Kate's speech of submission, applauding it wildly and calling it the 'choicest gem of the play'. H.N. Hudson asserted that *The Shrew* was worth 'All the volumes on household virtue that I know of'. Even the most successful and fiery of Victorian actresses to play the part of the Shrew, Ada Rehan, saw the taming of Kate as bringing her 'to the saving grace of woman'. In the first British production of the 'authentic' *Shrew*, one of the actors in the Induction was made up to resemble Shakespeare, then proceeded to take the role of Petruchio, brandishing the traditional whip, so that wife-taming became a Shakespearean virtue indeed.[20] 'Authentic' Shakespeare for the Victorians showed the beauties of wifely acquiescence. We probably do not need to remind ourselves that the same century, through the theories of Sigmund Freud, gave us the concept of normal female masochism.

VI

Amidst all this thirst for authenticity, there was a conceptual problem that editors had to wrestle with. If *The Shrew* was 'true' Shakespeare, then what was to be done with *A Shrew*? If *A Shrew* was also Shakespeare, then the wife-taming message was harder to associate unequivocally with his name. If *A Shrew* was not Shakespeare, then his originality went out of the window: *The Shrew* was massively borrowed from its earlier and cruder prototype and therefore less than authentic. The problem did not come to a head until the early twentieth century, but already towards the end of the nineteenth, we find editors entertaining the idea that *A Shrew* did not precede *The Shrew*, but instead derived from it. Victorian editors of Shakespeare were generally uncomfortable with the strong, outspoken women in Shakespeare's early plays. Furnivall, for example, expressed the strong hope that Shakespeare was not responsible for 'all the women's rant' in *Titus Andronicus*, the *Henry VI* trilogy, and *Richard III*.[21] To regard *A Shrew* not as a source but as a debased copy allowed them to associate the realism and patriarchy of *The Shrew* with 'authentic Shakespeare'. *The Shrew* and its message of wifely submission were the 'original'. *A Shrew*, with its freer relationship between Petruchio/Ferando and Kate, its many undercuttings of the shrew-taming moral, was, in a subtly sexualized language of transgression, a debased and brazen travesty of the 'manly' Shakespearean original, put together in all likelihood by itinerant actors as ignorant of dramatic art and as mean and destitute as the poor players within *A Shrew* itself.

The next stage of this editorial development is rather deliciously predictable. Widespread editorial agreement with the new textual theory by which *The Shrew* was original Shakespeare, or close to it, and *A Shrew* a 'vamped-up' copy came in the 1920s, along with the triumph of women's suffrage. The late-nineteenth- and early-twentieth-century struggle for women's rights made 'authentic Shakespeare' onstage in *The Taming of the Shrew* more and more uncomfortable. Increasingly, directors tried either to engage the play's topical potential directly – at least one production cast Kate as the 'new woman' – or to mitigate the tensions by staging the play as farce. Reviewers commented regularly on Kate's submission as unlikely to commend itself, as one of them put it, 'to the out-and-out feminists of the Women's Federation League or the generality of the shingled and Eton-cropped sisterhood'.[22] In 1926, two years before women's suffrage in Britain, Peter Alexander wrote an influential series of articles in the *Times Literary Supplement* contending yet once more that *A Shrew* was a 'later and degraded version' of Shakespeare's play and relying heavily on arguments first broached a half-century before. Other editors during the 1920s and later put Shakespeare at an even greater distance, arguing that his original play was lost, and that both *A Shrew* and *The Shrew* were derivative, although the latter was more strongly Shakespearean than the former.[23] At the same time that 'new women' were agitating for the vote in England, editors were burying the 'vamped-up' version of *A Shrew* deeper and deeper – like a shameful skeleton in the Shakespearean closet that had to be kept out of sight. Even editors who remained sceptical about Alexander's view of the relationship between the two plays displayed a nostalgia for past simplicities, as in Quiller-Couch's comment in the Cambridge edition (1928): 'avoiding the present times and recalling Dickens, most fertile of inventors since Shakespeare, with Dickens's long gallery of middle-aged wives who make household life intolerable by various and odious methods, one cannot help thinking a little wistfully that the Petruchian discipline had something to say for itself'.[24]

The textual arguments by which editors have convinced themselves (and others) that *A Shrew* is a contaminated version of *The Shrew*, or of an earlier play that was genuine Shakespeare, rest on an implicit prior ranking by which *The Shrew* is assumed to be 'what Shakespeare meant', so that deviations from it are invariably read as corruptions. In the two versions we have already noted of Kate's placing her hand beneath her husband's foot, for example, the standard argument is that 'the imitator, as usual, has caught something of the words of the original, which he has laboured to reproduce at a most unusual sacrifice of grammar and sense ... he has by omitting the words "in token of which duty" omitted the whole point of the passage'.[25] I have argued earlier that the 'imitator' is instead making a different point. Two other tell-tale passages for the derivative nature of *A Shrew* are drawn from the scene between Kate and the tailor. In the 'authorized' version Grumio protests to the tailor: 'Master, if ever I said "loose-bodied gown", sew me in the skirts of it and beat me to death with a bottom of brown thread' (IV.iii.131–2). The equivalent speech in *A Shrew* is, 'Master, if ever I said loose body's gown, sew me in a seam and beat me to death with [a] bottom of brown thread!' (p. 44, ll. 29–31). The criticism of *A Shrew* here is that 'the reporter is very close but the difference is enough to show his hand. "Sew me in the skirts of it" has meaning whereas the variation has none'.[26] The talk during the scene has been of facings, and facings quite commonly require the type of seam (although admittedly not quite the amplitude) in which a person could be sewn. Why does the idea of being sewn in a seam have no meaning? It requires no great powers of observation to recognize that facings in portraits of Elizabethan women's dresses are commonly sewn double, like what we would now call 'French seams'. The speech in *A Shrew* is more ludicrous than its counterpart in *The Shrew*, and also more deviously ribald if one takes the idea of being sewn in a lady's seam as relating to her person, not her clothes. But in what way is the passage clearly derivative? Only if one has already decided what constitutes 'good sense' in the text of the play, with variations representing nothing more than 'rant' or 'nonsense'. In the second passage, which follows hard upon the first, *A Shrew* has the following exchange:

> *San*. Dost thou hear, tailor? Thou hast braved many men: brave not me. Thou'st faced many men –
> *Tailor*. Well, sir.
> *San*. Face not me: I'll neither be faced nor braved at thy hands, I can tell thee! (p. 44, ll. 37–41)

The equivalent passage in *The Shrew* reads:

> *Grumio*. Thou hast faced many things.
> *Tailor*. I have.
> *Grumio*. Face not me. Thou hast braved many men; brave not me. I will neither be faced nor braved.
>
> (IV.iii.121–4)

In this case, editors argue, *A Shrew* misses the puns on 'faced' and 'braved', and therefore declares itself as the derivative version. But all that would be required for *A Shrew* to make as much 'sense' as *The Shrew* would be for the actor to indicate through gesture that the braving and facing he has in mind are punningly linked to the tailor's trade. *A Shrew*'s version of the passage is less explicit, but would hardly be regarded as corrupt if it were allowed to stand on its own: it is editorially suspect only because it does not replicate every nuance of *The Shrew*.

Perhaps the most damning flaw of *A Shrew* in the minds of those who have argued for its derivative status is its frequent Marlovian echoes. The argument here is that the ignorant actors who patched together the pirated version of the play threw in snatches of Marlowe whenever their memories failed them, creating a pastiche with no claim to independent literary integrity. Peter Alexander characterizes the putative compiler(s) as having 'a mentality very like that of ancient Pistol, and a head no more proof against the intoxication of tragic diction'.[27] That *A Shrew* contains numerous passages echoing *Tamburlaine the Great* and *Doctor Faustus* is undeniable, although some of the alleged parallels are too faint to be convincing. If we grant that text the same privilege of putative intentionality that is routinely granted to *The Shrew*, however, we can regard the Marlovian passages not as mere unassimilated bombast, but as deliberate stage quotations of tragedies well known to audiences in the early 1590s – quotations designed to create a ludicrous effect of mock heroic in their new and incongruous setting. In the Induction to *A Shrew*, for example, when the nobleman and his men first enter, his grand language echoes the famous speech with which Faustus first conjures up his devils:

> *Now that the gloomy shadow of the night,*
> *Longing to view Orion's drizzling looks,*
> *Leaps from th' Antarctic world unto the sky,*
> *And dims the welkin with her pitchy breath,*
> *And darksome night o'ershads the crystal heavens*
>
> (pp. 1–2, ll. 9–13)

What the Lord conjures up, however, is not demons but the drunken, sleeping Sly. The humour can scarcely be said to be subtle, but it might have been quite funny onstage. In the corresponding scene at the end of the play, when Sly is once again lying before the alehouse, the Tapster utters a parallel passage just before stumbling upon him:

> Now that the darksome night is overpassed,
> And dawning day appears in crystal sky,
> Now must I haste abroad. But soft, who's this?
> What, Sly?
>
> (p. 64, ll. 1–4)

The device is doubly ludicrous the second time, and helps to underline the return of Christopher Sly: his discovery, once again, takes centre stage. Marlovian echoes serve a similar comic, deflating function throughout the play, sometimes even taking the form of stage business. In the scene at Petruchio's house, *A Shrew*, unlike *The Shrew*, specifies that Petruchio / Ferando enters '*with a piece of meat upon his dagger's point*', echoing the hideously powerful moment in *Tamburlaine the Great Part I*, IV.iv in which Tamburlaine offers food at his sword's end to the conquered Bajazeth. The many Marlovian echoes of *A Shrew* help to keep the play firmly within the realm of farce, overturning any faint whisper of the heroic about Petruchio/Ferando's campaign against the shrew, undercutting any incipient claim to realism (of the kind so prominently made in *The Shrew*) before it has a chance to develop.

VII

Barring the discovery of new historical artifacts – such as a working manuscript of one or both texts in the same hand as the passages from *Sir Thomas More* believed to be in Shakespeare's – we are unlikely ever to settle the question of which play came first, or how much of either is genuine Shakespeare. We may settle such matters to our own satisfactions, but if past editorial opinion is any guide, what pleases us as explanation may not equally please those who come after us. To the author of the present essay, *A Shrew* sounds distinctly earlier, sounds as though it could perhaps contain bits of early Shakespeare and be designed to capitalize on the public passion for Marlowe during the early 1590s. Whether or not we label *A Shrew* as Shakespeare, we need to recognize that it is a more interesting, intriguing play than its long history of suppression would suggest. But what would be the point just now of insisting on the priority of one or another version? To do so would be to revert to the old editorial mode of creating hierarchies of texts which are invariably value-laden. I would suggest instead that we start thinking of the different versions of *The Taming of the Shrew* intertextually – as a cluster of related texts which can be fruitfully read together and against each other as 'Shakespeare'. To do that, of course, is to give up the idea that either Shakespeare or the canon of his works is a single determinate thing. It is to carry Shakespearean textual studies out of the filiative search for a single 'authentic' point of origin and into the purview of post-structuralist criticism, where the authority of the author loses its élan and the text becomes a multiple, shifting process rather than an artifact set permanently in print. In the case of *A Shrew* and *The Shrew*, it is also to interrogate the canonical version of a play we may no longer want to live with.

In twentieth-century productions of *The Shrew*, the patriarchal message of the piece has been evaded by many ingenious methods: Kate may wink at the audience even as she hoodwinks Petruchio, as in Mary Pickford's film version. Kate may be portrayed as a loveless neurotic who is cured by Petruchio through a kind of psychodrama that shows her her own excess. Quite often she abases herself out of love. Or the whole thing can be reduced to farce. At present, however, all these methods seem to have played themselves out onstage (and film), and there are signs that the equivalent critical readings are playing themselves out as well – not only among modern feminists, who find the text too alienating to be 'set right' by such strategies, but also among our students, who are increasingly unhappy with our usual readings emphasizing the mutuality of the taming and other such palliatives designed to smooth over the reality of Petruchio's domination. We can choose, of course, to remove the play quietly from the list of those we teach and discuss, as Shirley Garner and other perceptive readers have suggested we do.[28] Or we can bring back *The Shrew*'s long-suppressed intertext *A Shrew*, the tactic resorted to on the modern stage.

In the eighteenth century, readers of Shakespeare got the Sly ending to the play, while theatregoers saw the play cleansed of Sly and rechristened *Catherine and Petruchio*. Now the opposite pattern prevails: theatrical productions depend on the Sly framework to cast the whole patriarchal system constructed by the taming plot into doubt and unreality, while our texts banish Sly at the end and conclude with the 'reality' of Kate's capitulation. If *A Shrew* comes to be accepted by editors and readers as an acceptable intertext of *The Shrew* (whether as a first draft, source, or early derivative), then several things could happen. In editions of Shakespeare that offer composite texts of other plays, *The Shrew* could also become composite. In the same way that editors have regularly inserted the mock trial scene and other brief segments from the 1608 quarto of *King Lear* into the Folio text, so editors could insert the Sly episodes from the 1594 quarto *A Shrew* – and perhaps other material as well – into *The Taming of the Shrew*. A more satisfying alternative would follow the pattern of the newest editions of *King Lear* and print both texts in their entirety, one after the other. Such a format would preserve the integrity of each early version while offering readers a dazzling, unsettling empowerment: with only a slight stretching of the traditional rationale of copytext by which the best possible text is arrived at through the combination of variant early versions, readers would be freed, if the task appealed to them, to become their own editors, to create new combinations of the two texts that are as much 'Shakespeare' as the composite texts to which we are already accustomed in our standard editions of the plays.

But, it may be objected, such a procedure would be irresponsibly chaotic and ahistorical – it would take us much too far afield from the Renaissance itself, in which, whether we like it or not, patriarchy was as dominant and univocal as it is in *The Taming of the Shrew*. That is by no means clear. I have pointed to a process of naturalization by which the patriarchal ideology of *The Shrew* gradually became 'reality' in terms of public expectations in the theatre and readers' expectations of Shakespeare. But that process was not without its glitches, temporary reversals and ambivalences in any period – certainly not in the Renaissance itself. The same culture that preferred *The Shrew* to *A Shrew* also made space for an antidote. In the early seventeenth century, John Fletcher continued the story of Petruchio in *The Woman's Prize, or The Tamer Tamed*, in which Kate has died and Petruchio marries a second wife, Maria, who tames him as effectively as he had earlier tamed Kate, except that Maria's methods are draconian to the point of paramilitarism. When Shakespeare's *The Shrew* and Fletcher's *The Woman's Prize* were performed within a few days of each other at the court of Charles I in 1633, Shakespeare's *The Shrew* was 'liked', but Fletcher's play was 'very well liked'.[29] It is probably fair to say that patriarchy as a system has regularly been more consistent and orderly in the minds of historically inclined editors and readers than it has been in society at large. If we are to interrogate the canonical Shakespeare, then we need to interrogate the editorial assumptions underlying the texts by which we have come to 'know' him.

Notes

1. *The Taming of the Shrew* V.ii.179–80, cited from the New Cambridge *The Taming of the Shrew*, ed. Ann Thompson (Cambridge, 1984). Subsequent references to the play will be to this edition and indicated by act, scene, and line number in the text.
   This essay was presented at the University of Massachusetts, Amherst, as the *ELR* Lecture for 1990, now the Dan S. Collins Lecture in Renaissance Studies. The author would like to thank audiences at the University of Massachusetts, Arizona State University, Williams College, the University of Illinois at Chicago, the University of Wisconsin, and Yale University for invaluable comments and suggestions.
2. For discussion of recent performances, I am indebted to Tori Haring-Smith, *From Farce to Melodrama: A Stage History of* The Taming of the Shrew, *1594–1983* (Westport, CT, 1985), and to Graham Holderness, *Shakespeare in Performance:* The Taming of the Shrew (Manchester, 1989).
3. Thompson, pp. 1–3; the New Arden edition of *The Taming of the Shrew*, ed. Brian Morris (London, 1981), p. 3.
4. Scholarly opinion differs as to whether Shakespeare himself was a member of Pembroke's Men and whether *A Shrew* was actually performed by that company or by the Lord Chamberlain's Men at Newington Butts. There are also marked differences of opinion over which of these early *Shrews* was *A Shrew* and which may have been *The Shrew*. For representative views, see E.K. Chambers, *William Shakespeare: A Study of Facts and Problems*, 2 vols (Oxford, 1930), pp. 1324–8; *The Taming of the Shrew*, ed. Sir Arthur Quiller-Couch and John Dover Wilson (Cambridge, 1928), pp. vii–xxv, 99–126; *The Taming of the Shrew*, ed. H.J. Oliver (Oxford, 1984), pp. 29–34; and David George, 'Shakespeare and Pembroke's Men', *Shakespeare Quarterly* 32 (1981): 305–23.
5. Early editions I have consulted include *The Works of Mr. William Shakespeare; In Six Volumes*, ed. Nicholas Rowe (1709); *The Works of Shakespear … in Six Volumes*, ed. Alexander Pope (1720–25); *The Works of Shakespeare in Seven Volumes*, ed. Lewis Theobald (1733); *The Works of Shakespear in Six Volumes*, ed. Thomas Hanmer (1744); *The Works of Shakespear in Eight Volumes*, ed. William Warburton (1747); *The Plays of William Shakespeare, in Eight Volumes*, ed. Samuel Johnson (1765); Mr. William Shakespeare *his COMEDIES, HISTORIES, AND TRAGEDIES*, ed. Edward Capell (1768); and *The Plays and Poems of William Shakespeare in 10 Volumes*, ed. Edmond Malone (1790). Capell represents a transitional case in that the Sly materials are included in the text of his London 1768 edition

but branded as non-Shakespearean in the introduction and notes of his Dublin 1771 edition, *The Plays of Shakespeare*.

6. *Shakespeare's Plays in Quarto: A Facsimile Edition of Copies Primarily from the Henry E. Huntington Library*, ed. Michael Allen and Kenneth Muir (Berkeley, CA, 1981), p. xv; see also W.W. Greg, *The Shakespeare First Folio: Its Bibliographical and Textual History* (Oxford, 1955), pp. 210–16. For representative twentieth-century arguments about the derivative nature of *A Shrew*, see n. 23 below. For examples of dissenting opinion, to the effect that *A Shrew* is either early Shakespeare or Shakespeare's main source, see *The Taming of the Shrew*, ed. F.S. Boas (London, 1908); *The Works of Shakespeare: The Taming of the Shrew*, ed. R. Warwick Bond (Indianapolis, n.d.); *Narrative and Dramatic Sources of Shakespeare*, ed. Geoffrey Bullough, (London, 1966), I, 58; *Shakespeare's Comedy of 'The Taming of the Shrew'*, ed. William J. Rolfe (New York, 1881 [new edition, 1898]); W.J. Courthope, *A History of English Poetry* (London, 1895–1910), IV, pp. 467–74. To their credit, in *William Shakespeare: A Textual Companion* (Oxford, 1987), Gary Taylor and Stanley Wells leave open the question of the relationship between *A Shrew* and *The Shrew*.

7. Gary Taylor, 'Textual and Sexual Criticism: A Crux in *The Comedy of Errors*', *Renaissance Drama*, n. s. 19 (1988): 195–225.

8. For this point I am indebted to Margaret Downes-Gamble's paper 'The Taming-school: *The Taming of the Shrew* as Lesson in Renaissance Humanism and the Modern Humanities', forthcoming in a special issue of *Sixteenth Century Studies*, ed. Jean R. Brink. See also Thompson, pp. 13–14.

9. See, e.g., John C. Bean, 'Comic Structure and the Humanizing of Kate in *The Taming of the Shrew*', in *The Woman's Part: Feminist Criticism of Shakespeare*, ed. Carolyn Ruth Swift Lenz, Gayle Greene and Carol Thomas Neely (Urbana, IL, 1980, rpt. 1983), pp. 65–78; and Peter Berek, 'Text, Gender, and Genre in *The Taming of the Shrew*', in *'Bad' Shakespeare: Revaluations of the Shakespearean Canon*, ed. Maurice Charney (London, 1988), pp. 91–104. Both essays consistently misread *A Shrew* out of a desire to demonstrate Shakespeare's greater tolerance and humanity. For use of Kate's submission speech from *A Shrew*, see Ann Thompson's fine edition (n. 1 above), pp. 28–9.

Other interpretive articles with which I may not agree but to which my own thinking is indebted include Lynda E. Boose, 'Scolding Brides and Bridling Scolds: Taming the Woman's Unruly Member', *Shakespeare Quarterly* 42 (1991): 179–213; and her forth-coming essay '*The Taming of the Shrew*, Good Husbandry, and Enclosure'; Richard A. Burt, 'Charisma, Coercion, and Comic Form in *The Taming of the Shrew*', *Criticism* 26 (1984): 295–311; Joel Fineman, 'The Turn of the Shrew', in *Shakespeare and the Question of Theory*, ed. Patricia Parker and Geoffrey Hartman (London, 1985), pp. 138–59; Thelma Nelson Greenfield, 'The Transformation of Christopher Sly', *Philological Quarterly* 33 (1954): 34–42; Robert B. Heilman, 'The *Taming* Untamed, or, The Return of the Shrew', *Modern Language Quarterly* 27 (1966): 146–61; Barbara Hodgdon's forthcoming essay 'Katherina Bound, or Notes on Pla(k)ating the Structures of Everyday Life'; Richard Hosley, 'Was There a Dramatic Epilogue to *The Taming of the Shrew*?', *Studies in English Literature 1500–1900*, 1 (1961): 17–34; Sears Jayne, 'The Dreaming of *The Shrew*', *Shakespeare Quarterly* 17 (1966): 41–56; Ernest P. Kuhl, 'Shakespeare's Purpose in Dropping Sly', *Modern Language Notes* 36 (1921): 321–9; Karen Newman, 'Renaissance Family Politics and Shakespeare's *The Taming of the Shrew*', *English Literary Renaissance* 16 (1986): 86–100; Marianne L. Novy, 'Patriarchy and Play in *The Taming of the Shrew*', *English Literary Renaissance* 9 (1979): 264–80; Marion D. Perrit, 'Petruchio: The Model Wife', *Studies in English Literature 1500–1900* 23 (1983): 223–35; Michael W. Shurgot, 'From Fiction to Reality: Character and Stagecraft in *The Taming of the Shrew*', *Theatre Journal* 33 (1981): 327–40; Edward Tomarken's forthcoming essay 'The Discipline of Criticism: Samuel Johnson on Shakespeare'; Valerie Wayne, 'Refashioning the Shrew', *Shakespeare Studies* 17 (1985): 159–87; and Karl P. Wentersdorf, 'The Original Ending of *The Taming of the Shrew*: A Reconsideration', *Studies in English Literature 1500–1900* 18 (1978): 201–15. My thanks to Lynda Boose, Edward Tomarken and Barbara Hodgdon, who graciously shared their work in manuscript.

10. See Steven Urkowitz, *Shakespeare's Revision of* King Lear (Princeton, NJ, 1980); *The Division of the Kingdoms: Shakespeare's Two Versions of* King Lear, ed. Gary Taylor

and Michael Warren (Oxford, 1983); Urkowitz, 'Reconsidering the Relationship of Quarto and Folio Texts of *Richard III*', *English Literary Renaissance* 16 (1986): 442–66; Urkowitz, 'Good News about Bad Quartos', in *'Bad' Shakespeare: Revaluations of the Shakespeare Canon*, ed. Maurice Charney (London, 1988), pp. 189–206; Annabel Patterson, 'Back by Popular Demand: The Two Versions of *Henry V*', *Renaissance Drama*, n. s. 19 (1988): 29–62; and Leah Marcus, *Puzzling Shakespeare: Local Reading and Its Discontents* (Berkeley, CA, 1988). The present essay will be included in revised form in a book in progress under the tentative title of 'Unediting and Renaissance Shakespeare, Marlowe, Milton'.

11. *The First Folio of Shakespeare*, ed. Charlton Hinman (London, 1968), p. 7.

12. See, for example, *The Taming of the Shrew*, ed. Oliver, pp. 17–18.

13. *'The Taming of a Shrew' being the Original of Shakespeare's 'Taming of the Shrew'*, ed. F.S. Boas (London, 1908), p. 14, lines 169–71. Subsequent quotations from this edition will be indicated by page and line number in the text.

14. See Lawrence Stone, *The Family, Sex and Marriage in England, 1500–1800* (London, 1977); Joan Kelly, 'Did Women Have a Renaissance?' (1977), reprinted in *Women, History, and Theory: The Essays of Joan Kelly* (Chicago, 1984), pp. 19–50; and David Underdown's critique of Alice Clark's *Working Life of Women in the Seventeenth Century*, rev. ed by M. Chaytor and J. Lewis (London, 1982), in Underdown's 'The Taming of the Scold: The Enforcement of Patriarchal Authority in Early Modern England', in *Order and Disorder in Early Modern England*, ed. Anthony Fletcher and John Stevenson (Cambridge, 1985), pp. 116–36. Underdown accepts the theory of a general decline in the independence of women during the period, but argues that increased attention to the scold may signal increased opportunities for women in some segments of sixteenth- and seventeenth-century culture.

15. F.J. Furnivall, *The New Shakespeare Society's Transactions*, Series 1, no. 1 (London, 1874): 104. See also the New Arden edition of *The Taming of the Shrew*, ed. Brian Morris (London, 1981), pp. 62–3. John Russell Brown uses the appeal to realism in *The Shrew* to build a broad argument about increasing naturalism in acting styles during the age of Shakespeare, 'On the Acting of Shakespeare's Plays' (1953), rpt. in *The Seventeenth-Century Stage: A Collection of Critical Essays*, ed. G.E. Bentley (Chicago, 1968), pp. 41–54.

16. John Harington, *The Metamorphosis of Ajax*, ed. Elizabeth Donno (London, 1962), pp. 153–4; cited in Oliver, p. 34.

17. See G.E. Bentley, *The Professions of Dramatist and Player in Shakespeare's Time, 1590–1642*, one-volume paperback edition (1971 and 1984 rpt. Princeton, NJ, 1986); and Muriel C. Bradbrook, 'The Status Seekers: Society and the Common Player in the Reign of Elizabeth I', 1961, rpt. in Bentley, pp. 55–69.

18. *The Plays of William Shakespeare, in Eight Volumes*, ed. Samuel Johnson (1765), III, 99. For discussion of eighteenth-century adaptations, see Haring-Smith, pp. 7–22; and *Taming*, ed. Oliver, pp. 65–9.

19. See, for an example of women's response, Marianne Novy's introduction to her *Women's Re-Visions of Shakespeare* (Urbana, IL, 1990), p. 7.

20. For all these and other examples, see Haring-Smith, pp. 43–64. See also Susan J. Wolfson, 'Explaining to Her Sisters: Mary Lamb's *Tales from Shakespear*', in Novy, pp. 16–40, especially pp. 23–7.

21. *New Shakspere Society's Transactions* (1874): 95–103. See also William Benzie, *Dr. F.J. Furnivall: Victorian Scholar Adventurer* (Norman, 1983), pp. 194–6.

22. Thompson, p. 21.

23. See Peter Alexander, 'The Taming of a Shrew', *Times Literary Supplement*, Thursday, 16 Sept. 1926, p. 614. See also his '"II. Henry VI" and the Copy for "The Contention" (1594)', *Times Literary Supplement*, 9 Oct. 1924, pp. 629–30; and '"3 Henry VI" and "Richard, Duke of York"', *Times Literary Supplement*, 13 Nov. 1924, p. 730. For more recent refinements of the argument by which *A Shrew* is derived from *The Shrew* or from a common ancestor of both, see, e.g., Raymond A. Houk, 'The Evolution of *The Taming of the Shrew*', *PMLA*: 57 (1942): 1009–38; Henry David Gray, '*The Taming of a Shrew*', *Philological Quarterly* 20 (1941): 325–33; and G.I. Duthie, '*The Taming of a Shrew* and *The Taming of*

the Shrew', *Review of English Studies*, 19 (1943): 337–56. Similar arguments are made in almost every modern single-volume edition of the play; for dissenting views, see the sources in n. 6 above.

24. *The Taming of the Shrew*, ed. Sir Arthur Quiller-Couch and John Dover Wilson (Cambridge, 1928), p. xxvi. For another similar view, see A.L. Rowse, ed., *The Annotated Shakespeare, Vol. I: The Comedies* (New York, 1978), pp. 119–21.

25. Wilson, ed., citing, as nearly all discussions of the problem do, Samuel Hickson, 'Marlowe and the Old "Taming of a Shrew"', *Notes and Queries* 1 (1850): 194, 226–7, in the Cambridge edn, p. 179.

26. Wilson, ed., citing Hickson, Cambridge edn, p. 168.

27. Alexander, p. 614. All editorial argument about Marlovian borrowings rests ultimately on Hickson, n. 25 above. On Marlovian borrowings, see also Boas, pp. xxx–xxxii and 91–8, and nearly every modern edition of the play. My own argument that the Marlovian passages work as successful burlesque has been anticipated in part by a few editors, most prominently Quiller-Couch, pp. xxi–xxii.

28. '*The Taming of the Shrew*: Inside or Outside of the Joke?' in *'Bad' Shakespeare*, pp. 105–19.

29. Oliver, p. 64.

13

Shakespeare, Zeffirelli, and the Homosexual Gaze

William Van Watson

> And then, sir, would he gripe and wring my hand,
> Cry, 'O Sweet creature!' and then kiss me hard,
> As if he plucked up kisses by the roots
> That grew upon my lips; and then laid his leg
> Over my thigh, and sighed and kissed . . .

The passionate couple described above are not Antony and Cleopatra, or Hermia and Lysander, but Cassio and Iago (*Othello* III.iii.425–9). In his film of Giuseppe Verdi's opera version of the play (1986), Franco Zeffirelli superimposes Iago's recounting of this incident to Otello with an image of the naked, handsome body of the sleeping Cassio, who somnambulantly mouths Iago's sung words. The post-dubbing of the film, both as product of Italian cinema and as filmed opera, allowed for this use of aural–visual montage. Out of Cassio's body comes Iago's voice. This juxtaposition of male voices parallels the juxtaposition of male bodies referred to in Shakespeare's text, so that Zeffirelli's film purposefully emphasizes the homoerotic overtones of the original passage. In fact, the film at this point is nothing short of a homoerotic tease, as Cassio, bathed in a heated chiaroscuro, writhes and arches his back in sexual fantasy, caressing himself from head to groin, his genitalia threatening to erupt within the discreet limits of the frame at any moment. This homoerotic image of Cassio's blond, hairless and recumbent body emphasizes his ephebic, if not outright androgynous, nature. Zeffirelli cast the actor playing Cassio, Prince Urbano Barberini, in specific contrast to Otello's ostensibly masculine and dominant darkness, noting Barberini's similarity to Katia Ricciarelli, the soprano playing Desdemona: 'He, too, was blond like Desdemona, giving them a physical affinity to contrast even further with Otello' (*Autobiography*, p. 335). The undertow of Zeffirelli's film is not amiss, as the dramatic structure of Shakespeare's play is little more than a homoerotic web of disrupted male bonds into which the unsuspecting

Desdemona innocently intrudes. After all, it is Iago, not Desdemona, whom Othello 'loves not wisely, but too well' (V.ii.431). The Renaissance sleeping habits of the men, sharing the same bed shown explicitly by Zeffirelli in a scene between Roderigo and Iago, lends plausibility to Iago's claim of Cassio's supposed erotic dream. Such sleeping arrangements bespeak an intimacy of the male bonds, an intimacy emphasized by the fireplace which bathes the men's bedchamber in a warm light. For his part, Iago is not so much jealous of Othello's place with Desdemona as he is jealous of Cassio's place with Othello. In the opening party sequence, his policing jealous stare, combined with Desdemona's recurrent glances at her childhood friend, makes Cassio the preferred object of not only their gaze, but also Zeffirelli's camera.

For the better part of four centuries, the same Shakespearean scholars who have praised the Bard for his almost universal understanding of human psychology have been intent on straitjacketing his concept of human sexuality into a limited and conformist heterosexual polarity. There is, quite simply, more in heaven and earth, as well as in Shakespeare, than is dreamt of in this simple-minded homophobic philosophy. Certainly Valentine and Proteus mean more to one another in *Two Gentlemen of Verona* than their pursuit of Silvia means to either of them. Shakespeare's theatre is filled with such male bonding; many of his plays are little more than a male bonding ritual – *Henry V* and its showpiece, the St Crispin's Day speech, for instance. Admittedly, such male bonds in Shakespeare's plays usually remain safely within the realm of heterosexual male behaviour patterns, any homoerotic undercurrents remaining precisely that – undercurrents. Such relationships as that between Valentine and Proteus have traditionally been referred to by the euphemism 'Renaissance friendship', or what the Italians have called *eroica amicizia*, literally 'heroic friendship'. Peter Levi, Shakespeare's most recent biographer, writes: 'The romantic attachments of pairs of young men, bound up with ideas of love and honor, did in real life reach a hectic degree' (p. 33). It is certainly reasonable to believe that male–male relationships in Renaissance England were more affectively demonstrative than those of contemporary Anglo-American society. Consider one of Antonio's several impassioned addresses to Sebastian in *Twelfth Night*:

> I could not stay behind you: my desire
> More sharp than filed steel, did spur me forth:
> And not all love to see you (though so much
> As might have drawn one to a longer voyage)

(III.iii.4–7)

The eighteenth-century critic Edmond Malone comments on the effusive displays of emotion between Shakespeare's male characters, noting that 'such addresses to men, however indelicate, were customary in our author's time, and neither imported criminality nor were esteemed indecorous' (quoted in Pequigney, p. 30). Quite probably so. The sexual historian Philippe Ariès explains such 'Renaissance friendship' in relationship to homosexuality proper:

> I think that in certain cultures, e.g. Italian Quattrocento and Elizabethan England, there developed, out of an apparently asexual form of sentiment, a particular kind of manly love that verged on homosexuality; but it was a homosexuality that was undeclared and unadmitted, that remained a mystery, less through fear of prohibition than for a distaste for labelling oneself in the eyes of contemporary society as non-sexual or sexual. One hovered in a mixed zone that belonged to neither. (p. 71)

Unfortunately, the term 'Renaissance friendship' has also long functioned as the closet in which certain scholars have hidden their own homophobia. Simply because 'Renaissance friendships' existed does not mean that homosexual male relationships did not. During Renaissance times, the Catholic Church actually performed marriage ceremonies, wherein these ostensibly Platonic 'Renaissance friendships' were solemnized, only later to discover that a number of the friendly pairs had actually sexually consummated their vows. The sexual historian James M. Saslow writes: 'Montaigne reported several "marriages" between Portuguese men celebrated in a Roman Church in 1578; the couples lived together for some time before being arrested and burned' (quoted in Duberman, p. 95). A number of extant wills survive and attest to the homosexuality of these relationships (see Olivieri in Ariès, pp. 100–102).[1]

A more enlightened view shows Shakespeare's plays to be as pan-sexual as they are pan-social and pan-psychological. The point is simple. Homosexuality existed in Renaissance society, and Shakespeare knew it. Shakespeare's homosexual awareness is perhaps at its greatest in *Twelfth Night*. As a genre, comedy historically concludes with the pairing up of socially acceptable and even socially sanctioned couples. *Twelfth Night* follows this pattern, as Sir Toby ends up with Maria, Duke Orsino ends up with Viola, and Olivia ends up with Sebastian. However, if *Twelfth Night* is 'saddest of comedies', it is because the play is characterized by an acute sense of nostalgia for what has gone before: the same-sex pairings of Sebastian and Antonio, Olivia and Viola, and Duke Orsino and Cesario. This was particularly noticeable in the Andrei Serban 1989 production of the play for the American Repertory Theatre in Cambridge, Massachusetts. In Serban's version Orsino and Cesario repeatedly reclined in bed together, the 'Elephant' tavern where Sebastian and Antonio arranged to meet was identifiably transformed into a gay bar, and Viola and Olivia shared an openly sexual kiss *after* Viola discarded her disguise and revealed herself to be female. The play itself concludes with a lament for the same-sex relationships that might have been. Feste's closing song, 'When that I was and a little tiny boy', speaks of an androgynous time before the adoption of adult sex roles and the fall into becoming what Lacan has called 'sexed partial beings'. Despite such arguably sympathetic treatment regarding same-sex relationships, Shakespeare's theatre as a whole is far from championing homosexuality as a cause. In fact, when he does broach the topic it is more probably in order to deride the character in question. In this context, Hamlet's berating of the effeminate and Frenchified Osric comes to mind. In *Much Ado about Nothing*, Don Pedro's inability to find a woman who suits him makes his sexuality at least questionable, but in *The Merchant of Venice* Antonio's sexuality is not nearly so dubious. Here the character chastises himself for his love of another male, namely Bassanio. Such self-disgust reflects Antonio's internalization of the homophobic value system of the society which surrounded both him and Shakespeare. Nevertheless, in the same play, the fact that Solanio and Salerio understand Antonio well enough to taunt him implies at least a homosexual awareness on their part, and a possible homosexual dimension to their own relationship.

Furthermore, Shakespeare wrote with a homosexually aware audience in mind. Otherwise, lines such as Hamlet's 'Man delights not me – nor woman neither' would not play (II.ii.309). Christopher Marlowe's popular *Edward II* even stipulated an outright sympathetic response from its Elizabethan audience towards its overtly homosexual hero-king. Nevertheless, Zeffirelli has prudishly, homophobically and mistakenly claimed that there are no love scenes in Shakespeare 'for the simple reason that girls were played by boys and it would have been unseemly to attempt to show them intertwined on stage' (Zeffirelli, pp. 338–9). Despite Zeffirelli, it should be remembered that Elizabethan audiences saw adolescent males in such roles as Cleopatra seduce young men onstage on a regular basis. Treatment of the boys by the adult male actors was itself somewhat suspect. Prompted in part by the death of his own children from the plague, the playwright Ben Jonson took a special interest in what he considered the plight and abuse of these boy actors. As Jonson was a notorious womanizer who preferred liaisons exclusively with married women, it is highly unlikely that his own motivations regarding the boy actors were anything but altruistic.[2] In any case, although theatrical convention dictated that the boy be seen solely as the female character, there nevertheless existed a phenomenon known as 'personation', a term coined by John Marston in his play *Antonio and Mellida*. It is used to refer to the identification between the boy actor and his role, an identification which went beyond the bounds of standard acting techniques of the time. The Shakespeare critic Katherine E. Kelly refers to 'flaunting the qualities of the boy actor – sexually and verbally exuberant, punning, quick-witted and chiding'. She goes on to assert that 'repeated use of this strategy seems to have distinguished Shakespeare' (p. 84). On the narrative level, then, Shakespeare's audience empathized with scenes of heterosexual love, while on the level of theatrical convention they witnessed a vicarious game of homosexual cat and mouse. Even the conservative Shakespearean scholar S.L. Bethell has had to concede a 'multi-consciousness' to Shakespeare's audience (pp. 202–3).

Despite whatever sense of vicarious homosexuality may have existed in Shakespeare's theatre audience, the most compelling evidence for a homosexual sensibility in Shakespeare himself comes not from his plays but from his sonnets. The sonnet cycle is essentially a series of love poems written from Shakespeare to his patron, the Earl of Southampton, who, since he had more portraits painted of himself than any other nobleman of the age, was undoubtedly a very vain young man. Consequently, the hyperbolic compliments given him in the sonnets would probably have pleased him. In fact, such writers as Thomas Heywood, Barnabe Barnes, Gervase Markham and Thomas Nashe all composed poems in honour of Southampton. Still, the language of Shakespeare's sonnets far transcends the conventional bounds of literary praise with which most poets of the time lauded their patrons. Nevertheless, Levi, like generations of homo-phobic scholars before him, presumes to defend the relationship between the two men: 'Shakespeare and Southampton were not complete lovers, and the Sonnets are not about buggery' (p. 100). Whether or not Shakespeare and Southampton were complete lovers may remain a matter of conjecture, but the sonnets most certainly are about buggery. In fact, homoerotic imagery pervades the entire sonnet cycle. Consider the opening lines of Sonnet 52:

> So am I as the rich whose blessed key
> Can bring him to the sweet up-locked treasure,
> The which he will not every hour survey,
> For blunting the fine point of seldom pleasure.

The writer, Shakespeare, has a 'blessed key', or penis, which seeks 'the sweet up-locked treasure' of a sexual encounter with Southampton. Their times alone together are 'seldom', Shakespeare not having 'every hour' to 'survey' Southampton's charms. When the poet is able to sample his patron's 'up-locked treasure', it results in the 'blunting' of his 'fine-point', or loss of an erection. In his book *Such is My Love*, Joseph Pequigney provides a detailed analysis of Shakespeare's use of bawdy verbal imagery in the sonnets. Pequigney also recounts to what absurdly ludicrous lengths scholars have gone in order to desexualize their contents. Those same scholars who have argued the sexual connotations of such verbs as 'to have', 'to get' or 'to take' when referring to a female have suddenly and arbitrarily balked at the idea of the exact same terminology meaning anything sexual when it refers to a male.

As opposed to the more renegade Marlowe, who had gone so far as to declare the sacrilege that Jesus's love for John was 'an unnatural love', Shakespeare certainly never intended to flaunt whatever homosexual component there may have been to his nature. His sonnet cycle was written for the private perusal of Southampton, and was never intended for publication. It is only by an accident of history that the works ever entered the public domain. Southampton had bought Shakespeare his share in the Lord Chamberlain's Men, a gift of unorthodox generosity for the time, and in an insulting poem entitled 'Narcissus', the writer John Clapham faulted Southampton for needing 'an increase of manliness' (quoted in Levi, p. 96). Shakespeare, apparently scandalized, repeatedly urged his patron to marry. Maintaining a 'closeted' attitude is certainly in keeping with Shakespeare's overall personality. The dearth of legal records regarding him attests to the fact that he was nothing if not a well-behaved man of his time. Especially when compared to most of his playwright contemporaries, who left copious trails of legal documentation behind them, it is odd that Shakespeare was not involved in a single court case throughout his entire dramatic career. If he managed to avoid the wrath of the official censor, the Master of Revels, it was simply because his writing never really challenged the powers that were.

As a law-abiding citizen, Shakespeare would certainly have believed in keeping one's homosexuality quiet. Despite the openness of such figures as Marlowe, Sir Francis Bacon, and the poets William Drummond and Richard Barnfield, the latter of whom rivalled Shakespeare for the patronage of Southampton, homosexuality had been illegal in England since the Act of 1533 made sodomy punishable by loss of property and death. However, as the sexual historian David F. Greenberg explains: 'This new legislation had less to do with a change in attitude toward homosexuality or bestiality than with Henry's break with Rome which had just taken place' (p. 303). The laws, repealed, re-enacted and rewritten a number of times, functioned largely as a weapon in Henry's arsenal in his war against the monasteries and other political undesirables. In any case, it was at best only unevenly enforced. In 1540, for example, these laws served Henry well as a means for hanging the politically incorrect Lord Hungerford, allowing the royal household to confiscate his lands. In contrast, in 1541, when Nicholas Udall, author of the Tudor drama *Ralph Roister Doister* and headmaster at Eton, was involved in a sex scandal, he was allowed to go free because of his favourable political position *vis-à-vis* the regime. The anti-sodomy laws stayed basically intact during the reign of Elizabeth I. Later, when James I came to the throne in 1603, his affair with the Duke of Buckingham only served to make him wary of any potential political damage the issue of homosexuality might cause him. As a result, these laws were again left on the books. In any case, English Renaissance attitudes towards homosexuality were conflicted at best.

Essentially, Shakespeare was a social and political conservative. Not only does he respect authority in his works, but he recognizes a 'right' authority whose rightness is essentially in keeping with the concepts of the Divine Right of Kings and the metaphorical universe which characterized the *Weltanschauung* of his time. In Shakespeare, whenever authority is usurped, the usurper – whether Brutus or Macbeth, Bolingbroke or Richard III – must eventually atone for his sins; and when the proper chain of authority is upset, there are repercussions throughout the universe, including the natural order – the mad scene from *King Lear* serves as the most classic example. It is this same essentially conservative stance which ties Shakespeare to Franco Zeffirelli, as Zeffirelli is also intent, in an almost medieval manner, on there being some sort of metaphoric connection between the specific incident and the universal order as a whole. Zeffirelli asserts that 'some sort of plan is being worked out into which we all fit' (p. 249). Similarly, upon surviving the Allied bombing of Naples, Zeffirelli superstitiously claimed that 'the Madonna dell'Arco had worked another miracle' (p. 27). In his film *Jesus of Nazareth* (1976), the character of Joseph reveals the simple-minded religious roots of Zeffirelli's all-pervasive conservatism. Joseph exhorts the young Jesus: 'God gives us rules to keep our lives *straight*' (emphasis added). Zeffirelli's conservative religious views also explain his attitudes towards his homosexuality. He notes: 'My private life is what it is, but my religious convictions are unwavering. I believe totally in the teachings of the Church and this means admitting my way of life is sinful' (p. 241). Throughout his autobiography Zeffirelli vociferously exploits every opportunity to assail the leftist politics of Luchino Visconti, yet he remains quite reticent about the specific nature of his relationship with the older director. At his most candid, he cryptically refers to himself as being 'something more than an employee' of Visconti. Instead, he relegates explicit references to their sexuality to second-hand off-colour comments by Coco Chanel and Anna Magnani (p. 113). Magnani warns Zeffirelli: 'Though I love Luchino, I know he's a snake. You may be able to get at the good inside him, but you need a very special corkscrew' (p. 80). He prudishly claims that he was shocked at her 'vulgarity' even as he quotes it. Zeffirelli, law-believing if not exactly law-abiding, exiles his homosexuality to the closet, and this is where it is usually found in his films.

The fact that Zeffirelli has never made homosexuality the conscious and overt subject matter of his filmography should also be viewed from within the perspective of the Italian cinema as a whole. When Italian Neorealism burst onto the world film scene in 1945 with Roberto Rossellini's *Rome: Open City*, it brought with it a revitalization of homophobia and gay-bashing which has characterized the Italian cinema in a more or less modified form right up until the present day. Peter Bondanella describes the Nazis in Rossellini's masterpiece: 'Bergman is a monster; he is also pictured as an effeminate homosexual. Ingrid is a viperlike lesbian who seduces Marina with expensive presents and drugs' (p. 38). Here homosexuality and fascism mutually reinforce one another in their parasitic antipathy. From an historical perspective, such mutual identification of homosexuals as fascists, and vice versa, is especially reprehensible when it is remembered that homosexuals interred in Nazi concentration camps were the worst treated of Hitler's undesirables and died at a higher rate than any other group, including the Jews. Nevertheless, despite the homosexuality of two of Italy's foremost film directors, namely Pasolini and Visconti, such antipathetic treatment of homosexuality has persisted in the Italian cinema as much as it has in its more box-office-orientated American counterpart. While Pier Paolo Pasolini's *Teorema* (1968) might seem to present homosexuality in something of a positive light, his *Salò* (1975) seems to attack it. Pasolini never championed homosexuality as a cause, having never fully integrated it into his own personality. He comments: 'My homosexuality was something additional, something outside, it had nothing to do with me. I always viewed it beside me as an enemy' (quoted in Carotenuto, p. 25). Homosexuality appears somewhat less marginalized in the filmography of Visconti, but Visconti arguably maintains the same mutual identification of homosexuality with fascism in his *The Damned* (1969) that Rossellini had perpetrated two decades earlier. *Death in Venice* (1971) and *Ludwig* (1973) do deal with the topic openly, if very discreetly, yet neither film presents it in a positive manner. In *Death in Venice*, von Aschenbach's obsession with the young Tadzio only leads to his eventual death by the plague. Regarding *Ludwig*, Zeffirelli has convincingly argued that it is Visconti's most personal film. If so, then – as Vito Russo has pointed out in his landmark study of homosexuality in film, *The Celluloid Closet* – Visconti's most personal insight into the homosexual condition seems to be the disappointing realization that 'sleeping with the stable boy rots your teeth' (p. 254). Franco Brusati's *To Forget Venice* (1978) focused unequivocally on a homosexual couple, but by the end of this film the characters renounce their homosexuality as an impediment to personal growth. Similarly, Salvatore Samperi's film version of Umberto Saba's *Ernesto* (1979) violates the original ending of the novel as Ernesto recants his homosexuality and marries his boyfriend's sister. Only Paul Ree from Liliana Cavani's *Beyond Good and Evil* (1977) seems to have adopted a healthy attitude towards his homosexuality, even urging Friedrich Nietzsche to accept his own repressed drives, but Ree does so only from beyond the grave and only after being gang-raped.

In her now classic article, 'Visual Pleasure and Narrative Cinema', Laura Mulvey presents her theory of the gaze. In accordance with her feminist ideology, she associates the controlling impulse psychology assigns to scopophilia with a male-dominated society's agenda to control women. She claims that in standard Hollywood cinema 'the spectator identifies with the main male protagonist' (in Mast, p. 810). In brief, Mulvey argues that the history of cinema is predominantly the history of the active male subject who functions as bearer of the gaze upon the passive female object of the gaze. In studies of scopophilia made in Denmark in the 1970s, twice as many men as women reported experiencing excitement from the visual pleasure of watching heterosexually pornographic materials – 22 per cent as opposed to 11 per cent (Kutchinsky, in Kimmel, p. 237). Such results might seem to confirm Mulvey's point. She herself presents examples from Alfred Hitchcock and Josef von Sternberg in an effort to support her thesis that 'the male figure cannot bear the burden of sexual objectification. Man is reluctant to gaze at his exhibitionist self' (p. 810). However, there is more in heaven and earth, as well as in cinema, than is dreamt of in her philosophy too. The history of the cinema has also included women looking at men, women looking at women, and, perhaps most notably, men looking at men. Had Mulvey chosen her examples from the filmography of Jean Cocteau, Derek Jarman or Pedro Almodóvar, the clitocentric aspects of her argument might have fallen apart. Certainly she is correct in assigning Kim Novak the 'burden' of Jimmy Stewart's 'sexual objectification' in her discussion of Hitchcock's *Vertigo*. The reverse, however, is true in the case of Visconti's *Senso* (1954), wherein the repeatedly recumbent presence of Farley Granger as object of the lustful gaze of Alida Valli. In addition to the gaze between characters, there is also the gaze of the director (and, by extension, his audience) upon his subject matter. On this level, Granger is also the object of the gaze of Visconti. It is also on this level that Zeffirelli's homosexuality most frequently and furtively manifests itself. To assert the existence of a homosexual gaze does not necessarily remove the agenda for control from scopophilia itself, however. The axis of control merely shifts from the male–female polarity to the more Oedipal older male–younger male polarization, the older male burdening the younger male with sexual objectification. Such an exercise of voyeuristic power especially distinguishes the work of an older, already established director with relatively young unknown actors who are powerless in the industry. Zeffirelli's homoerotic treatment of such attractive previous unknowns as Michael York, Leonard Whiting, Graham Faulkner, Martin Hewitt, Prince Urbano Barberini and Jonathan Schaech merely serves to confirm this thesis.

When Zeffirelli made his film version of *The Taming of the Shrew*

(1967), he had already mounted stage versions of *Romeo and Juliet*, *Othello* and *Much Ado about Nothing* in England, as well as an Italian production of *Hamlet*. Nevertheless, most of his directorial work before this time had been in opera, as is evident from his exuberant stage business and use of supernumeraries in his *The Taming of the Shrew*. The play exhibits Shakespeare's conservative social position primarily as it manifests itself in his attitudes towards women. Shakespeare's relationship with his own wife remains somewhat enigmatic, as he and Anne Hathaway evidently spent most of their married life away from one another. Although there are references to Shakespeare's daughters, brother and illegitimate nephew moving to London to live with him, no such references exist regarding Anne. Instead, she remained permanently in Stratford-upon-Avon, an Elizabethan woman who apparently 'knew her place' in the male supremacist society of her time. Shakespeare's problematic views regarding women have prompted numerous publications in recent decades, and *The Taming of the Shrew* has been a prime target. In his book *Shakespeare on Film*, Jack J. Jorgens has commented: 'To a feminist, *Shrew* is ... a piece of male chauvinist wishful thinking' (p. 67). More daringly, Wilfrid Sheed has argued that the comedy is so misogynist that 'there is no way of making this play funny in modern times' (in Schickel, p. 169).[3] With his oft-repeated stance against abortion rights, Zeffirelli is hardly a friend of the feminists, and his film, at least superficially, seems to remain true to the misogyny of Shakespeare's original. Katherina's closing speech, wherein she places her hand beneath Petruchio's foot in token of her submission, was one of the few speeches in the play kept almost in its entirety in the film. However, the decision to play the speech in earnest was not Zeffirelli's, but Elizabeth Taylor's (Zeffirelli, p. 216). None the less, such sincerity is undermined as the scene concludes with Katherina's defiantly absenting herself in a moment when Petruchio leaves her unattended. In terms of a phallocentric agenda, perhaps more telling was the emphasis the film placed on the scenes wherein Petruchio, channelling all meaning through himself like a latter-day Adam, renames the world around him. He capriciously confounds day for night and the sun for the moon. Katherina is forced to acquiesce to such inanity – the female rendered subordinate, as Lacan has argued, by the very system of language she uses.

As by-products of the same phallocratically repressive society, homophobia and misogyny derive from a similar source. The gay activist writer John Stoltenberg has argued:

> Homophobia is totally rooted in the woman-hating that male supremacy thrives on. The male supremacist social hierarchy necessarily derogates both those who are female and those who are queer – namely, those who

are male anatomically but not male enough sociosexually.... The faggot is stigmatized because he is perceived to participate in the degraded status of the female.

(in Kimmel, p. 250)

Consequently, although *The Taming of the Shrew* focuses on the misogynistic aspects of Shakespeare's socially repressive sensibility, the play also provided Zeffirelli with ample opportunities for exhibiting both his homosexual and homophobic vision. In his *Brother Sun, Sister Moon* (1973) and *Jesus of Nazareth*, Zeffirelli maintained empathy and admiration for the characters of St Francis and Jesus, respectively, while still presenting the two protagonists as men who embodied certain traditionally 'feminine' characteristics. Such is not the case in the more polemically sexist *The Taming of the Shrew*. Here, instead, Zeffirelli invites the derision of the feminine in the caustic effeminacy of a variety of male characters. Hortensio, Bianca's ineffectual younger suitor, is rendered repulsively sissified, continually playing with his hair and nervously faltering on his own words. To a similar end, Gremio, Bianca's older suitor, is ridiculously costumed in an obnoxiously foppish pair of pantaloons. Later, the Tailor and the Haberdasher are portrayed even more effeminately, the Haberdasher fainting when Petruchio begins brutally tearing his handiwork apart.

Nevertheless, the text does provide Zeffirelli with occasion for a more good-natured sort of homosexual tomfoolery. Consider the following interchange which occurs upon Petruchio's arrival in Padua. He commands his servant, played in the film by Cyril Cusack:

> *Petruchio*: Villain, I say, knock me here soundly.
> *Grumio*: Knock you here, sir? Why sir, what am I, sir, that I should knock you here, sir?
> *Petruchio*: Villain, I say, knock me at this gate,
> And rap me well, or I'll knock your knave's pate.
> *Grumio*: My master is grown quarrelsome. I should knock you first,
> And then I know after who comes by the worst.

(I.ii.8–14)

Although the term 'to knock' may originally have served as a pun for 'to strike a blow', in Zeffirelli's film version it functions equally as well as a pun for copulation – in this case, between two men. Still later, Shakespeare's text makes an off-colour reference to the predominantly homosexual practice of analingus. As Petruchio courts Katherina, they engage in the following verbal joust:

> *Petruchio*: Come, come you wasp; i' faith, you are too angry.
> *Katherina*: If I be waspish, best beware my sting.

> *Petruchio*: My remedy is then, to pluck it out.
> *Katherina*: Ay, if the fool could find where it lies.
> *Petruchio*: Who knows not where a wasp does wear his sting? In his tail.
> *Katherina*: In his tongue.
> *Petruchio*: Whose tongue?
> *Katherina*: Yours, if you talk of tales, and so farewell.
> *Petruchio*: What, with my tongue in your tail? Nay, come again. Good Kate, I am a gentleman.
>
> (II.i.205–13)

Homophobic scholars intent on 'cleansing' Shakespeare have deleted precisely this passage from various editions of the play.[4] Zeffirelli includes it with Katherina sitting on a trap door atop Petruchio. This physicalized inversion of their relative positions in a male supremacist world functions as a visual correlative for the inversion of the sexual practice to which the bawdy alludes.

Nevertheless, Zeffirelli's homosexual sensibility is even more evident in his camerawork than in his subject matter, as it is this which is all-pervasive, and this which is the vehicle of the gaze. Despite his desire to become a bankable Hollywood director, Zeffirelli was not a product of the Hollywood studio system, so it is not surprising that his camerawork deviates from standard Hollywood practices. His first experiences behind the camera were as Visconti's apprentice, specifically as an assistant director on *The Earth Trembles* (1948). Thus, Zeffirelli's use of the homosexual gaze has been a matter of unintentional training as well as natural sensibility. The homosexual Zeffirelli opens his film of *The Taming of the Shrew* by parodying the heterosexual idea of woman as 'sexual object'. Here the camera follows Tranio's lustful gaze to an obese, ludicrously endowed blond prostitute, pointedly framed in a window. Later, Petruchio and Katherina's encounter with the bearded Vicentio on the road to Padua provides Zeffirelli with a similar opportunity for satire on the traditional gaze. When Petruchio tests Katherina by arbitrarily asserting that Vicentio is a woman, Katherina responds by calling the old man a 'young, budding virgin' and scrutinizes him as the object of her penetrating, controlling stare. A similar inversion of standard Hollywood practices characterizes Zeffirelli's treatment of Elizabeth Taylor through-out the film. Even when Katherina is first seen, it is more as bearer than as object of the gaze. As Elizabeth Taylor had the most famous eyes in cinema at the time, Zeffirelli could tease his audience with a metonymic close-up of one of her eyes looking out from between the shutters of an upstairs window. This pattern repeats itself later, when both Katherina and Bianca survey their prospective suitors below – the gender roles of Mulvey's theory of the gaze inverted yet again. After their visual interchange at the window, the dark-haired Katherina aggresses the more passively blonde Bianca, grabbing a phallic switch and threatening to disfigure her as object of the male gaze. Katherina cries: 'I'll mar thee 'til no man dare look on thee.' When this behaviour merely confirms Baptista in his preferential treatment of Bianca, Katherina breaks her adopted phallus over her knee. Petruchio then enters with his sword prominently displayed, something which happens recurrently in the film. Perhaps the most blatant example of phallic showmanship occurs when Petruchio attempts to drag Katherina away from the wedding reception. At this moment, Zeffirelli cuts to a punctuated close-up of Grumio's valiantly raised sword as, in an overtly calculated manner, it is illuminated with a flash of light. As phallocentrism suffers such coy and self-parodying homages, Katherina is left to retain her status as preferred bearer of the gaze throughout much of the film. After Petruchio has wooed her, she is locked in a room from which she peers at the scheming men below. Here the close-up of Taylor's famous eyes is enhanced by the bright colours of the stained-glass window out of which she looks. At her wedding, the intense ferocity of her gaze, abruptly revealed from beneath her veil, causes the priest to jump back in terror. It is through Katherina's gaze that Zeffirelli's camera takes in both the opulently displayed wedding gifts at the reception and the luxurious clothing the Tailor and Haberdasher later submit for her and Petruchio's approval. Throughout the film the camera repeatedly watches Katherina watch others (Petruchio, Baptista, Hortensio, the wedding guests, her servants, and so on) as she attempts to assess their vulnerabilities and control her own destiny. As Katherina verges on becoming the governing sensibility of the film, Zeffirelli's version actually tends to subvert the misogynist agenda of Shakespeare's play.

When Lucentio and Bianca first meet on a Paduan street, Zeffirelli's homosexualized camera spends as much time in adoring close-ups of Lucentio's face as it does Bianca's. Moments later, when the two characters espy each other again in front of her father Baptista's house, Zeffirelli actually privileges Michael York as Lucentio. While the camera contents itself with a two-shot of Bianca speaking with her father, it repeatedly returns to close-ups of York. (In fact, close-ups of York's face will become a signature of Zeffirelli's filmography, recurring in both *Romeo and Juliet* [1968] and *Jesus of Nazareth*.) In a still later scene, when Lucentio and Bianca are shown making love in a garden, the blond adolescent Biondello functions as lookout from a tree above. Here Zeffirelli's camera is at eye level with Biondello's buttocks, the first manifestation of what may be called his sodomizing gaze. In Zeffirelli's film version of *Hamlet* such camerawork is evident in the 'play-within-a-play' scene, which begins with a gratuitous close-up of the gymnasts' buttocks as they flip over one another. Despite these two clothed examples,

Zeffirelli's sodomizing camera usually seeks out naked male adolescent buttocks as the preferred object of its gaze. In this context, Martin Hewitt as David in two love scenes from *Endless Love* (1981), Graham Faulkner as St Francis in the town square in *Brother Sun, Sister Moon*, and Leonard Whiting as Romeo in the love scene from *Romeo and Juliet* come to mind. All these scenes were memorable for being emotionally charged, but critics have canonized Whiting's buttocks in particular, visible 'for more than seventeen seconds in three shots' (Donaldson, p. 169). Pauline Kael claimed that scenes from the film 'look like ads for *The Boy*' (p. 157), while John Simon noted 'fondly lingering shots of Romeo's bare bottom', arguing that Zeffirelli's film was 'a *Romeo and Juliet* for ... pederasts' (in Alpert, p. 208).[5]

As the first love tragedy in the history of Western theatre, *Romeo and Juliet* is arguably one of Shakespeare's most innovative works. Although Prince Escalus's authority is never challenged, the play does call into question the moral rectitude of the patriarchal order of Lords Capulet and Montague. In fact, the play is uniquely revolutionary among Shakespeare's works in its overwhelming sympathy for those who rebel against patriarchy. Zeffirelli is careful to establish the misogynist phallocentricity of this patriarchal order in the opening shots of his film. When the Capulet ruffians enter the square threatening to 'thrust' the Montague 'maids to the wall', the homosexual gaze of Zeffirelli's camera focuses on crotch level (I.i.21). Throughout the film Danilo Donati, Zeffirelli's costumer, calls further attention to the mannerist phallocentrism of Verona society with his brightly coloured 'fashion show in codpieces – two-toned with fringe and bows and laces' (Kael, p. 153). The prominent codpieces are merely a visual correlative for Sampson's barrage of phallically charged taunts, such as 'Me they shall feel while I am able to stand; and 'tis known I am a pretty piece of flesh', 'My naked weapon is out', and 'I do not bite my thumb at you, sir; but I / bite my thumb' (I.i.34–5, 40, 57–8). When the belligerent Tybalt first struts into the scene, the camerawork is even more elaborately attentive, panning upward to survey Michael York's calves and thighs, pausing at his crotch, and then continuing past his torso before finally framing his face in close-up. By placing the feud in such consciously phallocentric terms, Zeffirelli presents it as little more than the result of having two cocks, Montague and Capulet, in the one henhouse of Verona. The families thus have more in common than they have differences, as Romeo astutely realizes with his 'Here's much to do with hate, but more with love' (I.i.182).

Unlike the strident and garishly clad Tybalt, the more androgynously soft-spoken Romeo first appears carrying a flower, dressed in muted colours, his codpiece modestly hidden by his doublet. No camera flourishes announce his arrival. Instead, his apotheosis occurs in a softly lit long shot as he joins his cousin Benvolio, whose point of view the camera shares. As he approaches, Romeo walks into a close-up, the camera then following him in profile until he sits. When he finally reclines beside his cousin, the camera again shoots his face in close-up from above, and he talks of love. All this between Romeo and Benvolio is underscored with some of the most gently romantic theme music in the movie. That Zeffirelli employs such sensitive camerawork to privilege Romeo throughout the film comes as no surprise. Justifiably aware of the importance of the close-up, Zeffirelli cast Whiting in part because 'his looks were perfect for the role'. In fact, Zeffirelli considered Whiting 'the most exquisitely beautiful adolescent male I've ever met' (Zeffirelli, p. 228). In comparison, Zeffirelli's treatment of Juliet's first appearance is not nearly so adoring. She is first spied through an upstairs window across a courtyard in long shot. No romantic theme music accompanies her, and she is given no close-up at this juncture, but is seen only in long shot, medium shot or two-shots with either the Nurse or Lady Capulet. In this early part of the film, even Tybalt functions more as object of the gaze than does Juliet.

When Romeo and Juliet meet at the Capulet ball, Zeffirelli's homosexual camera again prefers Romeo. After an initial zoom when Romeo first sees Juliet, she then appears only from his point of view, either in long shot or two-shot, but always surrounded by other people. Although Juliet is the object of Romeo's gaze, Romeo remains the object of Zeffirelli's. Instead of focusing on Juliet, the camera repeatedly returns to close-ups of the enthralled Romeo. Juliet's first consistent and recurrent close-ups occur only when she, like Romeo, becomes bearer of the gaze, seeking out his face among the guests who listen to the singing troubadour. Later, when Romeo removes his mask and kisses Juliet's hand, he regains his status as preferred object of the gaze. Zeffirelli emphasizes this by having Romeo step back in response to the intensity of Juliet's look. Throughout the next sequence Zeffirelli's camerawork corresponds to the mutuality of the love sonnet by allowing Romeo and Juliet to function reciprocally as both bearers and objects of the gaze. Such a bisexualized approach saves the scene from degenerating into the sort of one-sided objectification associated with more conventional, phallocratically slanted camerawork. This is essential inasmuch as the play is predicated upon a belief in true love, not mere object narcissism. Nevertheless, Juliet does function more fully as object of the gaze in the beginning of the balcony scene, when Romeo eavesdrops on her from the garden below. The situation itself is implicitly charged with a power dynamic, as according to Lacanian psychoanalysis the invocatory drive reverberates with the same alienated agenda for control that characterizes scopophilia. Even at this juncture, however, Zeffirelli's homosexual sensibility prevails, the camera as likely as not maintaining its distance from Juliet, and intercutting shots of her with close-ups of Romeo as he watches. Although Juliet receives her share of close-ups during the film (she has the most extreme close-up of all when Romeo kisses her hand), Shakespeare did not conceive of her as a mere object for Romeo's gaze. She is an active heroine, whose initiative and willpower virtually take over the action of the play once Romeo has been banished to Mantua.

Perhaps more than any other Shakespearean character, Mercutio embodies the quintessentially ambivalent Elizabethan attitudes towards homosexuality. As Joseph Porter has pointed out in his study *Shakespeare's Mercutio: His History and Drama*, Zeffirelli's film is of historical importance if only for its recuperation of the 'semiotic complexities' of Mercutio, such 'complexities' deriving from the homophobic homosexual identity of the character, an identity shared by Zeffirelli, and perhaps by Shakespeare. Predictably, John Simon assailed such an interpretation of Mercutio as being 'creepily played by John McEnery' (in Alpert, p. 208). Still, this approach not only explains Mercutio's tragic sense of self-alienation, but also – and perhaps most importantly – it adds a critical intensity to his relationship with Romeo, making more credible Romeo's reflex to kill or be killed for his friend. As Jorgens has commented: 'There is a deep friendship, even love, between Romeo and Mercutio' (p. 84); while Romeo and Mercutio share almost as many tight close-ups as Romeo and Juliet, indicating the strong intimacy in this same-sex relationship.[6] In contrast to centuries of performance tradition, the Queen Mab speech in Zeffirelli's version does not degenerate into a vacuous exercise in Elizabethan rhetoric. Instead, it functions as a means for externalizing Mercutio's own internal conflicts. When Mercutio berates women for their victimized status in a male supremacist world, he actually tacitly chastises himself for his own victimized status as a repressed homosexual. As the true cause of Mercutio's misogyny threatens to break the surface, the inner conflict inherent in the speech escalates to near-hysteria. Alone and separated from his peers, this 'freaked-out Mercutio' emotionally collapses (Kael, p. 153). At this point, Romeo runs to him, and as he takes his head consolingly in his hands, the two share their first tight close-up, forehead to forehead. Moments later, when Benvolio and the others pull Mercutio away to the Capulet ball, his gaze remains longingly fixed upon Romeo. After the ball Mercutio searches for Romeo, who has already made his way into the Capulet garden. The following morning Mercutio interrogates Benvolio, displaying an inordinate interest in Romeo's whereabouts the previous night. Nevertheless, despite the mutual affection of Mercutio and Romeo, Mercutio can speak of love only in disparaging terms as 'French slop' (II.iii.48). For him, a homophobically repressed homosexual, real love constitutes a potentially traumatic discourse. Consequently, Mercutio takes refuge in humour and can express affection only in an alienated, nullifying manner, as he does before the Capulet ball when he mockingly makes as if to kiss one of his cohorts. He caustically bemoans the love-stricken Romeo:

> Alas, poor Romeo, he is already dead – stabb'd with a white wench's black eye, run through the ear with a love song, the very pin of his heart cleft with the blind bow-boy's butt-shaft.

(II.iii.15–18)

Here Romeo has been 'stabb'd', 'run through', and 'cleft' with a 'butt-shaft'. From Mercutio's homophobic-phallocentric perspective, love is tantamount to sodomy, as both threaten emasculation by rendering the male submissive and feminine. Mercutio's obsessive phallic punning carries with it a correspondingly devaluation of women and all things feminine. In his encounter with the Nurse, he greets her with an obscene gesture to accompany his line 'the prick of noon' (II.iii.119). He then grabs her veil, using it to improvise a pair of false breasts with which he parades derisively about the square. This done, he proceeds to crawl beneath the Nurse's skirts, only to make a hasty retreat as he gynephobically feigns passing out from the supposed stench.

Zeffirelli's camera finds an opportunity to contemplate the servant Peter's crotch when, on the steps of the church, he kicks up his heels and laughs at the Nurse. In a later scene in Mantua, Zeffirelli's direction creates an intimate moment when Romeo takes Balthasar's head in his hands before kissing him goodbye. While Zeffirelli's homosexual gaze manifests itself in such sensitive attentiveness to these minor characters, his filmic handling of Mercutio remains relatively uncomplimentary. The least attractive young male in Zeffirelli's cast of otherwise pretty boys, with his spindly legs and his haggard face, McEnery never bears the burden of sexual objectification. His close-ups repeatedly detail either an unappealing grimace or a squint. His tightest, longest-held solo close-up occurs with his face completely masked by a white handkerchief as he talks gibberish to Benvolio. Such treatment keeps the audience at an ambivalent distance from Mercutio in accordance with the character's own sense of self-alienation. As empathy for Mercutio is largely contingent upon his relationship with Romeo, they share tight close-ups during the brawl scene in which Mercutio is killed. In fact, Zeffirelli presents the deaths of both Mercutio and Tybalt as the result of overly intense male bonding. Tybalt's inflammatory pun that Mercutio 'consorts' with Romeo helps to precipitate their duel. At one point during their fight, Mercutio salivates and sharpens two rapiers on one another like knives, as if he is about to carve Tybalt up and eat him. As they confusingly attempt to assess the earnestness of their own duel, Mercutio and Tybalt function reciprocally as both objects and bearers of the gaze, much as Romeo and Juliet did during the Capulet ball.

When Mercutio is killed, it is his intimate bond with Romeo that inadvertently causes the accident. With regard to Mercutio's death, Donaldson has noticed that 'he experiences Romeo's touch rather than Tybalt's as the fatal contact' (p. 173).[7] In fact, Zeffirelli virtually presents Mercutio's mortal wound as being one of the heart when it is finally exposed from beneath his handkerchief. In a similar manner, through his use of fight choreography and handheld camera, Zeffirelli attributes Tybalt's death to an excessiveness of male intimacy as well. When both Romeo and Tybalt lose their rapiers, they fall to the ground writhing in an impassioned wrestling match. Their shirts are torn and open, exposing their torsos to the gaze of Zeffirelli's homoerotic camera. They separate, and Tybalt rearms himself. As he charges Romeo, Romeo quickly raises his rapier from his crotch in phallic similitude, a reiteration of Mercutio's earlier 'Here's my fiddlestick' gesture (III.i.49). Accidentally impaling himself on Romeo's rapier, Tybalt falls on top of him into yet another intimate and fatal male embrace.

In comparison to *Romeo and Juliet*, *Hamlet* is a relatively conventional work, falling firmly within the then already-established tenets of the genre of revenge tragedy. Hamlet reifies the exact same patriarchal ethic that *Romeo and Juliet* renders dubious. By its very nature revenge tragedy is implicitly conservative, presupposing a perennial playing out of justice's tit for tat, a metaphoric correlation between the actions of man and the universal order as a whole. In fact, as Zeffirelli's film clearly shows, the entire action of *Hamlet* takes place in a Lacanian manner, 'in the Name of the Father'. Hamlet, driven by grief, attempts to re-establish this ostensibly 'right' authority of 'the Law of the Father' by avenging the murder of his own. A similar sense of nostalgia for the father characterizes the bulk of the Zeffirelli filmography. Both *Jesus of Nazareth* and *Brother Sun, Sister Moon* recount the quest for their respective protagonists, Jesus and St Francis, for their spiritual fathers. Jesus's crucifixion ultimately results in his reunification with God, the Father, while *Brother Sun, Sister Moon* concludes with St Francis's meeting with the Pope. In *Endless Love*, Jade's family disintegrates into disaster largely because her father resists the traditional patriarchal role, exercising too little authority too late. Finally, *The Champ* (1979) culminates in a poignantly sentimental scene wherein the child T.J., played by Ricky Schroeder, screams for his dead father to wake up. As a child, Zeffirelli had seen the original 1931 version of the film with Wallace Beery, which left him quite affected. Zeffirelli's very existence as the illegitimate son of Ottorino Corsi, was something of an embarrassment to his father, and they had at best a problematic relationship. Corsi essentially neglected his son, taking an active interest in him only when he became an adult. Zeffirelli rejected such belated affection: 'I felt the moment had passed for the kind of father–son relationship he now wanted' (Zeffirelli, p. 60). Not surprisingly, then, a preoccupation with an absent or near-absent father becomes a hallmark of Zeffirelli's films. In his life he turned to a number of surrogates – Visconti, the opera director Tullio Serafin and the writer Donald Downes – to each of whom he dedicates his *Autobiography*. In emulating these three mentors, Zeffirelli attempted to evolve into a father to himself. Similarly, in his role as a director he saw himself as 'father to the kids' – his actors, designers and crew (Zeffirelli, p. 227).

Like Zeffirelli, Hamlet responds to the absence of his father by attempting to become a father to himself. In his book *Identity in Shakespeare*, James P. Driscoll speaks of Hamlet's maturation process in precisely these terms.[8] Some of the most sensitive camerawork in Zeffirelli's film occurs during Hamlet's dimly lit first encounter with his father's ghost. Paul Scofield's deep voice creates a sense of intimacy to which Zeffirelli's camera responds by filming the two characters in a series of tight interchanging close-ups. At one point, in a variation of the classic Hollywood over-the-shoulder shot, Zeffirelli's camera shoots the elder Hamlet's ghost from beside Hamlet's thigh, from what could only be called his crotch's point of view. Such camerawork indicates the phallo-centric bias of the patriarchal order Hamlet intends to champion. Zeffir-elli's use of the gaze in *Hamlet* reverberates throughout with a traditional phallocratic-patriarchal agenda of control, as Polonius, Claudius, Gertrude, Hamlet, Rosencrantz and Guildenstern all repeatedly spy upon one another from between porticoes, within windows, around corners, behind columns, arrases and walls. Such situations provide Zeffirelli with a third-party perspective, allowing his camera to assume an almost omniscient point of view of the action being watched. In addition, Zeffirelli's distinct predilection in the film for shooting down upon his subject matter from above similarly contributes to its pervasively patriarchal, ostensibly omniscient, God-the-Father sensibility.

As standard-bearer of such patriarchal phallocentricity, Hamlet carries a sword with him throughout much of the film. Unlike the more elegant rapiers of *Romeo and Juliet*, Hamlet's weapon appears both formidable and heavy. This sword functions as much as a crucifix as it does a phallic symbol, which, given Hamlet's medieval view of a metaphorical universe, are ideologically the same thing. Accordingly, Hamlet repeatedly holds his sword upright with the blade pointed down, so that it appears as a cross. He holds the sword in precisely this manner both in the movie poster and when Horatio and the castle guards swear themselves to secrecy regarding the appearance of the elder Hamlet's ghost, whose voice-over prompts them. In this scene, the camera prefers a tight close-up of the sword to one of Hamlet's face, something which also occurs when he contemplates killing Claudius. Zeffirelli's camera continually prioritizes the sword as enforcer of 'the Law of the Father' throughout the film. As such, it points at the guilty Gertrude even as it rests on the elder Hamlet's corpse during the opening scene. Later, in the bedroom scene, Hamlet uses the sword to his mother, and Zeffirelli exploits it as linking object between shots. Even in a relatively lyrical scene, such as when Hamlet lies on the ground in a lush field, his sword must stand conspicuously erect from out of the grass.

Hamlet's obsessive attempt to take his father's place extends to his interaction with Gertrude, their relationship in the film bordering on the explicitly incestuous. In their first scene Gertrude sets the tone, whispering to him like a lover, fretting over him, gazing upon him, fondling, touching, kissing and caressing him, so that Claudius's line 'The Queen his mother / Lives almost by his looks' rings especially true (IV.vii.11–12). When Hamlet takes his leave for England, theirs is a farewell scene between lovers firmly within the Classical Hollywood tradition, complete with a teary-eyed Gertrude and a mouth-to-mouth kiss. Zeffirelli has defined Hamlet in terms of this potentially incestuous bond: 'He is a boy taken in just at the moment when his affections would move away from his mother, but he dies too soon' (quoted in Cole, p. 440). While Shakespeare's youthful Hamlet supposedly studies at Wittenberg University, Zeffirelli's casting of the bearded Mel Gibson as a practically middle-aged 'boy' attached to his mother is at best odd. The close proximity in the ages of Gibson and Glenn Close argues for their identity as a couple. Furthermore, Close received top billing for the film alongside Gibson, indicating that she, not Helena Bonham-Carter, is really Gibson's leading lady. In contrast to the more womanly Close, Bonham-Carter, with her chubby cheeks and pouty mouth, appears as a mere girl, and her scenes with Gibson generally lack what Hollywood critics call 'chemistry'. For instance, the most intimate use of the gaze between Hamlet and Ophelia occurs in a crowded public place, at the performance of the playlet. Hamlet places his head on her lap, sitting submissively or even boyishly at her feet. An abrupt interchange between the two follows, especially mocking on Hamlet's part. A corresponding sequence of shot–countershot alternates close-ups of Ophelia from his point of view with close-ups of Hamlet from hers. This sequence is disrupted, however, as both Hamlet's focus and the camera's return obsessively to Gertrude, to whom his comments regarding the brevity of woman's love are addressed. Ophelia serves Hamlet here merely as she served Claudius and Polonius before: as bait, her role in Hamlet's life subordinated to Gertrude's.

The faithlessness of Gertrude, like that of Ophelia, provides Shakespeare and Hamlet with a rationale for venting the misogynistic impulses epitomized in Hamlet's blanket characterization: 'Frailty, thy name is woman' (I.ii.146). For Zeffirelli, it allows his reactive focus a transfer from homophobia to its misogynist corollary, as in *The Taming of the Shrew*. To this end he privileges Gertrude, editing her role far less than he does that of either Claudius or Horatio. Zeffirelli's preferential handling of the Hamlet–Gertrude relationship, with its incestuous undercurrents, is particularly evident in the scene wherein Hamlet confronts Gertrude with her treachery. It is the most warmly lit scene in the film; Gertrude's bedchamber is an intimate space whose thick walls and heavy draperies create a sense of privacy. Hamlet enters, his sword again conspicuously at his side. When he accuses Gertrude of complicity in his father's death, he throws her on to the bed, mounts her and violently thrusts his hips into her groin. At this juncture, Close literally screams that his words are 'like daggers', further emphasizing the phallic displacement of the situation. The amulet with Claudius's portrait that she wears around her neck not only ties her metaphorically to her husband, but also chains her to Hamlet himself, as he uses it to strangle her into submission. (In contrast, Hamlet earlier threw away a necklace chain he had given to Ophelia.) Zeffirelli's camera further binds Hamlet and Gertrude together in one of the two longest-held shared close-ups in the film. Their impassioned confrontation culminates in an explicitly sexual mouth-to-mouth kiss. When they pull apart, Zeffirelli's homosexual gaze prefers a close-up of Hamlet's face to one of Gertrude's, an inversion of standard Hollywood practice. As Gertrude disrupted the shot–countershot sequence between Hamlet and Ophelia, so the Oedipal apparition of the elder Hamlet's ghost brings to an end Hamlet's literal attachment to his mother. This sense of rupture extends to cinematic continuity as well, as Zeffirelli alternates shots of the ghost in a cool blue light in the doorway with unmatching shots of the doorway in the warm gold light of the hearth associated with Gertrude. Such alternation corresponds to the younger Hamlet's vacillation between two worlds, between his sense of duty to his father and his sense of passion for his mother. The gold light now frames Gertrude from behind as a halo, alluding to the redemptive effect of this confrontation.

In Zeffirelli's film the patriarchal father–son bond fully displaces the homoerotic tensions and intimate male friendships of his *Romeo and Juliet*. For instance, whereas Shakespeare, in his text, fully develops the character of Horatio as Hamlet's one true friend and confidante, Zeffirelli's film renders him a shadow figure, practically neutralizing his relationship with the title character. While Shakespeare's original gives Horatio almost twice as many lines as either Ophelia or Gertrude, Zeffirelli severely edits and almost obliterates the role. Shakespeare's Horatio and Hamlet share at least a true Renaissance friendship, if not more – a relationship of such intimate intensity that by the end of the play Horatio wants to accompany Hamlet in death, threatening his own suicide. Traditionally, Hamlet dies in Horatio's arms, Horatio's famous 'Good night, sweet prince' functioning as the empathetic climax of the play. Instead, Zeffirelli represses any potentially homoerotic tensions in the relationship between Hamlet and

Horatio by undermining its intimacy. The two share none of the tight close-ups that characterized his treatment of Romeo's relationship with Mercutio. Zeffirelli's Hamlet and Horatio hardly ever touch, and often do not even look at one another while they converse. Gibson's relatively more advanced age also serves to distance him from the noticeably younger actor playing Horatio, who, in Shakespeare's text, is either Hamlet's peer or near-senior. For instance, when Hamlet wishes Horatio farewell after their first scene together in the play, his line 'Your love is as mine to you' rings noticeably formal, even hollow (I.iii.254). At this point, instead of embracing they shake hands in a similarly stilted manner. By contrast, Hamlet's sworn enemy Laertes embraces him in forgiveness before dying in his lap. However, the homophobically determined treatment of the relationship between Hamlet and Horatio refuses to risk an embrace between the two men even at Hamlet's death. Instead, Zeffirelli's closing shot shows Hamlet lying alone on the floor, Horatio seated far enough from him so as not to touch him. The camera further enhances this sense of Hamlet's ultimate alienation by shooting the scene from the patriarchal above, and slowly pulling away into a distant long shot.

When Hamlet encounters Polonius in the library, he sits atop a bookshelf, affording the camera a crotch shot ostensibly from Polonius's point of view. Later, as Rosencrantz and Guildenstern bow in greeting to Claudius, Zeffirelli's sodomizing camera presents them quite literally from behind. At this moment Zeffirelli goes on to create an instance of visual–verbal montage by editing Shakespeare's text in such a way as to give Hamlet the line 'What an ass am I'. Nevertheless, such examples of the homosexual gaze are relatively scarce and do not determine the overall visual tone of the film. Instead, Zeffirelli recants the homoeroticism so prevalent in his treatment of the Verona youth, and finds no occasion in *Hamlet* for the exhibitionistic display of shirtless torsos or nude buttocks. In contrast to the brightly coloured tights and prominent codpieces of *Romeo and Juliet*, the sombre-toned medieval tunics of *Hamlet* merely serve to desexualize the male anatomy and render it shapeless. In fact, throughout the film Zeffirelli reactively suppresses his homosexual sensibility by generally disparaging the eroticization of the male. The youth who portrays the role of the queen with the players, for example, appears particularly unattractive in a garish red wig and hideous make-up. In a critical reference to the inherent narcissism of homosexuality, Zeffirelli's camera presents this adolescent in a derisively tight close-up mirror shot as he applies his copious cosmetics in preparation for the play. Later, in Ophelia's mad scene, Zeffirelli makes an even more derogatory comment on the eroticization of the male as tantamount to insanity itself. Here Ophelia brazenly accosts a castle guard whose marked youth, attractiveness, and formidably dominant physique contribute to 'burden' him with her 'sexual objectification'. Zeffirelli's camera further identifies him as such in one of the few overt instances of the homosexual gaze in the film, by shooting him in a close-up from Ophelia's desire-laden point of view. As active bearer of the gaze, she glides her hand down his torso and grabs a cylindrical piece of leather which hangs from his belt towards his crotch. The most explicit phallic symbol in the film, it is fondled by her in a provocatively masturbatory manner. Curiously enough, Zeffirelli's reactionary stance in the film regarding the homosexual sensibility does not extend to Osric, a character whom Shakespeare provides in his play primarily as an object for homophobic derision. Theatrical productions frequently costume the effeminately Frenchified Osric in pastels, lace and ruffles, and the character is portrayed with effusively effete gestures and affected speech. Instead, Zeffirelli neutralizes him, dressing Osric in muted tones and eliciting a subdued interpretation of the role from John McEnery, an actor who otherwise could certainly have exploited the character's homosexual overtones.

Arguably, the good-looking face of Mel Gibson as Hamlet serves Zeffirelli as the preferred object of his homosexual gaze. Particularly when Gertrude stares longingly at her son, Zeffirelli's camera does not hesitate to respond accordingly. However, in frame after frame, in close-up after close-up, in soliloquy after soliloquy, Hamlet looks at everything and nothing. His own gaze is disengaged, and Gibson's comparatively disengaging performance in the soliloquies further detaches these scenes from the visual politics of desire. By their very nature, these soliloquies preclude the presence of other characters who might 'burden' Hamlet with sexual objectification. During such passages, Zeffirelli's camera has no character's gaze with which it can empathize, nor does it autonomously eroticize Gibson as it did Whiting and York. Unlike them, Gibson's Hamlet does not play the role of male exhibitionist – at least not in the sexual sense. Instead, what Hamlet exhibits in soliloquy after soliloquy, in the crypt and at the cemetery, is his preoccupation with death, his concern whether 'To be or not to be' (III. i. 56). In his *Hamlet*, Zeffirelli replaces the eros of his earlier Shakespearean films with thanatos. He subverts the entire Lacan–Metz–Mulvey tradition by associating scopophilia not with the sexual drive but with the other basic Freudian drive, the death instinct. He opens his film with an image of death, the corpse of the elder Hamlet, as primary object of the shared gaze of Gertrude, Claudius and Hamlet himself. The intimacy of the scene between Hamlet and his father's ghost, as has already been discussed, is also noteworthy within this context. Hamlet shares an intimate and extensively held close-up with the skull of Yorick in the cemetery scene comparable only to that of him and Gertrude in the bedroom scene. Lying upon the ground, Hamlet holds the skull close to his face, almost as if to kiss it, staring at it eye socket to eyeball. As eros gives way to thanatos, the climax of the play, Hamlet's duel with Laertes, distinguishes itself sharply from Zeffirelli's hot-blooded cockfight of a Verona brawl. In contrast, Laertes is notably cold-blooded, a willing but calculating pawn in Claudius's plot. He and Hamlet fight not out of excessive passion, nor as a display of virility, but from a sense of patriarch-inspired moral rectitude. Theirs is a rigidly formalized duel, and the two, costumed in hoods and chain mail, function mutually as their own executioners. As such, their weapons are heavy and held repeatedly as crucifixes. *Hamlet* thus reaffirms Freudian thought, as Zeffirelli's thana-tized vision supersedes and represses his homosexual gaze.

More than two decades intervened between Zeffirelli's earlier Shake-spearean films and his *Hamlet*. His more advanced age partially accounts for his obsessiveness with death in this more recent work, as does his survival of a life-threatening automobile accident in 1969. In fact, this incident proved something of a turning point in Zeffirelli's life, prompting a sort of reconversion to his Catholic faith. He even made 'a vow to dedicate my work to God whenever possible' (Zeffirelli, p. 238). Such recommitment to religious roots led to his production of both *Brother Sun, Sister Moon* and *Jesus of Nazareth*. This stance helps explain the privileging of the sword–crucifix in *Hamlet*, as well as his comparative abandonment in the film of his earlier homoerotic sensibility. In his film *La Traviata* (1983) Zeffirelli reflected his own transgressive sexuality in that of Violetta. He argued that 'it is her sacrifice and religious sense of self-denial for a higher and impossible love that must ultimately make us weep for her' (Zeffirelli, p. 323). Zeffirelli thus asserts an ideological renunciation of his own sexuality – a renunciation that is evident in his latest Shakespearean film, a renunciation which corresponds to Hamlet's own renunciation of sexuality as proffered by Ophelia. To this end, Zeffirelli gives them a mute scene wherein Hamlet interrupts her embroi-dery and starts to kiss her, but decides not to.

As thanatized homage to patriarchy, the ghost behind Zeffirelli's film is not Visconti or even his own estranged father, but rather the most centrist patriarch of twentieth-century Shakespearean production, the man whose film version of *Henry V* first inspired Zeffirelli with a love of Shakespeare, his late personal friend, Sir Laurence Olivier. From Alan Bates to Ian Holm to Paul Scofield, Zeffirelli's cast contains a path of ex-Hamlets from the English theatre leading back to Olivier, and much of his film is indebted to the 1947 version made by the English actor. Olivier began his film with a funerary procession, whereas Zeffirelli begins with a funeral. Olivier marginalized the roles of Hamlet's peers while prioritizing that of Gertrude, and Zeffirelli follows suit. Olivier even cast a woman fourteen years his junior, Eileen Herlie, as his mother Gertrude. Both film versions forgo the sandy Danish coast of Elsinore for a craggy, rocky backdrop –

in Zeffirelli's case, location shooting in Stonehaven, Scotland. Both Gibson's and Olivier's Hamlets have dyed hair, conspicuously so in Olivier's black-and-white version.

Such comparisons are, of course, to a large degree superficial, as the two films are as essentially different as the two personalities who made them. They reveal, in addition to Zeffirelli's search for tradition, an obsessive nostalgia for patriarchy which has led him into an increasingly reactionary position, so much so that he has become an official in one of the neofascist parties, *Forza Italia*, currently in power in Italy's latest right-wing coalition government. Zeffirelli's self-proclaimed reactionary stance extends from feminist issues to leftist politics to his most virulent attacks on homosexuality – one gay-orientated publication dubbed him a 'monster who devours those like himself' (Della Valle, p. 73). The ideological, if not the personal, source of such homophobia stems from Zeffirelli's championing of the most conservative dictates of the Catholic Church. In contrast to Pasolini's intimate *The Gospel According to Matthew* (1964), Zeffirelli's version of the life of Christ returned to Hollywood conventions dating back to Cecil B. DeMille. His *Jesus of Nazareth* is on a classically epic scale, full of long shots and pans, replete with a blue-eyed Aryan Jesus and a cast of thousands, and populated with a long list of big-name stars from Anthony Quinn to Rod Steiger to Anne Bancroft to – yes – Sir Laurence Olivier.

This essay has attempted to suggest a transhistorical ambivalence regarding homosexuality extending from Shakespeare to Zeffirelli, and to examine the dynamic of Zeffirelli's peculiar homophobic homosexual sensibility as it has informed his Shakespearean filmography. Like homosexuality, the forbidden love of Romeo and Juliet must remain closeted, taking root beyond the realm of social sanction. Similarly, the survival of the marriage of Petruchio and Katherina seems contingent upon their spurning the equally repressive small-mindedness of Paduan society. As Petruchio sarcastically remarks, 'Padua offers nothing but what is kind' (V.ii.14). In its transgression of social mores, the interracial marriage of Otello and Desdemona in *Otello* also echoes the homosexuality of the film's director. Finally, the sexually charged interaction between Hamlet and Gertrude also lies uncomfortably outside the bounds of social acceptance. The incestuous undercurrents of their relationship verge on transgressing an even greater taboo than that of homosexuality.[9]

Zeffirelli's general preference for close-ups of the bearer, rather than the object of the gaze mostly allows his homosexual sensibility to privilege the youthful faces of such actors as Leonard Whiting and Michael York. In referring to Zeffirelli's homosexual gaze, it should be kept in mind that no worthwhile camerawork is ever too heavy-handedly one-sided. For instance, throughout *The Taming of the Shrew* the emphatic presence of

Elizabeth Taylor's cleavage, as costumed by Irene Sharaff, advertises her 'burden' of sexual objectification. Virtually the sole function of Natasha Pyne's Bianca, with her array of suitors, is as object of the male gaze. Consequently, Zeffirelli's primary concern was with the actresses' physical appearance. Similarly, he had originally rejected a chubby Olivia Hussey as Juliet, casting her only later because 'she had lost weight dramatically. Her magnificent bone structure was becoming apparent, with those wide expressive eyes and her whole angular self' (Zeffirelli, p. 226). Zeffirelli tellingly mentions neither talent nor training in this passage. Shakespearean film is still film, and therefore first and foremost a visual medium, so his preoccupation with the appearance of his actresses is not misplaced. The film critic Kenneth Tynan has remarked that 'too much has been written about how actors feel, too little about how they look' (in Mast, p. 657). Where Zeffirelli diverges from standard heterocentrist cinematic practice is not in his attentiveness with his actresses' appearance but with that of his actors.[10]

Notes

1. See also Greenberg, *The Construction of Homosexuality*, pp. 301–46.

2. See Riggs, *Ben Jonson: A Life*.

3. Nevertheless, the film did receive its share of critical praise. Roger Manvell writes: 'In the same tradition, but far more effective, is the film version of the sexist knockabout farce *The Taming of the Shrew* (189–90). Hollis Alpert was even more unbridled in his acclaim, calling the film at once both 'a quintessential rendering of the play' and 'an inspired improvement on the original' (quoted in Schickel, pp. 166–7).

4. The William J. Rolfe editions of the play from 1881 to 1909 are a prime, if somewhat Victorian, example.

5. In a classically homophobic manner, Simon offensively insists on the conflation of homosexuality and pederasty. Zeffirelli's decision to cast adolescents, as opposed to the long tradition of geriatric Romeos and Juliets, deserves praise, but is not as original as many scholars and film critics have believed. In the mid 1950s Dario Niccodemi had already mounted an Italian production of *Romeo and Juliet* with adolescents in the leading roles.

6. Unfortunately, for the purposes of this essay, the most blatant example of a shared homosexual gaze in the Zeffirelli filmography occurs not in one of his Shakespearean adaptations but in *Brother Sun, Sister Moon*. When Francis enters a room full of working peasants, he encounters a young, muscular man whose chest emerges from his open shirt. For a moment, they share an unmistakably homoerotic look which is then broken off. Francis then looks for him again among the wool dyers, but instead finds only an old man whose hands he takes into his own.

7. For a more extensive discussion of both Mercutio and the homosexual–phallic gaze as applied to the Verona youth, see Donaldson, *Shakespearean Films/Shakespearean Directors*. It was not my intention merely to repeat the arguments of his excellent chapter 'Let Lips Do What Hands Do', but some overlap has been unavoidable.

8. See Driscoll, *Identity in Shakespeare*, pp. 50–67. Driscoll speaks of Hamlet's *rite de passage* as essentially an attempt to integrate the various father figures in his life, specifically the elder Hamlet, Fortinbras and Horatio.

9. The relationships between Jade and David in *Endless Love* and Alfredo and Violetta in *La Traviata* also fall neatly within this context.

10. This homoerotic vision has persisted up to his latest film, *Sparrow* (1993), whose Jonathan Schaech Zeffirelli describes as 'beautiful, dark and ardent, timid in speech and arrogant in movement' (quoted in Mori).

References

Alpert, Hollis and Andrew Sarris, eds, *Film 68/69*, New York: Simon & Schuster, 1969.
Ariès, Philippe and Andre Bejin, *Western Sexuality: Practice and Precept in Past and Present Times*, New York: Basil Blackwell, 1987.
Bethell, S.L., 'Shakespeare's Actors', *The Review of English Studies* 1, 3 (July 1950).
Bondanella, Peter, *Italian Cinema: From Neorealism to the Present*, New York: Frederick Ungar, 1983.
Carotenuto, Aldo, *L'autunno della coscienza*, Turin: Boringhieri, 1985.
Cole, Toby and Helen Krich Chinoy, eds, *Directors on Directing*, Indianapolis, IN: Bobbs-Merrill, 1963.
Della Valle, Andrea, 'Gay che non amano i gay: Franco Zeffirelli', *Adam* 1, 1 (May 1994).
Donaldson, Peter S., *Shakespearean Films/Shakespearean Directors*, Boston, MA: Unwin Hyman, 1990.
Driscoll, James P., *Identity in Shakespeare*, Lewisburg, PA: Bucknell University Press, 1983.
Duberman, Martin Bauml, *et al.*, eds, *Hidden from History: Reclaiming the Gay and Lesbian Past*, New York: New American Library, 1989.
Eckert, Charles W., ed., *Focus on Shakespearean Films*, Englewood Cliffs, NJ: Prentice Hall, 1972.
Greenberg, David F., *The Construction of Homosexuality*, Chicago: University of Chicago Press, 1988.
Jorgens, Jack J., *Shakespeare on Film*, Bloomington: Indiana University Press, 1977.
Kael, Pauline, *Going Steady*, Boston, MA: Little, Brown, 1970.
Kelly, Katherine E. 'Shakespeare's Boy Actress', *Theatre Journal* 42, 1 (March 1990).
Kimmel, Michael S., ed., *Men Confront Pornography*, New York: Crown Publishers, 1989.
Lacan, Jacques, *Écrits: A Selection*, trans. Alan Sheridan, New York: Norton, 1977.
Levi, Peter, *The Life and Times of William Shakespeare*, New York: Holt & Company, 1989.
Manvell, Roger, *Theatre and Film*, Teaneck, NJ: Associated University Press, 1979.
Mast, Gerald and Marshall Cohen, eds, *Film Theory and Criticism*, New York: Oxford University Press, 1985.
Mori, Anna Maria, 'Sicilia vergine e martire: La capinera di Verga secondo Zeffirelli', *La Repubblica*, 10 June 1993.
Pequigney, Joseph, *Such is My Love: A Study of Shakespeare's Sonnets*, Chicago: University of Chicago Press, 1985.
Porter, Joseph A., *Shakespeare's Mercutio: His History and Drama*, Chapel Hill: University of North Carolina Press, 1988.
Riggs, David, *Ben Jonson: A Life*, Cambridge, MA: Harvard University Press, 1988.
Russo, Vito, *The Celluloid Closet*, New York: Harper & Row, 1981.
Schatz, Thomas, *Genius of the System*, New York: Pantheon, 1988.
Schickel, Richard and John Simon, eds, *Film 67/68*, New York: Simon & Schuster, 1968.
Shakespeare, William, *Hamlet*, ed. Harold Jenkins, New York: Methuen, 1982.
    Othello, ed. Julie Hankey, Bristol: Bristol Classical Press, 1987.
    Romeo and Juliet, ed. Richard Hosley, New Haven, CT: Yale University Press, 1965.
    The Taming of the Shrew, ed. Ann Thompson, New York: Cambridge University Press, 1984.
    The Taming of the Shrew, ed. William J. Rolfe, New York: American Book Company, 1909.
    Twelfth Night, ed. J.M. Lothian and T.W. Craik, London: Methuen, 1978.
Zeffirelli, Franco, *Zeffirelli: The Autobiography of Franco Zeffirelli*, New York: Weidenfeld & Nicholson, 1986.

Zeffirelli Filmography

Camping (1957); *The Taming of the Shrew* (1967); *Romeo and Juliet* (1968); *Brother Sun, Sister Moon* (1972); *Jesus of Nazareth* (1976); *The Champ* (1979); *Endless Love* (1981); *La Traviata* (1983); *Otello* (1986); *The Young Toscanini* (1988); *Hamlet* (1990); *Sparrow* (1993).

14

Engendering the Tragic Audience:
The Case of *Richard III*[1]

Phyllis Rackin

I

Although the First Folio classifies *Richard III* with Shakespeare's other English histories, the title pages of the Quartos suggest generic difference. In the case of *2 Henry VI*, the title page indicates both the episodic chronicle structure of the play and its historical subject: 'The First part of the Contention betwixt the two famous Houses of Yorke and Lancaster, with the death of the good Duke Humphrey: And the banishment and death of the Duke of *Suffolke*, and the Tragicall end of the proud Cardinall of *Winchester*, with the notable Rebellion of *Iacke Cade: And the Duke of Yorkes first claime unto the Crowne*'. The Quarto of *Richard III*, by contrast, designates at once its self-consciously dramatic form as tragedy, its origins as a script for theatrical performance, and its strongly centred focus on the male protagonist: 'The Tragedy of Richard the third, Containing, His treacherous Plots against his brother Clarence: the pittiefull murther of his iunocent nephewes: his tyrannicall usurpation: with the whole course of his detested life, and most deserved death. As it hath beene lately Acted by the Right honourable the Lord Chamberlaine his servants'.

In Shakespeare's time, the story of Richard III was repeatedly identified as tragic. Edward Hall had entitled his account of Richard's reign 'The Tragical Doynges of Kynge Richard The Thirde', Richard's story (along with those of Clarence, Hastings, Buckingham, and Jane Shore) was identified as a tragedy in *A Mirror for Magistrates*. Thomas Legge's Latin play *Richardus Tertius*, performed at Cambridge in 1579, is identified in contemporary texts as an exemplary tragedy, singled out by Sir John Harington and Thomas Heywood to illustrate the beneficial effects of tragic drama, and by Francis Meres in his list of 'famous tragedies'.[2] Yet another play about Richard, anonymously published in 1594 and entitled 'The True Tragedy of Richard III', begins with a dialogue between Truth and Poetrie that identifies 'Tragedia' as a player in the coming action and the subject of the play as a 'Tragedie' (Sig A3ʳ).

This essay is an attempt to delineate the ways the reconstruction of history as tragedy in *Richard III* transvalued the representations of women on Shakespeare's stage, and transformed the gendered relationship between actors and audience in the playhouse. I should begin, however, by acknowledging that the distinction between history and tragedy was by no means clear. The protagonists of tragedy, like those of history, were understood to be characters of high rank. Moreover, in the Renaissance as in antiquity, plays identified as tragedies frequently took their subjects from history. (Shakespeare himself is a good case in point: of the eleven plays designated as tragedies in the First Folio, all but *Romeo and Juliet* and *Othello* have historical subjects.)[3]

Despite the many similarities between the subjects of the two genres, contemporary descriptions of the ways they affected their audiences are strikingly different in regard to issues of gender. Anti-theatrical invective typically attacked all theatrical performance as effeminating, but the English history play offered a significant exception.[4] Thomas Nashe, in fact, used the example of the English history play to defend theatrical performance against its detractors: 'our forefathers valiant acts ... are revived', he declared, 'than which, what can be a sharper reproofe to these degenerate effeminate dayes of ours?' Commemorating the valiant deeds of heroic forefathers and celebrating the masculine virtues of courage, honour, and patriotism, the theatrical representation of English historical subjects could redeem theatrical performance as a means of reclaiming the endangered masculinity of the men in the theatre audience.

Tragedy, on the other hand, was likely to inspire womanly emotions in its spectators. According to Stephen Gosson, 'The beholding of troubles and miserable slaughters that are in Tragedies, drive us to immoderate sorrow, heaviness, womanish weeping and mourning, whereby we become lovers of dumpes, and lamentation, both enemies to fortitude.'[5] The claim that tragedy produced womanly softness in its spectators was not confined to anti-theatrical discourse. Sir Philip Sidney recounts a story from Plutarch in which the performance of a tragedy 'drewe aboundance of teares' from the eyes of a tyrant 'who, without all pitty, had murthered infinite nombers, and some of his owne blood' (pp. 177–8). Arguing for the salutary effects of tragedy, Sidney does not identify them as effeminating. The terms of his argument, however, suggest just that. He claims, for instance, that tragedy 'openeth the greatest wounds, and sheweth forth the Ulcers that are covered with Tissue'. As Gail Paster has demonstrated, men's bodies opened and wounded were gendered feminine; and the ulcer image directly parallels the terms in which Hamlet will address his guilty mother: 'Lay not that flattering unction to your soul, / That not your trespass but my madness speaks; / It will but skin and film the ulcerous place, / Whiles rank corruption, mining all within, / Infects unseen' (III.iv.145–9).

Women, in fact, were especially prominent in descriptions of the effects of tragedies on early modern audiences. In a 1620 recollection of a performance of *The Spanish Tragedy*, for instance, 'Ladyes in the boxes' are said to have 'Kept time with sighes and teares to [the player's] sad accents'. As Richard Levin points out, the numerous contemporary accounts that describe 'women weeping in the theatre' suggest a perception 'that women had a special sensitivity to, and perhaps a special preference for, pathetic plots and situations' (pp. 170–71).[6]

In *An Apology for Actors*, Thomas Heywood recounts three anecdotes to illustrate the beneficial effects of tragedies on their auditors. Two of them centre on women who had murdered their husbands. In the first, 'a towneswoman (till then of good estimation and report)' watching a play about a woman who had committed a similar crime 'suddenly skritched and cryd out Oh my husband, my husband! I see the ghost of my husband fiercely threatning and menacing me', and subsequently confessed her crime to the people about her in the audience. In the second, the particulars of the tragic plot are somewhat different, but they have exactly the same effect on the wicked woman: during the performance of a play in which a labourer, envied by his fellow-workers for his diligence, is murdered by having a nail driven into his temples, 'a woman of great gravity' becomes 'strangely amazed' and 'with a distracted & troubled braine oft sighed out these words: Oh my husband, my husband!':

> The play, without further interruption, proceeded, the woman was to her owne house conducted, without any apparant suspition, every one coniecturing as their fancies led them. In this agony she some few dayes languished, and on a time, as certaine of her well disposed neighbours came to comfort her, one amongst the rest being Church-warden, to him the Sexton posts, to tell him of a strange thing happening him in the ripping up of a grave: see here (quoth he) what I have found, and shewes them a faire skull, with a great nayle pierst quite through the braine-pan, but we cannot conjecture to whom it should belong, nor how long it hath laine in the earth, the grave being confused, and the flesh consumed. At the report of this accident, the woman, out of the trouble of her afflicted conscience, discovered a former murder. For 12 years ago, by driving that nayle into that skull, being the head of her husband, she had trecherously slaine him. This being publickly confest, she was arraigned, condemned, adiudged, and burned. (sig GI ᵛ, G2 ᵛ)

Heywood's lurid examples represent an extreme case. The plays he describes belong to the subgenre of domestic tragedy, an innovative dramatic form that moved down the social scale and into the home to find its subjects in a domestic space where female characters could and did play central roles (Dolan). Not all of the female spectators of tragedy were imagined as 'guilty creatures sitting at a play', and not all of the spectators of tragedy were imagined as women. None the less, the spectators were repeatedly and consistently described in contemporary accounts as moved to emotions and responses (compassion, remorse, pity, tears) that were understood as feminine. This conception of the effects of tragedy as feminizing, although not always explicitly stated, is remarkably consistent: it appears in arguments for and against the theatre, in the prologues and epilogues to plays, in accounts of actual experience as well as in prescriptive directions.

The Induction to *A Warning for Fair Women* (1599) begins with the stage direction: '*Enter at one doore, Hystorie with Drum and Ensigne: Tragedie at another, in her one hand a whip, in the other a knife*'. During the ensuing dispute with Comedie and Hystorie, Tragedie's feminine gender receives repeated emphasis. She is addressed by the others as 'mistris buskins' and 'my Ladie *Tragedie*', and she describes the kind of performance she requires as one that will produce feminine emotions in the audience:

> I must have passions that must move the soule,
> Make the heart heave, and throb within the bosome,
> Extorting teares out of the strictest eyes,
> ... Untill I rap the sences from their course ... (sig. A2^v, A3^r)

Over half a century later, Margaret Cavendish, the Duchess of Newcastle, described the effects of Shakespeare's tragedies in similar terms:

> in his Tragick Vein, he Presents Passions so Naturally, and Misfortunes
> so Probably, as he Peirces the Souls of his Readers with such a True Sense
> and Feeling thereof, that it Forces Tears through their Eyes. ...[7]

In direct contrast to Nashe's celebration of the history play, which imagines an audience of men inspired by the representation of a heroic masculine world to emulate the manly virtues of the forefathers, tragedy is repeatedly described as appealing to women as well as men; and its appeal to men is repeatedly described as directed towards their feminine sympathies, softening hard hearts, piercing guilty souls with remorse, ravishing the entire audience with the feminine passions of pity and fear, and forcing them to weep.

A similarly gendered difference characterized the subjects of the two genres. On the stage as in the audience, the exemplary subjects of tragedy – 'Gods and Goddesses, Kynges and Queenes' (Webbe, p. 249) – were understood to include women as well as men.[8] Because history sought to commemorate the past, reconstituted as a nostalgically idealized world of the fathers, women and sexuality occupied only marginal roles. Both tragedy and comedy, however, assigned important roles to women and marriage. In comedy, conflicts between older and newer social dispensations are characteristically resolved in marriage; in tragedy they often constitute the hero's predicament, which is typically defined at least partly in terms of his relationship to women. This is true not only in plays like *Romeo and Juliet*, *Othello* and *Antony and Cleopatra*, which centre on romantic relationships, but also in virtually every tragedy in the Shakespearean canon, with the possible exceptions of *Julius Caesar* and *Timon of Athens*.

Shakespeare's history plays opposed the troubling realities of cultural change by projecting a better world in the past; his tragedies played out those cultural contradictions in the struggles of an individual heroic figure destroyed by the irreconcilable conflicts they produced.[9] Deeply implicated in those contradictions, the ambivalent place of women in Shakespeare's world and the instability of the gender ideology that attempted to contain them were central issues in tragic drama (Rose; Callaghan).

II

The reconstruction of history as tragedy in *Richard III* is accompanied by a remarkable transformation in the representation and placement of female characters. Paradoxically, even as the female characters are ennobled, they are also disempowered. On the one hand, women are much more sympathetically portrayed. On the other, they lose the vividly individualized voices and the dangerous theatrical power that made characters like Joan and Margaret in the Henry VI plays potent threats to the masculine project of English history-making. Robert Weimann's distinction between *locus* and *platea* can be used to chart both the elevation of the female characters and their containment. Weimann associates the *locus* with the upstage site of mimetic illusion, 'aloofness from the audience and representational closure' which privileges the authority of the objects represented, the *platea* with the forestage where actors addressed their audiences, a liminal space where the authority of the represented narrative could be challenged by calling attention to the immediate theatrical occasion with all its subversive potential.[10] Although not always or necessarily literalized in specific locations on the physical stage, the different acting styles and different relationships between actor and audience that Weimann associates with *locus* and *platea* provide a useful basis for understanding the transformation of women's roles in *Richard III*.

Ennobled, the female characters move into the privileged *locus* of hegemonic representation, but this move also subsumes them into the patriarchal project of that representation, and distances them from the present theatre audience.

Because the traditional subjects of English history were the heroic deeds and dynastic struggles of kings and noblemen, the female characters in Shakespeare's other English history plays are typically defined in gendered antithesis by low social status and foreign nationality. The foreign tongues spoken by the Welsh woman in *1 Henry IV* and the French woman in *Henry V*, and the malapropisms that disfigure the speech of Mistress Quickly signal their inability to enter the official discourse of English history. In direct antithesis, all of the female characters in *Richard III* are highborn English women who speak in the undifferentiated, formal blank verse that constitutes the standard language of the playscript. Recruited in the service of the hegemonic project of the plot, the accession of Henry VII to the English throne, the women are also subsumed in its hegemonic discourse.[11] Even Margaret, the most powerful of Richard's female antagonists, speaks in the generalized rhetorical terms that constitute the normative language of the play.

Assuming their tragic roles as pitiable victims, female characters are no longer represented as dangerous, demonic Others. The subversive theatrical energy of the peasant Joan is replaced by the pathos of suffering English queens.[12] Margaret, the adulterous wife and bloodthirsty warrior of the Henry VI plays, is transformed into a bereaved and suffering prophet of divine vengeance for the crimes of the past. In the Henry VI plays, the female characters are defined as opponents to the masculine project of English history-making. In *Richard III*, all of the women support the desired conclusion of the historical plot, the foundation of the Tudor dynasty.

Although the overarching goal of the dramatic action in *Richard III* (as in all of Shakespeare's English histories and a number of his tragedies as well) is the maintenance of a legitimate royal succession, in this play, unlike the earlier histories, it is the male protagonist who opposes the patriarchal project. The threats to patrilineal succession represented in the *Henry VI* plays by Joan's sexual promiscuity and Margaret's adultery are replaced by Richard's murders and his deceitful effort to deny the legitimacy of his brother's innocent children, the rightful heirs to the throne he usurps, and even of Edward himself. In *Richard III*, the subversive power associated with female characters in the earlier plays is demystified, and all the power of agency and transgression is appropriated by the male protagonist. The threat of adultery is no longer real, and the character who threatens to displace legitimate heirs is not any adulterous woman but the slanderous man who brings the charge. Witchcraft, the quintessential representation of the dangerous power of women, is similarly reduced from a genuine threat to a transparent slander. Both Joan in *1 Henry VI* and Eleanor Cobham in *2 Henry VI* summon demons to the stage. In *Richard III*, however, there are only Richard's unsupported and obviously false charges against Queen Elizabeth and Jane Shore.

Joan in *1 Henry VI* is the prototype for the marginal and criminal status of the women in the *Henry VI* plays and also for their subversive, theatrical energy. Her very subversiveness, however, authorizes her dramatic power. As both Catherine Belsey and Karen Newman have observed, the custom of requiring witches to confess from the scaffold 'paradoxically also offered women a place from which to speak in public with a hitherto unimagined authority which was not diminished by the fact that it was demonic'. These public occasions were also theatrical. As both critics note, 'the crowds at trials and executions' were frequently described as 'beholders' or 'the audience', and 'Pamphleteers often describe[d] the scene of execution explicitly as a play.'[13]

Two episodes, one near the beginning of the play and one near its end, illustrate the way the powerful role of demonic other, occupied by women in the *Henry VI* plays, is now transferred to Richard. The longer of these is the second, the encounter near the end of Act IV between Richard and Queen Elizabeth, where Shakespeare altered his historical source in order to ennoble the character of the widowed queen. As Barbara Hodgdon observes, Shakespeare 'displaces those attributes the chronicler ascribes to the Queen onto Richard' (pp. 109–10). In Hall's version, Queen Elizabeth exemplifies female 'inconstancie', first promising her daughter Elizabeth (or, in the event of Elizabeth's death, her next daughter, the Lady Cecile) to Richmond, then, persuaded by promise of 'promocions innumerable and benefites', agreeing to Richard's demands:

> ... putting in oblivion the murther of her innocente children, the infamy and dishonoure spoken by the kynge her husbande, the lyvynge in avoutrie leyed to her charge, the bastardyng of her daughters, forgettyng also ye feithfull promes and open othe made to the countesse of Richmond mother to ye erle Henry, blynded by avaricious affeccion and seduced by flatterynge wordes, first delivered into kyng Richards handes her. v. daughters as Lambes once agayne committed to the custody of the ravenous wolfe. (pp. 391, 406)

Shakespeare's widowed queen, unlike Hall's, keeps faith with Richmond and adamantly refuses Richard's urgings to forget past wrongs. Insistently recalling the fate of her murdered children, she charges: 'No doubt the murd'rous knife was dull and blunt / Till it was whetted on thy stone-hard heart / To revel in the entrails of my lambs' (IV.iv.227–9). Shakespeare thus appropriates for Elizabeth's use against Richard the very arguments, and even the terms, by which the authoritative narrative voice in Hall's chronicle condemns her action.

In Shakespeare's representation, it is Richard and not Elizabeth – or any of the women – who becomes the sole object of condemnation. The women are deprived of theatrical power and agency, both of which are appropriated by Richard, along with their demonic roles. The audience is never allowed to see Elizabeth deciding to bestow her daughter on Richmond. All we get is Stanley's laconic report that 'the Queen hath heartily consented / He [Richmond] should espouse Elizabeth her daughter' (IV.v.7–8); and a number of critics have accepted Richard's judgement at the end of their encounter that the queen is a 'relenting fool, and shallow, changing woman'.[14] Like the other women in *Richard III*, Elizabeth serves as a kind of ventriloquist's dummy. She gives forceful and eloquent voice to Richard's crimes, but her own motives can remain ambiguous because they are finally irrelevant to the outcome of the plot. What is important is that Richmond marries her daughter; whether or when the queen gives her consent is of so little consequence that it is never clearly specified in Shakespeare's script.

The earlier incident is much more brief, a telling moment in Act I when Richard literally appropriates the demonic power of a woman's voice. Margaret of Anjou, sent at the end of *3 Henry VI* back to France (where her historical prototype died in 1482), returns unhistorically in *Richard III* like a voice from the dead to recall the crimes of the past and pour out curses on her old enemies. In Act I, Scene iii, she comes onstage as an eavesdropper who punctuates the dialogue with bitter comments delivered to the audience, unheard by the other characters. Finally, she moves forward to dominate the stage with a great outpouring of curses and denunciations, directed at each of the other characters in turn. When she comes to Richard, however, he interrupts the stream of malediction to turn Margaret's curses back upon herself. 'O, let me make the period to my curse!' she complains. 'Tis done by me', he replies, 'and ends in "Margaret"' (I.iii.216–38).

This exchange dramatizes what will be a major source of Richard's theatrical power – his appropriation of the woman's part.[15] Characterized throughout in terms of warlike masculinity and aggressive misogyny, Richard also commands the female power of erotic seduction. His monopoly of both male and female sexual energy is vividly portrayed in his seduction of Anne. The turning point comes when Richard lends her his sword and lays his breast 'naked' for her penetration (I.ii.177). Overwhelmed by Richard's aggressive passivity, Anne's resistance quickly collapses, whereupon Richard seals his sexual conquest by enclosing her finger with his ring. 'Look how my ring encompasseth thy finger,' he says. 'Even so thy breast encloseth my poor heart' (I.ii.203–4). Owner of both the sword and the naked breast, both penetrated ring and penetrating heart, Richard has become, as Rebecca Bushnell points out, 'both the man who possesses and the woman who submits' (p. 124).

The power that Richard takes from women is not only the power to curse and seduce; it is also the power to transcend the frame of historical representation, the ability to address the audience directly without the knowledge of the other characters, and the theatrical energy that serves to monopolize the audience's attention. The structure of Richard's exchange with Margaret is also the structure of the early scenes in the play: it is always Richard who has the last word – along with the first. Each scene is punctuated by soliloquies in which Richard addresses the audience, predicting the action to come, responding to the action just past, flaunting his witty wickedness, gloating at the other characters' weakness and ignorance, and seducing the fascinated auditors into complicity with his diabolical schemes.

The association between the transgressive, the demonic, and the theatrical is consistently used to characterize Richard. It is, in fact, associated with his story from its beginning in More's *History of King Richard the thirde* (*c.* 1513–18), written about thirty years after Richard's death, the source for the versions Shakespeare found in Hall and Holinshed.[16] In Shakespeare's representation, as in his sources, Richard's wickedness is repeatedly and explicitly associated with his characterization as an actor. These associations are established even in *3 Henry VI*. Just before his murder by Richard, Henry asks: 'What scene of death hath Roscius now to act?' (V.vi.10). Earlier in the play, Richard has a long soliloquy in which he identifies himself as a villain in exactly the same terms that Renaissance writers typically used to describe actors:

> Why, I can smile, and murther whiles I smile,
> And cry 'Content' to that which grieves my heart,
> And wet my cheeks with artificial tears,
> And frame my face to all occasions.
> . . .
> I can add colors to the chameleon,
> Change shapes with Proteus for advantages,
> And set the murtherous Machevil to school (III.ii.182–93)[17]

In *Richard III* Richard's identity as a master performer becomes the structural principle of the dramatic action. As Alexander Leggatt has observed, this 'is the only play of Shakespeare's to begin with a soliloquy by one of its characters'. Not only the central character in the *locus* of historical representation, Richard also monopolizes the *platea* of direct address to the audience; he 'is not just hero but chorus and presenter as well' (p. 32).[18] The early scenes of the play are punctuated by asides and soliloquies in which Richard announces his chosen dramatic role ('to prove a villain'), shares his wicked plots with the audience before stepping back into the frame of representation to execute them upon the other characters, and then returns to the *platea* to gloat about the efficacy of his performance.

By defining his villainy as theatrical *tour de force*, Richard invites the audience to suspend their moral judgement and evaluate his actions simply as theatrical performance. Significantly, the most striking instance of this manœuvre occurs in the soliloquy at the end of the scene when he seduces Anne. 'Was ever woman in this humor woo'd?' he asks the audience. 'Was ever woman in this humor won?':

> What? I that kill'd her husband and his father,
> To take her in her heart's extremest hate,
> With curses in her mouth, tears in her eyes,
> The bleeding witness of my hatred by,
> Having God, her conscience, and these bars against me,
> . . .
> Hath she forgot already that brave prince,
> Edward, her lord, whom I, some three months since,
> Stabb'd in my angry mood at Tewksbury?
> . . .
> And will she yet abase her eyes on me,
> That cropp'd the golden prime of this sweet prince
> And made her widow to a woeful bed? (I.ii.227–48)

This soliloquy, which ends the scene, goes on for thirty-seven lines, reminding the audience of the historical wrongs that should have made Anne reject his suit, flaunting the theatrical power that made her forget the past. Here, and throughout the first act of the play, Richard performs a similar seduction upon the audience. For the audience as for Anne, the seduction requires the suspension of moral judgement and the erasure of historical memory, since Shakespeare's contemporaries would have entered his theatre well aware of the demonic role that Richard had been assigned in Tudor historiography; but the sheer theatrical energy of his performance supersedes the moral weight of the hegemonic narrative.

The conflation of the historical seduction represented onstage with the theatrical seduction of the present audience, of the character Richard with the actor who played his part, and of the feminine character he seduces onstage with an audience placed in a feminine role, is implicit in two well-known anecdotes associated with the play from the beginning of the seventeenth century. In March 1602, John Manningham recorded in his diary an account of a 'citizen' in the audience 'upon a tyme when Burbidge played Rich. 3' who 'greue soe farr in liking with him, that before shee went from the play shee appointed him to come that night unto hir by the name of Ri: the 3'.[19] Another anecdote, not explicitly sexual, also attests the identification of Richard with the actor who played his part. Bishop Richard Corbet, a friend of Ben Jonson, described a visit to the site of the Battle of Bosworth Field in which his host, 'when he would have said, King Richard dyed, / And call'd – A horse! a horse! – he, Burbidge cry'de'.

Both these anecdotes point to a subtle but significant difference between conceptions of tragedy and history, a difference which helps to explain both the ennobling and the disempowering of the female characters in *Richard III*. Contemporary descriptions of the history-play genre focus on the historical objects of representation. Celebrating 'our domesticke histories', Thomas Heywood asks:

> what English blood sceing the person of any bold English man presented and doth not hugge his fame, and hunnye at his valor, pursuing him in his enterprise with his best wishes, and as beeing wrapt in contemplation, offers to him in his hart all prosperous performance, as if the personater were the man Personated.... What English Prince should hee behold the true portrature of that [f]amous King *Edward* the third, foraging France, taking so great a King captive in his owne country, quartering the English Lyons with the French Flowcr-delyce, and would not bee suddenly Inflam'd with so royall a spectacle, being made apt and fit for the like atchievement. So of *Henry* the fift. (1: sig B4ᵗ)

Thomas Nashe makes essentially the same claims for the theatrical performance of English history. For Nashe as for Heywood, the value of the history play is identified with the value of the objects of historical representation. '[W]hat a glorious thing it is', he insists, 'to have *Henrie* the fifth rcprcscntcd on the Stage, leading the French King prisoner.' He imagines 'How would it have joyed brave *Talbot* (the terror of the French) to thinke that after he had lyne two hundred yeares in his Tombe, hee should triumphe againe on the Stage and have his bones newe embalmed with the teares of ten thousand spectators at least (at severall times) who, in the Tragedian that represents his person, imagine they behold him fresh bleeding?' (4:238–9). The thought of the weeping spectators, however, leads inexorably to the thought of the 'Tragedian': the present actor who elicits the spectators' feminine tears replaces the historical character who constitutes the object of masculine emulation.

Conceived as historical drama, the play features the objects of representation. Conceived as tragedy, it features the theatrical power of the actor. In either case, the role of the protagonist is reserved for a male character, but so long as the protagonist is identified, like Heywood's Edward III or Nashe's (and Shakespeare's) Talbot, with the *locus* of historical representation, the transgressive power of theatrical performance can be mobilized by a woman like Joan (or a disorderly, effeminate man like Falstaff) to subvert the hegemonic narrative. Once the protagonist assumes the role of tragic hero, however, he can also dominate the *platea*. Not only the character privileged in the represented action, the tragic hero is also the actor privileged in theatrical performance. When Richard speaks to the audience, the *platea* begins to assume the function it would have in plays like *Hamlet* and *Macbeth* as the site of the soliloquies where the masculine subject of tragedy was to be constructed.[20]

III

The movement in *Richard III* from historical chronicle to tragical history is also a movement into modernity. Tragedy, as Catherine Belsey has shown, was deeply involved with the emergent conception of an autonomous masculine identity defined in performance. The history play was doubly associated with the past, not only with the traditional heroes of the historical chronicles it represented, but also with an older conception of masculine identity rooted in patrilineal inheritance. As a dramatic genre, moreover, tragedy represented the wave of the future, while the vogue of the history play was remarkably short-lived, beginning in the 1580s and ending soon after the accession of James I (Levy, p. 233; Rackin, pp. 30–32).

Both transitory and transitional, the Shakespearean history play was shaped by the same process of rapid cultural transformation that quickly produced its obsolescence as a dramatic genre. The plays combine two potentially contradictory versions of national and personal identity, rationalizing new conceptions of royal authority and masculine identity by reference to old models of patrilineal inheritance, amalgamating medieval cultural structures of dynastic succession with emergent concepts of personal achievement and private property. In so doing, they anticipate the new concept of feudalism that Richard Halpern describes as James I's 'major innovation on the absolutist claims of the Tudors', the conception of the crown as a piece of property inherited by the king. As Halpern explains:

> [The older] theory relies on a divine conception of *political* authority, which is mystically passed from the body of the ruling king to his successor; it regards the monarch as the political representative of God and therefore invests the office of kingship with certain unique qualities. The [emergent] 'feudal' theory, by contrast, envisions not a mysterious transmission of power but a legal transmission of property, with the king

as little more than a particularly privileged landlord. Political authority derives not from divine sanction but from the prerogatives of property ownership, and is conterminous with it. (pp. 220–23)

One way to state the problem in *Richard III* is in terms of the contradiction between these two models of royal authority. Representing the end of the old Plantagenet dynasty and its replacement by the House of Tudor, the project of the play is to ratify the property rights that Richmond acquired by his victory at Bosworth Field with the warrant of God's grace expressed throughout the play by prophecies, dreams and curses, and the patriarchal legitimacy that he appropriates by his marriage to Elizabeth.

The new conception of royal authority was implicated in new understandings of masculine identity. In the older, feudal model, not only a man's property, but also his title, status and personal identity were all determined by patrilineal succession. Increasingly, however, a man's status and identity were determined simply by his wealth. Instead of an inheritance, ratified by time and patriarchal succession, a man's place in the social hierarchy could now be achieved by his own performance. Ultimately, even the ideal of the landed hereditary aristocrat would give way to that of the self-made man. For the time being, the status and land purchased by new money were validated by genealogical fictions of aristocratic lineage.

This transition involved a transformation of the functions of marriage. In a society where social and economic status were based on patrilineal succession, the most important function of marriage was to contain sexuality and avoid the production of illegitimate children. In a society where the marital unit itself became the basis of social and economic status, marriage changed from being the instrument of reproducing patriarchy over time to the site of producing new wealth and status within its own time. As Karen Newman points out, by the 1590s the earlier conception of marriage as a necessary alternative to whoredom – as the lesser of two evils – was increasingly displaced by celebrations of ordered family life as the model and foundation for the good order of the state (Newman, p. 25). This transition is generally associated with the movement from Roman Catholic asceticism to Protestant celebration of marriage. However, it also involves the replacement of the notion that marriage is valuable only as a means of procreation of legitimate heirs by the belief that it is valuable in itself; and as such it can be seen as a concomitant of the transition from feudalism to an early form of capitalism in which the family was the basic unit of economic production among the emergent middle classes.

Authority was still gendered masculine and rationalized historically, but there were significant differences in the ways a man's place in the status hierarchy (and therefore his identity) was established. In the older, feudal model, status was grounded in land, inherited from an authorizing father and transmitted through the body of an effaced mother. In the newer model – the product of an emergent capitalism and an emergent nation-state – the material basis for power and authority was monetary wealth. That wealth did not need to be inherited; it could just as well be obtained by a man's own efforts, and it could be derived either from land or from some other source of monetary income, including the acquisition of a wealthy wife.

Transforming the structure and functions of the family, the cultural transformation that led in the long run from the masculine ideal of the hereditary feudal aristocrat to that of the self-made capitalist man also produced a new conception of women (Belsey, 'Disrupting'). Women became a form of property: acquiring a woman, like acquiring any other property, became a means of validating masculine authority and manhood. Within the feudal, dynastic model of cultural organization, a man was defined as his father's son, and the ideal woman was a chaste mother who transmitted the father's legacy. Once a man's status came to be defined by his own performance, however, the ideal woman became the marriageable heiress, the prize to be attained by a man's own efforts, the material basis for the establishment of his own wealthy household.

This is not to say, of course, that wealthy and aristocratic wives were not valued by feudal noblemen, or that chaste mothers had no place in the logic of bourgeois gender ideology. The simple schematic opposition I am proposing cannot begin fully to account for the richly textured variety of social practice and socially conditioned desire, for differences over time and across class, or the ways variations in the material conditions of individual lives qualified the force of prescriptive ideals. Even within the relatively closed discursive field of Shakespeare's English history plays, both models of the family and of gendered identity can be seen, although since history was a conservative genre, the patriarchal, feudal model predominates. The alternative performative model, although it becomes increasingly prominent in the second tetralogy, is much more fully elaborated in the comedies and tragedies.[21]

In the Henry VI plays, marriage is represented as dangerous and destructive to men. Both Henry VI and Edward IV reject prudent dynastic marriages in order to marry on the basis of personal passion; both marriages are represented as disastrous mistakes that weaken the men's authority as kings and destabilize the political order of their realms. *Richard III*, on the other hand, reaches its happy resolution in the marriage between Richmond and Elizabeth, the foundation of the Tudor dynasty. In so doing, it looks forward to Shakespeare's representation of Henry V, where the successful courtship of Katherine is presented as the culminating event of Henry's triumphant reign. The resolutions of those plots in marriage literalize the scripture from Proverbs, widely quoted in contemporary marriage handbooks and sermons: 'A good wife is the crown of her husband' (Newman, p. 15). Like a newly prosperous commoner who acquired a coat of arms in order to authorize his new wealth in genealogical fictions of hereditary entitlement, both kings authorize their possession of the lands they have won in military conquest by marrying women who can secure that land by genealogical authority to their heirs.

Although both marriages are historical facts, their deployment in Shakespeare's plays is a product of dramatic selection. Their location as the satisfying theatrical culminations of the represented stories also satisfies the ideological imperatives of an emergent capitalist economy and an emergent nation-state that increasingly employed the mystified image of a patriarchal family to authorize masculine privilege and rationalize monarchical power.[22] The 'mirror of all Christian kings' (II. Cho.6), Shakespeare's Henry V is also a prototype for the emergent ideal of modern masculinity, a gender identity that can be established only in the performance of heterosexual conquest. The act of sexual domination constitutes Henry's greatest triumph. The association of royal authority with the authority of a father in a family looks ahead, in fact, to Jacobean ideology, to Filmer's *Patriarcha*, to the emergent construction of the masculine paradigm as *paterfamilias*.

In keeping with this ideal, all the female characters in *Richard III* are related by blood or marriage to English kings and defined by their familial relationships – as wife, as prospective wife, as mother, as widow. Unlike the Henry VI plays, where both Joan and Margaret appeared onstage in masculine battledress and led armies on fields of battle, the female characters in *Richard III* are confined to domestic roles and domestic settings. The domestication and sexualization of women represents a movement into modernity; it adumbrates the rising barriers that were to confine respectable women within the household, defined as a separate, private sphere. *Richard III*, like the plays of the second tetralogy, is noticeably more modern in its representations of women, of gender roles, of the English state and of the family.

The movement into modernity reaches its culmination in the concluding speech, when Richmond seals his victory at Bosworth Field by announcing his intention to marry Elizabeth of York. It is only by appropriating Elizabeth's genealogical authority as the last survivor of the House of York that Richmond can authorize himself as king and authorize the legitimacy of the Tudor dynasty; only by becoming a *paterfamilias* that he can secure his new identity as king. Elizabeth, moreover, literalizes the legal status of a married woman as a *feme covert*, reduced to a disembodied name, a place-marker for the genealogical authority that Richmond's son will inherit.

The other female characters who appear in the play are also recruited in Richmond's project; and like Elizabeth, they are also sacrificed to it. Richmond's victory, in fact, re-enacts in benevolent form Richard's earlier appropriation of the feminine. Just as the play begins with Richard's appropriation of Margaret's power of subversive speech, it ends with Richmond's appropriation of the moral authority of bereaved and suffering women to authorize his victory. To serve that purpose, the female characters must lose their individuality and become an undifferentiated chorus of ritual lamentation, curse and prophecy that enunciates the providential agenda of the play. Recounting the crimes of the past, they speak as 'poor mortal-living ghost[s]' (IV.iv.26). Like the literal ghosts who appear on the night before the Battle of Bosworth Field, they announce the obliteration of patrilineal genealogy and invoke the higher authority of divine providence to validate Richmond's accession.[23]

In praying for Richmond's victory, the ghosts of Richard's victims speak for the entire nation, which is now identified as a helpless, suffering woman. This identification is reiterated in Richmond's final speech: 'Abate the edge of traitors, gracious Lord', he prays, 'that would reduce these bloody days again / And make poor England weep in streams of blood!' The suffering victim of Richard's bloody tyranny, England is also the cherished object of Richmond's compassionate concern. Both here and in his oration before the battle, Richmond characterizes himself as a loving, protective *paterfamilias*, and he also promises his soldiers the rewards that go with that role:

> If you do fight in safeguard of your wives,
> Your wives shall welcome home the conquerors;
> If you do free your children from the sword,
> Your children's children quits it in your age. (V.iii.259–62)

Richard, by contrast, resorts to jingoistic appeals to masculine honour and misogynist charges that Richmond is a 'milksop' and his soldiers are 'bastard Britains [i.e. Bretons], whom our fathers / Have, in their own land beaten, bobb'd, and thump'd'. 'If we be conquered', he says, 'let men conquer us' (V.iii.325–34).

At this point in the play, the audience is prepared to reject Richard's aggressively masculine rhetoric and respond instead as Richmond's 'loving countrymen' who desire to 'sleep in peace'. They are not, however, prepared to accept a female image of royal or theatrical authority. When Richmond invites the audience to join him in a prayer that the descendants of his union with Elizabeth will 'Enrich the time to come with smooth-fac'd peace, / With smiling plenty, and fair prosperous days', he appeals to their feminine desires for peace and prosperity and invokes the authority of their own female monarch to sanction his accession to the throne. But just as the Elizabeth whom Richmond marries can never appear onstage, the Elizabeth he foretells is never mentioned by name or identified as a woman.

Assuming the role of benevolent *paterfamilias*, Richmond constructs himself in direct antithesis to the solitary individualism of the tragic hero he supplants, the murderer of young princes, the character who defined himself from the beginning by his contempt for women and his separation from the loving bonds of kinship. None the less, the play ends as it begins, with a male character speaking from the *platea* empowered by his appropriation of the woman's part and his performative self-construction as the object of a feminized audience's desire.[24]

Notes

1. I am indebted to Roger Abrahams, Rebecca Bushnell, Jean Howard, Donald Rackin, and Carroll Smith-Rosenberg for careful readings and helpful criticisms of earlier versions of this essay.

2. See Harrington, p. 210; Heywood, sig F4^v; and Meres, pp. 319–20.

3. On the convergence of history and tragedy, see Lindenberger, pp. 72–8. For Aristotle the ideal tragic protagonist was 'highly renowned and prosperous – a personage like Oedipus, Thyestes, or other illustrious men of such families' – and also historical: Unlike comic poets, 'tragedians still keep to real names' (*Poetics* XIII, IX). Cf. Lope de Vega, p. 543: 'For a subject tragedy has history and comedy has feigning.'

4. Early modern beliefs about the effeminating effects of theatrical performance and attributions of feminine characteristics to actors have received considerable attention in recent criticism, but see especially Howard, 'Renaissance Antitheatricality', and Singh, pp. 99–122.

5. *Playes Confuted in five Actions*, p. 215. Gosson's charge that tragedy would incite womanly passions in its auditors had an ancient and respectable precedent in Book X of Plato's *Republic*, where Socrates condemned the sympathetic raptures stirred up by the tragedian as 'the part of a woman' (39). For a perceptive discussion of the effeminacy of the tyrant figure and the effeminating effects of his representation in tragedy, see Bushnell.

6. Levin quotes the description of the ladies in the *Spanish Tragedy* audience from Thomas May's *The Heir* (1620).

7. CCXI. *Sociable Letters* (1664), reprinted in *The Riverside Shakespeare* 1847, and also quoted in Levin, 'External Evidence', p. 12. For an impressive array of similar descriptions, see Levin's entire article.

8. This is a familiar list. On the marginal roles of women in Shakespeare's English history plays, see *Stages of History*, Chapter 4.

9. In the words of Herbert Lindenberger, 'Tragedy ... gives history a way of making "sense" out of what might otherwise be a chaos of events; or the catastrophe whose inevitability it demonstrates works to confirm our worst fears about the nature of events and, by one of those apparent paradoxes that we often find when we examine the effects of art, it ends up helping us to cope with an otherwise unbearable reality' (*Historical Drama*, p. 73).

10. See Weimann's *Shakespeare and the Popular Tradition*, pp. 73–85, 224–6, and 'Bifold Authority', pp. 409–10. For an excellent analysis of *Richard III* in terms of Weimann's theory, see Mooney.

11. As Nicholas Brooke has observed, 'the flexibility of private speech' in this play is almost entirely 'confined to Richard' (p. 108).

12. On the widespread use in English Renaissance drama of female characters, and

especially of bereaved mothers, as 'a symbolic focus of pity' rather than individual figures 'involved in ... action[s] through [their] own motive and volition', see McLuskie, p. 136 and Chapter 6 *passim*.

13. Newman, p. 67; Belsey, *The Subject of Tragedy*, pp. 190–91.

14. Antony Hammond, the editor of the Arden edition, states that 'Commentators have laboured to settle the impossible, whether Elizabeth's acceptance was real or feigned' (p. 296).

15. Cf. III.vii.51, when Buckingham will advise Richard to 'play the maid's part ... and take' the crown. See also Bushnell, pp. 118–26 for a brilliant exposition of this aspect of Richard's characterization.

16. See Hammond, pp. 77–8, for two striking examples, especially notable because, as Hammond points out, they occur in a passage that Shakespeare did not use in his play.

17. In addition to the repeated use of similar descriptions in anti-theatrical invective, it is noteworthy that Burbage himself, the actor who first played Richard's role, was compared in admiring contemporary descriptions to Proteus, the shape-shifter. For a good summary of Elizabethan descriptions of actors, including Burbage, see Montrose, pp. 56–7. On the image of Proteus as applied to actors, see Barish, pp. 99–107.

18. Compare Weimann's suggestive analysis in *Shakespeare and the Popular Tradition*, pp. 159–60.

19. A similar account, quoted by Schoenbaum, pp. 205–6, appeared in Thomas Wilkes's *A General View of the Stage* (1759), pp. 220–21.

20. For arguments that emphasize the differences between Richard and later tragic heroes, see Belsey, *Subject of Tragedy*, pp. 37–9; Adelman, p. 9. In Belsey's view Richard's isolation and self-assertion declare his alignment with the Vice 'rather than defining an emerging interiority'. To Adelman 'the effect' in Richard's final soliloquy 'is less of a psyche than of diverse roles confronting themselves across the void where a self should be'. She sees Richard as possessing a 'powerful subjectivity' in *3 Henry VI*, which is emptied out in *Richard III*, as he remakes himself 'in the shape of the perfect actor who has no being except in the roles he plays' (pp. 8–9). For a discussion that emphasizes Richard's status as prototype for the modern tragic hero, see Weimann, *Shakespeare and the Popular Tradition*, pp. 159–60. In Weimann's view, Richard 'marks the point of departure for modern tragedy ... the *Charakterdrama* of an individual passion and a self-willed personality' who combines the self-expressive threatrical energy of the traditional Vice with the 'mimetic requirements of a *locus*-oriented royal personage'. Weimann concedes that '*Richard III*, of course, only points the way', but he also insists that 'the pattern seems clear'.

21. For the distinction between patriarchal and performative masculinities, see Jeffords. Many critics have remarked on the patriarchal structures of Shakespeare's English chronicle plays, but see especially Kahn, Chapter 3. On the differing structures of masculine identity in the comedies, see Williamson.

22. Many writers have made this point, but see especially Williamson, Chapter 3, 'Patriarchy, Pure and Simple', and Schochet.

23. For a suggestive analysis of this function of the ghosts, see Hodgdon, p. 114.

24. On the exclusion of female characters from the *platea*, see Helms, pp. 554—65. Helms associates the male monopoly of the *platea* in public theatre plays with the fact that men's roles were played by adult shareholders in the companies, while women's roles were played by boy apprentices. See Forse for an argument that female parts were also played by adult shareholders, including William Shakespeare.

References

Adams, Hazard, ed., *Critical Theory Since Plato*, New York: Harcourt, 1971.

Adelman, Janet, *Suffocating Mothers: Fantasies of Maternal Origin in Shakespeare's Plays*, Hamlet to The Tempest, London: Routledge, 1992.

Anon., *The True Tragedy of Richard III*, London: Thomas Creede, 1594; rpt. Oxford: Malone Society, 1929.

——— *A Warning for Fair Women: A Critical Edition*, ed. Charles Dale Cannon, The Hague: Mouton, 1975.

Barish, Jonas, *The Antitheatrical Prejudice*, Berkeley: University of California Press, p. 1981.

Belsey, Catherine, 'Disrupting Sexual Difference: Meaning and Gender in the Comedies', in *Alternative Shakespeares*, ed. John Drakakis, London: Methuen, 1985, pp. 166–90.

——— *The Subject of Tragedy: Identity and Difference in Renaissance Drama*, London: Methuen, 1985.

Brooke, Nicholas, 'Reflecting Gems and Dead Bones: Tragedy versus History in *Richard III*', in *Shakespeare's Wide and Universal Stage*, ed. C. B. Cox and D. J. Palmer, Manchester: Manchester University Press, 1984.

Bushnell, Rebecca W., *Tragedies of Tyrants: Political Thought and Theater in the English Renaissance*, Ithaca, NY: Cornell University Press, 1990.

Callaghan, Dympna, *Woman and Gender in Renaissance Tragedy*, Atlantic Highlands, NJ: Humanities Press International, 1989.

Chambers, E. K., *The Elizabethan Stage*, 4 vols, Oxford: Clarendon, 1951.

Corbet, Richard, *Iter Boreale*, Furness 591.

Dolan, Frances E., 'Gender, Moral Agency, and Dramatic Form in *A Warning for Fair Women*', *SEL* 29 (1989): 201–18.

——— 'Home-Rebels and House-Traitors: Murderous Wives in Early Modern England', *Yale Journal of Law & the Humanities* 4 (Winter 1992): 1–31.

Forse, James H. 'Why Boys for (wo)Men's Roles? or Pardon the delay, "the Queen was shaving"', *Selected Papers from the West Virginia Shakespeare and Renaissance Association* 15 (1992): 6–27.

Furness, Horace Howard, Jr., ed. *The Variorum Edition of Shakespeare's* Richard III. Philadelphia, PA. Lippincott, 1908.

Gilbert, Allen, ed., *Literary Criticism: Plato to Dryden*, Detroit: Wayne State University Press, 1962.

Gosson, Stephen, *Plays Confuted in Five Actions*, Chambers 4:213–19.

Hall, Edward, *The Union of the Two Noble and Illustre Famelies of Lancastre & Yorke*, 1548, rpt. London: J. Johnson *et al.*, 1809.

Halpern, Richard, *The Poetics of Primitive Accumulation: English Renaissance Culture and the Genealogy of Capital*, Ithaca, NY: Cornell University Press, 1991.

Hammond, Anthony, ed., *The Arden Edition of Shakespeare's* King Richard III, London: Methuen, 1981.

Harington, Sir John, *A Preface, or rather a Briefe Apologie of Poetrie*, 1591, Smith 2:194–222.

Helms, Lorraine, '"The High Roman Fashion": Sacrifice, Suicide, and the Shakespearean Stage', *PMLA* 97 (1992): 554–65.

Heywood, Thomas, *An Apology for Actors*, London, 1612.

Hodgdon, Barbara, *The End Crowns All: Closure and Contradiction in Shakespeare's History*, Princeton, NJ: Princeton University Press, 1991.

Howard, Jean E., 'Renaissance Antitheatricality and the Politics of Gender and Rank in *Much Ado about Nothing*', in Howard and O'Connor, *Shakespeare Reproduced* 163–87.

Howard, Jean, E. and Marion F. O'Connor, eds, *Shakespeare Reproduced: The Text in History and Ideology*, London: Methuen, 1987.

Jeffords, Susan, 'Performative Masculinities, or, "After a Few Times You Won't Be Afraid of Rape at All"' *Discourse* 13 (1991).

Kahn, Coppélia, *Man's Estate: Masculine Identity in Shakespeare*, Berkeley: University of California Press, 1981.

Leggatt, Alexander, *Shakespeare's Political Drama: The History Plays and the Roman Plays*, London: Routledge, 1988.

Levin, Richard, 'The Relation of External Evidence to the Allegorical and Thematic Interpretation of Shakespeare', *Shakespeare Studies* 13 (1980).

——— 'Women in the Renaissance Theatre Audience', *Shakespeare Quarterly* 40 (1989).

Levy, F.J., *Tudor Historical Thought*, San Marino, CA: Huntington Library, 1967.

Lindenberger, Herbert, *Historical Drama: The Relation of Literature and Reality*, Chicago: University of Chicago Press, 1975.

McLuskie, Kathleen, *Renaissance Dramatists*, Atlantic Highlands, N.J.: Humanities Press International, 1989.

Meres, Francis, *Palladis Tamia, Wits Treasury*, 1598, Smith 2:309–24.

Montrose, Louis Adrian, 'The Purpose of Playing: Reflections on a Shakespearean Anthropology', *Helios* n.s. 7 (1980).

Mooney, Michael E., 'Language, Staging and "Affect": *Figurenposition* in *Richard III*', in *Shakespeare's Dramatic Transactions*, Durham, NC: Duke University Press, 1990, pp. 23–50.

Nashe, Thomas, *Pierce Penilesse his Supplication to the Divell*, 1592, Chambers 4:238–40.

Newman, Karen, *Fashioning Femininity and English Renaissance Drama*, Chicago: University of Chicago Press, 1991.

Paster, Gail Kern, '"In the spirit of men there is no blood": Blood as Trope of Gender in *Julius Caesar*', *Shakespeare Quarterly* 40 (1989): 284–98.

Plato, *Republic*, trans. Benjamin Jowett, rpt. Adams pp. 19–41.

Rackin, Phyllis, *Stages of History: Shakespeare's English Chronicles*, Ithaca, NY: Cornell University Press, 1990.

Rose, Mary Beth, *The Expense of Spirit: Love and Sexuality in English Renaissance Drama*, Ithaca, NY: Cornell University Press, 1988.

Schochet, Gordon, *Patriarchalism in Political Thought: The Authoritarian Family and Political Speculation and Attitudes Especially in Seventeenth-Century England*, Oxford: Blackwell, 1975.

Schoenbaum, Samuel, *William Shakespeare: A Compact Documentary Life*, New York: Oxford University Press, 1978.

Shakespeare, William, *The Riverside Shakespeare*, ed. G. Blakemore Evans, Boston, MA: Houghton Mifflin, 1974.

Sidney, Sir Philip, *An Apologie for Poetrie*, 1595, Smith I:148–207.

Singh, Jyotsna, 'Renaissance Antitheatricality, Antifeminism, and Shakespeare's *Antony and Cleopatra*', *Renaissance Drama* n.s. 20 (1989): 99–122.

Smith, G. Gregory, ed., *Elizabethan Critical Essays*, 2 vols, Oxford: Oxford University Press, 1904.

Vega, Lope de, *The New Art of Making Comedies*, 1609, trans. Olga Marx Perlzweig, Gilbert 541–8.

Webbe, William, *A Discourse of English Poetrie*, 1586, Smith I:226–302.

Weimann, Robert, 'Bifold Authority in Shakespeare's Theatre', *Shakespeare Quarterly* 39 (1988): 409–10.

——— *Shakespeare and the Popular Tradition in the Theater: Studies in the Social Dimension of Dramatic Form and Function*, ed. Robert Schwartz, Baltimore, MD: Johns Hopkins University Press, 1987.

Williamson, Marilyn, *The Patriarchy of Shakespeare's Comedies*, Detroit: Wayne State University Press, 1986.

15

The Virgin Not: Language and Sexuality in Shakespeare

William C. Carroll

'New plays and maidenheads', according to the Prologue of *The Two Noble Kinsmen*,

> are near akin:
> Much followed both, for both much money giv'n
> If they stand sound and well. And a good play,
> Whose modest scenes blush on his marriage day
> And shake to lose his honour, is like her
> That after holy tie and first night's stir
> Yet still is modesty, and still retains
> More of the maid to sight than husband's pains.
>
> (Prol. 1–8)

The endless renewal of the spoken word, the play whose every performance is almost but not quite the ordinary 'first night's stir', is comparable here to the virgin whose maidenhead is taken yet 'still is modesty', still *seems* 'more of the maid' than not. I want to take up here some of the ways in which plays and maidenheads are related, how Shakespeare's dramatic language represents sexuality. It will be necessary to narrow the focus considerably, of course – in terms of language and sexuality in Shakespeare, here, if anywhere, is God's plenty. My argument will therefore concern only female sexuality as a production of male discourse, and I mean to use the term 'sexuality' rather than 'gender' because I will examine the biological semantics at work in the plays. Some feminist theorists have argued that female sexuality is, in patriarchal discourse, unrepresentable – conceptually available only as lack, invisibility, or negation.[1] I will pursue that position through the different, sometimes contradictory ways in which the language of several early modern writers, particularly Shakespeare, represented female sexuality and biology. Ultimately, I will examine some of the mystifications of the Tudor–Stuart discourse of virginity, the *ne plus ultra*, so to speak, of female sexuality – looking particularly at how certain modes of discourse registered the presence or absence of virginity.

To begin with, female sexuality in Shakespeare's plays is invariably articulated as linguistic transgression – that is, a verbal replication of female obliquity. Often, the ordinary relation between signifier and signified has slipped, been dislocated or even reversed, the linguistic equivalent of the world turned upside down.[2] The chief rhetorical figure here is the pun. It's not surprising that Dr Johnson termed the pun Shakespeare's 'fatal Cleopatra', employing the supreme Shakespearean example of female sexuality to indicate how Shakespeare's masculine persuasive force, to borrow Donne's term, was weakened and deflected by the 'irresistible' fascinations of the feminized quibble. For the heroic, manly playwright, 'a quibble is the golden apple for which he will always turn aside from his career, or stoop from his elevation'.[3] In employing this terminology of swerve, fall and decline, Johnson touches on something important about the sexualized energy of the pun, as a linguistic field of subversion and transgression.[4] Yet Johnson has also suggestively reversed the actual analogy by transforming the beautiful Atalanta, who abandoned her race with Hippomenes to pick up the golden apples, into the male playwright distracted by effeminizing verbal structures. This gender reversal is necessary for Johnson's understanding of unstable language as feminine, and therefore seductive. Johnson thus suggests part of my argument here: that patriarchal discourse equates destabilizing verbal forms and female sexuality.

The pun and its inversion, the malapropism, permit the introduction into utterance of female sexuality without ever seeming to name or recognize it. The references may be comic – as in the Latin lesson in *The Merry Wives of Windsor*, and the English lesson in *Henry V*, with its mispronunciations of 'foot' and 'count' – or they may be sinister – as in the references to 'country matters' and 'country forms' in *Hamlet* and *Othello* – but such linguistic forms continually enact some type of subversion of the master discourse. When Bottom assures his fellows that they will meet in the woods, 'and there we may rehearse most obscenely' (*Dream* I.ii.100–01), we have little reason to doubt him.[5]

This kind of wordplay permits the eruption of female sexuality into ordinary utterance. In *Love's Labour's Lost*, for example, Costard has been put in Armado's custody as punishment for his transgression with Jaquenetta:

> *Armado*: Sirrah Costard, I will enfranchise thee.
> *Costard*: O, marry me to one Frances! I smell some *l'envoi*, some goose, in this.
> *Armado*: By my sweet soul, I mean setting thee at liberty, enfreedom-

ing thy person. Thou wert immured, restrained, captivated, bound.
                                                                (III.i.117–22)

In a complicated series of misunderstandings, Costard has come to equate
'*l'envoi*' with 'goose', a common slang term for a prostitute. So his fear
is that he will be forced to marry a prostitute named Frances. Her name,
in turn, has come from the mishearing of 'enfranchise' as 'one Frances' –
the word for liberation turns into its opposite, signifying a forced marriage.
Costard's linguistic incapacities have created a phantom virago, a loose
woman with designs on him. A similar betrayal of subconscious threats
occurs in *The Merry Wives of Windsor*, when Quickly mishears the answer
'pulcher' as 'polecats' during the Latin lesson. The lesson continues:

> *Evans*: What is your genitive case plural, William?
> *William*: Genitive case?
> *Evans*: Ay.
> *William*: *Genitivo: 'horum, harum, horum'*.
> *Quickly*: Vengeance of Jenny's case! Fie on her! Never name her,
> child, if she be a whore.
>
>   (IV.i.52–7)

Thus 'pulcher' becomes a slang word for 'whore', virtually the opposite of
the original word. And in one of Quickly's most remarkable transformations, 'genitive case' becomes 'Jenny's case' – the prostitute by name and,
considering her profession, her most valuable possessive as well; here a
grammatical term itself generates the sexual chimera. '*Horum*', of course,
predictably mutates into a verb. Through a kind of acoustical genius,
Costard and Quickly achieve a creation *ex nihilo*, the fabrication of
comically and sexually aggressive females – two ladies of the night,
Frances and Jenny – from the swerves and frictions of language.

If puns and malapropisms offer the sexual low road, the eruption of the
carnivalesque sexual into high discourse, then their linguistic opposite is
represented by a far more stylized form of verbal dislocation, the riddle.
However riddles are categorized, one common structural feature is that 'the
referent of the description' is withheld, to be guessed at by an audience –
all signifiers and no signified, in short.[6] This 'temporary threat of
discontinuity' Roger Abrahams aptly terms 'epistemological foreplay',
leading to the riddler's clarifying and satisfying solution to the problem –
providing the absent signified.[7] Shakespeare's plays encode female
sexuality in riddles so as to mystify it in terms of obliqueness or absence.
We may think immediately of such examples as the casket riddles in *The
Merchant of Venice*, which double the mystification, with one riddle on the
outside of each box and another on the inside, leading to another kind of
inside/outside riddle, as the treasure chest that contains the woman leads

to the woman that contains, and is, the sexual treasure. Bertram's riddle in *All's Well That Ends Well* also relies on synecdoches and verbal dislocations to encode Helen's aggressive (in his view) sexuality: 'When thou canst get the ring upon my finger, which never shall come off, and show me a child begotten of thy body that I am father to, then call me husband; but in such a "then" I write a "never"' (III.ii.57–60). Bertram has sworn, in the phrase which suggests my paper's title, 'to make the "not" eternal' (III.ii.22), to leave the riddle forever unresolved, epistemological foreplay with no climax.

In Shakespeare's first romance, however, the 'not' does and must remain eternal for Pericles. The riddle he reads encodes incest, the missing signified the daughter of Antiochus:

> I am no viper, yet I feed
> On mother's flesh which did me breed.
> I sought a husband, in which labour
> I found that kindness in a father.
> He's father, son, and husband mild;
> I mother, wife, and yet his child.
> How they may be and yet in two,
> As you will live resolve it you.

> > *(Pericles* Sc.i.107–14)

It is worth recalling here that Shakespeare, as Goolden has noted, has altered his sources by making the missing signified of the 'I' in this riddle be not the father, but the daughter.[8] This change not only 'sharpens the focus on the princess', as Gorfain notes,[9] but defines female sexuality as absence – and, if the riddle is answered, as transgression. In a final example, when Mariana appears before the Duke at the end of *Measure for Measure*, her riddling responses to his questions lead him to conclude: 'Why, you are nothing then; neither maid, widow, nor wife!' (V.i.176–7). But the Duke's 'nothing' is then re-presented in Mariana's riddling self-proclamation:

> My lord, I do confess I ne'er was married,
> And I confess besides, I am no maid.
> I have known my husband, yet my husband
> Knows not that ever he knew me.

> > (V.i.183–6)

Once again, the power of negation, of the 'not', becomes the defining category of a woman's sexuality. Mariana's riddle that 'my husband / Knows not that ever he knew me' anticipates the paradox of the former virgin who 'still retains / More of the maid to sight', but also begins to lead us towards darker and more tragic moments in the plays, particularly to

Othello, who kills the wife he knew not he knew.

If puns and riddles occlude female sexuality by displacing it from the plays' high discourse, we might expect a less oblique representational strategy in the names given to female sexuality, and to the female genitalia specifically, but the realm of the referential, as we will see, is no less one of mystification. Usually, the name given to the female sex organs in Shakespeare's plays is a variant of the patriarchal metaphors of absence or containment: the O, the pit, ring, case, box, casket, the subtle hole, her C's, U's, and T's, the lake, pond, swallowing tomb, the placket, chimney, the fault,[10] and so on. Here are the images, now familiar from psychoanalytic and philological scholarship, of absence, emptiness, darkness, fall, invisible depth. From the 'unhallowed and bloodstained hole' (II.iii.210) and 'detested, dark, blood drinking pit' (II.iii.224) of *Titus Andronicus*, to the 'sulphurous pit' (*Lear* F IV.v.125) of *Lear*, Shakespeare produces one misogynistic representation after another; virtually all of them suggest that the female genitalia, in one way or another, locate 'hell ... darkness ... burning, scalding, stench, consumption' (*Lear* F IV.v.124–5).[11]

The most contested and paradoxical category of semantic description, however, is the category of the virgin, who is metonymically defined by the names given to her hymen. The religious and psychological value of virginity was, of course, under interrogation in early modern England. On the one hand, the cult of the Virgin Mary taught, as Marina Warner has noted, 'that the virginal life reduced the special penalties of the Fall in women and was therefore holy. Second, the image of the virgin body was the supreme image of wholeness, and wholeness was equated with holiness.' The virgin body was believed to be perfectly sealed up, 'seamless, unbroken'. This belief was based in part on inaccurate medical knowledge – 'the hymen was thought to seal off the womb completely ... caulking the body like tar on a ship's timbers', as Warner notes, though Renaissance anatomists, as we will see, were not as certain as this formulation.[12] The virgin's body, to employ a vocabulary derived from Bakhtin, is 'classical', with its key orifice closed, rater than 'grotesque'. The hymen thus became the most important fetishized commodity possessed by a woman, a barrier both physical and spiritual, a sign from God marking the Second Eve. As Mary Douglas has shown, the 'body's boundaries can represent any boundaries which are threatened or precarious';[13] the hymen is an ultimate threshold, a barrier to men, marking the fall into sexuality, the transition from maiden to woman, the making of the virgin not. The hymen's liminal status gives it an enormous symbolic importance as a construct of patriarchal discourse.[14]

The cult of the Virgin, however, was under attack in Reformation England, and even Queen Elizabeth's appropriations of Catholic iconology as the Virgin Queen did not overcome the sceptics and iconoclasts.[15]

Elizabeth's own dalliances were public gossip, even her monthly gynaecological status, and Ben Jonson could speculate to Drummond of Haw-
thornden that Elizabeth 'had a Membrana on her which made her
uncapable of men, though for her delight she tryed many, at the comming
over of Monsieur, ther was a French Chirurgion who took in hand to cut
it, yett fear stayed her & his death'.[16] There was also a strong libertine
tradition which demystified and subverted the value of virginity. Catullus,
for one, furnished the Renaissance its standard comparison between the
natural world and sexuality, pre-eminently through the unplucked flower
that loses its bloom (LXII.39–47). He also commodifies virginity, suggesting that the maidenhead can be precisely divided to reflect the economic
stakes of those who have invested in it:

> Your maidenhead [*virginitas*] is not all yours but
>   in part your parents';
> Your father has a third, your mother is given a
>   third,
> Only a third is yours.

$$(LXII.62–4)^{17}$$

This passage stands behind Chapman's continuation of 'Hero and Leander',[18] among other texts, and leads to paradoxical arguments that virginity
is not a something, an intact hymen, but a nothing. Marlowe's witty
argument, in 'Hero and Leander' Sestiad I, is typical. Virginity and
marriage, the narrator argues, are completely different:

> This idol which you term virginity
> Is neither essence subject to the eye,
> No, nor to any one exterior sense,
> Nor hath it any place of residence,
> Nor is't of earth or mould celestial,
> Or capable of any form at all.
> Of that which hath no being, do not boast;
> Things that are not at all, are never lost.

$$(I.269–76)$$

The libertine argument may be aimed at seduction, but it also turns on a
definition of absence and negation that can lead in more disturbing
directions. Iago taps into the vision of the 'not', the no-thing, when he tells
Othello: 'Her honour is an essence that's not seen. / They have it very oft
that have it not' (*Othello* IV.i.16–17). The handkerchief may be offered as
a substitute membrane which can be seen, handled, and passed back and
forth, but virginity itself is one of those 'things that are not at all', 'they
have it very oft that have it not'. The thing itself can be known only through

signs, thereby permitting a semiotic slippage which can be manipulated by an Iago for his own ends.

Paroles' dialogue on virginity with Helen in *All's Well That Ends Well* follows the same line of sophistic logic. His argument proceeds from the libertine assumption: 'It is not politic in the commonwealth of nature to preserve virginity', because 'loss of virginity is rational increase' (I.i.124–6).[19] Virginity is a paradoxically self-annihilating commodity: 'by being once lost [it] may be ten times found; by being ever kept it is ever lost. . . . 'Tis a commodity will lose the gloss with lying: the longer kept, the less worth' (129–30, 150–51). Time forbids the quotation of this entire dialogue, but it ends with an elaborate personification which inverts the gender and age of the virgin:

> Virginity like an old courtier wears her cap out of fashion, richly suited but unsuitable, just like the brooch and the toothpick, which wear not now. Your date is better in your pie and your porridge than in your cheek, and your virginity, your old virginity, is like one of our French withered pears: it looks ill, it eats drily, marry, 'tis a withered pear it was formerly better, marry, yet 'tis a withered pear.

> (I.i.152–60)

Turning the young maiden into the old courtier, this passage moves towards an equation between the hymen and male impotence; for every intact virgin, it seems, another male has failed. Helen's response to Paroles – 'Not my virginity, yet . . .' (line 161)[20] – provides the first instance of the rhetoric of negation which resurfaces later in the play in the central riddle, already quoted, in which Bertram says: 'I have wedded her, not bedded her, and sworn to make the "not" eternal' (III.ii.21–2), and in Diana's challenge to the King in the final scene: 'Good my lord, / Ask him [Bertram] upon his oath if he does think / He had not my virginity' (V.iii.186–8).

The language which Shakespeare employs to signify virginity thus generally trades on various forms of paradoxical negation, but the names given to the hymen itself suggest both positive and negative categories. The name 'hymen', to begin with, signifies both the god of marriage, and marriage generally, as well as the physical membrane; the same word thus figures the object which defines the virgin, and the ritual which demands the loss of that object.[21] The state of virginity thus exists only as a condition of potential loss. The god of marriage makes two formal appearances in Shakespeare: first, at the end of *As You Like It*, to 'join in Hymen's bands' (V.iv.127) the four couples; and again in the opening scene of *The Two Noble Kinsmen*, accompanied by a traditionally dressed virgin, 'encompassed in her tresses, bearing a wheaten garland' (I.i.is.d.). Neither play includes a description of the god himself.[22]

More metaphorically, the hymen is a 'maidenhead', a usage which the

OED dates from the mid thirteenth century. Shakespeare uses the term frequently, often in the sense of a commodity, a thing to be acquired or taken, or a trophy of male conquest and possession. Thus Jack Cade asserts in *The First Part of the Contention* (*2 Henry VI*): 'There shall not a maid be married but she shall pay to me her maidenhead, ere they have it' (IV.vii.118–20). But Shakespeare also understands the symbolic inversion at work in this name, by which the head of a maiden becomes a maidenhead, resulting at times in fantasies of punishment and dismemberment.[23] In *Romeo and Juliet*, Samson promises to be civil with the maids:

> I will cut off their heads.
> *Gregory*: The heads of the maids?
> *Samson*: Ay, the heads of the maids, or their maidenheads, take it in what sense thou wilt.
>
> (I.i.22–5)

This displacement figures in several of the plays, but particularly in *Measure for Measure*, where the plot lines converge in the figure of the executioner, Abhorson, and his new assistant, the bawd Pompey. As Ragozine's head is substituted for Claudio's, so is Mariana's maidenhead substituted for Isabella's.[24]

The hymen is further objectified as a *valuable* object; thus Laertes warns Ophelia not to open 'your chaste treasure ... / To [Hamlet's] unmastered importunity' (*Hamlet* I.iii.31–2). Virginity is a rare jewel but, as Marlowe puts it in 'Hero and Leander': 'Jewels being lost are found again, this never; / 'Tis lost but once, and once lost, lost for ever' (ii.85–6). In *Pericles*, Boult threatens 'To take from you [Marina] the jewel you hold so dear' (*Pericles* Sc.xix.180), following the Pander's (or Bawd's) command to him: 'Crack the ice of her virginity, and make the rest malleable' (Sc.xix.167–8). Thus virginity is valuable, rigid, reflective, and fragile – an irresistible challenge to possess, not a spiritual state but merely a physical condition.

In perhaps the most common metaphoric name, virginity is an unplucked flower, usually a rose; to penetrate the hymen is to deflower. The metaphoric origins of this ancient comparison are easy enough to imagine, and the usage in Shakespeare, and certainly in all of Renaissance literature, is pervasive; I will mention here only the 'little western flower' struck by the 'bolt of Cupid', in *A Midsummer Night's Dream*: 'Before, milk-white; now, purple with love's wound' (II.i.165–7). Some contemporary scientific treatises, however, liberalized the flower metaphor in their anatomical descriptions. In *The Anatomie of the Bodie of Man* (1548), for example, Thomas Vicary uses the metaphor of 'deflouring', but reserves the term 'flowres' as a specific name for the menses, a term which had become common usage among Renaissance anatomists, midwives and physicians.[25] In his *Microcosmographia* (1615), however, Helkiah Crooke brings biology and metaphor more closely together. 'The Caruncles [small pieces of flesh and membrane] are foure', Crooke says in his description of the hymen, 'and are like the berries of the Mirtle, in every corner of the bosome one'. All these parts and others, taken 'together make the forme of the cup of a little rose halfe blowne when the bearded leaves are taken away. Or this production', he goes on, 'with the lappe or privity may be likened to the great Clove Gilly-flower when it is moderately blowne' (223 [*sic*: actually 235]). No wonder Perdita, just five years earlier, did not want 'streaked gillyvors, / Which some call nature's bastards' (*The Winter's Tale* IV.iv.82–3) in her garden. Crooke's attempt to bring the semantic domains of metaphor and biology together was echoed in other anatomies, including the anonymous *Aristotle's Master Piece*, where the hymen

> is like the bud of a rose half blown, and this is broken in the first act of copulation with man: and hence comes the word *Deflora* to deflower; whence the taking of virginity, is called deflowering a virgin: for when the rose bud is expanded, virginity is lost.[26]

The flower is thus both a metaphor and, through acts of transference and supposed observation, allegedly also a close description of the thing itself.

Crooke goes on to further definitions of the hymen: 'It is called *Hymen quasi Limen*, as it were the entrance, the piller, or locke, or flower of virginity' (223 [*sic*: 235]), and later, 'they call it *Claustrum virginitatis, the lock of virginity*: for which their opinion they bring testimonies out of the holy scriptures' (255) – namely, the custom of displaying the virginal blood on the wedding sheets. Some anatomies also offer as a name the term '*Cento*', which translates as 'patchwork'. Thus the liminal threshold must be locked and contained, yet the membrane itself is almost indescribably fragile, mere threads.[27]

Shakespeare employs one name which puns on all the dislocations and mystifications that we have already examined – that is, the virgin knot (thus my title again). What was a virgin knot? It is equated with but apparently distinct from the so-called marriage knot and the true-lover's knot. The true-lover's knot is the iconographic image of the elaborately encoiled and overlapping thread, with no beginning or end, which unites true lovers via a 'knot formed of two loops interwined' (*OED*) – a kind of early Möbius strip, used as an *impresa* or perhaps worn on the sleeve; the *OED* offers examples from the fourteenth century. Examples may be seen as well in portraits of the time – such as that of Sir Henry Lee (1568) in the National Portrait Gallery – in emblem books, and, in *The Two Gentlemen of Verona*, in Julia's proposal to 'knit' up her hair 'in silken strings / With twenty odd-conceited true-love knots' (II.vii.45–6). The 'true-love' was also a kind of flower which was said to resemble the true-lover's knot – which leads us back to the flower of the hymen itself.[28]

The marriage knot, on the other hand, was the mystic union of two lovers through marriage, what Milton termed 'the inward knot of marriage, which is peace & love' and 'the holy knot of marriage'.[29] The marriage knot could not be dissolved by man, as Spenser noted: 'His owne two hands the holy knots did knit, / That none but death for ever can divide' (*Faerie Queene* I.12.37.1–2); marriage is 'the knot, that ever shall remaine' (*Amoretti* 6.14).[30] Shakespeare's usage is straightforward: Warwick in *The True Tragedy of Richard Duke of York* (*3 Henry VI*) refers to the 'nuptial knot' (III.iii.55); Capulet plans to 'have this knot knit up tomorrow morning' between Juliet and Paris (*Romeo* IV.ii.24), and in *Cymbeline* those who marry are said 'to knit their souls ... in self-figured knot' (II.iii.114–16). The knot of love may also indissolubly link friends or family: Gloucester in *1 Henry VI* refers to the 'knot of amity' to be gained through the alliance with France (V.i.16), Malcolm describes 'those strong knots of love' which are Macduff's family (*Macbeth* IV.iii.28), and Agrippa claims that the marriage between Antony and Octavia will make Antony and Octavius 'brothers, and ... knit your hearts / With an unslipping knot' (*Antony* II.ii.132–3). Hippolyta in *The Two Noble Kinsmen* elaborates the metaphor in this description of the friendship of Pirithous and Theseus:

> Their knot of love,
> Tied, weaved, entangled with so true, so long,
> And with a finger of so deep a cunning,
> May be outworn, never undone.

> (I.iii.41–4)

The marriage knot or true-lover's knot cannot be 'undone', 'untied' or 'dissolv'd', then. It is for ever.[31]

But the virgin knot is something else. In *Pericles*, Marina is determined to preserve her honour:

> If fires be hot, knives sharp, or waters deep,
> United I still my virgin knot will keep.
> Diana aid my purpose.

> (Sc.xvi.142–4)

And Prospero warns Ferdinand not to be another Caliban with Miranda:

> If thou dost break her virgin-knot before
> All sanctimonious ceremonies may
> With full and holy rite be ministered ...

> (*Tempest* IV.i.15–17)

And so Bertram's riddle in *All's Well* turns on this pun – 'I have wedded her, not bedded her, and sworn to make the "not" eternal' (III.ii.21–2) – on both the marriage knot and the virgin knot; he resists the eternal knot by refusing to untie the physical knot. Clearly, the virgin knot – an external figure for the hymen within – is meant to be 'untied' or broken in marriage. But what kind of a knot is it? A square knot? A double half-hitch? Surely not a sailor's knot? For Othello, the word conveys everything ugly about what he thought had been his virgin wife: turning the fountain of his life into 'a cistern for foul toads / To knot and gender in' (*Othello* IV.ii.63–4).

There were at least two contending mythological accounts of the virgin knot. In 'Hero and Leander' Sestiad v, Chapman refers to the general union of lovers in his long narrative of Hymen's own wedding. The god of marriage himself was eternally bound, when Juno's priest took

> the disparent silks, and tied
> The lovers by the waists, and side to side,
> In token that thereafter they must bind
> In one selt sacred knot each other's mind.

> (v.355–8)

But if the 'sacred knot' will never be dissolved, another ritual is also invoked:

> The custom was that every maid did wear,
> During her maidenhead, a silken sphere
> About her waist, above her inmost weed,
> Knit with Minerva's knot, and that was freed
> By the fair bridegroom on the marriage night,
> With many ceremonies of delight.

> (v.389–94)

Minerva – said to be a perpetual virgin in some Renaissance accounts – seems a plausible choice here, yet Chapman's identification of the knot with Minerva is probably a mistake, as D.J. Gordon has suggested.[32]

A second mythological account – certainly the traditional one – is given by Ben Jonson in his masque *Hymenai*, where the eternal knot and the knot to be dissolved seem to blend together. 'Reason' describes the dress of the bride, including

> The zone of wool about her waist,
> Which, in contrary circles cast,
> Doth meet in one strong knot that binds,
> Tells you, so should all married minds.

> (lines 173–6)[33]

The description of the 'personated bride' in the stage directions offers a bit more information: 'her zone, or girdle about her waist, of white wool, fastened with the Herculean knot' (lines 51–2). Jonson's own footnote offers this explanation: 'That was *nodus Herculeanus* [Hercules' knot], which the husband at night untied in sign of good fortune, that he might be happy in propagation of issue, as Hercules was, who left seventy children' (p. 517). Jonson cites as his authority Sextus Pompeius Festus, who indeed specifies the number seventy, though the great majority of authorities suggested a more modest number: Rabelais, for instance, describes Hercules as one of the 'certain fabulous fornicators . . . who made women of fifty virgins in a single night'. Even Christian critics of pagan eroticism, such as Clement of Alexandria, held the line at fifty, as Jonson himself did in *The Alchemist* (II.ii.39).[34] The knot of Hercules, in turn, may be associated with the Amazonian belt, the 'golden belt of Thermodon', as Golding translated it (*Metamorphoses* IX.233). In one of his twelve labours, Hercules defeated the Amazon Hippolyta and seized the belt or girdle she wore, freeing the way, in effect, for Theseus' capture of Hippolyta. The figure of the Amazon, as several scholars have shown, represents an effeminizing, demonized female power, suppressed and contained within patriarchal discourse.[35] Queen Elizabeth, herself frequently compared both to Minerva and to an Amazon, is pictured in two of the Armada portraits with an elaborate knot on her dress precisely in front of her genitals; her virginity is thus signified as intact, just as the maidenhead of England is now safe from the Spanish attack.[36]

But whether the virgin knot derives from Hercules, from Minerva, or from biological semantics, it also remains a 'not', a negation. If it is understood as the '*Hymen quasi Limen*', it is a liminal no-thing, perhaps a knot or puzzle to be undone, a zero, a 'nothing'.[37] Some contemporaries speculated that there was no such thing as the hymen as a matter of biological fact. In his long section on the female reproductive system in *De usu partium*, the premier reference work in the period, Galen never mentions the hymen, and indeed, there seemed to early modern writers no defined *use* for it – except to mark by its absence the loss of virginity. Adherents of the so-called one-sex model of the human body, moreover, either do not mention the hymen or cannot relate it to anything equivalent in the male system.[38] In *Microcosmographia*, Crooke is consistently definitive in his comments, but turns exceedingly tentative in his description of the hymen, referring to what 'many will have to bee a slender membrane. . . . This they say is broken in the devirgination.' For the 'true History of the Hymen', though, Crooke refers to other texts rather than to any actual observation (233 [*sic*: 235]). In the 'Questions' at the end of this chapter, moreover, Crooke's answers raise more questions: 'Almost all Physitians thinke that there is a certain membrane . . . which they call Hymen. This membrane they say is perforated in the middest' (255). In

examining the claim that a virgin will bleed when the hymen is first
deflowered – the sole function of the hymen from a male point of view –
Crooke invokes textual precedent, but it is not clear: '*Falopius* yeeldeth to
this opinion, *Columbus* writeth that he hath seene it, [but] *Laurentius*
sayeth' that after many dissections of young maidens 'hee could never
finde it though he searched curiously for it with a Probe; which (sayth he)
might have beene felt to resist the Probe if there had beene any such thing,
and therfore he thinketh that it is but a meere fable. Yet notwithstanding
thus far he giveth credite to *Columbus* and *Falopius*, that hee thinketh there
is sometimes such a membrane found', but it may be only an 'Organicall
disease' or malformation. The letting of blood by the virgin, then, may not
always occur, and is no sure sign of virginity. 'Wee must therefore',
Crooke concludes, in a passage which must have unsettled many a man at
the time, 'finde out some other locke of Virginitie' (256). Similarly, in *The
Anatomy of Melancholy* (1621), Robert Burton takes up the argument
about whether the sign of virginity is the hymeneal blood, quoting
authorities from the Bible, the Greeks, the Egyptians, the Carthaginians,
and so forth; revealing the instability of this sign of virginity, Burton
concludes that as a test for virginity, hymeneal blood is 'no sufficient trial',
according to some authorities, 'And yet others again defend it.'[39] A similar
doubt is registered in *Aristotle's Master Piece*, where the anonymous
author describes various ways in which the requisite signs of the hymen's
presence may fail to appear. The conclusion registers a zone of uncertainty
and potential anxiety:

> when a man is married and finds the tokens of his wife's virginity, upon
> the first act of copulation, he has all the reason in the world to believe her
> such, but if he finds them not, he has not reason to think her devirginated,
> if he finds her otherwise sober and modest: Seeing the Hymen may be
> broken so many other ways, and yet the woman both chaste, and virtuous.
> Only let me caution virgins to take all imaginable care to keep their virgin
> zone entire, that so when they marry, they may be such as the great
> Caesar wished his wife to be, not only without fault but without suspicion
> also.[40]

But no wife can be without a 'fault', in all the senses of that term; the
'tokens' of virginity are unstable, and if the husband 'finds them not, he
has not reason to think' his wife is not a virgin. Ambrose Parey, on the other
hand, is not tentative or qualifying at all:

> it is worth observation, that in all this passage there is no such membrane
> found, as that they called *Hymen*, which they feigned to be broken at the
> first coition. Yet notwithstanding *Columbus*, *Fallopius*, *Wierus*, and
> many other learned men of our time think otherwise, and say, that in
> Virgins a little above the passage of the urine, may be found and seene

such a nervous membrane, placed overtwhart [*sic*] as it were in the middle way of this necke, and perforated for the passage of the courses [i.e. menses]. But you may finde this false by experience.

(Book 3, p. 130)

Parey notes the contradictions among different authorities, including midwives, as to the supposed location of the membrane. Those who rely on the appearance of hymeneal blood as the sign of virginity are making a mistake, he argues, giving as one incredible example a story of prostitutes who have learned to *counterfeit* virginity, by putting into their vaginas 'the bladders of fishes, or galles of beasts filled full of blood, and so deceive the ignorant and young lecher, by the fraud and deceit of their evill arts, and in the time of copulation they mixe sighes with groanes, and womanlike cryings, and the crocodiles teares, that they may seeme to be virgins, and never to have dealt with man before' (Book 24, p. 938). Virginity is here reduced to one of the performing 'arts', constituted by nothing more than a set of manipulable signs; but as we have seen, even the existence of virginity's physical manifestation, the hymen, was always constituted by secondary and tertiary signs and emblems. That these could be manipulated, or could not be relied upon to convey any truth about women, is the surprising discovery of much contemporary medical discourse, which questions the very existence of the hymen. If the virgin might actually be a harlot, then the 'lock' of virginity is no sure thing. Maybe, maybe not. The evidence of the hymen's presence depends on the status of the sign, which can only (perhaps) point to its absence. As Parey mused on the contradictions of the hymen: 'But truly of a thing so rare, and which is contrary to nature, there cannot be any thing spoken for certainty' (Book 24, p. 938).

Thus the mystery of virginity that attracts, confuses, and bedevils many of the male characters in Shakespeare's plays, the fetishized commodity that is and is not. The plays circle round this mystification through an oblique language of indirection and negation. The not/knot pun slides further and further from its signified, unable to name it but unable to escape it. Flute tells us: 'A paramour is, God bless us, a thing of naught' (*Dream* IV.ii.14), allowing sexual transgression and emptiness to mate in a pun. Ophelia takes up Hamlet's suggestive pun in similar language:

> *Hamlet*: Be not you ashamed to show, he'll not shame to tell you what it means.
> *Ophelia*: You are naught, you are naught.

(III.ii.137–40)

And Richard III confounds Clarence's guard:

> Naught to do with Mrs Shore? I tell thee, fellow:

He that doth naught with her – excepting one –
Were best to do it secretly alone.

(Richard III I.i.99–101)

We may even begin to hear more complex resonances in Viola's paradoxical self-declarations: 'I am not that I play' *(Twelfth Night* I.v.177) and 'I am not what I am' (III.i.139).

In the Shakespearean language of sexuality, then, a woman is not a virgin whose knot is nought because she has been naught. Virginity is continually invoked, described, celebrated, occluded, denied and denounced, and language can only obliquely represent it. It remains a kind of negation *ex creatio*. 'What I am and what I would', Viola tells the audience, 'are as secret as maidenhead' *(Twelfth Night* I.v.206–7).

Notes

1. One of the best discussions of sexuality in the early modern period is Mary Beth Rose, *The Expense of Spirit: Love and Sexuality in English Renaissance Drama* (Ithaca, NY, 1988).

2. For a recent analysis of the crisis of the sign in this period generally, see Barry Taylor, *Vagrant Writing: Social and Semiotic Disorders in the English Renaissance* (Toronto, 1991). The 'world turned upside down' trope, in relation to women, is analysed in Natalie Zemon Davis's classic essay, 'Women on Top', in *Society and Culture in Early Modern France* (Stanford, CA, 1975).

3. *Samuel Johnson: Rasselas, Poems, and Selected Prose*, ed. Bertrand H. Bronson (New York, 1958), p. 252.

4. There is a substantial body of critical commentary on the Renaissance use of the pun; see in particular the luminous work of M.M. Mahood, *Shakespeare's Wordplay* (London, 1957), and Sigurd Burckhardt, *Shakespearean Meanings* (Princeton, NJ, 1968). See also William C. Carroll, *The Great Feast of Language in 'Love's Labour's Lost'* (Princeton, NJ, 1976).

5. Freud remarks that the malaprop 'does not possess [any inner] inhibition as yet, so that he can produce nonsense and smut directly and without compromise' (Sigmund Freud, *Jokes and Their Relation to the Unconscious*, ed. James Strachey (New York, 1960), p. 185).

6. Roger D. Abrahams, 'The Literary Study of the Riddle', *Texas Studies in Language and Literature* 14 (1972), p. 187. On the distinction between 'oppositional' and 'non-oppositional' riddles, see Alan Dundes, 'Toward a Structural Definition of the Riddle', in *Analytic Essays in Folklore* (The Hague, 1975).

7. Abrahams, 'The Literary Study of the Riddle', p. 182.

8. P. Goolden, 'Antiochus's Riddle in Gower and Shakespeare', *Review of English Studies* n.s. 6 (1955): 245–51.

9. Phyllis Gorfain, 'Puzzle and Artifice: The Riddle as Metapoetry in "Pericles"', *Shakespeare Survey* 29 (1976), p. 14. Ruth Nevo describes this riddle as 'dream work methodized', in *Shakespeare's Other Language* (London, 1987), pp. 39–41.

10. See John H. Astington, '"Fault" in Shakespeare', *Shakespeare Quarterly* 36 (1985): 330–34. See also Janet Adelman's suggestive comments on this pun in *Hamlet*, in *Suffocating Mothers* (London, 1992), pp. 23–4, 252–3.

11. Shakespeare uses a few terms that appear in contemporary anatomies and midwifery books – the mother, the lap – but they are exceptions to the general pattern. The 'mother' was the uterus (cf. Lear's 'O, how this mother swells up toward my heart', *Lear* F II.ii.231).

The 'Lap or Privities' was 'that part into which the necke of the wombe determineth, and is seated outwardly at the forepart of the share bone, and is as it were a skinny addition of the necke, as *Galen* speaketh ... aunswering to the prepuce or foreskin of a man' (Helkiah Crooke, *Microcosmographia: A Description of the Body of Man* [London, 1615], p. 237; subsequent textual references are to this edition). Hamlet's request of Ophelia – 'Lady, shall I lie in your lap?' (*Hamlet* III.ii.107) – is thus quite explicit, as the ensuing dialogue indicates. The best overview of English Renaissance gynaecological knowledge is Audrey Eccles, *Obstetrics and Gynaecology in Tudor and Stuart England* (Kent, OH, 1982).

12. Marina Warner, *Alone of All Her Sex: The Myth and the Cult of the Virgin Mary* (New York, 1976), pp. 72–4.

13. Mary Douglas, *Purity and Danger: An Analysis of the Concepts of Pollution and Taboo* (London, 1984), p. 115. For a discussion of the ways in which 'sexual states and functions are used as markers of social identity', using modern ethnographic evidence, see Kirsten Hastrup, 'The Semantics of Biology: Virginity', in *Defining Females*, ed. Shirley Ardener (New York, 1978).

14. Cf. the answer in *The Problemes of Aristotle, with other Philosophers and Phisitions* (London, 1597) to the question 'Why doth a woman love that man exceeding well, who had hir maidenhead?': 'Is it bicause that as the matter doth covet a forme of perfection, so doth a woman the male? or is it by reason of shamefastnes? for as that divine *Plato* saith, shamefastnes doth follow love. It is reason that the love and esteeme of him who loosed the bonds of hir credite and shame. Or is it bicause the beginning of great pleasure, doth bring a great alteration in the whole, bicause the powers of the minde are greatly delighted, and sticke and rest immoveably in the same? And therefore *Hesiodus* giveth counsell to marry a maide' (14ᵛ). In his essay on 'The Taboo of Virginity', Freud offers a more sophisticated but equally gender-biased explanation of the same alleged phenomenon: 'The maiden whose desire for love has for so long and with such difficulty been held in check, in whom the influences of environment and education have formed resistances, will take the man who gratifies her longing, and thereby overcomes her resistances, into a close and lasting relationship which will never again be available to any other man. This experience brings about a state of "thraldom" in the woman that assures the man lasting and undisturbed possession of her and makes her able to withstand new impressions and temptations from without' (Sigmund Freud, *Sexuality and the Psychology of Love*, ed. Philip Rieff (New York, 1963), p. 70).

15. On the Elizabethan appropriation of the cult of the Virgin, see Frances A. Yates, *Astraea: The Imperial Theme in the Sixteenth Century* (London, 1975), pp. 29–120; Roy Strong, *The Cult of Elizabeth* (Berkeley, CA, 1977); Louis Adrian Montrose, '"Shaping Fantasies": Figurations of Gender and Power in Elizabethan Culture', *Representations*: 2 (1983): 61–94; and C.L. Barber and Richard P. Wheeler, *The Whole Journey: Shakespeare's Power of Development* (Berkeley, CA, 1986), pp. 23–38.

16. Carole Levin, 'Power, Politics and Sexuality: Images of Elizabeth I', in *The Politics of Gender in Early Modern Europe*, eds Jean R. Brink *et al.*, *Sixteenth Century Essays and Studies* 12 (1989), pp. 95–110; *Ben Jonson*, ed. C.H. Herford and Percy and Evelyn Simpson (Oxford, 1925–52), I.142.

17. Guy Lee, ed., *The Poems of Catullus* (Oxford, 1990), p. 75.

18. Stephen Orgel, ed., *Christopher Marlowe: The Complete Poems and Translations* (Harmondsworth, 1971), 'Hero and Leander', Sestiad V.473–8. Textual quotations from Marlowe and Chapman are from this edition.

19. Erasmus makes this argument in *Proci et puellae* (1523); see *The Colloquies of Erasmus*, trans. Craig R. Thompson (Chicago, 1965, pp. 86–98). For a concise discussion of the Renaissance doctrine of Increase, with special attention to Shakespeare's sonnets, see J.W. Lever, *The Elizabethan Love Sonnet* (London, 1956), pp. 189–201. Donne (the attribution is in doubt) argues in Paradox XII, 'That Virginity is a Vertue', that 'surely nothing is more unprofitable in the Commonwealth of *Nature*, then they that dy old maids, because they refuse to be used to that end for which they were only made ... *Virginity* ever kept is ever lost' (John Donne, *Paradoxes and Problems*, ed. Helen Peters (Oxford, 1980), pp. 56–7). Cf. Comus's argument in Milton's 'Comus': 'List Lady, be not coy, and be not cozen'd / With that same vaunted name Virginity; / Beauty is nature's coin, must not be

hoarded, / But must be current, and the good thereof / Consists in mutual and partak'n bliss, / Unsavory in th'enjoyment of itself. / If you let slip time, like a neglected rose / It withers on the stalk with languish't head' (*John Milton: Complete Poems and Major Prose*, ed. Merritt Y. Hughes [New York, 1957], lines 737–44, p. 107). Even the anti-libertine argument employed the same rhetoric, as may be seen in the thirteenth-century homily *Hali Meidenhad*: 'Maidenhood is a treasure that, if it be once lost, will never again be found. Maidenhood is the bloom that, if it be once foully plucked, never again sprouteth up' (*Hali Meidenhad*, ed. Oswald Cockayne [London, 1866], p. 10).

20. Helen's line strikes me as not necessarily a textual crux, as some editors have thought – thus Bevington's *The Complete Works of Shakespeare*, I.i.165n, as well as the Riverside edition – but as her serious musing on Paroles's comic paradoxes: '*Not* my virginity'.

21. So in Catullus' famous wedding song, the god is summoned by the singing of virgins: '"o Hymenæe Hymen, / o Hymen Hymenæe", / ut lubentius, audiens / se citarier ad suum / munus, huc aditum ferat / dux bonae Veneris, boni / coniugator amoris' (LXI.39–45). ['"O Hymeneal Hymen, / O Hymen Hymeneal", / So that the more gladly, hearing / Himself summoned to his proper / Duty, he may make approach here / As the bringer of good Venus / And good love's uniter': Lee, *Poems of Catullus*, pp. 58–9.]

22. Cartari, in *Le imagini de i'dei* (Lyons, 1581), offers an illustration of Hymen with the following commentary: 'Hymen was shown by the ancients in the form of a handsome young man crowned with a diversity of flowers, in his right hand a lighted torch and in his left hand a red veil (or it could be saffron) with which new brides covered their head to face the first time they went to their husbands. And the reason for this . . . is that the wives of priests among the ancient Romans almost always wore a similar veil. Because they were not allowed to divorce, as others were, the covering of the bride with the veil came to mean the desire for the marriage never to be dissolved. This does not preclude also the symbolic meaning of the chaste modesty of the bride, which is the same as Pudor, respected by the ancients so much that it was worshipped like a god' (quoted in John Doebler, *Shakespeare's Speaking Pictures* [Albuquerque, NM, 1974], p. 37).

23. Cf. Lear's vision of the simpering dame, 'Whose face between her forks presages snow' (*Lear* F IV.v.117).

24. In *Pericles*, Boult tells Marina: 'I must have your maidenhead taken off, or the common executioner shall do it' (Sc.XIX.153–4).

25. Thomas Vicary, *The Anatomie of the Bodie of Man* (1548), eds F.J. and Percy Furnivall (London, 1888), pp. 77–8. According to Ambrose Parey, the term 'flowers' is used 'because that as in plants the flower buddeth out before the fruits, so in women kinde this flux goeth before the issue, or the conception thereof' (*The Workes of that famous Chirurgion, Ambrose Parey*, trans. Thomas Johnson [London, 1634], Book 24, p. 945). Textual references are to this edition; I will refer to Parey by his Englished name rather than Pare. James Rueff, in *The Expert Midwife* (London, 1637), employs the same terminology of deflowering (also describing former virgins as 'robbed of their best Iewll' [Book 2, p. 59].

26. *The Works of Aristotle, The Famous Philosopher* (New York, 1974), p. 18. This description is quoted again in *Aristotle's Experienced Midwife* (in *The Works*, pp. 80–81), and in *Aristotle's Last Legacy* (in *The Works*, p. 233). The textual history of these spurious works is obscure; Eccles locates copies of the *Master Piece* from 1694, the *Last Legacy* from 1690, and the *Midwife* from 1700, but all are 'certainly derived from much older works' (Eccles, p. 12). In the case of the *Problemes of Aristotle* – usually included with the other three works – printed copies exist from 1595. In Hoby's translation of Castiglione's *Courtier* (1561), however, Lord Gasper reports 'a great Philosopher in certaine Problemes of his, saith' that a woman always loves the man who 'hath been the first to receive of her amorous pleasures' (Baldassare Castiglione, *The Book of the Courtier*, trans. Sir Thomas Hoby [London, 1928], p. 199) – i.e. the passage from *The Problemes of Aristotle* quoted in note 14 above. The modern editor cites Aristotle's *Physics* as a source, but Thomas Laqueur (*Making Sex: Body and Gender from the Greeks to Freud* [Cambridge, MA, 1990], p. 277, n. 23) reports that this idea cannot be found there. The reason is that it comes from the spurious *Problemes*, apparently from an edition much earlier than the earliest known version listed in the STC. By 1615, the idea has become completely conventional: 'Whence is the

Proverb (as it hath been said) *Maydens love them that have their maydenhead*' (Richard Brathwaite, *A Strappado for the Divell* [London, 1615], M3ʳ).

27. '*Claustrum*' was also used in *Aristotle's Master Piece*, pp. 10, 18. For '*Cento*', see Rueff, *The Expert Midwife*, Book 2, p. 52.

28. For Sir Henry Lee's portrait, see Roy Strong, *Gloriana: The Portraits of Queen Elizabeth I* (New York, 1987), p. 141, plate 149. Cf. the title of Richard Brathwaite's excruciatingly long retelling of the Pyramus and Thisby story: *Loves Labyrinth: Or the True-Lovers Knot* (London, 1615). The *OED* gives *Hamlet* IV.v.39 as a reference to the true-love flower, where Ophelia sings of 'sweet flowers, / Which bewept to the grave did – not – go / With true-love showers'. Cf. also Vaughan's remarkable poem 'The Knot', where the heavenly Virgin is addressed: 'Thou art the true Loves-knot; by thee / God is made our Allie, / And mans inferior Essence he / With his did dignifie. / For Coalescent by that Band / We are his body grown, / Nourished with favors from his hand / Whom for our head we own. / And such a Knot, what arm dares loose, / What life, what death can sever? / Which us in him, and him in us / United keeps for ever' (*The Complete Poetry of Henry Vaughan*, ed. French Fogle [New York, 1964], lines 5–16, p. 302). Phillip Stubbes complains of the fashion in 1583, noting the 'sleeves ... tyed with true-looves knottes (for so they call them)' (Phillip Stubbes, *Anatomy of the Abuses in England*, ed. F.J. Furnivall [London, 1877–9], I.74).

29. *The Complete Prose Works of John Milton*, ed. Ernest Sirluck (New Haven, CT, 1959), *D.D.* 2.269.31, *M.B.* 2.467.30. The author of *Hali Meidenhad* notes: 'Look around, seely maiden, if the knot of wedlock be once knotted, let the man be a dump or a cripple, be he whatever he may be, thou must keep to him' (p. 32).

30. J.C. Smith, ed., *Spenser's Faerie Queene* (Oxford, 1909), I.12.37.1–2; Ernest de Selincourt, ed., *Spenser's Minor Poems* (Oxford, 1910).

31. Milton allows that 'the knot of marriage may in no case be dissolv'd but for adultery' (*Complete Prose Works. D.D.* 2.240.29); while Donne prays in erotic language for a separation from the knot in 'Holy Sonnet XIV': 'Yet dearly I love you, and would be loved fain, / But am betrothed unto your enemy, / Divorce me, untie, or break that not again, / Take me to you, imprison me, for I / Except you enthral me, never shall be free, / Nor ever chaste, except you ravish me' (*John Donne: The Complete English Poems*, ed. A.J. Smith [London, 1976], p. 314). Cf. Leantio's dying words for Bianca in Thomas Middleton's *Women Beware Women*, ed. J.R. Mulryne (London, 1975): 'My heart-string and the marriage-knot that tied thee / Breaks both together' (IV.ii.44–5).

32. In 'Chapman's Use of Cartari in the Fifth Sestiad of "Hero and Leander"', *Modern Language Review* 39 (1944): 280–85, D.J. Gordon suggests that Chapman inferred an allusion to Minerva in Cartari's phrase, 'In quo Deam Virginensen vir invocabat'; yet in other passages of Cartari which Chapman has obviously read, the identification with Hercules is quite clear: 'Cingulum id Herculano nodo vinctum'. Cartari, in turn, is simply paraphrasing (as he acknowledges) Sextus Pompeius Festus: 'Hunc Herculaneo nodo vinctum' (*Sexti Pompei Festi: De Verborum Significatu Quae Supersunt Cum Pauli Epitome*, ed. Wallace M. Lindsay [London, 1913], p. 55). Chapman may have made an association with Minerva's shield, with which the maiden warrior-goddess defended her virtue. On the iconography of Minerva's shield, see James Nohrnberg, *The Analogy of the Faerie Queene* (Princeton, NJ, 1976), pp. 456–7. For a broader study, see Rudolf Wittkower, 'Transformations of Minerva in Renaissance Imagery', *Journal of the Warburg Institute* 2 (1938–9): 194–205.

33. Ben Jonson, *The Complete Masques*, ed. Stephen Orgel (New Haven, CT, 1969). Textual references are to this edition. In *Aristotle's Master Piece*, 'the Zone, or girdle of chastity', is defined as the hole in the middle of the hymen, through which the menses flow (p. 18). The terminology of the 'Zone' may derive from Catullus' famous phrase, 'zonam soluere virgineam', 'to undo a virgin's girdle' (Lee, *Poems of Catullus*, LXVII.28, p. 112).

34. *The Five Books of Gargantua and Pantagruel*, trans. Jacques Le Clercq (New York, 1936), p. 390; *Clement of Alexandria*, trans. G.W. Butterworth (London, 1919), p. 69. Sextus Pompeius Festus seems to have been the first to escalate the number ('septuaginta'), which was also copied by Cartari. Natalis Comes (Chapter Seven of the *Mythologiae*) gives the number as fifty. At some point, moreover, a further escalation in Hercules' sexual power took

place, as he is said not just to impregnate fifty (or seventy) virgins, but to do it in a single night (so Jonson at *Alchemist* II.ii.39).

35. See Celeste Turner Wright, 'The Amazons in Elizabethan Literature', *Studies in Philology* 37 (1940): 433–56; Winfried Schleiner, '*Divina virago*: Queen Elizabeth as an Amazon', *Studies in Philology* 75 (1978): 163–80; Gabriele Bernhard Jackson, 'Topical Ideology: Witches, Amazons, and Shakespeare's Joan of Arc', this volume, p. 142 ff.; and Simon Shepherd, *Amazons and Warrior Women: Varieties of Feminism in Seventeenth-Century Drama* (New York, 1981).

36. See Strong, *Gloriana*, pp. 130 (pl. 138) and 132 (pl. 139). In other portraits, a pearl or other jewel holds the same symbolic place on her dress – pp. 127 (pl. 136), 129 (pl. 137) and 151 (pl. 168).

37. In a very suggestive essay, David Willbern traces 'Shakespeare's Nothing', in *Representing Shakespeare*, ed. Murray M. Schwartz and Coppélia Kahn (Baltimore, MD, 1980). See also the brilliant commentary on the sexual economy of the 'O' in James L. Calderwood, *A Midsummer Night's Dream* (London, 1993).

38. Thomas Laqueur's definitive study, *Making Sex: Body and Gender from the Greeks to Freud*, has no entry in its Index under 'hymen'; the subject is significantly absent throughout. Neither of the two most popular midwifery books available in England in this period – Eucharius Roesslin, *The byrth of mankynde* (London, 1540; 13 editions), and James Guillemeau, *Child-Birth or, The Happy Deliverie of Women* (London, 1612; 2 editions) – ever mentions the hymen, even in their descriptions of the female reproductive system. In *The Sicke Womans Private Looking-Glasse* (London, 1636), John Sadler makes a single, one-line reference to the hymen (Chapter I, p. 5).

39. Robert Burton, *The Anatomy of Melancholy*, ed. Holbrook Jackson (London, 1932), III.iii.2 (p. 284).

40. *Aristotle's Master Piece*, in *The Works of Aristotle, The Famous Philosopher*, p. 20.

16

Circumscriptions and Unhousedness: *Othello* in the Borderlands

Carol Thomas Neely

Since writing my essay 'Women and Men in *Othello*' in 1973, I have had much time and many incentives to rethink *Othello*.[1] I have been brought face to face with issues I overlooked earlier by teaching the play in many contexts and teaching women's studies and women writers' courses, including work by many contemporary women writers of colour. Simultaneously, I have been influenced by the turn towards history in Renaissance studies and by the critique of essentialism and emphasis on difference in feminist theory. A recent opportunity to write a theorized feminist autobiographical essay allowed me to analyse how my various 'homes' (social, institutional, theoretical) enforced exclusions.[2] The now glaring omissions of race and of historical context in my *Othello* essay are the most obvious example. The consequences of these omissions have been astutely pointed out, especially by Walter Cohen and Ania Loomba.[3] Omission of these issues is, of course, characteristic of most feminist and psychoanalytic work, including that on *Othello*, written in the 1970s and 1980s, and has been widely criticized.[4]

Recently, critics have begun to explore more fully the issue of race in the play and its treatment in criticism and in productions. A number of scholars have begun to retrieve the discourse on Africa developing in England in the later sixteenth and early seventeenth centuries, and to understand the play within this context.[5] But in these essays, the issue of gender often drops out of sight (once again). Karen Newman's discussion, one of the few to keep Othello and Desdemona, race and gender continuously in view, produces what I think are too stable analogies between Desdemona's gender, reduced to her sexuality, and Othello's race, reduced to his skin colour – linking them by virtue of their apparently homologous monstrousness.[6] Analyses which ignore gender or analogize it to race cannot address the ways in which race and gender and sexuality inflect each other. Indeed, a number of recent essays, focusing on race in the play, have the effect of marginalizing or simplifying Desdemona's role, or of blaming her for the tragedy.[7] I have found similar problems in classroom discussion where, it seems, some category slips out of focus while another emerges as *the* primary 'cause' of the tragedy.

In this essay, I analyse how the categories of gender, race and sexuality are inseparable, unstable, disunified, and mutually constitutive. In thinking through these issues I have found especially useful Anthony Barthelemy's analysis of the developing early modern meanings of Moor (12–17); Ania Loomba's rigorous analysis of the interactions of race and class and gender in *Othello* (*Gender*, pp. 48–62); and cogent arguments by feminist theorists about the theoretical and political dangers of 'ranking' oppressions and formulating one kind of 'difference' as prior to, constitutive of, or separable from other kinds.[8] Especially useful and provocative has been Judith Butler's work on the performativity of gender and sexuality, including her essay on *Paris is Burning* in *Bodies that Matter*, in which she argues (against the Lacanian symbolic's assumption of 'the primacy of sexual difference in the constitution of the subject') that the film suggests 'that the order of sexual difference is not prior to that of race or class in the constitution of the subject', and that 'the entire psychoanalytic paradigm needs to be subjected to this insight' (p. 130).[9] By undertaking such an analysis, I hope to avoid falling into the binary traps which lurk everywhere in the enterprise of criticism, especially perhaps *Othello* criticism: it is seen as a tragedy of either jealousy or honour (Andreas, pp. 39, 41) – either Othello or Iago is to blame; either race or gender is the primary issue. I am trying not to privilege, reify or erase any of these categories, but to understand their historical emergence through their mutual construction.

As a cautious first step, I choose to defer the word 'race' or 'racism' in my analysis in order to explore how precursors to our current concepts of 'race' and 'racism' were gradually emerging and being consolidated in England in the late sixteenth century, and how those negotiations play themselves out in *Othello*.[10] Anthony Barthelemy usefully discusses the blurred and disjunctive early modern meanings of 'Moor' – derived from and referring to a geographical location (inhabitants of Mauritania – or Africa more generally); to adherents to a religion (non-Christians, especially Muslims); or to physiognomy (less white, non-white, or black skin colour); 'the only certainty is that the person referred to is not a European Christian' (p. 7). *Othello*, through relentless iterations of 'Moor', generates a similar range of meanings of 'Moor' in relation to non-Moor or European, and perhaps moves towards some consolidation of these meanings only to disunify them again.

The play presents diffuse, disjunctive and shifting representations of Othello's Moorishness, while Iago, from his opening taunt – 'An old black ram / Is tupping your white ewe' (I.i.88–9) – purveys a narrow, derogatory, colour-specific definition. Brabantio expresses amazement that Desdemona could 'Fall in love with what she feared to look on' – 'In spite of nature, / Of years, of country, credit, everything' (I.iii.96–8). He sandwiches three precise differences – age, geography, status – between two broad ones – 'nature' and 'everything' – but does not refer to skin colour. Iago persuades Roderigo that Desdemona will soon 'disrelish the Moor' because she will require 'loveliness in favor, sympathy in years, manners and beauties' (II.i.228), mixing personal attributes ('favor', 'years') with cultural ones ('manners') and implying skin colour indirectly. Later, he tactfully revises his list for Othello's benefit, calling Desdemona perverse for refusing 'many proposed matches / Of her own clime, complexion, and degree' (III.iii.233–4). Othello himself agonizes about the cause of her fantasized disaffection, considering – and rejecting – three kinds of difference: 'Haply for I am black, / And have not those soft parts of conversation / That chamberers have, or for I am much declined / Into the vale of years – yet that's not much' (III.iii.267–70). He names outright the colour Iago euphemizes, ignores geography altogether, and translates 'degree' or status into the more easily acquired chamberers' 'manners'. In these negotiations about Othello's difference and Moorish difference, we can see the play moving, largely under Iago's impetus, towards the consolidation of disjunctive differences of country, clime, manners, age, culture, status, into colour prejudice and racial hierarchy. England in the period was perhaps likewise moving towards a more narrowly biological/ physiological definition of Moors or Africans, but it would be a long time before disparate ideas of difference would be unified into our modern concept of 'race'.[11]

For similar reasons I want to forgo the terms 'colonial' and 'colonialism' in my discussion, although I think Ania Loomba makes apt use of them. But neither Venice's situation in the Mediterranean in the play nor England's relation to Africa in the period is very accurately conveyed by the notion of colonialism as we now understand the term.[12] The many allusions in *Othello* to Mediterranean places and peoples: to Florence, Venice, Cyprus, Rhodes, Barbary, Aleppo, Palestine, and to Ottomites, Turks, pagans, Anthropophagi, Egyptians – don't represent European hegemony (indeed, the Ottoman Empire controlled much of the land around the Mediterranean, both in the play and at the time when it was written, making Venice and Cyprus vulnerable to attack and colonization). They manifest instead the diverse, fruitful, competitive, troubling interactions and exchanges of countries, cultures, religions, customs, peoples in the borderlands of Christian Europe, the Ottoman Empire, and partly Christian, partly Muslim, partly pagan Africa. Hence I do not find it useful to characterize Othello as a colonial subject. He is a freed slave,[13] an immigrant to Venice, and a Venetian citizen and General, a converted

Christian. It may be appropriate to think of him as a *mestizo* because he is constituted by, shot through with, different and contradictory cultural formations: African and European, slave and General, non-Christian and Christian, wanderer and defender of Venice. Such contradictions – as Gloria Anzaldúa, theorizing the hybrid or *mestizo/a* consciousness of outside–insiders, affirms – can be a source of identity, power and creativity as well as of self-division, impotence and self-abnegation. Before his marriage, Othello seems to have assumed this *mestizo* status productively.

Othello, then, is represented as Moorish, *mestizo*, a General, an 'extravagant and wheeling stranger' (I.i.136) who marries late. Desdemona is represented as coming to the opening scene's wedding night from a different, apparently more unified place – from the chambers of her father's house, where, as a 'maiden never bold of spirit' (I.iii.94), her white daughterly dutifulness is expressed in obedient performance of 'house-affairs' and 'Shunning' of marriage to the 'wealthy curled darlings of our nation' (I.ii.68). But at her culturally approved passage from daughter to wife, she moves from maidenly 'shamefastness' ('her motion blush'd at her self' [I.iii.95–6]) to the forthright enactment of her desires, and chooses to elope with a Moorish General instead of being handed a husband of her father's choosing. This violent 'unhousing' triggers conflicts and contradictions within the enclosed space of white, Venetian, aristocratic, daughterly femininity.[14] So Othello is an outsider who chooses to move inside – inside Venice, inside Christianity, and inside marriage to Desdemona. She is an insider who chooses, 'by downright violence, and scorn of fortunes' (I.iii.249), to break out of her house, her milieu and her country, choosing to go with Othello to Cyprus, a European outpost. It is by means of the divisions within and between them, divisions catalysed by the intersection of genders, cultures, and sexualities, that their tragedy erupts.[15]

Marriage, Othello says, is 'the very head and front of my offending' (I.iii.80), and it is marriage which precipitates differences into cleavages in three intersecting ways. First, Desdemona and Othello enter marriage to satisfy opposite (and internally contradictory) needs. Othello will put his 'unhoused free condition' into 'circumscription and confine' for 'love' of the 'gentle Desdemona' (I.ii.25–6). I find no evidence that he is represented as marrying to whiten himself, as Loomba (p. 54) hesitantly suggests, or to secure his (already achieved) 'assimilation' (which the marriage threatens and destroys). Rather, Othello seeks to find a place to 'house' his *mestizo*, 'wheeling' self, to have it *confirmed*, shared, and – as his handkerchief gift signifies – 'subdued' (III.iv.57). As he says – 'When I do love thee not, / Chaos is come again' (III.iii.92–3). In contrast, Desdemona marries Othello to get away from home, from 'guardage', from the 'circumscription' and security which have shaped her life as an elite, white

Venetian daughter; but she also wants comfort along with adventure. Their wedding night – not in her father's house or in a new home, but at the place of travellers, the Inn of the Sagittar, sign of the hybrid centaur's translation into a fixed constellation – signifies the precarious potential of this *mestizo* match in the borderlands, as does their journey to Cyprus, a contested Mediterranean island associated with love and war.

Second, the marriage is interracial – or, as I want to say, intercultural. 'Miscegenation' – the cultural mixture whose grossness Iago calls up – is not a single or uniformly postulated union of opposites. In different cultural settings, miscegenation serves different purposes, transgresses different boundaries, creates different status conflicts, and hence is received differently depending on its gendering, on the historical moment, and on the cultural perspective of the viewer.[16] In medieval and early modern Muslim culture, according to Bernard Lewis, intermarriage between Muslim men and women of different (even lower) status – Jewish, Christian, slave, black – was partly sanctioned by religion, law and custom even as prejudice against Africans became more prevalent in the seventh and eighth centuries. The superior status of the man in marriage gave him the authority to translate and elevate his wife, erasing her origins and socializing her into his culture (pp. 85–91). From the point of view of Islamic/Moorish culture, Othello's marriage would be sanctioned. From the perspective of white Venetian culture within which the now-Christian Othello resides, however, the marriage is transgressive because Othello's maleness gives him higher status, whereas Desdemona's cultural insiderness (in which skin colour becomes suddenly salient) gives her higher status, and because she elopes. Much more analysis of the different valences, functions and representations of differently gendered miscegenation in different historical and literary contexts is needed to test varied hypotheses about its functioning.

bell hooks and Lynda Boose both note that black man/white woman matches occur more frequently and are more sanctioned than their opposite – in early modern drama, in nineteenth-century American fiction, and in twentieth-century American film: for example, *Guess Who's Coming to Dinner* and *Jungle Fever*. hooks attributes this asymmetry to negative stereotypes of black women, and to the fact that black men and white women are next to each other on the race-and-gender status hierarchy which places white men at the top and black women at the bottom; hence matches between white men and black women are maximally transgressive as the black woman moves from the bottom to the top of the hierarchy and must be assimilated into the white man's family (*Ain't I a Woman*, pp. 61–71). Boose, in contrast, attributes the taboo nature of white male/woman of colour miscegenation, and the romanticized versions of the opposite mixture in literary representation to the discovery by travellers, especially Best, that blackness was genetically more powerful than whiteness in marking lineage. Hence, a black man's and a white woman's offspring confirm the parthenogenetic fantasy of patriarchy, whereas a black woman's and a white man's offspring 'resignify all offspring as the property of the mother' ('Getting', p. 46).

There is yet a third way in which this marriage's particular intersection of genders and cultures is represented as generating historically specific contradictions and colliding family narratives. Both Desdemona and Othello are shown to view marriage as conventionally reproducing the regulatory family norms of their cultures of origin. Both explicitly assume that they will replicate the role of the same-gender parent, and that their spouse will replace the other-gendered parent. But the regulation of gender and sexual relations in Othello's Moorish family and Desdemona's Venetian one, as these are represented in the play, are at odds. Desdemona, performing before the Senate the denied wedding ritual, declares that in marriage she becomes her mother, shifting obedience from her father to her husband:

> I am hitherto your daughter: but here's my husband:
> And so much duty as my mother show'd
> To you, preferring you before her father,
> So much I challenge, that I may profess,
> Due to the Moor my Lord.

(I.iii.185–9)

Later (in Folio text) she articulates her wifely subordination as specifically sexual: 'My heart's *subdued* / Even to the utmost pleasure of my Lord' (I.iii.250–51; emphasis added). In contrast, the ritualized gender relations which Othello's mother's handkerchief symbolizes and inculcates are those in which magical, 'amiable' female power and love subdue male sexual desire and inconstancy. The handkerchief's history inscribes it as a transmitter of female power and heritage (Neely, *Broken*, pp. 128–9), as woven by a (Moorish?) sibyl, and passed on with instructions to Othello's mother by a (Moorish?) 'Egyptian charmer' who

> Told her, while she kept it
> T'would make her amiable, and *subdue* my father
> Entirely to her love: but if she lost it,
> Or made a gift of it, my father's eye
> Should hold her loathly, and his spirits should hunt
> After new fancies.

(III.iv.56–61; emphasis added)[17]

Put side by side, these two narratives of family sexual and gender dynamics and family reproduction reveal the contradictory position of women (and men) in the patriarchies which they uphold; on the one hand women are prescribed to be obedient daughters and wives; on the other hand they are imagined as sexually desirable and powerful stabilizers of the family, controllers of husbands (and producers of children). These roles may be accorded different emphases in different cultures – and cultural insiders may imagine women who are outsiders as especially threatening and powerful.[18] Men must fulfil equally contradictory roles: they must retain authority over their wives and allow their sexuality to be subdued and contained by them. The differences represented in the narratives starkly illuminate the complicated cross-cultural Oedipal dynamics of *this* marriage: Desdemona must simultaneously take her (Venetian) mother's and her (Moorish) mother-in-law's place, while Othello must simultaneously take his (Moorish) father's and his (Venetian) father-in-law's place. In order to understand how this conflict plays itself out, I will see the handkerchief not only as the symbol of Desdemona's honour, sexuality and deflowering which Othello constructs, or as the signifier of Othello's male sexual anxieties which other critics have analysed,[19] but as the emblem of Moorish women's magical sexual power and control over male sexuality, as its history signifies. The handkerchief narrative can be seen to represent something of Othello's, or Shake-speare's, or English, or early modern imagined relations to real Moorish families and to the myth of African men's sexual excess as 'reported' in travellers' tales (see Note 21 below). I want to explore how acknowledging the occluded place of this cultural marker – Moorish female sexuality – might refocus the play.[20]

Feminist theorists have compellingly shown how the occlusion of women of colour and their sexuality/ies from analysis can be a cause, a symptom, or a consequence of prematurely unifying ideology or sub-jectivity around gender *or* race *or* sexuality or comparing 'women' and 'Blacks', a problem neatly encoded in the anthology title, *All the Women are White, All the Blacks are Men, But some of Us are Brave*.[21] Indeed, the category of Moorish women's sexuality is absent from most discussions of the handkerchief and of *Othello*. Similarly, African female sexuality is often elided in the critics' claims about and selections from contemporary travel narratives, and to some extent in the narratives themselves. While commentators show that early modern attitudes towards Africans included amazement and horror at prodigious lustfulness, their selected quotations refer primarily to the sexual drives and huge members of black men whose multiple women merely certify male prowess: one man 'hath as many wives as he is able to keep and maintaine', concubines, and 'swarmes of harlots'.[22] Likewise, at the time of *Othello* there are as yet no certain representations of Moorish women in the drama. Barthelemy says that Marston's *Sophonisba* (1606) is probably the first stage play to represent a Moorish waiting woman (p. 124). The sexual and social devaluing such representation would effect in Marston's Zanthia and in Zanche in Webster's *White Devil* (1611) is, however, foreshadowed in the offstage female Moor/Negro whose impregnation by Lancelot is joked about in *The Merchant of Venice* (III.v.34–9).[23]

The powerful Moorish female sexuality represented in the handkerchief, when acknowledged, provides a new vantage point from which to view the divisions, conflicts and destructions which the play enacts. It permits an emphasis on how both Othello and Desdemona, by marrying, become vulnerable and culturally fractured beings. She is torn between the imperative to identify with and represent the magic power imaged in the handkerchief and the wifely duty her mother models. Othello's 'circum-scription' in marriage, instead of enabling and solidifying his 'occupa-tion(s)', in all possible senses of the word, ironically destroys those things which provide him with a home and an identity – his generalship in Venice, the subordination of his lieutenants, his friendship with Brabantio and Cassio, and his marriage to Desdemona, the wife in whom he has 'garner'd up [his] heart' (IV.ii.58). I want to argue (in contrast to Loomba, pp. 48–9) that neither protagonist simply moves from one pole of their 'category' to the other: Desdemona from subversive (white) female assertiveness to stereotypical female passivity; Othello from (male) Europeanized assim-ilation to internalized Moorish self-denigration.[24] Each's hard-won *mestizola* identity breaks down under the pressure of competing and contradictory prescriptions and desires, exacerbated by Iago's stereotype-mongering.

Desdemona, like Othello, is torn by her culture's conflicting demands on daughters and wives, by Venetian and Moorish cultural expectations, and by the conflicting claims she and Othello make on each other. Hence she misunderstands the tale of the handkerchief, its symbolic importance, her structural identification with it, and Othello's jealousy, and lies about its loss. After Othello bewhores her, her sense of isolation and alienation – from Venice, from her father, from Othello and from herself – is represented through her identification not with Othello's powerful mother or her dutiful one, but with her mother's maid, Barbary, whose name and fate associate her with northern Africa, and hence with Moorish female sexuality in the play. But in contrast to the powerful sibyl, the Egyptian charmer, and the mother of *Othello*, Barbary is a servant who is killed by her love and sexuality rather than controlling them; she is dislocated and disempowered sexually and socially, as Desdemona discovers herself to be.[25]

Desdemona's identification with her during the willow scene, as she seeks to use the magic of the wedding sheets to subdue Othello, is poignantly appropriate. In Barbary's willow song, which Desdemona makes use of to explore her own mutually exclusive choices, the maid, powerless to control her lover's inconstancy and madness, weeps for his loss; she contradictorily accuses him of falsehood, forgives his 'scorn', and dies (IV.iii.51,54). Just these contradictions mark Desdemona's own dying words, which speak alternately angry self-assertion, wifely obedience, and self-erasure. She accuses Othello ('Oh, falsely, falsely murder'd' [V.ii.118]), declares her own innocence ('A guiltless death I die' [123]), and acquiesces in her (now) self-destructive duty ('Nobody, I myself', 'Commend me to my kind lord' [125–6]). Analysing the place of Moorish female sexuality allows us to see that Desdemona, like Othello, dies divided, still owing duty as her mother did to her lord, but also identifying with her suppressed 'dark' double – her Moorish mother-in-law refigured as the abandoned servant, Barbary. Emilia, more angered than Desdemona is at husbands who 'pour our treasures into foreign laps' (IV.iii.88), participates in the identification when she likewise dies singing the refrain of the willow song at her death, while defending Desdemona's chastity and attacking the 'cruel Moor' Othello has become (V.ii.249–50).[26]

Just so, Othello's final speech, more familiarly, narrates potentialities, both individual and cultural, constructions both Moorish and Venetian, which, present throughout, are now violently at odds. He imagines himself once more as the traveller in Aleppo (like Cyprus a precarious or contested Christian stronghold, but *inside* the Ottoman Empire). He identifies with both legitimate authority ('I have done the state some service'. 'I smote him thus.') and treachery, with power and weakness, with Europeanness and with Moorishness. These are embodied in the figures of the base Judaean or Indian (either one representing a non-Christian tribe or 'race'), of the malignant and turban'd Turk (representing religious, political and moral subversion, although in Aleppo the Turk is a colonized native), and of the circumcised dog, representing perhaps the infidel, feminized impotence of the Jew.[27] The death of Othello, like that of Desdemona, acts out the cultural divisions within and between them which the contradictions of the cross-cultural union have brought to the surface, which Iago's poison has enlarged, and which their unhousedness has rendered deadly.[28] Tellingly, after Desdemona's death and at his own, Othello's literal blackness remains virtually unspoken by himself or by others; it is diffused once again into a moral, geographical or religious category. In Emilia's references, her only ones in the play, the literal, physiological meaning slides back into the symbolic and moral one: 'O, the more angel she, / And you the blacker devil!' (V.ii.130–31); 'She was too fond of her most filthy bargain' (V.ii.157). Similarly, as the handkerchief's meaning is reinscribed, its connection with Moorish female sexuality is attenuated as it becomes 'an antique token my father gave my mother' (V.ii.216–17). Catalysed by Othello's marriage to Desdemona and Iago's narrative of this union, the play's movement towards the consolidation of complex cultural

differences into categories of 'black' and 'white' dissipates after Desdemona's and Othello's deaths. In the last moments Iago becomes a
scapegoat, absorbing the denigrating epithets of 'slave' and 'dog',
formerly used against Othello but now dissociated from exclusively racial
implications. The visual sign of difference – Othello, Emilia and Desdemona, in their 'tragic lodging' on the bed – must be 'hid' (V.iii.364, 366).
The movement towards our own consolidated conception of 'race' is
emergent, but not yet completed, in *Othello*.

Notes

1. The essay was first published in *Shakespeare Studies* 10 (1977): 133–58; was
reprinted, revised, in *The Woman's Part: Feminist Criticism of Shakespeare*, ed. Carolyn
Lenz, Gayle Greene and Carol Neely (Urbana: University of Illinois Press, 1980); and
reprinted, further revised, in my *Broken Nuptials in Shakespeare's Plays* (New Haven, CT:
Yale University Press, 1985), itself reprinted by the University of Illinois Press, 1993.
Writing a new preface for this paperback edition encouraged me to place the book in the
context of current critical developments.

2. First circulated at 'Gender and Cultural Difference', a seminar chaired by Madelon
Sprengnether at the 1991 Tokyo International Shakespeare Congress, and subsequently
published as 'Loss and Recovery: Homes Away from Home', in Greene and Kahn, eds,
Changing Subjects.

3. Loomba, *Gender*, pp. 40, 41, 57, 60; Cohen, 'Political', pp. 23, 25. See also Loomba,
'Color', pp. 19–22, 24–5, for an analysis of how my 'Constructing the Subject' continues
to privilege gender over other differences and white Western women over other women, and
to confine women to the private sphere.

4. For example, Cavell; Gohlke; Greenblatt; Garner; Greene, 'This'; Kahn; Snow;
among many others. Some recent essays which return the play to its historical context – for
example, Maus and Wayne – likewise disregard issues of race.

5. See early essays by Fiedler, Hunter and Jones; and more recent essays by Bartels,
Barthelemy, Berry, Cowig, Orkin; and by Loomba, Boose, Parker, and Singh, in Hendricks
and Parker, eds, *Women, 'Race', and Writing*.

6. Parker's essay has a similar trajectory. See Loomba, 'Color', pp. 20–21, for a
criticism of analogizing race, class, and gender oppressions.

7. Compare Andreas, Little, and Singh with earlier essays by Cavell, Greenblatt, and
Snow.

8. See, for example, Anzaldúa; Moraga and Anzaldúa; Hull; hooks; and Spelman,
especially Chapters 5 and 6.

9. I am also indebted to Judith Butler's lecture, delivered at a Queer Theory Conference
at the University of Illinois, Urbana, in March 1992, which outlined an earlier version of her
published argument.

10. I don't mean to claim that these terms should not be used of earlier periods (even
though they did not appear until the late nineteenth century); nor would I deny that the play
produces or elicits (in Neill's formulation [p. 395]) responses appropriately deemed 'racist'
in its audiences and critics. Lynda Boose ('Getting', pp. 35–45), asks a series of pertinent
questions which go to the heart of the difficulties in trying to understand, from the vantage
point of our own post-slavery, post-colonial, post-nineteenth-century biological conceptions
of race, what sorts of differences the early modern period imagined and constructed in those
who were alien to it. She argues that Western white racism evolves under a regime of
capitalism and slavery within a system of patriarchy which cannot accept miscegenation's
genetic challenge to male dominance.

11. Boose ('Getting'), drawing on Renaissance sources, explores how racial difference

begins to get separated out from a *mélange* of other differences in ways that are difficult to trace. Her essay, encountered after mine was drafted, supports many of my hypotheses. Anthony Barthelemy analyses a stage of the process in Pory's introduction of 'Moor' in his translation of Leo Africanus (pp. 12–16). Bernard Lewis traces the beginnings of racial consciousness and prejudice in the Islamic world after the seventh century under the impetus of increasing trade of black slaves from Africa eastward into Muslim territory. Winthrop Jordan sees racially based colour prejudice as developing in the New World in the early seventeenth century, with the beginnings of the slave trade.

12. As I understand the secondary sources, by 1604 England had no settlements in Africa, made no efforts to convert the inhabitants, and engaged only in sporadic trade with African regions. In the sixteenth century the English had underwritten a few triangular slave voyages; they entertained ambassadors from Moorish countries as from European ones (Tokson, p. 4), and brought 'Blackamoors' to England to train as translators. Subsequently, in 1596, Elizabeth ordered the exchange of at least 89 Blackamoors as slaves to Spain to repay a German merchant for his trouble and expense in returning 89 English prisoners from Spain to England. This incident and the exact history, status, and number of Blackamoors in England needs much more research and analysis. Elizabeth's emphasis on the need to repay the merchant's favour seems defensive, and her argument for acceding to his deal is that England (not Blackamoors) is 'populous', and that the Blackamoors are expendable not because they are black but because they are not subjects or Christians, and many Christian subjects are out of work. (The Communiqué is quoted in Loomba, *Gender*, p. 63, note 5, and is widely misinterpreted, I think.) Meredith Skura's discussion of the difficulties of assuming the existence of a discourse of colonialism in early-seventeenth-century England is useful and shrewd. For a related examination of the emergence of the idea of the fetish and the idea of utopia out of interactions between Europeans and others, especially Africans, in the early modern period, see my forthcoming 'Women/Utopia/Fetish: Disavowal and Satisfied Desire in Margaret Cavendish's *New Blazing World* and Gloria Anzaldúa's *Borderlands/La Frontera*'.

13. He was most probably 'sold to slavery' by an 'insolent foe' (I.iii.137–8) in Africa to the Turks, who had been bringing slaves from Africa into the Ottoman Empire since the fifth century. He achieved his 'redemption thence' (I.iii.138) perhaps by buying it or by manumission, as was common for slaves in the Arab world, who were then granted many of the rights of free citizens, including the right to hold positions of power like Othello's as General (Lewis, Chapter 1).

14. Compare Stallybrass, 'Patriarchal Territories', and Boose, *Fathers*, Introduction, for analyses of how female chastity and the daughter's place within the family, marriage, and culture generate social contradictions.

15. It is important to note that Othello's Moorishness is construed as negative difference (by him and by others in the play) *only after* and in relation to his marriage to Desdemona (Loomba's point, pp. 49, 58), only by white men, and especially by Iago, who calls out this cultural difference to regain his military position and reforge his homosocial bond into a vowed 'marriage' with Othello. I don't have space here to discuss Iago's role in pushing the play's conflicts towards contradictions, but it needs to be more fully addressed.

16. bell hooks's analysis of why differently gendered, mixed-race marriages are differently received at different periods in American history is useful in thinking about these issues (*Ain't I a Woman*, pp. 60–70). Loomba (*Gender*), carefully examines how the intersections of race, class and gender make this particular marriage a threat. Boose ('Getting') argues that unions between black men and white women, typical of early modern romance, are less threatening than those between white men and black women, since the fact that black children result derails patriarchal fantasies of parthenogenesis, manifests the children as the mother's property, and becomes the repressed narrative which generates, eventually, a 'violent system of racial anathema' (p. 46). Neither hooks's nor Boose's analysis precisely delineates the tensions of this particular mixed-race couple. Iago's opening taunts to Brabantio support Boose's hypothesis by emphasizing the offspring of the mixed sexual union seen as contaminating Brabantio's family line: 'the devil will make a grandsire of you' ... 'You'll have coursers for cousins and gennets for germans.' The children of the mixed match in which a 'Barbary horse ... covers' Desdemona (I.i.91,

110–13) are not, however, specified as black, and there is no further allusion to them in the play.

17. Othello's description of the containment of his own 'affects' before the Senate (I.iii.263) might be seen as embodying the beginning of this process rather than necessarily signalling his fear of sexuality.

18. See Catherine Belsey's discussion of how the role of mother disrupts early modern European patriarchal hierarchy (pp. 155–60); and see below on Moorish women.

19. Compare Snow; Cavell; Parker, pp. 94–5; Boose, 'Othello's Handkerchief'.

20. Many of the essays in Hendricks and Parker, *Women, 'Race', and Writing in the Early Modern Period*, likewise focus on this suppressed figure, especially Boose; Hall; Callaghan; Ferguson. Callaghan notes that Jewish women in Renaissance drama are often less 'racialized', more assimilable than are Jewish men (p. 170). Kim Hall, however, makes the interesting point that whereas male writers de-emphasize Cleopatra's 'blackness', women writers such as Elizabeth Cary, Mary Sidney, and Emilia Lanier emphasize it in the process of authorizing European women. In Loomba's essay, as in her book, this identity is central through her explicit positioning of herself as a post-colonial Indian woman. But it continues to be occluded in other recent discussions of *Othello*, especially those which limit their focus to Desdemona's white femininity and Othello's black masculinity, and map contemporary reinscriptions of this relationship back on to *Othello*: see Little; Andreas; Singh.

21. See references in note 6 above. Walter Cohen both alluded to and sidestepped the problem in his plenary lecture at the 1992 SAA meetings when he noted that the discourse of colonialism created a new category, native women, but did not go on to explore the function of this category.

22. Jordan, quoting Purchas and Leo Africanus (pp. 33–4); see also Tokson, pp. 16–17. There are a few references to African female lasciviousness, some of them from travellers in later periods (e.g. Jordan, p. 35).

23. He would seem to be one of the few white men in drama imagined as fathering a mixed-race child, but only as a joke. Other instances of the occlusion of African women are Jordan's titling the section of his book on the myth of African venery 'Libidinous Men', and discussing only one play, *Othello*, in it (pp. 32–43); and Eliot Tokson's book *The Popular Image of the Black Man in English Drama*, which subsumes black women under the category of black men, not taking gender difference into account.

24. Parker discusses how the play 'crosses gender and racial identities', and is filled with 'split chiastic exchanges and divisions' (pp. 97, 98), but has a tendency to homologize all forms of monstrous otherness. Nor does Othello undergo the opposite transformation from Moor to white, as Fiedler argues (p. 191). Almost everyone who talks about Othello's development falls into some kind of racial stereotypes which my framing of the play may not avoid either. Fiedler writes: '[Othello] has become, in short, *colorless*, ... which means that he no longer functions archetypally even as a stranger, much less a black' (p. 191).

25. The maid's name associates her with 'Barbary', the territory in northern Africa which Iago has already identified with foreignness, bestiality and dark skin by his reference to Othello in the first scene as a 'black ram' and a 'Barbary horse'. But Desdemona's maid, Barbary, is, like Othello, a servant in Venice; her skin colour is occluded; she is betrayed by love, not, apparently, race; and her tale is Europeanized by the willow, a conventional Western emblem of betrayed love.

26. Gilbert and Gubar succinctly formulate the function of a 'dark double', especially in their discussion of Bertha Mason in *Jane Eyre*, pp. 359–63.

27. James Shapiro's recent work traces the ways in which circumcision symbolized, for Christian Europe, the abjection and danger of the Jews. Boose ('Getting') asks of the otherness of Jews, Turks, and Blacks to Renaissance Europe: 'Did circumcision possibly set up a covert sense of bodily difference – not the difference of "nature" signified by skin color but the difference that made Muslim and Jew synonymously alien and, for a culture unused to the idea of such mutilation enacted upon male genitals, made that alienness as disturbing, deeply threatening, and by consequence as negatively value-laden to Christians in the late sixteenth century as later centuries have imagined skin color and/or physiognomy' (p. 40)?

28. Neill aptly remarks of Iago's concoction of racial poisons: 'It is a technique that works close to the unstable ground of consciousness itself; for it would be almost as difficult

to say whether its racial anxieties are ones the play discovers or implants in an audience as to say whether jealousy is something Iago discovers or implants in Othello' (p. 395).

References

Andreas, James R., 'Othello's African Progeny', *South Atlantic Review* 57 (1992): 39–57.

Anzaldúa, Gloria, *Borderlands/La Frontera: The New Mestiza*, San Francisco: Spinsters/ Aunt Lute Press, 1987.

Bartels, Emily, 'Making More of the Moor: Aaron, Othello, and Renaissance Refashionings of Race', *Shakespeare Quarterly* 41 (1990): 433–54.

Barthelemy, Anthony, *Black Face, Maligned Race: The Representation of Blacks in English Drama from Shakespeare to Southerne*, Baton Rouge: Louisiana State University Press, 1987.

Belsey, Catherine, *The Subject of Tragedy: Identity and Difference in Renaissance Drama*, London: Methuen, 1985.

Berry, Edward, 'Othello's Alienation', *SEL* 30 (1990): 315–33.

Boose, Lynda, 'The "Getting of a Lawful Race": Racial Discourse in Early Modern England and the Unrepresentable Black Woman', in Hendricks and Parker, pp. 35–54.

―――― 'Othello's Handkerchief: "The Recognizance and Pledge of Love"' *English Literary Renaissance* 5 (1975): 360–74.

Boose, Lynda and Betty Flowers, eds, *Daughters and Fathers*, Baltimore, MD: Johns Hopkins University Press, 1989.

Butler, Judith, *Bodies that Matter: On the Discursive Limits of 'Sex'*, New York and London: Routledge, 1993.

Callaghan, Dympna, 'Re-reading Elizabeth Cary's *The Tragedie of Mariam, Faire Queene of Jewry*', Hendricks and Parker, pp. 163–77.

Cavell, Stanley, *The Claim of Reason*, Oxford: Oxford University Press, 1979, pp. 481–96.

Cohen, Walter, 'The Discourse of Empire in the Renaissance', Plenary Session Talk, Shakespeare Association of America Annual Meeting, Kansas City, 1992.

―――― 'Political Criticism of Shakespeare', in *Shakespeare Reproduced*, ed. Jean Howard and Marion O'Connor, London: Methuen, 1987, pp. 18–46.

Cowig, Ruth, 'Blacks in English Renaissance Drama and the role of Shakespeare's *Othello*', in *The Black Presence in English Literature*, ed. David Dabydeen, Manchester: Manchester University Press, 1985, pp. 1–25.

Ferguson, Margaret W., 'Juggling the Categories of Race, Class, and Gender: Aphra Behn's *Oroonoko*', in Hendricks and Parker, pp. 209–24.

Fiedler, Leslie, *The Stranger in Shakespeare*, New York: Stein & Day, 1972.

Garner, Shirley N., 'Shakespeare's Desdemona', *Shakespeare Studies* 9 (1976): 233–52.

Gilbert, Sandra and Susan Gubar, *The Madwoman in the Attic*, New Haven, CT: Yale University Press, 1979.

Gohlke (Sprengnether), Madelon, '"All that's spoke is marred": Language and Consciousness in *Othello*', *Women's Studies* 9 (1982): 157–76.

Greenblatt, Stephen, *Renaissance Self-Fashioning from More to Shakespeare*, Chicago: University of Chicago Press, 1980, pp. 232–54.

Greene, Gayle, '"This that you call love": Sexual and Social Tragedy in *Othello*', this volume, p. 47.

Greene, Gayle and Coppélia Kahn, eds, *Changing Subjects: The Making of Feminist Literary Criticism*, New York and London: Routledge, 1993.

Hall, Kim F., 'I Rather Would Wish to be a Black-moor: Beauty, Race, and Rank in Lady Mary Wroth's *Urania*', in Hendricks and Parker, pp. 178–94.

Hendricks, Margo and Patricia Parker, eds, *Women, 'Race', and Writing in the Early Modern Period*, New York and London: Routledge, 1994.

hooks, bell, *Ain't I a Woman: Black Women and Feminism*, Boston, MA: South End Press, 1981.

―――― *Talking Back, Thinking Feminist, Thinking Black*, Boston, MA: South End Press, 1989.

Hull, Gloria, Patricia Scott and Barbara Smith, eds, *All the Women are White, All the Blacks are Men, But Some of Us are Brave*, Old Westbury, NY: Feminist Press, 1982.

Hunter, G.K., 'Othello and Colour Prejudice', in *Dramatic Identities and Cultural Traditions*, New York: Barnes & Noble, 1978, pp. 31–59.

Jones, Eldred, *The Elizabethan Image of Africa*, Charlottesville: University Press of Virginia, 1971.

Jordan, Winthrop, *White Over Black: American Attitudes Toward the Negro, 1550–1812*, Chapel Hill: University of North Carolina Press, 1968.

Kahn, Coppélia, *Man's Estate: Masculine Identity in Shakespeare*, Berkeley: University of California Press, 1980.

Lewis, Bernard, *Race and Slavery in the Middle East: An Historical Enquiry*, Oxford: Oxford University Press, 1990.

Little, Arthur, '"An Essence that's not seen": The Primal Scene of Racism in Othello', *Shakespeare Quarterly* 44 (1993): 304–24.

Loomba, Ania, *Gender, Race, Renaissance Drama*, Manchester: Manchester University Press, 1989, pp. 38–64.

—— 'The Color of Patriarchy: Critical Difference, Cultural Difference, and Renaissance Drama', in Hendricks and Parker, pp. 17–34.

Maus, Katharine Eisaman, 'Proof and Consequences: Inwardness and its Exposure in the English Renaissance', *Representations* 34 (Spring 1991): 29–52.

Moraga, Cherrie and Gloria Anzaldúa, eds, *This Bridge Called My Back: Writings by Radical Women of Color*, Massachusetts: Persephone Press, 1981.

Neely, Carol, *Broken Nuptials in Shakespeare's Plays*, New Haven, CT: Yale University Press, 1985. Reprinted Urbana: University of Illinois Press, 1993.

—— 'Constructing the Subject: Feminist Practice and the New Renaissance Discourses', *English Literary Renaissance* 18, 1 (Winter 1988): 5–18.

—— 'Women/Utopia/Fetish: Disavowal and Satisfied Desire in Margaret Cavendish's *New Blazing World* and Gloria Anzaldúa's *Borderlands/La Frontera*', in *Heterotopia: Postmodern Utopia and the Body Politic*, ed. Tobin Siebers, Ann Arbor: University of Michigan Press, 1994, pp. 58–95.

Neill, Michael, 'Unproper Beds: Race, Adultery, and the Hideous in Othello', *Shakespeare Quarterly* 40:4 (1989): 383–412.

Newman, Karen, '"And wash the Ethiope white": Femininity and the Monstrous in Othello', in her *Fashioning Femininity and English Renaissance Drama*, Chicago: University of Chicago Press, 1991.

Orkin, Martin, 'Othello and the Plain Face of Racism', *Shakespeare Quarterly* 38 (1987): 166–88.

Parker, Patricia, 'Fantasies of "Race" and "Gender": Africa, Othello, and Bringing to Light', in Hendricks and Parker, pp. 84–100.

Shakespeare, William, *The Merchant of Venice*, Arden edn, ed. John Russell Brown, London: Routledge, 1988.

—— *Othello*, Arden edn, ed. M.R. Ridley, London: Routledge, 1989.

Shapiro, James, Lecture, University of Illinois, Urbana, April 1991.

Singh, Jyotsna, 'Othello's Identity, Postcolonial Theory, and Contemporary African Rewritings of Othello', Hendricks and Parker, pp. 287–99.

Skura, Meredith, 'Discourse and the Individual: The Case of Colonialism in *The Tempest*', *Shakespeare Quarterly* 40 (1989): 42–69.

Snow, Edward, 'Sexual Anxiety and the Male Order of Things in Othello', *ELR* 10 (1980): 384–412.

Spelman, Elizabeth, *Inessential Woman: Problems of Exclusion in Feminist Thought*, Boston, MA: Beacon, 1988.

Stallybrass, Peter, 'Patriarchal Territories: The Body Enclosed', in *Rewriting the Renaissance: Discourses of Sexual Difference in Early Modern Europe*, ed. Margaret Ferguson *et al.*, Chicago: University of Chicago Press, 1986, pp. 123–42.

Tokson, Elliot, *The Popular Image of the Black Man in English Drama, 1550–1688*, Boston, MA: G.K. Hall, 1882.

Wayne, Valerie, 'Historical Differences: Misogyny and Othello', in *The Matter of Difference: Materialist Feminist Criticism of Shakespeare*, ed. Valerie Wayne, Ithaca, NY: Cornell University Press, 1991, pp. 153–80.

17

Afterword: What Happens in *Hamlet*?

Lisa Jardine

> *Ophelia*: My lord, as I was sewing in my closet,
> Lord Hamlet, ... comes before me.[1]

At least twice in my published work over the past ten years my attention as a historicizing, feminist reader of Shakespeare has been drawn to the figure of Hamlet's mother, Gertrude.[2] She was, indeed, one of the original textual stimuli for my setting out to write *Still Harping on Daughters*: the fact that so much had been made, on behalf of or against the cause of women, of the very little she is given to say in the play was one of the early examples I noted of a pressing need to reconsider our approaches to the female figures in Shakespeare. When I returned to her in 1991 it was to suggest even more strongly that the critical reader's confidence of Gertrude's guilt in the play depended upon culturally customary transferences of blame which remain all too recognizable to us today: we have no difficulty in understanding the way in which blame for the incestuous marriage entered into by Old Hamlet's brother, Claudius, is passed across to Gertrude as if she were its instigator.

Whenever we give attention to the figure of Hamlet's mother it is, I think, as part of an attempt to understand the cultural dynamics of blame, and its relation to questions of gender. She is virtually silent on her own behalf (Gertrude speaks fewer lines than any other major character in the play); her depth as a protagonist is accumulated out of the responses to her of others. Thus she captures for feminist critics the constructedness of femaleness which has absorbed us for more than a decade.

The crux in the play for all explorations of the condition of Gertrude's so-called 'guilt' is the closet scene of Act III Scene iv. Here, critics feel, we are bound to find the key to understanding that complexity of feeling which T.S. Eliot captured so vividly in his influential essay on the play:

> The essential emotion of the play is the feeling of a son towards a guilty mother ... Hamlet (the man) is dominated by an emotion which is

inexpressible, because it is in excess of the facts as they appear.... Hamlet is up against the difficulty that his disgust is occasioned by his mother, but that his mother is not an adequate equivalent for it; his disgust envelops and exceeds her.[3]

Yet the closet scene is more ostentatiously stage-managed, more contrived within the suffocating court atmosphere of watching, controlling and generalized espionage, than any other scene in the play. The 'intimate' conversation between Hamlet and his mother there is entirely the brainchild of Claudius's master of surveillance, Polonius:

> *Polonius*: ... if you hold it fit, after the play
> Let his queen-mother all alone entreat him
> To show his grief, let her be round with him,
> And I'll be plac'd, so please you, in the ear
> Of all their conference.[4]

> *Polonius*: My lord, he's going to his mother's closet.
> Behind the arras I'll convey myself
> To hear the process. I warrant she'll tax him home,
> And as you said – and wisely was it said –
> 'Tis meet that some more audience than a mother,
> Since nature makes them partial, should o'erhear
> The speech of vantage. Fare you well my liege.
> I'll call upon you ere you go to bed,
> And tell you what I know.
>   *King*: Thanks, dear my lord.[5]

Gertrude is a decoy, to lure Hamlet into the self-revelation which he has adeptly avoided, and which will decide Polonius and Claudius as to whether he is a danger to the state. Like Ophelia in the 'nunnery' scene, Gertrude embarks on her audience with her son in the full knowledge that they are deliberately overheard.[6] Unlike Ophelia (who simply 'walks' where Hamlet will 'as 'twere by accident' encounter her), by summoning her son to her most private quarters she formally signals to him that their meeting will be in the strictest confidence. Here, then, are grounds for accusations of betrayal: from the outset Gertrude connives in misleading Hamlet more formally and more fully than does the dutifully obedient Ophelia.

Why did I not notice, on earlier occasions on which I looked at the female figures in *Hamlet*, the carefully contrived espionage which is the crucial condition in the play for that raw exchange of intimacies in the closet scene? The question is, naturally, a rhetorical one. But before I try to answer it, let us look briefly at some of the implications of that recognition – of our registering Polonius's confident insistence that Hamlet is bound to reveal his emotional all to his mother, and that any analysis of the closet scene ought therefore to take account of the fact that circumstances have been arranged so that this private transaction can be covertly observed.

In *The English Secretorie* (1592) Angel Day defines the closet as follows:

> Wee do call the most secret place in the house appropriate vnto our owne priuate studies, and wherein we repose and deliberate by déepe consideration of all our waightiest affaires, a *Closet*, in true intendment and meaning, a place where our dealings of importance are shut vp, a roome proper and peculier onely to our selues. And whereas into each other place of the house, it is ordinary for euery néere attendant about vs to haue accesse: in this place we do solitarie and alone shutte vp our selues, of this we kéepe the key our selues, and the vse thereof alone do onely appropriate vnto our selues.[7]

Within the organization of rooms in the English country house of the period, the total privacy of the closet is signified by its location as the final room in a run of chambers serving increasingly 'private' functions – the reception room opening into the retiring room, opening into the bedroom, off which is found the closet (sometimes the closet is even concealed within a chimneypiece, or the depth of a wall).[8] But as Alan Stewart has recently pointed out, the aura of utter seclusion which the closet acquires depends to some extent on the social formality of the gentlewoman or man's withdrawing to it:

> In Lady Margaret Hoby's diary ... the (private) closet is placed in contrast to her (public) bedchamber, where she is often accompanied by her gentlewomen, acting as a sign to distinguish public praying – that is, praying in company – from private, solitary praying which takes place in her closet. For example, on Thursday 13 September 1599 she concludes her day 'then I wrought tel almost :6:, and praied with Mr. Rhodes [her chaplain], and priuatly in my Closett'.... When Lady Margaret goes into her closet, she does not merely withdraw to privacy, but rather she enacts that withdrawal publicly, and records it textually, indicating a space of secrecy outside the knowledge of the household.... The closet is thus constructed as a place of utter privacy, of total withdrawal from the public sphere of the household – but it simultaneously functions as a very *public* gesture of withdrawal, a very public sign of privacy.[9]

Of the domestic spaces occupied or traversed on a daily basis by the early modern gentlewoman, her closet was the sole place over which she ostensibly exercised total control, her one truly privy or private place.

Because what goes on in the closet is – uniquely amongst the activities in the early modern gentrified household – customarily solitary, a suggestion of the illicit, the indiscreet, certainly the secretive, hovers over those infrequent occasions when men and women encounter one another there, a *frisson* of likely indiscretion audible in Ophelia's anxious account of Hamlet's intrusion 'all unbrac'd' into her private quarters in Act II Scene i.[10] For beyond Hamlet's dishevelled appearance, his very entry into the entirely unsupervised, solitary intimacy of Ophelia's closet suggests an erotic entanglement. When Hamlet responds to his mother's summons, and comes to her closet, he intrudes where customarily a woman would entertain only her husband or lover. For an adult son, intimations of erotic possibility are almost inevitable; the son crosses into the enclosure of his mother's privacy to encounter her as a sexualized subject.

The King of Denmark's close adviser and Councillor of State, Polonius, has no legitimate place within the intimate space of Gertrude's closet; his presence fatally confuses privacy with affairs of state. The erosion of privacy which has already been effected by the constant surveillance which has characterized Claudius and Polonius's management of the state of Denmark here reaches its logical conclusion: the state invades the Queen's inner sanctum, and in the ensuing confusion it is defiled by a botched and mistaken act of violence.

The instructions issued by Polonius to Gertrude are that she should reprimand her son for his behaviour towards Claudius:

> *Polonius*: A will come straight. Look you lay home to him.
> Tell him his pranks have been too broad to bear with
> And that your Grace hath screen'd and stood between
> Much heat and him. I'll silence me even here.
> Pray you be round.[11]

Performing before Polonius, Gertrude frames her reproach formally; believing himself alone, Hamlet responds familially. The upshot is that the language of public disapproval collides with that of personal hurt, coloured by the present reminders of maternal sexuality:

> *Hamlet*: Now mother, what's the matter?
> *Gertrude*: Hamlet, thou hast thy father much offended.
> *Hamlet*: Mother, you have my father much offended ...
> *Gertrude*: Have you forgot me?
> *Hamlet*:   No, by the rood, not so.
> You are the queen, your husband's brother's wife,
> And, would it were not so, you are my mother.[12]

Reproved for his offensive behaviour (with the familiar 'thou' of maternal scolding), Hamlet retaliates with the more grievous 'offence' against his deceased natural father of his mother's remarriage to his brother. The marriage is technically illicit, and serious matter under canon law; within the closet it takes on an aura of secrecy and deception, as if it has been 'discovered' by Hamlet (yet the marriage appears to bother no one else in the court of Denmark). Whereas Hamlet, as he proceeds fully to reveal, continues to suffer the deeper smart of the usurped place of the two men whose part he takes – his father supplanted by Claudius in his mother's bed; himself supplanted on the throne by Claudius, who also now stands in affection between himself and his mother.

In an important essay on *Hamlet*, reprinted in the present volume (p. 104), Jacqueline Rose suggests that Eliot's judgement of the play as an aesthetic failure ('Hamlet is up against the difficulty that his disgust is occasioned by his mother, but that his mother is not an adequate equivalent for it; his disgust envelops and exceeds her') can be turned around – that the intensity of feeling produced in Hamlet by his mother's sexual inscrutability captures the essence of femininity. For Hamlet, Gertrude is unmanageable in the enigmatic and indecipherable quality of her sexuality, 'the Mona Lisa of literature':

> By choosing an image of a woman [the Mona Lisa] to embody the inexpressible and inscrutable content which he identified in Shakespeare's play, Eliot ties the enigma of femininity to the problem of interpretation itself. . . . Freud himself picks up the tone in one of his more problematic observations about femininity when he allows that critics have recognized in the picture:
>> the most perfect representation of the contrasts which dominate the erotic life of women; the contrast between reserve and seduction, and between the most devoted tenderness and a sensuality that is ruthlessly demanding – consuming men as if they were alien beings. . . .
> What other representation, we might ask, has so clearly produced a set of emotions without 'objective correlative' – that is, in excess of the facts as they appear? T.S. Eliot's reading of *Hamlet* would therefore seem to suggest that what is in fact felt as inscrutable, unmanageable or even horrible (ecstatic in both senses of the term) for an aesthetic theory which will allow into its definition only what can be controlled or managed by art is nothing other than femininity itself.[13]

Rose names the problem for Hamlet in the closet scene as femininity, and identifies the 'buffoonery, ecstasy, the excessive and unknowable' of his subsequent behaviour as the recognizable response of a man who cannot deal with that problem.

If we set this version of Hamlet's difficulty in relation to Gertrude within the context I have been describing, what do we get? In the terms of intimacy, privacy, and enclosure away from the public domain which I have been exploring, the problem which confronts Hamlet in the closet scene is one of contradictory, inconsistent and incompatible messages.

Hamlet is summoned to the intimate space into which his mother has (publicly) withdrawn: he crosses into what he believes to be the domestic sphere, expecting the entire secrecy of an intense conversation between mother and son. But the presence of an intruder means that privacy is already absent; his exchanges are already coloured by public interpretation as they are uttered. The competing and conflicting signs which Hamlet receives from his mother are the product of an insecure separation of private and public domains, intimate and state spaces. The enigma of femininity (in Freud's and Rose's terms) cannot be fully grasped historically without registering that it takes its shape from this insufficiently clear demarcation of discourses and domains – from the elision of the demands of social and secret (sexual) intercourse.

When the intimacies of the early modern closet are interpreted from a public perspective, then the intimate transaction is perceived as erotically charged. Just as Hamlet's uncomprehending buffoonery in Ophelia's closet was readily interpreted as thwarted eroticism, so Hamlet's retreat from his mother's closet – backwards, in disorder, dragging a dead body – implies an erotic situation he has been unable to deal with. Thus the physical spaces of intimacy in the early modern play readily lend themselves to a psychoanalytic interpretation. Psychoanalytic readings of and responses to the play, *Hamlet*, register the fact that neither the audience nor Hamlet can comprehend his mother, Gertrude. Our modern interpretation, in other words, is that of a world which no longer honours spatial thresholds between differing registers of publicness and privacy, but which nevertheless registers the difficulty.

'Is it the King?' asks Hamlet, after he has run through with his rapier the figure concealed behind the tapestry hanging. And indeed, the only person Gertrude might reputably have entertained in her closet is her husband. As if to underscore this limitation, the ghost of Hamlet's father appears 'in his nightgown' – in the kind of state of undress which only a woman's most intimate companion could affect in such a place. In response, Hamlet fills the space of intimacy with an excess of sexually explicit accusation levelled against his mother in respect of her conduct with Claudius, accusations in which his constant invoking of the mismatch between brother and brother renders both men vividly present:

> Look here upon this picture, and on this,
> The counterfeit presentment of two brothers.
> See what a grace was seated on this brow,
> Hyperion's curls, the front of Jove himself,
> An eye like Mars to threaten and command,
> A station like the herald Mercury
> New-lighted on a heaven-kissing hill,
> A combination and a form indeed

Where every god did seem to set his seal
To give the world assurance of a man.
This was your husband. Look you now what follows.
Here is your husband, like a mildew'd ear
Blasting his wholesome brother.[14]

The effect is yet again to produce a redundancy of male presences in Gertrude's closet, competing for her personal attentions. Alongside the body of Polonius and the distressed person of her son, the physical attributes of two husbands are vividly conjured up, two consorts in the innermost space of the erotic and potentially carnal, eliciting from Hamlet the accusation: 'O shame, where is thy blush?'.

What is excessive in this closet is the presence of all these men, together with the withholding of a promise of emotional (or possibly erotic) satisfaction. What the audience experiences is Gertrude's promiscuous entertaining of too many men in her inner chamber, and her reluctance to commit her loyalties except under emotional duress.

'[Hamlet's] disgust envelops and exceeds [his mother],' wrote Eliot. '[T]he fact that it is a woman who is seen as cause of the excess and deficiency in the play, and again a woman who symbolizes its aesthetic failure, starts to look like a repetition,' writes Rose. A troubling excess – emotions too large for the scale of the offences caused – has been a feature of all Hamlet criticism since Eliot's classic essay. Hamlet's 'excessive' feelings in terms of desire (inexpressible emotion) immediately make concrete and specific his mother as focus of attention for her guilt – she is pronounced guilty not as a judgement on her actions, but as a condition of her presence in the play in relation to Hamlet. Faced with the impossibility of resolving the uncertainties surrounding his father's death, Hamlet turns his attention instead upon his mother. If Hamlet's feeling is excessive, it is because his sense of his mother's guilt exceeds what could possibly fit the facts of the plot. Or, as another critic puts it, the play's enigma is the gap between 'Hamlet's vehement disgust and the Gertrude who is neither vehement nor disgusting'.[15]

Hamlet's emotion concerning his mother's remarriage, painfully revealed in the secrecy of the closet, is 'excessive' – there is too much of it. Eliot himself related this 'too much' to an editorial argument – there is too much of what Shakespeare is thinking about to pin on to the bare bones of an inferior play by Kyd, with which he is supposedly working. There is, however, another source of 'excess' in *Hamlet*, which conforms intriguingly closely to Rose's suggestions that 'buffoonery, ecstasy, the excessive and unknowable [are] terms in which we have learnt to recognize (since Freud at least) something necessarily present in any act of writing ... which suppresses them ... only at a cost'. The play-text of *Hamlet* with which we all, as critics, work is a conflation of three texts, and is at its most conflated in the closet scene.

All modern editions of *Hamlet* use the second quarto of 1604 (Q2) as their core text, and incorporate material from the 1623 first folio (F), together with some material from the first 'bad' quarto of 1603 (Q1). The result is a 'conflated' text, whose component texts are succinctly described in the New Cambridge edition of the play as follows:

> Q1 is generally recognised as a 'bad' quarto: a corrupt, unauthorised version ... of Shakespeare's play. It runs to 2,154 lines.... Q2 is not well printed, but is generally held to be based on Shakespeare's own manuscript, his 'foul papers'; that is, the completed draft, as opposed to a fair copy, which he submitted to his company. This is the fullest of the three versions, 3,674 lines.... The third basic text is ... the First Folio (F). A number of passages found in the second quarto, amounting to 222 lines, are omitted, but five new passages, totalling 83 lines, are added, giving a total for the play of 3,535 lines [16]

Editorial practice is, roughly, to take the Q2 text and 'restore' to it the 83 lines found only in the first folio (but without deleting the 222 lines which are in Q2 but not in F, thus producing a text 3,757 lines long). A certain number of further lines and emendations are introduced on the basis of Q1. The result is a play-text which, if performed in its entirety (as the Royal Shakespeare Company did in 1992), runs for nearly five hours.

Twenty-seven lines in the Q2 version of the closet scene do not occur in F, but are customarily returned to the text by the editor, thus increasing its length significantly. Almost all these occur in Hamlet's outbursts against his mother. The restoration of the 'lost' lines from the second quarto, largely reshaped in the folio version of the play, has the effect of literally *repeating* many of the sentiments expressed. The excess and repetition to which both Eliot and Rose draw attention, in other words, are a feature of the editorial process of textual conflation and accretion, as much as of the dramatist's original design. Every modern edition of *Hamlet* (including the one Eliot was using) has – literally – too much text in the scene between Hamlet and Gertrude; there is textual excess even before the critic sets to work on it. And lo and behold, what an outstandingly alert and sensitive reader like Eliot detects in the scene is excessive emotion – too much emotionally going on in the text to be sustained by the plot structure.

Excess is 'present in the act of writing' in *Hamlet* because the received text contains more than one version of the 'act of writing' the closet scene.[17] This should not, however, deter us in locating the emotional crux of the encounter between Gertrude and Hamlet here, in this scene. For we might well want to argue that it is precisely because the exchanges between them carry such a heavy emotional freight that the dramatist worked over and reworked them in successive stagings, or textual renderings of the play. In any case, it is a tribute to the critical ear of both Eliot and Rose that their insistence on the curiously repetitive and ecstatic nature of Hamlet's pronouncements is matched by the discovery that the text of *Hamlet* is, at this point in the play, literally excessive.

Why did I fail to note the crucial significance of surveillance for the closet scene in *Hamlet* when I wrote critically about Gertrude before? At a banal level, closets were not the focus of social historians' attention until recently, thus the possibility had been lost of identifying the specificity of location of the scene as crucial for the plot. But this is not an adequate explanation. What has happened between 1983, when I first noted the critics' unreasonable demand that Gertrude should bear the burden of guilt for Hamlet's crisis of indecision, and now is that feminist critics have moved from identifying the problem to using their textual skills on the text of the play to explore possible answers (however partial). As Rose writes elsewhere:

> What requires explanation . . . is not that Gertrude is an inadequate object for the emotions generated in the play, but the fact that she is expected to support them. Hamlet's horror at Gertrude (like the horror Eliot sees behind the play) makes her a focus for a set of ills which the drama shows as exceeding the woman *at the same time* as it makes her their cause. It has often been pointed out that Hamlet's despondency seems to centre more on his mother's remarriage than it does on his father's death even after the revelation of his uncle's crime. Eliot does suggest that it is in the nature of the sentiments dealt with in *Hamlet* – a son's feelings towards a guilty mother – that they are unmanageable by art. But he does not ask why it is, in the play as in his own commentary, that the woman bears the chief burden of the guilt.[18]

In 1983 it was contentious enough simply to point out that Gertrude does not deserve the critics' blame for Hamlet's tortured and confused state of mind. The question 'What happens in *Hamlet*?', asked and answered with such patriarchal confidence by John Dover Wilson in 1935, nowadays requires a more reflective and complicated response. Once it has been pointed out that Gertrude is neither complicit in the murder of Old Hamlet, nor in any way in control of what has happened to the throne of Denmark, what is it that has happened which makes her remain so dramatically culpable? The question Rose asks goes further: why does Gertrude continue to carry the play's burden of guilt so recognizably today? In other words, in 1994 the feminist critic wrestles with the problem of the persistence of patriarchy beyond the historically specific circumstances of the play's conception. Retrieving the signification of the closet goes some way towards bridging the social historical gap between early modern gender anxiety and our own.

The essays in this volume chart almost twenty years of critical attention given to the issue of gender in Shakespeare's plays. As a collection they do indeed, as the title suggests, trace a history, something like the kind of record to be found in the front of an Elizabethan family Bible – key names in the genealogy of critical descent, accompanied by a brief record or reminder of the vital contribution they have made to a still thriving dynasty. They provide a vivid record of the development I have just described – from courageous early essays identifying the problem for feminist critics both with the plays of Shakespeare themselves, and with critical inter-pretations which ignore the particular problems of gender raised, through to struggles to recognize the growing complexity of the problems to be tackled, and the increasingly strong demands for attention of other critical voices – notably those of race and ethnicity.

Anyone who believes, as I do, that in readings of Shakespeare are to be found the critical pulse-points of any period will read these essays attentively. They chart the growth in maturity of feminism as they track the shifting preoccupations of the critics. I suspect that every critic represented here, given the chance, would want to alter their essay in some way in the light of their current understanding both of Shakespeare and of feminism. Many of those represented here have taught critics like myself to reconsider judgements they reached in their earlier published writings (as Carol Neely acknowledges in her essay on *Othello*, pp. 302 ff.). For-tunately, the fortunes of our published works evade our grasp: we have here a lasting testimony to the achievement of that little band called the 'feminist critics of Shakespeare'. We've come a long way.

Notes

1. *Hamlet* II.i.77–84. All quotations are from the Arden edition, edited by Harold Jenkins.
2. *Still Harping on Daughters* (Harvester, 1983); '"No offence i' th' world": *Hamlet* and Unlawful Marriage', in F. Barker and P. Hulme, eds, *Uses of History: Marxism, Post-Modernism and the Renaissance* (Manchester University Press, 1991), pp. 123–39.
3. Eliot, 1932, in *Selected Prose of T.S. Eliot*, ed. Frank Kermode (London: Faber, 1975), pp. 144–5.
4. *Hamlet* III.ii.183–7.
5. *Hamlet* III.iii.27–35.
6. The 'accretion', '*Hamlet within*: Mother, mother, mother', of Q2 and F, discarded by modern editors, surely registers the limited, local culpability of Gertrude in conspiring to have her familial exchange with her son spied upon.
7. Angel Day, *The English Secretorie* (Richard Iones, London, 1592), 109, quoted by Alan Stewart, *The Bounds of Sodomy* (Princeton, NJ: Princeton University Press, forthcoming).

8. See, for example, the plan by John Smythson for additions to Haughton House, Nottinghamshire, 1618 and his plan for a terrace range at Bolsover *c.* 1630, reproduced as plates 191 and 177 respectively in Mark Girouard, *Robert Smythson and the Elizabethan Country House* (New Haven, CT: Yale University Press, 1983).

9. Stewart, *The Bounds of Sodomy*, Chapter 5, 'Epistemologies of the Early Modern Closet'.

10. Stewart argues compellingly that it is the innuendo surrounding encounters in the closet which fuels the suggestion that the gentleman's private secretary (who licitly works with him in the privacy of his closet) might be having some kind of erotic relationship with his employer.

11. *Hamlet* III.iv.1–5.

12. *Hamlet* III.iv.8–16.

13. Rose, 'Hamlet – the *Mona Lisa* of Literature', p. 104.

14. *Hamlet* III.iv.53–65.

15. Cedric Watts, *Harvester New Critical Introductions to Shakespeare: Hamlet* (Sussex: Harvester, 1988), pp. xxiv–v.

16. Philip Edwards, ed., *Hamlet* (Cambridge: Cambridge University Press, 1985), p. 9.

17. We might add that Q1 contains a further, almost entirely distinct version of the most emotionally complex component in this scene, the 'Look here upon this picture' speech. See G. Holderness and B. Loughrey, eds, *The Tragicall Historie of Hamlet Prince of Denmarke* (Hemel Hempstead: Harvester Wheatsheaf, 1992), p. 80.

18. J. Rose, 'Sexuality in the Reading of Shakespeare: *Hamlet* and *Measure for Measure*', in J. Drakakis, ed., *Alternative Shakespeares* (London: Methuen, 1985), pp. 95–118 [101].

Notes on Contributors

Deborah Barker is an Assistant Professor of English at the University of Mississippi. She has published articles on Kate Chopin (in *Beyond the Bayou: Re-Searching Kate Chopin*, ed. Lynda S. Boren and Sara deSaussure Davis [1992]) and William Faulkner, and she is currently completing a book on representations of female visual artists in nineteenth-century American fiction.

Catherine Belsey chairs the Centre for Critical and Cultural Theory, University of Wales, Cardiff. Her books include *The Subject of Tragedy: Identity and Difference in the Renaissance* (1985); *John Milton: Language, Gender, Power* (1988); and *Desire: Love Stories in Western Culture* (1994). She is joint editor with Jane Moore of *The Feminist Reader: Essays in Gender and the Politics of Literary Criticism* (1989).

William C. Carroll is Professor of English at Boston University. He is the author of *The Great Feast of Language in Love's Labour's Lost* (1976) and *The Metamorphoses of Shakespearean Comedy* (1985); and editor of Middleton's *Women Beware Women* for the New Mermaid Series. Among his forthcoming works are *Shakespeare and the Discourse of Poverty* and the Arden edition of *The Two Gentlemen of Verona*.

Carol Cook has taught at Oberlin College, Vassar College, and Princeton University. Her work on Shakespeare and gender has appeared in such journals as *Theatre Journal* and *PMLA*, and in such essay collections as *Shakespearean Tragedy and Gender* and *Shakespeare Left and Right* (1991).

Gayle Greene is Professor of English and Women's Studies at Scripps College, Claremont, California. She has co-edited *The Woman's Part: Feminist Criticism of Shakespeare* (1980), *Making a Difference: Feminist Literary Criticism* (1985), and *Changing Subjects: The Making of Feminist Criticism* (1993). She has written two books on contemporary women's fiction – *Changing the Story: Feminist Fiction and the Tradition* (1992) and *Doris Lessing: The Poetics of Change* (1994) – and writes regularly for *The Nation*. Greene is currently working on a book on cancer and the environment.

Gabriele Bernhard Jackson is Professor of English at Temple University. She is the author of *Vision and Judgment in Ben Jonson's Drama* and editor of *Every Man in His Humor* in the Yale Ben Jonson series. She has published articles on Tudor and Stuart drama, with particular attention to Ben Jonson and Shakespeare, as well as on eighteenth-century poetry. Currently, she is working on a book-length study of early modern visual and textual representations of viragos.

Lisa Jardine is Professor of English and Dean of Arts at Queen Mary and Westfield College, University of London. She is the author of *Francis Bacon: Discovery and the Art of Discourse* (1974); *Still Harping on Daughters: Women and Drama in the Age of Shakespeare* (1983); and *Erasmus, Man of Letters: The Construction of Charisma in Print* (1993). With Anthony Grafton she is the author of *From Humanism to the Humanities* (1986); and with Julia Swindells the author of *What's Left? Women and Culture in the Labour Movement* (1990). She is currently working on a general book on the European Renaissance, entitled *All Our Worldly Goods: The Legacy of the European Renaissance*; and she has a book on Shakespeare in press: *Reading Shakespeare Historically*.

Coppélia Kahn, author of *Man's Estate: Masculine Identity in Shake-speare* (1981), is Professor of English at Brown University. She has co-edited several anthologies, most recently *Changing Subjects: The Making of Feminist Literary Criticism* (1993), and has written articles on Shakespeare, Renaissance drama, and feminist theory. Her book in progress, on the sexual politics of masculine subjectivity in Shakespeare's Roman works, will be published in Routledge's Feminist Readings of Shakespeare series.

Ivo Kamps is Assistant Professor of English at the University of Mississippi. He is the editor of *Shakespeare Left and Right* (1991), and the author of the forthcoming *Staging History: Historiography, Ideology, and Literary Form in the Stuart Drama*. He has edited *Materialist Shake-speare: A History* (1995). He has co-edited *The Phoenix* with Lawrence Danson for the Oxford complete works of Thomas Middleton (1995).

Leah Marcus teaches English at the University of Texas, Austin. She is the author of *Childhood and Despair* (1978), *The Politics of Mirth* (1986), *Puzzling Shakespeare: Local Readings and Its Discontents* (1988), and is currently finishing an edition of the writings of Queen Elizabeth I and a book entitled *Unediting the Renaissance*, which will include a revised and expanded version of the essay on *The Taming of the Shrew* included in the present volume.

Carol Thomas Neely, Professor of English and Women's Studies at the University of Illinois, Urbana–Champaign, is co-editor of *The Woman's Part: Feminist Criticism of Shakespeare* (1980). She is the author of *Broken Nuptials in Shakespeare's Plays* (1985) and articles on Shakespeare, sonnet sequences and feminist theory, including 'Constructing the Subject: Feminist Practice and the New Renaissance Discourses'. She has an essay forthcoming on the feminist utopias of Margaret Cavendish and Gloria Anzaldúa, and is currently working on a book on the gendering of madness in Early Modern England, tentatively entitled *Did Madness have a Renaissance?*

Marianne Novy has written *Love's Argument: Gender Relations in Shakespeare* (1984); and *Engaging with Shakespeare: Responses of George Eliot and other Women Novelists* (1994). She has edited *Women's Revisions of Shakespeare: On Responses of Dickinson, Woolf, Rich, H.D., George Eliot and Others* (1990); and *Cross-Cultural Performances: Differences in Women's Revisions of Shakespeare* (1993). Professor of English at the University of Pittsburgh, she is also the 1994–5 Director of the Women's Studies Program there. She is currently writing about adoption in literature and culture.

Joseph Pequigney, Professor of English at the State University of New York at Stony Brook, is the author of *Such is My Love: A Study of Shakespeare's Sonnets* (1985). He has also written on Milton and Marvell, and is currently at work on studies of some representations of homosexuality in English Renaissance writers. His 'Sodomy in Dante's *Inferno* and *Purgatorio*' appeared in *Representations* (1991).

Phyllis Rackin is Professor of English in General Honors at the University of Pennsylvania, and a past president of the Shakespeare Association of America (1993–4). Her articles on Shakespeare and related topics have appeared in such journals as *Shakespeare Quarterly*, *PMLA*, and *Theatre Journal*, and various anthologies. Her most recent book is *Stages of History: Shakespeare's English Chronicles* (1990). She is currently working with Jean Howard on a feminist study of Shakespeare's history plays, *Engendering a Nation: Shakespeare's Chronicles of the English Past*.

Jacqueline Rose is a lecturer in English at the University of Sussex. She is the author of *The Haunting of Sylvia Plath* (1991) and *Sexuality in the Field of Vision* (1986).

Ann Thompson is Professor of English and Head of Department at Roehampton Institute, London. Among her many publications are *Shakespeare's Chaucer* (1978); *The Taming of the Shrew* (ed., 1984); *Shakespeare, Meaning and Metaphor* (with John O. Thompson, 1987); *'King Lear': The Critics' Debate* (1988); *Teaching Women: Feminism and English Studies* (ed. with Helen Wilcox), and *Which Shakespeare?* (1992). Her current research includes a new edition of *Hamlet* for Arden 3, for which she is also the General Editor. She also holds General Editorship of *Feminist Readings of Shakespeare* (a forthcoming series from Routledge). Together with Sasha Roberts, she is working on an anthology entitled *Women Readers of Shakespeare, 1600–1900*.

Valerie Traub is an Associate Professor in the English Department at Vanderbilt University. She is the author of *Desire and Anxiety: Circulation of Sexuality in Shakespearean Drama* (1992). She is currently working on discourses of female erotic pleasure in the early modern period.

William Van Watson is currently a Lecturer in Film Studies at Washington University in St Louis. He is the author of *Pier Paolo Pasolini and the Theater of the Word* (1989); and of articles on Rossellini, Fritz Lang, Pasolini, Molière and Madonna. He has also translated works by Umberto Giordano, Toscanini, Pasolini and Frank Wedekind, and provided subtitles for films by Mario Monicelli. He has taught in Italy as well as in the United States. Upcoming projects include a chapter on Paula Abdul for a book on MTV, and co-authorship of a book on homosexuality and lesbianism in Italian cinema.

Index